W9-ADN-615

Varieties of Literary Experience

Contributors

M. H. Abrams
Jacques Barzun
Eric Bentley
Germaine Brée
Cleanth Brooks
Calvin S. Brown
Stanley Burnshaw
John Ciardi
Edward Dahlberg
Angel del Río
Leon Edel
John Gassner
Stephen Gilman
Harry Levin
Henri Peyre
Philip Rahv
Gregor Sebba
Lionel Trilling

Varieties of Literary Experience

Eighteen Essays in World Literature

EDITED BY

STANLEY BURNSHAW

NEW YORK UNIVERSITY PRESS

1962

Library of Congress Catalog Card Number: 62–11513
Manufactured in the United States of America
Design and typography by Ernst Reichl

To the Memory of

ÁNGEL DEL RÍO

Contents

Introduction

A DECENT EDITOR OF A NEW VOLUME of critical essays should no doubt begin by apologizing for its existence: not only are there already more such books than one could possibly read, but the best critics aren't critics at all—they are creative artists or lovers! "The best account of a painting can well be a sonnet or an elegy," said Baudelaire; "the best of all critics is a poet." Rilke made no secret of his grand contempt when he declared, in one of his *Letters to a Young Poet,* that "works of art are of infinite loneliness and with nothing to be so little reached as with criticism. Only love can grasp and hold and fairly judge them."

It may well be true that we print more criticism than is good for us, but to ask critics to stop producing is to ask readers to stop talking; for what is criticism but conversation—at its best, exalted conversation—written down for the eye to hear? If people who read are eager to tell others about their pleasures or their miseries, why should they be silenced? No law compels anyone to listen. Every reader (except the professional, who needs to know what his peers are saying) enjoys the absolute freedom to pick and choose among the numberless voices. Or he can ignore them all in favor of the original work that set off the clamor—whereupon he may end up a critic himself, and thus add to the sin of our time.

Though most criticism takes the humbler form of prose, its genesis is not essentially different from that of a sonnet or an elegy—which is to suggest that all excellent criticism is inspired. It is inspired, of course, by an involvement with a novel, a play, or a poem, and therefore at second remove; but that such an experience can be as stirring or as illuminating as a first-hand involvement with reality, hardly needs to be argued. What should be considered, rather, is the part played in the resulting critical essay by the impelling imaginative force that Rilke described as love and Shelley as sympathy. The value of all critical thinking hinges upon its control. Proust pointed to the danger of subordination when he warned that "the moment our reasoning intelligence tries to judge works of art, there is no longer anything fixed or certain; one can prove anything one wishes to." Let discursive thinking take over, and criticism dissolves into pointlessness, for each work of art has a logic peculiarly its own which is at odds with the everyday variety. What matters above all is the critic's impassioned involvement and the meaningful kinships laid bare by the vision of sympathy. Whether praise or blame happens to ensue is not important if the sources of the judgment are ultimately the same. Even the fiercest of critical attacks may be rooted in compassion.

The title of this volume calls for explaining, especially the first part, with its echo of William James. By dropping the definite article from *The Varieties of Religious Experience* and changing the adjective, I intend neither depth nor mystery. A reader prone to pry may smile at my disclaimer, that I simply could not find more faithful words for describing this assemblage of eighteen essays—on writers, novels, plays, poems, movements, themes, ideologies, approaches—each of which embodies a set of assumptions, a style, and a method of its own.

Such variety, deliberately sought for, seems worth adducing at a time when every critic is supposedly enrolled in one of a handful of "schools." To be sure, certain schools exist, but I do not see how the most rewarding critics can be properly fitted into any of them. And even among those who might be said to belong, the differences are more interesting than the agreements. As in all literary pigeonholing, the singulars quite transcend their groups.

So much for the main title of the book. The five words that follow are another matter, and though they might lead to a variety of questions, they particularly suggest that we ask ourselves what we mean by the term "world literature." If it denotes a library of volumes, each section of which contains the complete published writings of a specific language, then "world literature" has only academic interest: it could be experienced by few if any living persons, for one can experience only as many literatures as the languages he commands. Most readers (including most scholars and critics) can never be truly at home in more than a very few foreign tongues. Hence "world literature" *as it is read* is by no means the totality of writings produced by the peoples of the world—not the alien originals at all but domestic imitations.

All this may be obvious enough until we remind ourselves that every piece of literature in translation is a very different thing from the work from which it was transported. The domestic imitation is made of different words. We "know" this, of course; we "know" that every translation is a new work; and yet we approach it not as we approach a new work originally written in our own language but with a special and pervasive awareness of difference. And we make charitable allowances, even to the extent of downgrading the translation by seeing the original enclosed in a halo of imagined superiority to whatever we find in the words before us. This curiously impeding awareness operates not only with dissatisfying translations. No matter how affecting the words before us, we "know" that the work they derived from must surely have been better, for we quite properly assume that something precious has been lost. The moment we become aware that we are reading a translation, the normal relation between book and reader breaks down. The translated book is, of course, no longer quite foreign—but neither is it "genuinely" English. What then can it be but a species of limbo literature?

Though such a question would always seem ungracious, it sounds particularly so today when translators are more productive than ever before and publishers promise them support. Dazzled by the first revelations of a goldening age, many readers may quickly reverse their ancient habits, and, in pursuit of the new, long-hidden joys, push aside everything including thoughts they long held to be true. Somewhere along this enchanted line, they may start telling themselves that all the essential differences between first-hand and second-hand literatures are merely a matter of theory, and then with a pragmatic wave of the hand, dismiss these differences as no longer worth considering. Merrily bound for the other extreme, they may even find themselves believing that the impossible has been accomplished: that the translation "problem" has at last been solved for all time.

Other readers, however, especially those with a weakness for books about literature, are likely to remain unchanged; for if recent criticism has contributed anything importantly new it has been to point up the implications of the ever obvious fact that a book is a matter of words. It is always and overwhelmingly a matter of words—as colors are the painter's materials, so are words the writer's; but whereas colors have no fatherland, words are stopped at each linguistic frontier. It is *Zapiski iz Podpolya* for readers of Russian and *Notes from the Underground* (or *Letters from the Underworld*) for readers of English: from title to conclusion, two structures of different words, which is also to say: two different structures. But in all such structures we find, in addition to the words, a variety of abstractable creations. How many, we may never be able to say; nor does the arithmetic count.

What matters is that certain of these creations can be carried over from language to language without decisive loss—story, plot, fable, myth, allegory, generalized analogy. Ideas can also be translated to the extent that two languages possess terms that are reciprocally appropriate. Occasionally idioms may show something like a one-to-one correspondence, as will some elements of form in the gross. But such types of equivalence are as much as can be hoped for at best, for if literature is made of language, then it is changed when its language is changed—changed for better or worse, but in every case changed.

Nobody will deny that these statements hold true of poetry—besides, given certain aids, every reader can experience foreign poems in their original words [1]—but what of prose? That the English tongue possesses some fine works of fiction in translation is beside the point; their excellence has nothing to do with their difference from what they purport and are taken to be. And it is mainly because excellence here does away with full awareness of difference that readers need to realize what can happen even to prose in the process of change.

No handier example can be suggested, I think, than the following passage from *Tonio Kröger*, since Thomas Mann himself presided at the ceremony of analysis that took place at Colorado College in the spring of 1941.[2] Some thirty teachers and students of German had been asked to translate this paragraph from the middle of the story:

> Und Tonio Kröger fuhr gen Norden. Er fuhr mit Komfort (denn er pflegte zu sagen, dass jemand, der es innerlich so viel schwerer hat als andere Leute, gerechten Anspruch auf ein wenig äusseres Behagen habe), und er rastete nicht eher, als bis die Türme der engen Stadt, von der er ausgegangen war, sich vor ihm in die graue Luft erhoben. Dort nahm er einen kurzen, seltsamen Aufenthalt.

[1] As I have tried to show in *The Poem Itself* (Holt, Rinehart and Winston, 1960).
[2] As reported by Hans Rosenhaupt, in *The History of Ideas News Letter*, III, No. 3 (July 1957), pp. 60–63. Reprinted by permission of Dr. Rosenhaupt.

The discussion began with the fifth word: why had Mann used, instead of *gegen,* the archaic *gen?* Was there some connection with Siegfried's trip north to Iceland? Mann explained that he had striven for a balladesque atmosphere. As for the fourth word, *fuhr,* he had used it in the sense of *zog;* hence *traveled* would be too "pedestrian." *Norden* had been intended in what Mann called "a certain symbolical sense." *Er fuhr mit Komfort* had been written with technical comfort in mind. The word *innerlich* gave rise to much difficulty. *Schwer haben* turned out to be a deliberate understatement. *Anspruch haben* was finally translated as *entitled,* though Mann regretfully permitted the omission of *gerecht* (*rightfully*) for the greater good of simplicity in translation. *Creature comfort* was too explicit for *äusseres Behagen,* he said; and as for *rastete,* there was simply no exact English equivalent. The penultimate *seltsamen* had a dreamlike or fantastic connotation for the author; but *fantastic* was a bit exaggerated, *strange* would be unmelodious. The best solution was *a brief, enchanted stay.* After eighty minutes of deliberation, the following version was accepted by all present, including Thomas Mann, who considered it to be more faithful than any of the three published renderings of the same passage: [3]

[3] And Tonio Kröger journeyed northward. He traveled comfortably (for he was wont to say that any one who has so much more distress of soul than other people may justly claim a little external comfort), and he did not rest until the towers of the cramped city which had been his starting-point rose before him in the gray air. There he made a brief, strange sojourn.

—Trans. by Bayard Q. Morgan (German Publication Society, 1914)

And Tonio Kröger traveled north. He traveled with comfort (for he liked to say that anyone who was so much more disturbed internally than other people had a perfect right to a little external comfort), and he never stopped until the towers of the narrow city from which he had come rose up before him into the grey air. There he made a brief, strange stop-over.

—Trans. by Kenneth Burke (Alfred A. Knopf, 1925)

And Tonio Kröger travelled north. He travelled in comfort (for he was wont to say that anyone who had suffered inwardly more than other people had a right to a little outward ease); and he did not stay until the towers of the little town he had left rose up in the grey air. Among them he made a short and singular stay.

—Trans. by H. T. Lowe-Porter (Alfred A. Knopf, 1936)

> And Tonio Kröger went north. He went in comfort, for he always said that anyone who had so much more to bear inwardly than other people was surely entitled to a little outer ease. And he did not stop until there rose before him in the gray sky the spires of the cramped little city from which he had once set out. There he made a brief, enchanted stay.

Faced with such a demonstration in rendering so small a part of so long a story, a reader may throw up his hands. Frost was all too right! —"Poetry is that which gets lost from verse or prose in translation."—the quotation repeated again and again: it cannot be repeated too often. And yet, the "poetry" is by no means the main element contributing to the massed-up effectiveness of a foreign novel or play rendered into English. Its untranslatable charges of meaning may prove crucial only in isolated passages or they may inform every sentence from beginning to end; but even when this poetry is lost or weakly imitated, other important structures may remain in the domesticated version—the many "abstractable creations" noted earlier and the new constructions (character, situation) to which they give rise. All such things of course owe their existence to the original words from which they have now been cut off; but the life they lead and the power they exert no longer depend on those words.

They depend on the newfound words that compose their natures, which is to say that differences always arise. How many or how decisive depends on the "veil," if we think of translation as that which hangs between the original and our eyes. The veil distorts, as it must; it conceals; at times it darkens. But there is still much to be seen. The image behind it glows with curious light. And like every object viewed through a veil, it may sometimes seem to us finer than it really is. Not necessarily because we endow it with virtues we should like it to possess (as some Frenchmen have done with Poe), but rather because of the texture of the veil. Is there any reason why a prose translation cannot, as literature in a new language, be superior to the original? Is the King James Bible, for example, less great than the Hebrew? Even such exhilarating questions can only affirm the fact of difference. They should also make us alert to our limits, especially when we try to see all that a critic tells us he has seen in a work of world literature. How easy to forget that his sometimes seemingly excessive pronouncements or incredible findings, in a Dostoevski novel, for example, developed in the course of his involvement with *Zapiski iz Podpolya,* whereas we may have read only a book entitled *Notes from the Underground,* or *Letters from the Underworld.* Better to realize why such readers as ourselves must always stand outside: not only the original work but every critique it engenders will always remain not quite within reach, clad in obscuring veils.

With one exception, the contributions to this volume developed out of lectures prepared for my seminar in World Literature at New York University, begun in September 1958. A few of the essays have already been printed, and due acknowledgment is hereby made to *The Sewanee Review, Saturday Review,* the *Partisan Review, The Massachusetts Review, The Literary Review,* and the *Hispanic Review.* I am indebted also to Jacques Barzun, from whom I first learned of the *Tonio Kröger* report in *The History of Ideas News Letter,* and to Arthur Armstrong, for his translation of the essay by the late Ángel del Río.

The passages quoted in the texts have been included by the generous permission of the owners of their respective copyrights.

New York, N. Y. S. B.
January 1962

Varieties of Literary Experience

Five Ways of Reading *Lycidas*

M. H. ABRAMS

MOST MODERN CRITICS base their theories on the proposition that a poem is an object in itself. And all critics endorse enthusiastically at least one statement by Matthew Arnold, that the function of criticism is "to see the object as in itself it really is." The undertaking is surely valid, and laudable; the results, however, are disconcerting. For in this age of unexampled critical activity, as one poetic object after another is analyzed under rigidly controlled conditions, the object proves to be highly unstable, and disintegrates. In the pages of the critics we increasingly find, under a single title, not one poem, but a variety of poems.

Milton's *Lycidas* is a convenient case in point, because it is short enough to be easily manageable, has been explicated many times, and is almost universally esteemed. If not every reader goes all the way with Mark Pattison's judgment that it is "the high-water mark of English Poesy," still critics agree about its excellence as closely as they ever do in evaluating a lyric poem. My point is that, on the evidence of their own commentaries, critics agree about the excellence of quite different poems. They present us not with one *Lycidas,* but with discriminable types of *Lycidas*—five types, I have announced in my title. I feel confident that with a little more perseverance I could have distinguished at least seven, to equal William Empson's types of ambiguity. But in these matters distinctions, as Mr. Empson's procedure demonstrates, can be rather arbitrary. And even five types of *Lycidas* are enough to confront the literary theorist with an embarrassing problem: Is a poem one or many? And if it is one, how are we to decide which one?

I

For the first type, take *Lycidas* as it was commonly described in the period between the first volume of Masson's monumental *Life of Milton* (1859) and the critical age ushered in by T. S. Eliot and I. A. Richards a generation ago. This traditional reading (in which I was educated) was epitomized by J. H. Hanford in his *Milton Handbook.* Individual discussions varied in emphasis and detail; but when in that lost paradise of critical innocence readers looked at *Lycidas,* they agreed that they saw an elegiac poem about Edward King, a contemporary of Milton's at Christ's College, who had been drowned when his ship suddenly foundered in the Irish Sea. To depersonalize his grief and elevate its occasion, Milton chose to follow the elaborate conventions of the pastoral elegy as these had evolved over the 1800 years between the Sicilian Theocritus and the English Spenser; he ended the poem with a traditional consolation at the thought of Lycidas resurrected in heaven, and found in this thought the strength to carry on his own concerns. In two passages, many commentators agreed—they often called them digressions—Milton uttered his personal concerns under a thin fictional disguise. In one of these Milton expressed his own fear that "th' abhorred shears" might cut him off before he could achieve the poetic fame to which he had dedicated his life. In the other Milton, through St. Peter, voiced a grim warning to the corrupt English clergy of his time.

Writing in 1926, on the extreme verge of the New Criticism, Professor Hanford was so imprudent as to close his discussion with the statement that "*Lycidas* bears its meaning plainly enough on its face." It contains, to be sure, a minor verbal crux or two, such as the nature of the "two-handed engine at the door"; but, he roundly asserted, "there has been little room for disagreement regarding its larger features."

Only four years later E. M. W. Tillyard published in his *Milton* an analysis of *Lycidas* which in its opening tucket sounded the new note in criticism:

> Most criticism of *Lycidas* is off the mark, because it fails to distinguish between the nominal and the real subject, what the poem professes to be about and what it is about. It assumes that Edward King is the real, whereas he is but the nominal subject. Fundamentally *Lycidas* concerns—

But before we hear what *Lycidas* is really about, we ought to attend to Tillyard's distinction between "nominal" and "real" poetic meaning. For this modern polysemism, which splits all poems —or at least the most noteworthy poems—into two or more levels of meaning, one overt and nominal (which other readers have detected) and the other covert but essential (whose discovery has usually been reserved for the critic making the distinction), is extraordinarily widespread, and we shall find it repeatedly applied to *Lycidas*. The levels of meaning are identified by a variety of names. Tillyard elsewhere distinguishes between conscious and unconscious, and direct and oblique meanings. Other critics make a parallel distinction between manifest and latent, ostensible and actual, literal and symbolic, particular and archetypal significance. And at the risk of giving away a trade secret, it must be confessed that most of the time, when we critics come out with a startling new interpretation of a well-known work, it is through the application of this very useful interpretative stratagem.

The procedure, of course, is indispensable in analyzing works for which there is convincing evidence that they were written in the mode of allegory or symbolism. But it is worth noting that the distinction was developed by Greek commentators, interested in establishing Homer's reputation as a doctor of universal wisdom, who dismissed Homer's scandalous stories about the gods as only the veil for an esoteric and edifying undermeaning. The same strategy was adapted by Philo to bring the Old Testament into harmony with Greek philosophy, and by the Church Fathers to prove that the Old Testament prefigured the New Testament, and by medieval and Renaissance moralists in order to disclose, behind Ovid's pagan and ostensibly licentious fables, austere ethical precepts and anticipations of the Christian mysteries. To the cultural historian it appears that the distinction between nominal and real meaning has not infrequently been used as a handy gadget to replace what an author has said with what a commentator would prefer him to have said.

We are braced now for Tillyard's disclosure of the real subject of *Lycidas*. "Fundamentally *Lycidas* concerns Milton himself; King is but the excuse for one of Milton's most personal poems." The main argument for this interpretation is that *Lycidas* is generally admitted to be a great poem, but "if it is great, it must contain deep feeling of some sort"; since this feeling is obviously not about King, it must be about Milton himself. Milton, Tillyard maintains, expressed his own situation and feelings and attitudes, not only in the obviously allegorical passages about driving afield and piping with Lycidas, or in the passages on fame and the corrupt clergy, which had been called personal by earlier critics, but from beginning to end of the poem. How radical Tillyard's formula is for translating objective references into subjective equivalents is indicated by his analysis of the poem's climactic passage:

> The fourth section purports to describe the resurrection of Lycidas and his entry into heaven. More truly it solves the whole poem by describing the resurrection into a new kind of life of Milton's hopes,

> should they be ruined by premature death or by the moral collapse of his country. . . . Above all the fourth section describes the renunciation of earthly fame, the abnegation of self by a great egotist, and the spiritual purgation of gaining one's life after losing it.[1]

Only such an interpretation, Tillyard claims, will reveal the integrity of the poem, by making it possible "to see in *Lycidas* a unity of purpose which cannot be seen in it if the death of King is taken as the real subject." Furthermore, the value of the poem really resides in the ordered and harmonized mental impulses for which the objective references are merely a projected correlative: "What makes *Lycidas* one of the greatest poems in English is that it expresses with success a state of mind whose high value can hardly be limited to a particular religious creed."

From this interpretation and these grounds of value John Crowe Ransom (to speak in understatement) disagrees,[2] and so provides us with a third type of *Lycidas.* His premise is that "anonymity . . . is a condition of poetry." Milton very properly undertook to keep himself and his private concerns out of his memorial verses, and to do so assumed the identity of a Greek shepherd, the "uncouth swain" of the last stanza, who serves as a *dramatis persona,* a "qualified spokesman," for the public performance of a ritual elegy. As for the problem with which Tillyard confronted us—if the passion is not for King, for whom can it be except Milton himself?—Ransom solves it by dissolving it. There is no passion in the poem, and so no problem. "For Lycidas [Milton] mourns with a very technical piety." The pastoral conventions are part of the poetic "make-believe," and the whole poem, whatever more it may be, is "an exercise in pure linguistic technique, or metrics; it was also an exercise in the technique of what our critics of fiction refer to as 'point of view.' "

[1] See also Tillyard's analysis of *Lycidas* in *Poetry Direct and Oblique* (revised version, London, 1948), pp. 81–84.

[2] John Crowe Ransom, "A Poem Nearly Anonymous," in *The World's Body* (New York, 1938), pp. 1–28.

This is the poem, at any rate, that Milton set out to write and almost succeeded in writing. But his youth and character interfered and forced into the poem three defiant gestures of "rebellion against the formalism of his art," and this unfortunate registration of Milton's temperament makes the poem only half-way anonymous. One of these rebellious gestures is the liberty Milton took with his stanzas, which are almost anarchically irregular and include ten lines which do not rime at all. Another is St. Peter's speech; in Ransom's comment on this passage, we hear a voice out of the past—the Cavalier critic gracefully but firmly putting the stiff-necked and surly Puritan in his place: it expresses, he says, "a Milton who is angry, violent, and perhaps a little bit vulgar. . . . Peter sounds like another Puritan zealot, and less than apostolic." The third instance of Milton's self-assertion is his "breach in the logic of composition"; that is, he shifts from the first-person monologue with which the poem opens to dialogues with Phoebus and others, then abruptly to the third person in the last stanza, where the uncouth swain is presented in "a pure narrative conclusion in the past [tense]." It follows that Ransom's concluding evaluation turns Tillyard's precisely inside out. The sustained self-expression, on which Tillyard had grounded both the unity and excellence of the elegy, according to Ransom breaks out only sporadically, and then so as to violate the integrity and flaw the perfection of the poem. "So *Lycidas,* for the most part a work of great art, is sometimes artful and tricky. We are disturbingly conscious of a man behind the artist."

One might, of course, demur that, given Ransom's own criteria, two of the items he decries as arrogant gestures of Milton's originality are exactly those in which he closely follows established conventions. The scholarly annotators—at whom, as he passes, Ransom turns to smile—tell us that the models for Milton's stanzas, the elaborate *canzone* employed by several Italian lyrists of the sixteenth century, were not only variable in structure but also included unrimed lines for the sake of that seeming ease and freedom which is the aim of an art that hides art. As for St. Peter's diatribe, Milton inherited the right to introduce rough satire against the clergy into a pastoral from a widespread convention established by Petrarch, who was not vulgar, nor a Puritan, nor even a Protestant. In Ransom's third exhibit, one element—Milton's putting the elegy into a narrative context in the conclusion, without a matching narrative introduction—is not, apparently, traditional. But it is at any rate odd to make Milton out to assert his own egoism in the passage that specifically assigns the elegy to another person than himself; a person, moreover, who is the entirely conventional rural singer of a pastoral elegy.

But this begins to seem captious, and does not represent the measure of my admiration for the charm and deftness of Mr. Ransom's essay, which thrusts home some important and timely truths about the dramatic construction of *Lycidas* by the artful device of overstatement. It is, one might hazard, a virtuoso exercise in critical point of view.

Let the commentary by Cleanth Brooks and John Hardy, in their edition of Milton's *Poems* of 1645,[3] represent *Lycidas*, type four. At first glance it might seem that to these explicators the poem is not really about King, nor about Milton, but mainly about water. They turn to the first mention of water in lines 12–14 and discover at once the paradox that the "tear" which is the "meed" paid to Lycidas by the elegiac singer is of the same substance, salt water, as the "wat'ry bier," the sea on which the body welters. As the poem develops, they say, "the 'melodious tear' promises to overwhelm the 'sounding Seas.'" For the tear is the elegy itself, which derives its inspiration from the "sacred well" of the muses, and flows on through a profusion of fountains, rivers, and streams, in richly ambiguous interrelations of harmonies, contrasts, and ironies, until, by the agency of "resurrection images," all of which "have to do with a circumvention of the sea," we are transferred to a transcendent pastoral realm where Lycidas walks "other streams along" and the saints wipe the tears forever from his eyes.

[3] Cleanth Brooks and John Hardy, "Essays in Analysis: *Lycidas*," in *Poems of Mr. John Milton* (New York, 1951), pp. 169–86.

The base of the critical operation here is the assumption that "the 'poetry' resides in the total structure of meanings." The primary component in this structure is "imagery," of which the component parts are so organically related, through mutual reflection and implication, that it does not matter where you start: any part will lead you to the center and to the whole. The key to both the form and value of *Lycidas,* then, which Tillyard had found in the ordering of mental impulses, and Ransom in the all-but-successful maintenance of impersonal elegiac conventions, Brooks and Hardy locate in the evolution and integration of the imagery:

> *Lycidas* is a good poem not because it is appropriately and simply pastoral and elegiac—with . . . all the standard equipment—but because of its unique formal wholeness, because of the rich "integrity" of even such a single figure as that in the lines "He must not flote upon his wat'ry bier/Unwept. . . ."[4]

It turns out, however, that these images are only provisionally the elements of the poem, since in Milton they are used as vehicles for a submerged but essential component, "certain dominant, recurrent symbolic motives." For the fact, hitherto mainly overlooked, is that "Milton is a symbolist poet to a considerable extent."[5] Accordingly we must again, as in Tillyard's essay, penetrate the ostensible meaning to discover the real meaning of *Lycidas,* though a real meaning which in this case is an abstract concept. "What," they ask, "is the real subject" of *Lycidas?*

> If Milton is not deeply concerned with King as a person, he is deeply concerned, and as a young poet, involved, with a theme—which is that of the place and meaning of poetry in a world which seems at many points inimical to it.

[4] *Ibid.,* p. 259.
[5] *Ibid.,* pp. 256, 250.

Specifically, the early part of the poem presents the despairing theme that nature is neutral, emptied of the old pastoral deities ("to say nymphs are ineffectual is tantamount to denying their existence"); and this concept is transcended only by the movement from philosophic naturalism to Christian supernaturalism, in the pastoral imagery of the conclusion in heaven.

Perhaps other readers share my disquiet at this discovery. Leaving aside the question whether it is valid to assume that *Lycidas* is essentially a symbolist poem of which the real subject is a theme, there remains the difficulty that the theme seems to be startlingly anachronistic. Milton, we are told, writing in the 1630's and echoing a complaint about the nymphs which is as old as Theocritus' first Idyll, presents us with the world-view involving "an emptied nature, a nature which allows us to personify it only in the sense that its sounds seem mournful. . . . The music of nature . . . has also been stilled." But wasn't it a Victorian poet who said this, in an elegy published not in 1638 but in 1850?

> And all the phantom, Nature, stands—
> With all the music in her tone,
> A hollow echo of my own,—
> A hollow form with empty hands.

As for the concept imputed to Milton, with respect to the place of poetry in an inimical world, that "Nature is neutral: it is not positively malignant, but neither is it beneficent"—isn't this exactly the thesis laid down in 1926 by I. A. Richards in a very influential little book, *Science and Poetry*? In our own age, Mr. Richards said,

> the central dominant change may be described as the *Neutralization of Nature,* the transference from the Magical View of the world to the scientific. . . . There is some evidence that Poetry . . . arose with this Magical View. It is a possibility to be seriously considered that Poetry may pass away with it.[6]

[6] I. A. Richards, *Science and Poetry* (London, 1926), pp. 47–48.

At any rate, it is by a notable sleight of explication that Brooks and Hardy convert to the real meaning that Nature does not sympathize with the poet's sorrow and "has no apparent respect for the memory of Lycidas" the very passage in which Milton explicitly states the contrary: that nature, which had responded joyously to Lycidas' soft lays when he was alive, now mourns his death:

> Thee, Shepherd, thee the Woods, and desert Caves,
> With wild Thyme and the gadding Vine o'ergrown,
> And all their echoes mourn.

We go on to the fifth type of *Lycidas,* the archetypal version, which entered the critical ken after the vogue of the writings in comparative anthropology of James G. Frazer and in analytical psychology of C. G. Jung. This mode of criticism, like the last, begins by isolating images or patterns of imagery; now, however, the focus is on images which reflect the agents and events of myth or folklore. The favorite legends are those which (according to some folklorists) concern beings who were once nature deities—the dead and risen gods of Syria, Egypt, and Greece associated with the dying or reaping of the crops in the fall and their revival in the spring.

Richard P. Adams, investigating "The Archetypal Pattern of Death and Rebirth in *Lycidas,*" [7] discovers that the poem is throughout "a remarkably tight amalgam of death-and-rebirth imagery." These images begin with the initial reference to the evergreen plants, the laurel, myrtle, and ivy, and continue through the allusions to the hyacinth, the rose, and the violet, which had their mythical genesis in the blood of a mortal or deity. The many water-images are here interpreted as fertility symbols; the allusion to the death of Orpheus is said to bring in a myth whose similarities to "the deaths of Adonis, Attis, Osiris, and other fertility demi-

[7] Richard P. Adams, in *Publications of the Modern Language Association,* LXIV (1949), pp. 183–188.

gods have been pointed out by modern scholars"; while the poet's speculation that the body of Lycidas perhaps visits "the bottom of the monstrous world" parallels the descent into water and the dragon fight "which is often a feature of death-and-rebirth cycles."

Adams is content with a fairly traditional interpretation of the subject of *Lycidas:* Milton's concern was not with Edward King but "with the life, death, and resurrection of the dedicated poet, and specifically with his own situation at the time." Northrop Frye, however, in his essay on "Literature as Context: Milton's *Lycidas,*"[8] contends that the "structural principle" of the poem, the formal cause which "assimilates all details in the realizing of its unity," is "the Adonis myth," and that "Lycidas is, poetically speaking, a god or spirit of nature, who eventually becomes a saint in heaven." The archetypal reading here provides us with a new principle of unity, a new distinction between ostensible and implicit meaning, and a new version of what the poem is really rather than nominally about. In an earlier essay, Frye put the matter bluntly: "Poetry demands, as Milton saw it, that the elements of his theme should be assimilated to their archetypes. . . . Hence the poem will not be about King, but about his archetype, Adonis, the dying and rising god, called Lycidas in Milton's poem."[9]

II

It will not do to say, as one is tempted to say, that these five versions of *Lycidas* really give us the same poem in diversely selected aspects and details. The versions differ not in selection or emphasis but in essentials. Each strikes for the heart of the poem; each claims to have discovered the key element, or struc-

[8] In *The Proceedings of the Second Congress of the International Comparative Literature Association,* ed. W. P. Friederick, University of North Carolina Studies in Comparative Literature, XXIII (1959), 44–55.

[9] Northrop Frye, "Levels of Meaning in Literature," *Kenyon Review,* XII (1950), pp. 246–262.

tural principle, which has controlled the choice, order, and interrelations of the parts, and which establishes for the reader the meaning, unity, and value of the whole. Nor will it help put Humpty Dumpty together again, to combine all these critical modes, as some commentators recommend, into a single criticism which has the virtues of each and the deficiency of none. To provide a coherent reading, a critical procedure must itself be coherent; it cannot be divided against itself in its first principles. A syncretic criticism is invertebrate; it will yield not an integral poem, but a ragout.

When there is such radical and many-sided disagreement about the real but nonliteral and esoteric meaning of the poem, the best hope of remedy, I think, lies in going back to Milton's text and reading it with a dogged literalness, except when there is clear evidence that some part of it is to be read allegorically or symbolically. This is what I propose, very briefly, to attempt. In a way, this puts me in a favorable position. A drawback in writing as a new critic is that it would be embarrassing to come out with an old reading; whereas I can plead that I have deliberately set out to labor the obvious, and can take comfort from the number of earlier critiques with which I find myself in agreement.

Looked at in this way, *Lycidas* turns out to be in some sense—although at times a very loose sense—about Edward King, about Milton, about water, about the problem of being a poet in an inimical world; and it is undoubtedly about at least one God (Christ) who died to be reborn. But it is about none of these in the central way that it is about certain other things that, to the literal-minded reader, constitute the essential poem Milton chose to write.

First, it is about—in the sense that it presents as the poetic datum, Milton's elected fiction—a nameless shepherd, sitting from morning to evening in a rural setting and hymning the death of a fellow poet-pastor, who is not Edward King, but specifically, Lycidas. The reason all our interpreters except Ransom treat the stated elegist rather casually, if at all, is that they tend to take as premise that a poem is an object made of words. So indeed it is. But as a starting point for criticism, it would be more inclusive and suggestive to say that a poem is made of *speech,* for the reason that the term "speech" entails a particular speaker. In *Lycidas* the speaker is an unnamed rustic singer, presented and described before the close of the poem, whose speech refers to a state of affairs, describes the appearance and quotes the statements of other speakers, including Phoebus, Camus, and St. Peter, expresses his own thoughts and changing mood, and conveys, by immediate implication, something of his own character. This poem is therefore clearly a dramatic lyric, with a setting, an occasion, a chief character, and several subordinate characters (who may, however, be regarded as representing the speaker's own thoughts, objectified for dramatic purposes as standard *personae* of the pastoral ritual).

Tillyard is surely right, as against Ransom (and earlier, Dr. Johnson), in finding deep feeling in the poem, but he confronts us with the spurious alternative that the feeling must be either about King or about Milton himself. The feeling is occasioned by the death of Lycidas and the thoughts plausibly evoked by that event; and it is experienced and expressed not by Milton, but by a singer Milton is at considerable pains to identify as someone other than himself. Precisely what Milton himself thought and felt during the many hours—probably days—in which he labored over *Lycidas,* despite Tillyard's assurance, is beyond all but the most tenuous conjecture; although it is safe to say that, among other things, he was thinking how he might put together the best possible pastoral elegy. But we know precisely what the uncouth swain thought and felt because the expression of his thoughts and feelings constitutes the poem, from the bold opening, "Yet once more, O ye Laurels . . . ," up to, but not including, the closing eight lines, when the author takes over as omniscient narrator: "*Thus* sang the uncouth Swain. . . ."

Readers of the poem at its first appearance, in 1638, knew that it was one of thirteen *Obsequies to the Memorie of Mr. Edward*

King, and undoubtedly some also knew (what the edition of 1645 specified) that the J. M. who signed the last obsequy was John Milton, whose circumstances and relations to King bore some resemblance to those presented in the poem. Such knowledge, however, does not displace but adds a particular historical reference to the two chief persons of the literal poem. *Lycidas* is not simply "about" King; it is a public ceremonial on the occasion of King's death, and the decorum of such a performance requires that the individual be not only lamented but also honored. And how could King be honored more greatly than to be made an instance of the type of poet-priest, identified by the traditional name "Lycidas," and to be lamented by a typical pastoral singer—in Ransom's phrase, a "qualified spokesman" for the public performance of a ritual elegy—whose single voice is resonant with echoes of poets through the ages mourning other poets untimely cut off? My insistence here may seem to be much ado about trivia, and, provided we are ready to fill out the details when pertinent, it can be a harmless critical shorthand to say that it is Milton who sings a lament for Edward King. But entirely to disregard these elementary circumstances may be the beginning of critical arrogance, which can end in our substituting our own poem for the one Milton chose to write.

The pastoral singer sets out, then, both to lament and to celebrate Lycidas. But consideration of this particular death raises in his mind a general question about the pointless contingencies of life, with its constant threat that fate may slit the thin-spun thread of any dedicated mortal prior to fulfilment and so render profitless his self-denial. This doubt, it should be noted, is not an ulterior "theme" beneath the ostensible surface of the poem. It is, explicitly, a topic in the thought of the lyric speaker, a stage in his soliloquy, which the speaker's continued meditation, guided by the comments of other imagined characters, goes on to resolve. This turn away from Lycidas to the circumstance of those who have survived him is not insincere, nor does it constitute a digression or an indecorously personal intrusion. It is entirely natural and appropriate; just as (to borrow a parallel from J. M. French) it is altogether fitting and proper for Lincoln, in the course of the *Gettysburg Address,* to turn from "these honored dead" to concern for "us the living." [10] After all, the doubts and fears of the lyric speaker concern the insecurity of his own life only insofar as he, like Lycidas, is a member of the genus Poet, and concern the class of poets only insofar as it shares the universal human condition.

While initially, then, we may say that the presented subject in *Lycidas* is a pastoral singer memorializing the death of a dedicated shepherd poet-and-priest, we must go on to say that—in a second and important sense of "subject" as the dynamic center, or controlling principle, of a poem—its subject is a question about the seeming profitlessness of the dedicated life and the seeming deficiency of divine justice raised in the mind of the lyric speaker. That the rise, evolution, and resolution of the troubled thought of the elegist is the key to the structure of *Lycidas,* Milton made as emphatic as he could. He forced it on our attention by the startling device of ending the elegy, in a passage set off as a stanza in ottava rima, not with Lycidas, but with the elegist himself as, reassured, he faces his own destiny with confidence. But there is no occasion for Lycidas to feel slighted by this dereliction, for has he not been left in heaven, entertained and comforted by a chorus of Saints, and given an office equivalent to St. Michael's, as guardian of the western shore?

III

If this, in barest outline, is the subject and the structural principle of the poem, what are we to make of the thematic imagery which, in the alternative interpretation by Brooks and Hardy, motivates and controls its development?

Lycidas indeed, as these critics point out, incorporates many

[10] See J. M. French, "The Digressions in Milton's *Lycidas,*" *Studies in Philology,* L (1953), 486.

water and sheep-and-shepherd images; it also has song-and-singer images, floral images, stellar images, wide-ranging geographical images, even a surprising number of eye, ear, and mouth images. The usual strategy of the modern critic of imagery is to pull out a selection of such items and to set them up in an order which is largely independent of who utters them, on what occasion, and for what dramatic purpose. Freed from the controls imposed by their specific verbal and dramatic contexts, the selected images readily send out shoots and tendrils of significance, which can be twined into a symbolic pattern—and if the critic is sensitive, learned, and adroit, often a very interesting pattern. The danger is that the pattern may be largely an artifact of the implicit scheme governing the critical analysis.

From our elected point of view, the images in *Lycidas* constitute elements in the speech—some literal and some figurative, allegoric, or symbolic—which serve primarily to express the perceptions, thoughts, and feelings of the lyric speaker. These images constitute for the reader a sensuous texture, and they set up among themselves, as Brooks and Hardy point out, various ambiguities, contrasts, and harmonies. But in *Lycidas,* the procession of images is less determining than determined. If they steer the meditation of the speaker, it is only insofar as they cooperate in doing so with more authoritative principles: with the inherited formulae of the elegiac ritual, and with these formulae as they in turn (in Milton's inventive use of pastoral conventions) are subtly subordinated to the evolving meditation of the lyric speaker himself. In effect, then, the imagery does not displace but corroborates the process of feelingful thought in the mind of a specified character. This, it seems to me, is the way Milton wrote *Lycidas;* there is no valid evidence, in or out of the poem, that he constructed it—as T. S. Eliot might have done—out of a set of ownerless symbols which he endowed with an implicit dynamism and set to acting out a thematic plot.

For the mythic and archetypal interpretation of *Lycidas,* as it happens, there is a more plausible basis in Milton's ideas and characteristic procedures. As a Christian humanist of the Renaissance, Milton was eager to save the phenomena of classical culture, and thus shared with the modern archetypist an interest in synthesizing the ancient and modern, the primitive and civilized, pagan fable and Christian dogma, into an all-encompassing whole. And Milton knew, from diverse ancient and Renaissance mythographers, about the parallel to the death and resurrection of Christ in ancient fables and fertility cults—about what in *Paradise Lost* he called the "reviv'd Adonis" (IX, 440), and the "annual wound" of Thammuz, identified with Adonis by the Syrian damsels who lamented his fate "in amorous ditties all a Summer's day" (I, 446–452). But these facts are not adequate to validate a reading of *Lycidas* as a poem which is really about Adonis, or any other pagan fertility god. In *Lycidas* Milton makes no allusion whatever to Adonis, and he refers to Orpheus only to voice despair that even the Muse, his mother, was helpless to prevent his hideous death. In his references to these fables in *Paradise Lost*, Milton specifies that the story of the Garden of revived Adonis is "feign'd," lists Thammuz-Adonis among the "Devils [adored] for Deities," and describes the mother of Orpheus as "an empty dream" (VII, 39). For though a humanist, Milton is a Christian humanist, to whom revelation is not one more echo of archetypal myths but the archetype itself, the one Truth, which had been either corrupted or distortedly foreshadowed, "prefigured," in various pagan deities and fables. There is a world of difference between Milton's assumption that there is only one religion and Blake's archetypal assertion that "All Religions are One."

Furthermore, by conflating Christian and non-Christian story into equivalent variations on a single rebirth pattern, an archetypal reading tends to cancel dramatic structure by flattening the poem out, or even—in the extreme but common view that we get closer to the archetype as we move back along the scale toward the vegetational cycle itself—by turning the poem inside out. For if we regard the rebirth theme as having been revealed in the opening passage on the unwithering laurel, myrtle, and ivy, and as merely reiterated in later passages on Orpheus, on water, on sanguine flowers, and in the allusion to Christ and the risen Lycidas, then the denouement of the poem lies in its exordium and its movement is not a progress but an eddy.

The movement of *Lycidas,* on the contrary, is patently from despair through a series of insights to triumphant joy. We can put it this way: read literally, the elegy proper opens with the statement "Lycidas is dead, dead ere his prime"; it concludes with the flatly opposing statement "Lycidas your sorrow is *not* dead." Everything that intervenes has been planned to constitute a plausible sequence of thoughts that will finally convert a logical contradiction into a lyric reversal by the anagnorisis, the discovery, that for a worthy Christian poet-priest a seeming defeat by death is actually an immortal triumph.

Milton achieves this reversal by a gradual shift from the natural, pastoral, and pagan viewpoint to the viewpoint of Christian revelation and its promise of another world, the Kingdom of Heaven. He carefully marks for us the stages of this ascent by what, to contemporary readers, was the conspicuous device of grading the levels of his style. For as Milton said in the treatise *Of Education,* issued seven years after *Lycidas,* decorum (including "the fitted stile of lofty, mean, or lowly" to the height of the matter) "is the grand master peece to observe." The problem of decorum had been particularly debated in connection with the pastoral, which had troubled Renaissance theorists by the duplicity of its stylistic requirements, since it typically dealt with high matters under the lowly guise of a conversation between uncouth swains. Milton's comment on the fitted style probably was an echo of Puttenham's statement that "decencie," or "decorum"—the just proportioning of the "high, meane, and base stile"—is "the chiefe praise of any writer"; and Puttenham had also pointed out that, though the normal level of pastoral was the "base and humble stile," the form was often used "under the vaile of homely persons and in rude speeches to insinuate and glaunce at greater matters." [10]

Accordingly Milton's singer opens the poem with a style higher than the pastoral norm: "Begin, and somewhat loudly sweep the string" is what he bids the muses, echoing the "*Sicelides Musae, paulo maiora canamus*" with which Virgil had elevated the pitch of his fourth, or "Messianic," Eclogue. (Puttenham had remarked concerning this pastoral that, because of its lofty subject, "Virgill used a somewhat swelling stile" and that under the circumstances, "this was decent." [11]) The initial level of *Lycidas* suffices for the early pastoral and pagan sections on sympathizing nature, the nymphs, and the death of Orpheus. But this last reference evokes the despairing thought: what boots the ascetic life for those who, like Lycidas, stake everything on a treacherous future? The immediate comfort occurs in a thought in which the highest pagan ethics comes closest to the Christian: the distinction between mere earthly reputation and the meed of true fame awarded by a divine and infallible judge. The concept is only tangentially Christian, however, for the deities named in this passage, Phoebus and Jove, are pagan ones. Nevertheless "that strain," the singer observes, "was of a higher mood," and he therefore readdresses himself to Arethuse and Mincius, waters associated with the classical pastoralists, as a transition back to the initial key: "But now my *Oat* proceeds. . . ."

The next modulation comes when St. Peter raises by implication the even more searching question why a faithful shepherd is taken early, while the corrupt ones prosper. He himself gives the

[10] George Puttenham, *The Arte of English Poesie* (1589), in *Elizabethan Critical Essays*, ed. G. G. Smith (London, 1904), II, 27, 40, 155.

[11] *Ibid.*, p. 156. In his Epistle and gloss to Spenser's *Shepherd's Calendar*, one of the chief models for *Lycidas*, E. K. had also emphasized the question of stylistic decorum in the pastoral. He observed of the October Eclogue, which concerns poetry, that the style is properly "more loftye than the rest," and that at its inspired close Spenser's "verse groweth so big, that it seemeth he hath forgot the meanenesse of shepheards state and stile." (*Spenser's Minor Poems*, ed. Ernest De Selincourt, 1910, pp. 101, 104.)

obscurely terrifying answer: the two-handed engine stands ready to smite at the door; infallible justice dispenses punishment as well as rewards. This time the "dread voice" has been not merely of "a higher mood" but of an entirely different ontological and stylistic order, for it has "shrunk" the pastoral stream and frightened away the "Sicilian Muse" altogether. It is not only that the voice has been raised in the harsh rhetoric of anger but that it belongs to a pastor, and expresses a matter alien to the world of pagan pastoral. A Christian subject is here for the first time explicit. The appearance and speech of Peter, although brought in, as Milton said in his subtitle, "by occasion," is far from a digression. It turns out, indeed, to be the climax and turning point of the lyric meditation, for without it the resolution, in heaven, would seem to have been contrived through Christ as a patent *deus ex machina.* The speech of Peter has in fact closely paraphrased Christ's own pastoral parable (John 9:39–41; 10:1–18) addressed to the Pharisees, in which He too had denounced those who remain blind to the truth, who climb into the sheepfold, and who abandon their sheep to the marauding wolf, and had then identified Himself as the Good Shepherd who lays down His life for His sheep—but only, He adds, "that I might take it again." Once Christ, the shepherd who died to be born again, is paralleled to the dead shepherd Lycidas, though by allusion only, the resolution of the elegy is assured—especially since Peter, the Pilot of the Galilean Lake, is the very Apostle who had been taught by Christ, through faith and force of example, to walk on the water in which he would otherwise have drowned (Matthew 14:25–31). The elegiac singer, however, is momentarily occupied with the specific references rather than the Scriptural overtones of Peter's comment, with the result that the resolution, so skilfully planted in his evolving thought, is delayed until he has tried to interpose a little ease by strewing imaginary flowers on Lycidas' imagined hearse. But this evasion only brings home the horror of the actual condition of the lost and weltering corpse. By extraordinary dramatic management, it is at this point of profoundest depression that the thought of Lycidas' body sinking to "the bottom of the monstrous world" releases the full implication of St. Peter's speech, so that the lyric singer makes the leap from nature to revelation, in the great lyric peripety:

> Weep no more, woeful Shepherds weep no more,
> For Lycidas your sorrow is not dead,
> Sunk though he be beneath the wat'ry floor . . .
> So Lycidas, sunk low, but mounted high,
> Through the dear might of him that walk'd the waves. . . .

This consolation is total, where the two earlier ones were partial. For one thing, we now move from the strict judgment of merit and demerit to the God who rewards us beyond the requirements of justice with the free gift of a life eternal. Also, the elegist has had the earlier promises of reward and retribution by hearsay from Apollo and Peter, but now, in a passage thronged with echoes from the Book of Revelation and soaring, accordantly, into an assured sublimity of style, he has his own imaginative revelation, so that he, like St. John in that Book, might say: "And I saw a new heaven and a new earth." His vision is of a Lycidas who has lost his life to find a better life in a felicity without tears; in which even that last infirmity of noble mind, the desire for fame, has been purged "in the blest Kingdoms meek of joy and love," the earthly inclination to Amaryllis and Neaera has been sublimated into the "unexpressive nuptial Song" of the marriage of the Lamb, and the pastoral properties of grove, stream, and song serve only to shadow forth a Kingdom outside space and beyond the vicissitude of the seasons. But the meditation of the lyric singer, as I have said, is ultimately concerned with the dead as they affect the living; so, by way of the Genius of the shore, we redescend to the stylistic level of plain utterance and conclude with the solitary piper at evening, facing with restored confidence the contingencies of a world in which the set and rise of the material sun are only the emblematic promise of another life.

IV

We are all, I am sure, by now aware of a considerable irony: I undertook to resolve the five types of *Lycidas* into one, and instead have added a sixth. But of course, that is all a critic can do. A critique does not give us the poem, but only a description of the poem. Whatever the ontological status of *Lycidas* as an object-in-itself, there are many possible descriptions of *Lycidas*—as many, in fact, as there are diverse critical premises and procedures which can be applied to the text.

In the bewildering multiplication of assumptions and procedures in the present age, it would be useful to have a safeguard against confusion, and a safeguard as well against the sceptical temptation to throw all criticism overboard as a waste of time. I would suggest that we regard any critique of a poem as a persuasive description; that is, as an attempt, under the guise of statements of fact, to persuade the reader to look at a poem in a particular way. Thus when a critic says, with assurance, "A poem means X," consider him to say: "Try reading it as though it meant X." When he says, "*Lycidas* is really about Milton himself," quietly translate: "I recommend that you entertain the hypothesis that *Lycidas* is about Milton, and see how it applies." From this point of view, the best interpretation of *Lycidas*—we can say, if we like to use that philosophical idiom, the reading which approximates most closely to *Lycidas* as an object-in-itself—is the one among the interpretations at present available which provides the best fit to all the parts of the poem in their actual order, emphases, and emotional effects, and which is in addition consistent with itself and with what we know of Milton's literary and intellectual inheritance and his characteristic poetic procedures.[13]

The persuasive description of *Lycidas* which I have sketched

[13] See R. S. Crane's analysis of critical interpretations as hypotheses for investigating the structures of poems, *The Languages of Criticism and the Structure of Poetry* (Toronto, 1953), pp. 164–183.

must be judged by the degree to which it satisfies these criteria of correspondence and coherence. To be sure it has a serious handicap, when measured against the startling discoveries in recent years of what *Lycidas* is really about. It is singularly unexciting to be told at this date that *Lycidas* is really what it seems—a dramatic presentation of a traditional pastoral singer uttering a ritual lament and raising in its course questions about untimely death and God's providence which are resolved by the recognition that God's Kingdom is not of this world. But surely this is the great commonplace in terms of which Milton, as a thoroughly Christian poet, inevitably thought. We cannot expect his innovations, on this crucial issue, to be doctrinal; the novelty (and it is entirely sufficient to make this an immense feat of lyric invention) consists in the way that the pastoral conventions and Christian concepts are newly realized, reconciled, and dramatized in the minute particulars of this unique and splendid poem.

I would not be understood to claim that the alternative readings of *Lycidas* I have described are illegitimate or their discoveries unrewarding. They freshen our sense of old and familiar poems, and they force readers into novel points of vantage that yield interesting insights, of which some hold good for other critical viewpoints as well. I am as susceptible as most readers to the charm of suddenly being brought to see a solidly dramatic lyric flattened into an ornate texture of thematic images, or to the thrill of the archetypal revelation whereby, as Jane Harrison described it, behind the "bright splendors" of "great things in literature" one sees moving "darker and older shapes." But in our fascination with the ultra-violet and infra-red discoveries made possible by modern speculative instruments, we must take care not to overlook the middle of the poetic spectrum. The necessary but not sufficient condition for a competent reader of poetry remains what it has always been—a keen eye for the obvious.

LYCIDAS

John Milton

Yet once more, O ye laurels, and once more,
Ye myrtles brown, with ivy never sear,
I come to pluck your berries harsh and crude,
And with forced fingers rude
Shatter your leaves before the mellowing year.
Bitter constraint and sad occasion dear
Compels me to disturb your season due:
For Lycidas is dead, dead ere his prime,
Young Lycidas, and hath not left his peer.
Who would not sing for Lycidas? He knew 10
Himself to sing, and build the lofty rime.
He must not float upon his watery bier
Unwept, and welter to the parching wind,
Without the meed of some melodious tear.
Begin, then, Sisters of the sacred well,
That from beneath the seat of Jove doth spring,
Begin, and somewhat loudly sweep the string.
Hence with denial vain and coy excuse;
So may some gentle Muse
With lucky words favor my destined urn, 20
And as he passes turn
And bid fair peace be to my sable shroud.
For we were nursed upon the selfsame hill,
Fed the same flock, by fountain, shade, and rill.
Together both, ere the high lawns appeared
Under the opening eyelids of the morn,
We drove afield, and both together heard
What time the gray-fly winds her sultry horn,
Battening our flocks with the fresh dews of night,
Oft till the star that rose at evening, bright, 30
Toward heaven's descent had sloped his westering wheel.
Meanwhile the rural ditties were not mute,
Tempered to the oaten flute;

Rough Satyrs danced, and Fauns with cloven heel
From the glad sound would not be absent long,
And old Damoetas loved to hear our song.
  But, oh! the heavy change, now thou art gone,
Now thou art gone, and never must return!
Thee, Shepherd, thee the woods and desert caves,
With wild thyme and the gadding vine o'ergrown, 40
And all their echoes mourn.
The willows, and the hazel copses green,
Shall now no more be seen,
Fanning their joyous leaves to thy soft lays.
As killing as the canker to the rose,
Or taint-worm to the weanling herds that graze,
Or frost to flowers, that their gay wardrobe wear,
When first the white-thorn blows;
Such, Lycidas, thy loss to shepherd's ear.
  Where were ye, Nymphs, when the remorseless deep 50
Closed o'er the head of your loved Lycidas?
For neither were ye playing on the steep
Where your old bards, the famous Druids, lie,
Nor on the shaggy top of Mona high,
Nor yet where Deva spreads her wizard stream:
Aye me! I fondly dream
"Had ye been there"—for what could that have done?
What could the Muse herself that Orpheus bore,
The Muse herself, for her enchanting son,
Whom universal nature did lament, 60
When by the rout that made the hideous roar
His gory visage down the stream was sent,
Down the swift Hebrus to the Lesbian shore?
  Alas! what boots it with uncessant care
To tend the homely slighted shepherd's trade,
And strictly meditate the thankless Muse?
Were it not better done as others use,
To sport with Amaryllis in the shade,
Or with the tangles of Neaera's hair?
Fame is the spur that the clear spirit doth raise 70
(That last infirmity of noble mind)

To scorn delights, and live laborious days;
But the fair guerdon when we hope to find,
And think to burst out into sudden blaze,
Comes the blind Fury with th' abhorrèd shears,
And slits the thin-spun life. "But not the praise,"
Phoebus replied, and touched my trembling ears;
"Fame is no plant that grows on mortal soil,
Nor in the glistering foil
Set off to the world, nor in broad rumor lies, 80
But lives and spreads aloft by those pure eyes
And perfect witness of all-judging Jove;
As he pronounces lastly on each deed,
Of so much fame in heaven expect thy meed."
  O fountain Arethuse, and thou honored flood,
Smooth-sliding Mincius, crowned with vocal reeds,
That strain I heard was of a higher mood.
But now my oat proceeds,
And listens to the Herald of the Sea
That came in Neptune's plea. 90
He asked the waves, and asked the felon winds,
What hard mishap hath doomed this gentle swain?
And questioned every gust of rugged wings
That blows from off each beakèd promontory.
They knew not of his story;
And sage Hippotades their answer brings,
That not a blast was from his dungeon strayed,
The air was calm, and on the level brine
Sleek Panope with all her sisters played.
It was that fatal and perfidious bark, 100
Built in the eclipse, and rigged with curses dark,
That sunk so low that sacred head of thine.
  Next, Camus, reverend sire, went footing slow,
His mantle hairy, and his bonnet sedge,
Inwrought with figures dim, and on the edge
Like to that sanguine flower inscribed with woe.
"Ah! who hath reft," quoth he, "my dearest pledge?"
Last came, and last did go,
The Pilot of the Galilean Lake;

Two massy keys he bore of metals twain 110
(The golden opes, the iron shuts amain).
He shook his mitered locks, and stern bespake:
"How well could I have spared for thee, young swain,
Enow of such as for their bellies' sake,
Creep and intrude, and climb into the fold!
Of other care they little reckoning make
Than how to scramble at the shearers' feast,
And shove away the worthy bidden guest.
Blind mouths! that scarce themselves know how to hold
A sheep-hook, or have learned aught else the least 120
That to the faithful herdman's art belongs!
What recks it them? What need they? They are sped;
And when they list, their lean and flashy songs
Grate on their scrannel pipes of wretched straw;
The hungry sheep look up, and are not fed,
But swoln with wind and the rank mist they draw,
Rot inwardly, and foul contagion spread;
Besides what the grim wolf with privy paw
Daily devours apace, and nothing said.
But that two-handed engine at the door 130
Stands ready to smite once, and smite no more."
Return, Alpheus, the dread voice is past
That shrunk thy streams; return, Sicilian Muse,
And call the vales, and bid them hither cast
Their bells and flowerets of a thousand hues.
Ye valleys low, where the mild whispers use
Of shades, and wanton winds, and gushing brooks,
On whose fresh lap the swart star sparely looks,
Throw hither all your quaint enameled eyes,
That on the green turf suck the honeyed showers, 140
And purple all the ground with vernal flowers.
Bring the rathe primrose that forsaken dies,
The tufted crow-toe, and pale jessamine,
The white pink, and the pansy freaked with jet,
The glowing violet,
The musk-rose, and the well-attired woodbine,
With cowslips wan that hang the pensive head,

And every flower that sad embroidery wears;
Bid amaranthus all his beauty shed,
And daffodillies fill their cups with tears, 150
To strew the laureate hearse where Lycid lies.
For so to interpose a little ease,
Let our frail thoughts dally with false surmise.
Aye me! Whilst thee the shores and sounding seas
Wash far away, where'er thy bones are hurled,
Whether beyond the stormy Hebrides,
Where thou perhaps under the whelming tide
Visit'st the bottom of the monstrous world;
Or whether thou, to our moist vows denied,
Sleep'st by the fable of Bellerus old, 160
Where the great Vision of the guarded mount
Looks toward Namancos and Bayona's hold;
Look homeward Angel now, and melt with ruth;
And, O ye dolphins, waft the hapless youth.
  Weep no more, woeful shepherds, weep no more,
For Lycidas, your sorrow, is not dead,
Sunk though he be beneath the watery floor,
So sinks the day-star in the ocean bed,
And yet anon repairs his drooping head,
And tricks his beams, and with new-spangled ore 170
Flames in the forehead of the morning sky.
So Lycidas sunk low, but mounted high,
Through the dear might of Him that walked the waves,
Where other groves, and other streams along,
With nectar pure his oozy locks he laves,
And hears the unexpressive nuptial song,
In the blest kingdoms meek of joy and love.
There entertain him all the Saints above,
In solemn troops, and sweet societies,
That sing, and singing in their glory move, 180
And wipe the tears forever from his eyes.
Now, Lycidas, the shepherds weep no more;
Henceforth thou art the Genius of the shore,
In thy large recompense, and shalt be good
To all that wander in the perilous flood.

Thus sang the uncouth swain to th' oaks and rills,
While the still morn went out with sandals gray;
He touched the tender stops of various quills,
With eager thought warbling his Doric lay:
And now the sun had stretched out all the hills, 190
And now was dropped into the western bay;
At last he rose, and twitched his mantle blue:
Tomorrow to fresh woods, and pastures new.

Why Diderot?

JACQUES BARZUN

I

WHENEVER I AM LOOKING FOR enjoyment from literature and the arts, and also when, in the modern manner, I "study" them for clues to intellectual or social history, I find myself most drawn to the geniuses whose fame is unsettled. Of the ancients I prefer Euripides and Lucian; in recent times, William James, Walter Bagehot, and Samuel Butler; before them, Berlioz and Diderot. Their works and characters pull me back again and again to speculate and admire.

This preference may be temperamental in part, just as their incomplete or grudging recognition is in part accidental. But my choice is also rational, like the state of their reputations, and both are possibly instructive. Of course, if the situation is to tell us something new, we must be sure that we have got hold of a truly great mind, and not merely an approximation of one. Nor should we confuse what I call unsettled fame with obscurity. The group of geniuses I have in mind are figures known, at least by name, to all who discuss ideas and their history. Nor has praise been withheld from my chosen men. Their distinction lies in the perennial disquiet they inspire. Their praise is mixed with doubts. Most significant, perhaps, the reasons for valuing their work are many and conflicting. In a word, the men and their achievements resist classification.

The effect of this lack of pliability upon the ordinary critic is extraordinary. Thus in the excellent *Oxford Companion to French Literature* one reads that Diderot "had not the patience and method to produce any single great work." This comes after the statement that the direction of the *Encyclopédie* was "the most notable of his contributions to the advancement of knowledge, and a vast burden of which, with great courage and perseverance, he bore the main share." Apparently perseverance is not patience and the *Encyclopédie* is not a work of method. What is more, this estimate of Diderot's character tells us that he was "affable, generous, a faithful friend . . . bubbling over with ideas, enthusiasm and coarse gaiety; at the same time violent and unbalanced."

I attach great importance to such summaries in reputable handbooks, for they reflect in their bland confusion the general uncertainty I speak of; and they naturally spread it farther, to the newcomers for whom such books are intended. In these same pages Diderot's great works—and particularly that masterpiece, *Rameau's Nephew*—are listed as "minor philosophical works," while the doctrine to which they contribute in this minor way is said to be philosophical determinism. Diderot was "an experimental materialist" who anticipated "in some respects later evolutionary ideas." He was in addition an "ardent moralist" and "the founder of art criticism in France," though "his underlying principles are full of fallacies." I am reminded by these wondrous judgments of the "authoritative" literature on Berlioz thirty years ago, when I began wading through its naive incoherence and factual inaccuracy.

For this state of affairs, which recurs and will recur in the history of civilization, I discern two causes: profound originality and transcendent imperfection. I say transcendent to suggest a superior quality, that of work produced at a time when perfection along established ways is no longer of any value. For example, after the tales of Voltaire—after *Candide* especially—and after Rousseau's *Confessions,* no possibility is left of insinuating philosophy, morality, and psychology agreeably, through narratives couched in a diction limpid and calm. Nothing less than the scabrous irregularities of *D'Alembert's Dream* and the vulgar language and detail of *Rameau's Nephew* satisfy the need to re-establish contact with common life.

Men such as Diderot, then, are *uncompleting* men because they are finders and initiators, not concluders and finishers. That is why they puzzle the tidy minds of the academy, whose valuable role is to affix labels and put away in glass cases. Diderot, they rightly say, cannot be "associated with a stabilized genre" (this failure sounds ominous) "much less with a single recognized masterpiece." Here one might demur. If *Rameau's Nephew* is not a masterpiece, then the term had best be abandoned. "Recognized" is again a matter of opinion. If Goethe and Freud recognized in Diderot a master of reality, he can wait for the professors of literature. Meantime we grant them that Diderot is not of those who, to the sound of public acclaim, drive the last nail into the edifice their predecessors have built. Rather, they destroy and build anew, groping and stumbling at times, seeming paradoxically full of old ideas as well as of new, and unable to point to unmistakable followers because posterity altogether, in all its diversity and warfare, follows in their steps.

Their very career, in a worldly sense, is untoward. Here is Diderot, a great figure in his own day, courted by the crowned heads of states and of intellect, a hero in the struggle for liberty of thought, a voluminous, indefatigable writer not one of whose productions is without originality or importance, yet whose ultimate greatness depends on three or four works, written relatively late in life, nearly lost, and published half a century after his death. In life, his friends might dub him *"le philosophe"* and Voltaire liken him to Plato, but the high performance justifying these epithets was hidden from those who spoke them.

II

Under "Diderot" in Flaubert's *Dictionary of Accepted Ideas* we read: "Always followed by d'Alembert"; and under "Encyclopédie," which the joining of the names evokes, we find: "Quaint and old-fashioned; but even so, thunder against." To get at Diderot, to read him, understand him, and love him, one must push to one side the gigantic and successful enterprise to which he devoted thirty years of his life. Not that the twenty-eight folio volumes of the encyclopedia, packed with knowledge and doctrine, wit and good prose, are a negligible achievement. They testify to Diderot's enormous intelligence, just as the story of the vicissitudes endured by the solitary editor defines his heroic character. But on the scale of the eighteenth century the work was but a mass medium for spreading culture. Diderot himself described it in terms we recognize as good advertising copy: "a complete library"—"lavishly illustrated"—"no one who wants to be up to date can afford, etc. . . ." But strange as it may seem after the consequences, good and evil, that have been ascribed to the *Encyclopédie,* Diderot's superhuman labors to produce it were but his tribute to the spirit of the day. One proof of this is that the work was a great commercial success. Many of the "best people" were encyclopedists. To write the text Diderot found a hundred contributors. To write his late masterpieces or to read them aright he found only himself, and we are still "discovering" him 175 years after his death.

There is even a subtle contradiction between the bearing of the *Encyclopédie* and Diderot's innermost convictions. The idea of knowledge codified and portable, of enlightenment by system, went against Diderot's earliest and deepest perceptions. If ever the editor wondered why he was striving so hard to put that loaded alphabet in order, he may have told himself that he was doing it only to clear the public mind for receiving his own fluid speculations. He did not, of course, reason in this way, so far as I know; I only make up this internal dialogue to render the contrast I see between the plain business of the *Encyclopédie* and the evocative meaning of the final great works. Yet my fancy is not wholly without warrant. In his *Letter on the Blind,* just before Diderot enters the long tunnel of editorial work, he gives as it were a last look at reality and exclaims: "I cannot conceive why people do not grow bored reading so much and learning nothing."

For his own part, Diderot had been reading a great deal since early youth, when he was a very fair student of the arts and sciences, particularly mathematics. He had made his bohemian way in Paris by tutoring in that science, by translating from English and Italian, which he had mastered alone, and by other hackwork. But none of this was meant to foster a respectable career as man of letters. Diderot was a hot, passionate, rebellious youth. He quarrelled with his well-loved father over marrying, and was even sent to prison on that account. And for his earliest *Pensées* (1746) Diderot used Shaftesbury's name to cover his own, so that he might express his faith in "enthusiasm," in rash deviation from eighteenth-century taste.

What is more, this fledgling philosopher spoke in a new voice. His prose was rapid, trenchant, sinewy. One might suppose that these adjectives apply as much to Voltaire, but the two styles are worlds apart: Diderot's tone becomes less and less "polite" as he becomes more and more himself. He relies increasingly on colloquialism—and hence on dialogue—to achieve what he seeks, which we should today call "realism." He is dissatisfied with anything less than the exactitude of intimacy and concreteness, and he says so:

> In general any language is poor in words adequate to the uses of writers with a lively imagination. They are as badly off as intelligent

> foreigners—the situations they invent, the delicate nuances of character they perceive, the naturalness *[naïveté]* of the depictions they want to give, make them continually depart from ordinary modes of speech and make them use turns of phrase that are always admirable provided they are neither precious nor obscure. . . . The license taken with the common tongue is overlooked, the truth of the rendering alone strikes us.

This is the creed of a literary Romantic, dated 1749, the year of Goethe's birth. Nor is it with Diderot an isolated intention, a vagary. His "psychology" (as we say today to mean his view of man), his artistic tastes, his morality, his science, his metaphysics, and his ultimate philosophy are in tune with this new *impatience.* Diderot wants to cut through the resilient web of conventional words and tested generalities so as to reach and grip the reality that flashes and beckons to him from between the joints of the neoclassic. And the first particle of that new truth shows him that Descartes' founding universal reason on the thinking self is an illusion. Men are diverse, each is unique, individualism and pluralism follow: "Since I am someone who acts thus and so, anyone who could act otherwise could not be me."

In the relativism of that sentence and in others about "matter capable of thought," critics have found Diderot's materialism and determinism. The propriety of using these terms can be plausibly argued, but then their definition has to be made so singular that they cease to have the common meaning in order to denote a position peculiar to Diderot. It would seem simpler to begin by saying what Diderot meant. Whatever he was, he cannot be classed with those who take comfort in the explanation that matter-in-motion alone exists, giving rise to human consciousness as an "epiphenomenon" which chemistry will one day explain. Diderot believes the opposite:

> Man is the sole starting point and end to which everything must finally be related. It would be absurd to put a cold, insensitive, speechless being in place of man, for if you banish man . . . from

> the face of the earth, this sublime and moving spectacle of nature will be but a sad and lifeless scene—the universe will be hushed, silence and darkness will regain sway . . . why should we not indeed make man the center of all that is?

Deciding to do so does not, it is true, account for the mystery of life, but that is a mystery which it is permissible to fail to solve. When Diderot supposes "thinking matter," he is but trying to get rid of the dualism of soul and body, like Goethe, Coleridge, the elder Darwin, and other vitalists half a century later. It was Diderot's "lively imagination" that enabled him to seize by direct intuition the primacy of life and the likelihood of organic evolution. These notions present difficulties, like all philosophic beliefs, and it is not my concern to prove them right or wrong in whole or in part. They show the direction of Diderot's thought and his intellectual temper and it is these I am concerned with. They announce a tendency which takes its rise in the late eighteenth century and dominates the early nineteenth; it lacks an historically ratified name; but supposing the thing and the name each properly understood, it could be called pragmatism.

Certainly William James, had he studied Diderot, would not have disowned him as a forerunner. They have in common the sense, rare in philosophers and undeveloped in the ordinary man, of the native and irremediable variety, the autonomous confusion of things. Hegel had this sense only to clamp down a waffle iron over the plastic mass. Other philosophers assure themselves that the disorder is but Appearance. Very few are sufficiently radical empiricists to adopt stubborn rules in the philosophical task of making order out of chaos, saying to themselves: "Remember! Concreteness, direct contact with the given, first and last!"

It is very likely that this rule is no more reliable than any other. The algebraist, for example, does pretty well when he leaves concreteness behind and leaps across the void of abstraction—as Diderot the mathematician was fully aware. But I am describing a philosophical complexion, and one must admit that the empirical pluralist, whose obsession is to find out first what the experience feels like, tastes and smells and thinks like, and only afterwards connects it, in patches, to create local order—such a philosopher avoids many errors and makes many discoveries. His temper is in fact the generator of novelty. Since I have paired Diderot and William James, it is apposite to give an example of Diderot's concreteness in psychological method, which is also a specimen of his originality in self-knowledge. The passage is from his *Letter on the Deaf and Dumb for the Use of Those Who Can Hear and Speak:*

> Sensation does not follow the successive unfolding of speech. If it could dictate to twenty mouths, each mouth uttering its word, all the preceding ideas would be expressed together. That is indeed what sensation would wonderfully perform on an ocular keyboard.

III

On this "ocular keyboard," I presume, the world played with Diderot's unconscious a duet to which he listened in order to transcribe it. His views on art and on morality reflect his determination not to tamper with his own naive, uncorrected impression. If he interprets it, he must do so without distorting the given; if he explains, he amplifies merely, and does not explain away. It is characteristic that in the great dialogue called *D'Alembert's Dream*, the true philosopher is man *dreaming*. Only in that state can he at once perceive and convey the nature of life. Waking, he suffers from too many constraints; the presence and the expectations of an interlocutor and a woman would spoil the deliverance. When Diderot wants to push farther the exploration of the self and examine the coercion of wild impulse by society, he makes use of Rameau's nephew to render plausible the inner dialogue of a double self, id and ego, each embodying a Reason the other cannot assimilate or defeat. It is the nephew, a Panurge-like character speaking in the accents of a modern novelist—Joyce or Céline—who points out to the philosophic "I" that the aim of being a good man by fulfilling one's duty to society is self-contradictory.

The repression that society exerts on appetite, that is, on the creature's urge to survive, master its environment, and enhance its share of life, is fitful but inescapable. The upshot of the struggle is what fills the prisons and the pages of history—pain, violence, and disgrace, the warping of character and the tragic downfall of ambitious talents. But that same erratic force is also the cause of the world's false standards. Diderot is not resigned to the hypocrisy which the good must put up with, and sometimes imitate, in order to live. As he says in *Rameau's Nephew,* in the whole kingdom everybody must dance his little cowardly dance of social flattery. Only one man walks—the King—and even he goes through contortions if he is ruled by a mistress.

Such is the price of civilization, which makes Diderot long for the primitive simplicity of Tahiti, or—what comes to the same thing—makes him understand the calculating selfishness of the disabused, typified by the wastrel Rameau. Yet Diderot is not a cynic and he cannot return to a primitive existence. He knows as well as Rousseau that there is no "going back to nature." In this predicament he solaces himself with the anodyne of his age: sentimentality. When warmth of feeling and cold egoism press equal claims upon the philosopher, the only escape is into a storybook tenderness contrasting the two and making virtue triumph. Hence the absurd stories inserted in Diderot's most lifelike dialogues, the maudlin passages in his art criticism, and the bad plays which were his contribution to the new bourgeois drama.

That this weakness was cultural rather than individual need hardly be demonstrated. Sentimentality afflicted all the great writers of the century, from the puritanical Richardson (whom Diderot worshipped as a psychologist) to Richardson's opposite, Fielding; and from the worldly wits, Voltaire, Sterne, and Beaumarchais, to the grave young lyricist Goethe. Goethe purged himself of the fault by writing *Werther,* but it has continued to plague other oppressed spirits down to our day, when it occurs in its inverted form of contrived brutality.

In Diderot we must take this blemish as accidental and dwell on the vision which his sentimentality seems to contradict. For it was from passion, not enlightenment, that the whole bent of his genius was naturalistic. He loved the actual. When he first undertook the Encyclopedia as a translator of the English work by Chambers, he noticed that his author relied on books for his information about crafts and trades, and that the books were wrong. Diderot decided to visit the craftsmen's shops and set things straight. Before the end of his eleven volumes of plates, he had five assistants doing nothing else but verify processes and draw tools and machines from life.

The originality of this outlook is shown by the discrepancy between it and what d'Alembert propounds in his Preface to the same work. The mathematician has little use for trade and technology. Only science interests him—science, the glory of the modern age, because it is universal and abstract and certain. Feeling, which is not subject to scientific inquiry, appears to d'Alembert as an inconvenience, like the imperfections in the glass of a telescope. And the practical arts, less "difficult" than science, always empirical and ridden with imperfection, form but the crude foundations of the cultural edifice.

Against this prevailing view, Diderot's origins and upbringing spoke consistently with his judgment and his tastes. The son of a cutler, he knew the value of technology in the making of civilization. Again like Rousseau, he had made his way upward from a social class well below that of the comfortable bourgeoisie, and he saw society as much more chaotic than "polite." Once at the top he kept his impressions and some of the manners of his beginnings: in all Europe only Diderot conversing with Catherine the Great could have seized her knee to make her listen to an argument. This naturalness was of a piece with his complaint to his family about the portrait that was painted of his father: "What you have done, you and the painter, is altogether worthless. I asked you for my everyday father and you have sent me nothing but my Sunday one."

It would be rash to make of Diderot a democrat, even by anticipation. The significance of his naturalism is not primarily political. It lies in the realm of what is now called culture. By being himself *à outrance,* he supplied a fresh model of human consciousness. To know this new man we must recognize intuitively how it is that an appreciation of the work of craftsmen and inventors goes with a respect for strong feeling and a skepticism about the social order. It is a very modern combination. Diderot was in fact developing a new sensibility. Diderot is *artiste* in a way in which Voltaire, for all his poetry, is not. And the new sensibility, as the coming age of Romanticism was to prove, was that of the artist in the comprehensive sense of the man whose perceptions and judgments are first and last esthetic, regardless of subject matter.

IV

That sensibility, Diderot did not, of course, achieve completely —or perhaps he lost part of it when young, under the pressure of circumstance. In middle life he thought back with regret to the days when he looked "*vif, ardent, et fou.*" But the fire thus freely shown did not die. Of all the men of his generation Diderot is the only one in whom I see the signs of a Faustian spirit and a Faustian quest. Like Faust, he abandoned a dry and mechanical interpretation of life and grew into an awareness that nature is alive.

Similarly, Diderot passes in his lifetime from the conception of art as a judicious sort of manufacture, subject to rules and graced with *je ne sais quoi,* to the conception that art is an unconscious study of nature—"foreknown by imagination or genius and rendered in cold blood." His own practice was increasingly that of the romanticist observer who quarries nature and himself for the materials of his art. Whether it is the description of female homosexuality in *La Religieuse* or the battle of wits in *Rameau's Nephew,* the author is making fiction and morality out of autobiography and the lives and deeds of his contemporaries. His art is historical and documentary in the manner consecrated only after Diderot's death, by the nineteenth century.

As a critic, Diderot frames as propositions what he believes in as a creator. This in itself is a departure from the neo-classic order of events, in which the canons of taste pre-exist and determine production. In his youth Diderot had studied music; in his old age he calls for what amounts to music drama. In this he was not alone; the emancipation of music was one of the first signs, in the eighteenth century, of the approaching artistic revolution. But in the criticism of painting Diderot was a solitary pioneer. His *Salons* were the first journalistic reports upon the fine arts, and despite all subsequent cavils they have not been equaled for liveliness, judgment, and critical audacity. They stand in the history of reviewing with Lessing's *Hamburgische Dramaturgie,* with the critical journalism of Berlioz, Baudelaire, and Shaw.

Here again Diderot's touchstone is the reality he sees, but used with superior judgment. Take, for example, his words on Boucher in 1761:

> What color! What variety! What a wealth of forms and ideas! The man has everything except Truth. No part of his compositions would please if separated from the rest. But the whole will captivate you. You will ask yourself, "Where in the world has anybody seen shepherds dressed with such rich elegance? What occasion has ever brought together in the open country, under the arches of a bridge and far from any house, so many men, women, and children, cattle, sheep, dogs, bottles of straw, water, fire, a lantern, braziers, cauldrons, and pitchers? . . . What a racket of miscellaneous objects!" You feel the absurdity of it and yet you cannot leave the picture. It will not let you go. You come back to it. The vice is so agreeable, the extravagance so inimitable and so rare.

To a love of external reality akin to the desire for an "everyday father," a love which is in large measure accessible to all once the spell of convention and abstraction is broken, Diderot added the less common love of emotional truthfulness. Long cultivated, this power is what enabled him to throw out in his dialogues so many remarkable hints of later systems, such as the famous argument by which Diderot tries to convince Rameau of the necessity of moral education: "If your little savage were left to himself and to his native blindness, he would in time join the infant's reasoning to the grown man's passions—he would strangle his father and sleep with his mother."

We have a glimpse of Diderot's method—if method it was—in the frequent asides that interrupt his dialogues. For example, after a wonderful pantomine by Rameau in behalf of expressiveness in music, Diderot asks himself: "Did I admire? Yes, I did admire. Was I moved to pity? I was moved. But a streak of derision was interwoven with these feelings and denatured them." It is reasonable to suppose that the dialogue form became his chosen medium because of its adaptability to this sort of interruption and introspection. The novel in the eighteenth century was too rigid and monotone to permit the nuance-seeking which became Diderot's chief concern as thinker and writer. The dialogue form is not dramatic but dialectical; it is not narrative but anecdotal. Its advantages are precisely those which the artist-philosopher requires, permitting him to render the dramatic and narrative quality to be found in ideas, without having to delay the movement or distort the shape of the regular play or novel form.

This latitude does not mean that the writer of dialogues can let his pen run on as statement and rejoinder occur to him, nor again that his work is but the parceling out of arguments and objections among lay figures. One has only to compare with Diderot's the dialogues of Hume "Concerning Natural Religion" to see the difference between a philosopher *tout court* and one who is also an artist. Diderot's figures are vivid creatures, even when asleep, as is d'Alembert in the famous *Dream*. In *Rameau's Nephew*, as Goethe pointed out, the aimlessness is a superficial appearance. The work has the tightest weave imaginable and is cut to a perfect model. In fact, since Plato and Lucian, literature affords but few examples of mastery in this difficult though oft-attempted genre. In the last two hundred years, unless one takes Peacock's novels as dialogues (which is legitimate), Diderot stands alone: Wilde and Landor and Santayana, admirable as they are, lack both his originality and his power.

His originality could, of course, be illustrated much more fully than I have done. His remarkable views on sexuality, on pragmatic religion, on the emancipation of women, and on innumerable issues of esthetics and social philosophy would make a long list. And it would justify the claim that he belongs among the half-dozen geniuses that stand out among the great galaxy of eighteenth-century minds. This small company of the incomparable are: Lessing and Kant, Goethe and Burke, Rousseau and Diderot.

The Songs in *Mother Courage*

ERIC BENTLEY

THE SONG OF SHELTER[1]

[Scene 10]

In March a tree we planted
To make the garden gay.
In June we were enchanted:
A lovely rose was blooming
The balmy air perfuming!
Blest of the gods are they
Who have a garden gay.
In June we were enchanted.

When snow falls helter skelter
And loudly blows the storm
Our farmhouse gives us shelter.
The winter's in a hurry

But we've no cause for worry.
Cosy are we and warm
Though loudly blows the storm:
Our farmhouse gives us shelter.

"THE SONG OF SHELTER" is the last song in *Mother Courage*, yet it can be discussed first as showing how singing functions dramatically in Brecht's plays. "The Song of Shelter" is the entire written content of a scene (10). Yet the content of the song would not give you the scene. The scene consists of a gesture or, rather, a posture: Kattrin and her mother pull the wagon themselves now. Exhausted, they have stopped. A voice is heard from inside a farmhouse. The drama of the scene is in the relationship of the voice to the two listeners. The singer has shelter; the listeners do not. This is the final upshot of the song. The conception is distanced and decorated by a preceding stanza celebrating the singer's participation in the beauty of the garden. But Brecht used to point out to actors the error of singing the song chiefly with the roses in mind. The voice must sing not only joy in the garden's beauty but complacency in possession of the house.

This scene, which needs no dialogue, also needs no movement. It is a tableau, an image. Movement is left entirely to the music—handled by an unseen singer.

No dialogue. The scene belongs to a girl who cannot speak: Kattrin, who will be killed in the next scene.

We have to ask ourselves how many dramatists can do so much with a pause in the action filled only by an off-stage singing voice.

Some are indoors "in the warm"; others outside in the cold. Brecht tends to divide mankind that way. Class struggle? Perhaps. But it might be more accurate to say class antagonism without struggle. And the word "class" has some misleading connotations. The lines of *The Threepenny Film* are closer to the point:

Und die Einen sind im Dunkeln
Und die Andern sind im Licht—

"Some there are who live in darkness/Some there are who live in light." Brecht's poetry is one long defence of those who live in the darkness—like Kattrin.

The little song tends, then, to universalize the statement the play is making here. Brecht's songs generally have this tendency. Sometimes they have it supremely. The preceding song—of Solomon—is an instance. It presents, like "The Song of Shelter," one of Brecht's leading conceptions. It also sums up *Mother Courage.* The play tells the story of the killing of Courage's three children: the Honest Son, the Brave Son, and the Kind Daughter. The song takes an instance of honesty (Socrates), of bravery (Caesar), and of kindness (St. Martin) and shows how all are killed. The singers (the Cook and Courage herself) do not forget their own position: they are identified with Solomon, whose wisdom was knowing the futility of wisdom, and with those who have obeyed the Ten Commandments to no effect.

THE SONG OF SOLOMON

[Scene 9]

You've heard of wise old Solomon,
  You know his history.
He thought so little of this earth,
He cursed the hour of his birth
  Declaring: all is vanity.
How very wise was Solomon!
  But all the world knew what was what
Before the setting of the sun:
  His wisdom 'twas that put him on the spot.
So thank your stars if you have none.

And Julius Caesar, who was brave,
  You saw what came of him.
He sat like God on an altar-piece
  And yet they tore him limb from limb
While his prestige did still increase.

"Et tu, Brute! I am undone!"
  And all the world knew what was what
Before the setting of the sun:
  'Twas bravery that put him on the spot.
So thank your stars if you have none.

You all know honest Socrates
  Who always spoke the truth.
They owed him thanks for that, you'd think,
Yet they put hemlock in his drink
  And swore that he was bad for youth.
How honest was the people's son!
  But all the world knew what was what
Before the setting of the sun:
  'Twas honesty that put him on the spot.
So thank your stars if you have none.

Selfless Saint Martin could not bear
  His fellow creature's woes.
  He met a poor man in the snows
And gave him half his cloak to wear:
  So both of them fell down and froze.
What an unselfish paragon!
  But all the world knew what was what
Before the setting of the sun:
  Unselfishness had put him on the spot.
So thank your stars if you have none.

God's Ten Commandments we have kept
  And acted as we should.
  It has not done us any good.
O you who sit beside a fire,
Pray help us now: our need is dire!
Strict godliness we've always shown,
  But all the world knew what was what
Before the setting of the sun:
  Our godliness has put us on the spot.
So thank your stars if you have none.

The summing-up is approximately placed just before the final catastrophe of the story: the shooting of Kattrin. Such placing is, perhaps, obvious enough. Something about Brecht's play-making that may easily escape attention is the relation of this song to "The Great Capitulation" (scene 4), which comes just after the first catastrophe: the shooting of Swiss Cheese. The two songs are twin pillars supporting the play as a whole. They make complementary statements. The first speaks of the necessity of defeatism, of going down on your knees "to God Almighty if you please!" The second records what the fruits of such piety are. Everything runs downhill in this play—in the action and in the thinking. But if you read it backwards, it is optimistic. The fruits of the piety wouldn't be there but for the piety. The piety wouldn't be there but for the capitulation. Moral: don't capitulate—an optimistic injunction, if ever there was one! If the play doesn't quite back it up, it would nonetheless like to, as witness the enormous sympathy for the one who does not capitulate: Kattrin. No absence of empathy and identification there!

THE SONG OF THE GREAT CAPITULATION

[Scene 4]

Long, long ago, a green beginner,
  I thought myself a special case.
(None of your ordinary, run of the mill girls, with my looks and my talent and my love of the higher things!)
I picked a hair out of my dinner
  And put the waiter in his place.
(All or nothing. Anyway, never the second best. I am the master of my fate. I'll take no orders from no one.)
Then a little bird whispers!
        The bird says: "Wait a year or so
        And marching with the band you'll go
        Keeping in step, now fast, now slow,
        And piping out your little spiel.

Then one day the battalions wheel
And you go down upon your knees
To God Almighty if you please!"

My friend, before that year was over
I'd learned to drink their cup of tea.
(Two children round your neck and the price of bread and what all!)
When they were through with me, moreover,
They had me where they wanted me.
(You must get in with people! If you scratch my back, I'll scratch yours. Never stick your neck out!)
Then a little bird whispered!
The bird says: "Scarce a year or so
And marching with the band she'd go
Keeping in step, now fast, now slow,
And piping out her little spiel.
Then one day the battalions wheel
And she goes down upon her knees
To God Almighty if you please!"

Our plans are big, our hopes colossal.
We hitch our wagon to a star.
(Where there's a will, there's a way. You can't hold a good man down.)
"We can lift mountains," says the apostle.
And yet: how heavy one cigar!
(You must cut your coat according to your cloth.)
That little bird whispers!
The bird says: "Wait a year or so
And marching with the band we go
Keeping in step, now fast, now slow,
And piping out our little spiel.
Then one day the battalions wheel
And we go down upon our knees
To God Almighty if you please!"

"The Great Capitulation" is the second song of Mother Courage herself, and it contains her story. "The Song of Fraternization" contains Yvette's story. The simplest alternative to capitulating is fraternizing—if you can't lick 'em, join 'em—it seems preferable. The stories of failure that this play otherwise consists of are offset by the success story of Yvette. She comes up in the world while all the others come down or stay down. "It pays to fraternize"—I find myself speaking ironically because, of course, the Yvette episode is ironical. As usual, the song contains the essence. The one positive thing in Yvette's life is over before our tale begins: she has been in love.

THE SONG OF FRATERNIZATION

[Scene 3]

Scarce seventeen was I when
  The foe came to our land
And laid aside his sabre
  And took me by the hand.
    And we performed by day
    The sacred rite of May
    And we performed by night
    Another sacred rite.
    The regiment, well exercised,
    Presented arms, then stood at ease,
    Then took us off behind the trees
    Where we fraternized.

Each of us had her foe and
  A cook fell to my lot.
I hated him by daylight
  But in the dark did not.
    So we perform by day
    The sacred rite of May
    And we perform by night
    That other sacred rite.
    The regiment, well exercised,
    Presents its arms, then stands at ease,

Then takes us off behind the trees
Where we fraternize.

Ecstasy filled my heart, O
My love seemed heaven born!
But why were people saying
It was not love but scorn?
The springtime's soft amour
Through summer may endure
But swiftly comes the fall
And winter ends it all.
December came. All of the men
Filed past the trees where once we hid
Then quickly marched away and did
Not come back again.

Directors will have to take care, when casting an Yvette, to pick an actress who can not only suggest what she is and will become but what she once was, what she once felt.

Songs in 2 and 3 contain the story of Eilif and Swiss Cheese, respectively, but with various indirections, various effects of distance. "The Fishwife and the Soldier" is actually sung by Eilif, but he takes no responsibility for the contents. It is something his mother taught him, and he had learnt it by rote. He identifies himself not with the song but with the Soldier in it who cries, "the life of a hero for me!" Heaven knows how the little incident would end if his mother did not chance to be eavesdropping so that she can give the song the ending which Eilif would scarcely care to confront. She does know what she is singing, but there is no indication that, even now, Eilif gets the point. For him it is just a nice war song. The total achievement of this song resembles that of the charade of the black cross in the previous scene. Both times the end of the play is prefigured in the beginning. Brecht uses the old pattern of oracle and fulfillment with considerable emphasis in this play, if with some humor and irony. Some may think it too fatalistic a pattern for a "social" playwright, but Brecht's point is precisely that fatality rules where people will not rule, where they have capitulated, where they are on their knees.

THE SONG OF THE FISHWIFE AND THE SOLDIER

[Scene 2]

To a soldier lad comes an old fishwife
And this old fishwife, says she:
"A gun will shoot, a knife will knife,
You will drown if you fall in the sea.
Keep away from the ice, if you want my advice,"
Says the old fishwife, says she.
The soldier laughs and loads his gun, then grabs his knife and starts to run:
"It's the life of a hero for me!
From the north to the south I shall march through the land
With a knife at my side and a gun in my hand,"
Says the soldier lad, says he.

When the lad defies the fishwife's cries,
The old fishwife, says she:
"The young are young, the old are wise,
You will drown if you fall in the sea.
Don't ignore what I say or you'll rue it one day,"
Says the old fishwife, says she.
But, gun in hand and knife at side, the soldier steps into the tide:
"It's the life of a hero for me!
When the new moon is shining on shingle roofs white
We are all coming back: go and pray for the night,"
Says the soldier lad, says he.

And the fishwife old does what she's told—
Down upon her knees sinks she:
"When the smoke is gone, the air is cold,
Your heroic deeds won't warm me!

See the smoke, how it goes! May God scatter his foes!"
  Down upon her knees sinks she.
But, gun in hand and knife at side, the lad is swept out by the tide:
  He floats with the ice to the sea.
And the new moon is shining on shingle roofs white
But the lad and his laughter are lost in the night:
  He floats with the ice to the sea.

Courage's partial unawareness coupled with Eilif's total unawareness of the meaning and relevance of the song gives us irony within irony. It is Brecht's custom to make his songs flash significance this way and that. When Helene Weigel sings "your heroic deeds won't warm me!" her inflection, coupled with a plural form of "your" which we don't have in English, makes the line refer to all the Nazis and potential Nazis in the audience.

How bold and unabashed Brecht is in resorting to artifice! It is not at all likely that mother and son would meet in this way, let alone that a song could just happen to be divided between them in this way. Yet in the theatre, that natural home of the unnatural, all this passes off with an air of spontaneity.

In 1949 I attended a meeting of a Communist youth group in East Berlin at which Brecht was questioned by the young Reds about the new production of his play. One of the young people questioned the whole mode of Eilif's behavior in this song, and asked specifically why he performed a weird sword dance between the stanzas. Brecht immediately stuck his cigar in his mouth to gain time—as he had done when questioned by the Unamerican Committee in Washington two years before. Then he very mildly said: "There are two answers to that. One is: people do perform such dances. The other is: why not?"

Perhaps the boldest example of Brechtian theatre in all of *Mother Courage* is the Chaplain's singing the story of the death of Jesus just before Swiss Cheese is shot. This "Song of the Hours" is often omitted from German productions, and was omitted from the early printings of my own rendering of the play. I now think it should always be included—both in performance or in reading. However, I don't think the reason for the omission was ever the fear of offending anyone's religious susceptibilities. These would be much more offended by other things that were never omitted. What seemed to faze many theatre people was the difficulty of adding so weighty an item to an already very weighty scene. But surely the sheer audacity would carry it? It is the extreme case of universalizing the meaning of a scene in the lyrics. Though the analogy of Swiss Cheese and Christ may at first seem flippant, in the actual treatment it turns out not to be. (Gottfried von Einem, the composer, has subsequently had no trouble at all making a dignified choral work from this song.) Brecht's Christ is —inevitably—the good boy in a world that crucifies goodness. Since it is stupid to be good under such conditions, this is a stupid Christ, however sweetly amiable. But beneath Brecht's recognition of stupidity is his compassion.

THE SONG OF THE HOURS

[Scene 3]

In the first hour of the day
Simple Jesus Christ was
Carted as a murderer
Before the heathen Pilate.

Pilate found no fault in him,
No cause to condemn him,
So he sent the Lord away.
Let King Herod see him!

Hour the third: the Son of God
Was with scourges beaten,
And they set a crown of thorns
On the head of Jesus.

And they dressed him as a king.
Joked and jested at him.
And the cross to die upon
He himself must carry.

Six: they stripped Lord Jesus bare.
To the cross they nailed him.
When the blood came gushing, he
Prayed and loud lamented.

Each upon his cross, two thieves
Mocked him like the others.
And the bright sun crept away
Not to see such doings.

Nine: Lord Jesus cried aloud
That he was forsaken.
In a sponge upon a pole
Vinegar was fed him.

Then the Lord gave up the ghost
And the earth did tremble.
Temple curtain split in two.
Cliffs fell in the ocean.

Evening: they broke the bones
Of the thieves beside him.
Then they took a spear and pierced
The side of gentle Jesus.

And the blood and water ran
And they laughed at Jesus.
Of this simple son of man
Such and more they tell us.

The Song of "Mother Courage" the character is also the Song of *Mother Courage* the play. The sound of the song and the sight of Mother Courage singing it on or beside her wagon—these began as the most stunning theatrical "effect" in the play and have become symbols of the play, its grandeur, and its meaning for many people in many countries.

THE SONG OF MOTHER COURAGE

[Prologue]

Here's Mother Courage in her wagon!
  Hey, Captain, let them come and buy!
Beer by the keg! Wine by the flagon!
  Let your men drink before they die!
Sabres and swords are hard to swallow:
  First you must give them beer to drink.
Then they can face what is to follow—
  But let 'em swim before they sink!
        Christians, awake! The winter's gone!
        The snows depart. The dead sleep on.
        And though you may not long survive,
        Get out of bed and look alive!

Your men will march till they are dead, sir,
  But cannot fight unless they eat.
The blood they spill for you is red, sir,
  What fires that blood is my red meat.
For meat and soup and jam and jelly
  In this old cart of mine are found:
So fill the hole up in your belly
  Before you fill one underground!
        Christians, awake! The winter's gone!
        The snows depart. The dead sleep on.
        And though you may not long survive,
        Get out of bed and look alive!

[Scene 7]

If war don't suit your disposition
  When victory comes you will be dead.
War is a business proposition,
  Not with cream-cheese but steel and lead!

Too many seek a bed to sleep in:
  Each ditch is taken, and each cave,
And he who digs a hole to creep in
  Finds he has dug an early grave.
And many a man spends many a minute
  In hurrying toward some resting place.
You wonder, when at last he's in it,
  Just why the fellow forced the pace.

[To Follow Scene 8]

Up hill, down dale, past dome and steeple,
  My wagon always moves ahead.
The war can care for all its people
  So long as there is steel and lead.
Though steel and lead are stout supporters,
  A war needs human beings too.
Report today to your headquarters!
  If it's to last, this war needs you!
    Christians, awake! The winter's gone!
    The snows depart. The dead sleep on.
    And though you may not long survive,
    Get out of bed and look alive!

[To End the Play]

Dangers, surprises, devastations—
  The war takes hold and will not quit.
But though it last three generations,
  We shall get nothing out of it.
Starvation, filth, and cold enslave us.
  The army robs us of our pay.

Only a miracle can save us
  And miracles have had their day.
    Christians, awake! The winter's gone!
    The snows depart. The dead sleep on.
    And though you may not long survive,
    Get out of bed and look alive!

The song has a double action. Its words, from beginning to end, are bottomlessly cynical, blackly pessimistic. Yet people come away from the play in general, and from this song in particular, saying: "I doubt that any other play has paid such homage to mankind's greatest virtue, its heroic determination to somehow, almost anyhow, keep on pulling the wagon further on. . . ." This is Tennessee Williams speaking, and it is possible that ignorance of German has led him to be guided too exclusively by the music and by visual images. Yet what he says is neither pointless nor wholly wrong. The words of this song are, to a degree, cancelled by the act of singing them. One may be a pessimist, but to sing one's pessimism is to transcend it. To sing one's pessimism humorously adds another twist. Humor also has a double action. It contains an admission of defeat: "nothing to be done." But, like song, it is itself a kind of victory. You exorcize these dreadful thoughts by uttering them humorously. Mother Courage is always saying cynical things but not for one moment do we take her for a cynical person—unless all cynical persons are doing the same thing: overcoming despair by humorous indulgence in it.

To achieve real despair in this song, Brecht had to take it away from Mother Courage and write that last stanza without humor, for a chorus of soldiers:

Dangers, surprises, devastations—
  The war takes hold and will not quit.
But though it last three generations,
  We shall get nothing out of it.
Starvation, filth, and cold enslave us.
  The army robs us of our pay.

Only a miracle can save us
And miracles have had their day.

The German for "song" is "Lied." Therefore we need a word for the sung parts of Brecht's plays, which he called in the German text "Die Songs." There being none, perhaps we should simply take what the German says and spell it phonetically: "Zonks." You are no Brechtian till you can speak knowingly of Brecht's Zonks, die Zonks der Sreepenny Ohperah, dair Barbarah-Zonk, etc.

It does not resemble the English folk-song—or the Irish one as Mr. O'Casey likes to introduce it into his plays. It does not resemble the songs in *The Beggar's Opera.* There Gay's idea was to set new words to old tunes of any kind. It was also his conception that the dialogue could be interrupted at any time by these musical quotations, however brief. One could even jump straight from one quotation to another. All of which is a far cry from the songs of *The Threepenny Opera,* which are almost never musical quotations and never mere snatches. The first thing we notice is that the Brechtian song is an individual item, clearly marked off from its context, like an individual number in vaudeville.

The song, then, is an interruption of dialogue, but it would perhaps be less misleading to say that in Brecht's plays the dialogue is an interruption of the songs—in other words, that the songs are the heart of the matter.

When, in my preface to *Seven Plays by Brecht,* I took the position that "epic theatre is lyric theatre," an intelligent Marxist critic accused me of unclarity. What I principally meant, however, is very clear indeed: that the lyrics are the core of the play.

There have been dramas based on lyrics before. The *Peribañez* and the *Knight from Olmedo* of Lope de Vega are probably based on the little ballads contained within them. But this is a matter of plot and character. The lyrics from which Brecht's plays spring, or on which they rest, so to speak, do not contain his plots and characters: they expound his themes. This is perhaps the most surprising thing about a Brecht play: that *the songs, which we expect to be at once frivolous and peripheral, are dead serious and central, all appearance to the contrary notwithstanding.*

A shrewd Catholic critic, Henri Gouhier, has written of *The Threepenny Opera:* "The intimate collaboration of Bertolt Brecht and Kurt Weill rejuvenates the formula of musical comedy in entrusting to the part that is sung the expression of whatever goes beyond mere incidents. . . ." This is the other end of my own statement: musical theatre is redeemed from the banality of mere intrigue by the Brechtian songs, which reinforce incident with interpretation.

Mahagonny began as but a group of lyrics in *Die Hauspostille,* Brecht's first book of poems (1927). From the beginning they have tunes—perhaps of Brecht's own invention, and certainly not by Kurt Weill. Then comes "The Little Mahagonny" of Brecht and Weill, still not too much more than a setting of some songs. But drama is bursting out all over: and the end-product is one of the (in every sense) big musical plays of our day.

The versatility of Brecht gave an impression of lack of continuity. He would set each play in a different place and time, and establish a completely different style of dialogue. The songs represent a constant element. The places and times of Brecht's "actions" are such that they are equally hospitable to the same songs. "The Solomon Song" occurs in both *The Threepenny Opera* and *Mother Courage!* Why? Because the same themes come up in both, and especially the theme of this song: the futility of the virtues. *Mother Courage* also contains a song that goes all the way back to *Die Hauspostille:* the "Fishwife and the Soldier." Brecht's thoughts about the military life are neither "a cliché of the nineteen-thirties" nor simply derivative from his Marxism. They represent a profound preoccupation from one end of his work to the other.

But if Brecht puts his themes into his songs, he puts his theatrical genius into them too. As Gouhier remarks, in speaking of *The*

Threepenny Opera, Brecht and Weill impose on the part that is sung a "rhythm such as cannot be sung without being acted." So true is this that many Brecht songs can, so to speak, be acted without being sung. *Lotte Lenya acts her songs.* This fact can be appreciated even by listeners to her recordings, for her voice acts the songs. Conversely, it can be fatal to give a Brecht lyric to a singer. The histrionic values tend to be swallowed up in the vocal ones. I have been present when Brecht fired a singer who was doing "The Song of Shelter" in *Mother Courage.* "Far too beautiful," was his only comment. He knew that one had no sense of a serving maid in a kitchen singing at her work: one felt transported to a concert hall where singing *is* the work.

As a model of that Brechtian singing which is really acting I would instance not only Madam Lenya but also Frau Trude Hesterberg—Frau Peachum on the Columbia recording of the complete *Threepenny Opera.* Her rendering of "The Ballade of Sexual Submissiveness" is one of the great things in the Brechtian repertoire.

Frau Hesterberg told me she ran a nightclub in Munich in the early twenties, and one day a strange young man came to be auditioned, small, dark, owlish, reserved. She was sure he had come to the wrong address. Then he sang to the guitar in a thin, piercing voice. He wasn't good but he was curiously arresting. "There's something very unusual about your material," she said, "where did you pick up these songs?" He said: "They're my own." It was Bertolt Brecht, and the kind of thing he wrote in those days is preserved in *Die Hauspostille,* complete with the tunes he used. I do not know if he composed these tunes. The book attributes them to no one. But I append them here since they have never appeared in any American book. And I preface them with a translation of my own fitted to one of them, so that readers who know music can try it out.

To learn these lyrics—words and music—is the best possible introduction not only to the poetry but to the theatre of Brecht.

HYMN OF THE RED ARMY SOLDIER

BY BERTOLT BRECHT ENGLISH WORDS BY ERIC BENTLEY

(to be sung to the tune given below)

Because beneath its leaden sun
This land of ours is eaten bare,
It spat us out on freezing highways,
It spat us out on byways dark.

Though washed in snow until the spring
The army is red summer's child.
The fall brought snow. When it was winter
The army's heart froze in the wind.

In those years Freedom was a word
That often fell from lips of ice,
And some had tiger's fangs that followed
After the red, inhuman flag.

And when by night the red moon swam
Our fellows tied their horses up,
And in the fields talked of the future,
Then fell asleep, tired by the march.

The rain it rained, the dark wind blew;
To sleep on stones was very sweet.
The rain removed from weary eyelids
Not the dirt only but our sins.

And when at night the sky grew red
They took it for the red of dawn.
It was a fire. The dawn came later.
But Freedom never came, my boys!

And so wherever they might be,
They said: this finally is hell.
But all the hells that once were final
Gave place to others finally.

So many hells were still to come.
But Freedom never came, my boys!
And now if what arrived were Heaven
They would not be around to see.

When we ourselves are eaten bare
(Our hearts as leaden as the sun),
The army spits our skin and bones out
Into a hole not deep but cold.

With bodies hardened by the rain,
With hearts disfigured by the ice,
With empty, bloody hands and grinning,
We enter now YOUR PARADISE.

"Hymn of the Red Army Soldier."

I. Lektion, Kap. 2. Von Jakob Apfelböck

In mil- dem Lich-te Ja - kob Ap - fel-böck, erschlug den

Va-ter und die Mut-ter sein und schloß sie beide in den Wäsche-

schrank, und blieb im Hau - se üb - rig, er al - lein. usw.

"Of Jacob Apfelböck." A ballad about a juvenile delinquent. He has committed parricide and matricide.

"Hymn of Orge." Sung by Baal in the play *Baal,* and expressing a happily anal viewpoint which today might please Professor Norman O. Brown.

"Orge's Answer." In similar vein but not in the play.

"Ballad of the Adventurers." Sung by Baal in *Baal*.

"Ballad of the Pirates." The tune was later to be used, with rhythmic changes, for "The Song of Mother Courage." Brecht identifies this tune as a French one entitled, "L'étendard de la pitié." I have made unavailing efforts to find any other record of a tune or song of this title.

Mahagonny-Lieder

I

II
Wer in Ma-ha-gon-ny blieb, brauchte je-den Tag fünf
Dol - lar. Und wenn er's be - son - ders trieb,
brauch-te er viel-leicht noch ex - tra. A - ber da-mals
blie-ben al - le in Ma-hagon-nys Po - ker-drink-sa - loon.
Sie ver-lo-ren in jedem Fal-le, doch sie hat-ten was da-von.
Auf der See und am Land wer-den al-len Leu-ten ih - re
quasi recitativo, parlando
Häu - te ab - ge - zo - gen, dar - um sit - zen al - le
Leu - te und ver - kau - fen al - le Häu - te, denn die
Häu - te wer-den je-der-zeit mit Dol-lars auf - ge-wogen.

III
An ei - nem grau - en Vor-mit-tag, mit - ten im
Whis-ky, kam Gott nach Ma - ha - gon - ny, kam
Gott nach Ma - ha - gon - ny. Mit - ten im Whis-ky be-
merk - ten wir Gott in Ma - ha - gon - ny.
Sauft ihr wie die Schwämme mei - nen gu - ten Wei - zen
Jahr für Jahr? Kei - ner hat er - war - tet, daß ich
kä - me; wenn ich kom - me jetzt, ist al - les gar?
An - sa - hen sich die Män-ner von Ma - ha-gon - ny,
parlando
ja! sag - ten die Män - ner von Ma - ha - gon - ny.

Alabama Song

The words to all these songs (pp. 68–72) are known to the record-buying public from the Brecht-Weill opera, *Rise and Fall of the City of Mahagonny*. These are not Weill's tunes but something far more primitive—perhaps of Brecht's composing. The English is Brecht's own. He did not know English then, but had heard the popular American songs of that time (around 1925).

"Of the Man Baal." The poem that prefaces the play *Baal*.

"Of the Seduced Girls." Seduced, drowned, and rotting, in fact.

"Legend of the Dead Soldier." A ballad that tells how the Kaiser drafted even a corpse, which accordingly had to die a hero's death a second time. An English version of this ballad, as well as "Hymn of the Red Army Soldier," is sung by the translator, Eric Bentley, on a tape recording which forms part of a program broadcast in 1961 by WBAI (New York), WGBH (Boston), KPFA (San Francisco), KPFK (Los Angeles), and of which there is a copy in the Poetry Room, Lamont Library, Harvard University, as also in the Library of Speech Recordings, 803 Business Building, Columbia University.

As for the music to *Mother Courage:* Some of the songs, set by Paul Dessau and sung by Germaine Montero, are available on a twelve-inch disc distributed by Vanguard Records. Some have been recorded, too, by the original Berlin cast and the discs are usually available from Deutsche Schallplatten, Deutscher Buch Export, Leninstrasse 16, Leipzig C. 1.

The Writer and Our Time: Malraux, Sartre, Camus

GERMAINE BRÉE

THE LAST FEW YEARS have witnessed the publication of a number of critical studies dealing with a composite image of "the contemporary writer" whom they analyze, arraign, and judge in relation both to a situation supposedly characterizing our time and to a vague function which literature should supposedly fulfill. We are, it seems, infected by the deadly bacillus "Eurocoque," if I may misuse an image coined by the poet Ivan Goll to suggest spiritual vacuum, a disease which the writer is spreading among us. We are, moreover, a "bankrupt civilization" to the bankruptcy of which the writer is contributing instead of bringing a cure.

"Hamletism," wrote a critic[1] recently, ". . . lives again. . . . The contemporary sense of nothingness paralyzes [in the writer] the capacity for action as well as utterance." Haunted by the ghost of the murdered father-image of God, overpowered by the consequent void and responsibility, the writer, we are told,

[1] Charles I. Glicksberg, *Literature and Religion,* Southern Methodist University Press, 1960.

becomes "inarticulate." An inarticulate Hamlet, to be sure, opens up new perspectives. The thought of the silence presiding over our twentieth-century literature, although hardly self-evident, is not wholly unpleasant to those of us whose bookshelves groan under the weight of the volumes produced out of this "paralyzed capacity for utterance." I know of no divining-rod for distinguishing among the inarticulate, for literature is perforce the domain of the articulate. If Malraux, Sartre, or Camus, to mention the three French writers most often referred to, ever suffered from "paralysis" when action or expression were called for, then the term "paralysis" calls for redefinition.

Clearly we are dealing with a myth—a composite to which Marx and Freud have obviously contributed. The vocabulary if not the method of Sartrean psychoanalysis, when divorced from Sartre's system of values and diluted and applied to literature by less entertaining epigones, is also responsible for some of the more dismal trends in recent criticism. Writing is often considered, if not exactly an "evasion," then a way *out*, invented in cases of psychological and social desperation. Literature is viewed as the avowal of a defeat. Reinforced by such terms as "the world of existence," "collective guilt," and "original sin," and accompanied by the inevitable atom bomb, both the "birth trauma" and the "Oedipus complex" are making a comeback.

A related approach is that of critics who continue to assess literature according to social rather than individual values. They are headed straight back to the highroad shared by Marxist, humanist, and religious critics alike. Writing is judged in relation to a social function ascribed to it by the critic: the better the function is fulfilled, the better the literature. Since, in all three cases, the values to be served are related to an emerging "future" or to an ideal state of humanity, the critic enjoys broad prerogatives. He evaluates the degree and nature of the writer's commitment, pointing out the omissions, distinguishing between the valid and the nonvalid, the partisan and the "authentic." This type of criticism rests on the familiar and much discussed assumption that the fictional worlds which writers create are of the same nature as the world in which they live and that they refer to some known structure inherent in "our-being-in-the-world-and-in-history," to borrow a widely used existentialist term.

Thus perched upon the critic's knee, the writer is a mere ventriloquist's dummy. His work is dissolved into fragmentary quotations, hand-picked and projected into a context furnished by the critic, highly edifying no doubt, but all too often insufferably dull, moralistic, didactic, and dogmatic—in fact the exact opposite of creative. From this *Ubuesque* [2] operation of "deliterarization," if I may coin a word, emerges the paralyzed Hamlet, a writer short of breath and saddled by history with a task too heavy for his frail shoulders.

This is a sketchy and not altogether unbiased picture, for it is true that "To be or not to be . . . a writer" has been a live issue among writers themselves. "The writers that preceded us," wrote Camus, "when they doubted, doubted their own talent. Today, artists question the very meaning of their art, of their existence." This statement calls for qualification. For some 150 years, since the days of Romanticism, writers, particularly in France, have questioned the meaning of their art and they have done this increasingly as the years went by. W. H. Sobel in *The Writer in Extremis* [3] examines some of the forms that this question took among the German expressionists, and with respect to France I need do no more than mention Lautréamont, Mallarmé, Rimbaud, Valéry, and the surrealists. But since these writers answered the question by producing literary works—varying, to be sure, widely in scope and in value—we have some reason to suspect that, like Descartes', theirs is a provisional doubt which it might be dangerous to construe as the sign of a helplessly schizoid frame of mind. Rather it may be a first and necessary step toward a reorientation, a vigorous affirmation. The vocabulary used by Camus is pertinent. A writer may

[2] King Ubu, the burlesque hero of the play by Alfred Jarry, invented a machine for the "decerebration" of his subjects.

[3] Walter H. Sobel, *The Writer In Extremis*, Stanford University Press, 1959.

"doubt" his talent; he "questions" his art, and through his work, he may answer both his doubts and his questions. It should prove enlightening to approach the question of the writer's attitude toward literature from his own point of view.

I

Essentially Proust's great novel, *In Search of Time Lost*,[4] is built around the question of the validity of literature. It reaches a first climax and a dead point when the narrator is brought face to face with the realization that writing, to which he intends to devote his life, may well be an insignificant activity. The passage is widely known. The narrator's first doubts appear one evening at Tansonville, the Swann estate where he is staying with Gilberte Swann, his childhood friend, now married to one of the Guermantes clan. He has picked up a volume of the journals of the Goncourt brothers and has read a description—amusingly written by Proust himself in the manner of the Goncourts—of the society in which he moved. The discrepancy between the truth as he has seen it and its literary rendering makes him question the validity of literature. Some time later, the question arises again:

> During the railway journey back to Paris, I fell to thinking of my lack of literary talent which I had early suspected along the Guermantes way, and had recognized with still more sadness on my daily walks with Gilberte at Tansonville before going home to dinner very late in the night, and which, the evening before leaving that country estate, while reading some pages from the journal of the Goncourt brothers, I had very largely attributed to the *vanity and falseness of literature*. This idea, less painful perhaps but still more dispiriting if I explained it, not by a deficiency peculiar to me personally, but as due to the non-existence of the

[4] This is the exact translation of Proust's title *A la recherche du temps perdu*, which C. K. M. Scott–Moncrieff rendered as the Shakespearian *Remembrance of Things Past*.

ideal in which I had formerly believed, had not recurred to me for a long time past, but now it struck me anew and with more crushing force than ever.[5]

This doubt, not of his own talent but of literature itself, has to be resolved by the narrator if he is to escape from the nihilism into which he is plunged and to start to write. The answer, when it comes, comes to him from within. To write is, in essence, an act of faith. The subsequent fate of the pages written will remain unknown to the writer. Art, as Proust says, is "a last Judgment." In a not altogether Mallarméan sense, books, paintings, musical compositions are "throws of the dice," militating against their own nothingness—the nothingness of their creators, and, consequently, of all human beings.

The writers who followed Proust—Malraux, Sartre, and Camus more particularly—raised the same question but in a different context and from a different point of view. It was Malraux, whose whole work rests on an almost desperate questioning of art, who, in *Man's Hope,* tersely raised a question which went straight to the root of what Camus later called the modern writer's "bad conscience," his doubts concerning the legitimacy of his calling. Malraux formulated the question in terms of painting, in a short dialogue that takes place in Madrid during the Spanish Civil War. Two men, both dedicated to art—an art dealer, Alvear, and an art historian, Scali, who is fighting with the Republican armies—talk as the battle circles around them. It is the younger man, Scali, who raises the question:

"In the churches of the south where we fought, I saw large spots of blood side by side with paintings. . . . Paintings . . . lose their force."

"We need other paintings, that's all," said Alvear.

"That's placing works of art pretty high," Scali answered.

[5] Marcel Proust, *Remembrance of Things Past,* trans. by C. K. M. Scott–Moncrieff, Random House, II, 983.

"Not works: art." . . .

"Art is of small importance in the face of suffering and unfortunately no painting holds up in the face of spots of blood." [6]

In this brief dialogue we easily discern the two themes that were to dominate the discussion throughout the next twenty years: "We need other paintings" and "art is of small importance in the face of suffering." Albert Camus wrote in almost identical terms:

> The radical questioning of art by the artist has many reasons and only the loftiest need be considered. Among the best explanations is the feeling the contemporary artist has of lying or of indulging in useless words if he pays no attention to the sufferings brought about by history.[7]

It is clear that the terrain of the debate had shifted since Proust. In 1947, shortly after World War II, when Sartre set out to define the conditions of an art valid for his time, he emphasized the fact that the writer's self-questioning was linked to a sudden overwhelming sense of responsibility in the face of the historical experience of the thirties and forties: "We were brutally thrown back into history," he notes in *What Is Literature?*, the essay in which he contrasts the point of view of the writers formed during the years of World War II with that of their predecessors.

As writers, all three men had acquired a new sense of the global historical context in which they were, to use a Sartrean term, "situated," and with it they had a sense of the great mass of human beings and of the depth and immediacy of its suffering. For writers this twofold sense could be doubly paralyzing, and it surely gave new and disconcerting dimensions to the very notion of "man" as expressed in our humanistic literature. When Proust's narrator questions the validity of literature, it is within a private

[6] André Malraux, *L'Espoir* (Paris: Gallimard, 1937), pp. 270–71.

[7] Albert Camus, Lecture given at the University of Uppsala, 1957: *Resistance, Rebellion, and Death* (Knopf, 1960) p. 250.

context. Malraux, Sartre, and Camus place it in a global and historical context. All three have a strong feeling that they belong to a human community at a crucial moment in the history of the human race—hence their self-questioning.

The preoccupation of these writers with the events of history has a double origin. Part, of course, stems from the violent events in which all three participated to a greater or less degree; the other lies in the overwhelming attention they gave to various philosophies of History, all more or less directly connected with the ideas of Hegel and Marx. The 1930's mark a cleavage with the past: unemployment, social unrest, the growth of fascism, the Spanish Civil War, concentration camps in Nazi Germany, the oncoming of World War II. It was part of the prevailing climate of those years inevitably to think of History as a determining and fascinating form of Fate and to turn to Hegelian or Marxist dialectics the better to come to terms with the present by applying to it a "logic of becoming" which could give it meaning. Malraux, Camus, and Sartre were thus oriented toward a questioning of the meaning of History, and hence of the responsibility of the writer, of the part he should play in events, and to question this in the light of a philosophy of History—the Marxist—which all three came to reject in some of its aspects after having at one time accepted its conclusions. Hence the emergence in France of a literature of "debate and self-questioning" of which Victor Brombert speaks in his study of "the intellectual hero" in French fiction,[8] a central theme of which is the relation of the individual to History.

In the nineteenth century, History had on the whole been regarded somewhat as an archeological exercise, the knowledge of a past from which one could draw a certain wisdom concerning affairs of state which was applicable to the present. As the concepts of Hegel and Marx, though diluted, became familiar, History appeared as a unit: past, present, and future were indivisible.

[8] Victor Brombert, *The Intellectual Hero: Studies in the French Novel, 1880–1955*, Lippincott, 1961.

The sense of "being-in-history" did not at first carry with it any very dire consequences. Submission to an historical destiny coincided with a belief that it would take the form of a more or less painless and inevitable movement toward a better society, carrying on the values of the present while discarding the errors. The writer's responsibility did not lie so much in the course of events, which were felt to be inevitable, as in his art. But when, fortified by a type of political thought derived from Hegel and Marx, which justified any means toward achieving the ends of History, the more alarming aspects of our twentieth-century history appeared, a crucial conflict developed within the consciousness of the writers. It was linked to the question of the value of the individual human being. Human nature, according to Marxist thought, is plastic and can be molded at will; man is malleable and has therefore no intrinsic dignity outside his social function, nor for that matter has the artist.[9]

That a conflict might arise between the social role of the arts and the artist's inner sense of commitment to an experience which might not fit this mold, was not at first apparent. It was only slowly that a debate took shape concerning the relation of the artist to History, a debate which was eventually to turn into an indictment of History and, after a first period of hesitation, into a reaffirmation of the place of art as one of the highest forms of human activity. This debate involved two generations at least, the two that followed Proust's generation, and it is reflected fairly well in the novel.

II

A first group of novels—Jules Romains' *Men of Good Will* (1932–1947), Duhamel's *The Pasquier Chronicle* (1933–1945),

[9] Marx himself had great respect for the dignity of the individual and for his capacity to act positively and freely in harmony with the determining forces of History. The consequences of his definition of men as molded by their social environment, however, were soon redefined by others to include also the notion of the historical "guilt" of any opposition to the "correct" evolution of history.

Martin du Gard's *The Thibaults* (1922–1940)—showed a deep concern with History. All three authors attempted to reconstruct a period of time, the one leading to World War I. Behind them, of course, stood Tolstoy's impressive *War and Peace*, but with 1914 so close to their experience they could not share Tolstoy's detached and *a posteriori* vision. The advent and character of World War I had profoundly disturbed all three men; and yet their novels have in common an attempt to explain *away* the scandal of that war. It was obvious to these authors that the historic process had misfired somewhere along the line. Through their novels they were trying both to diagnose the error and to prevent its recurrence.

For Duhamel, World War I is an inhuman, tragic event, due in great part to our folly in having allowed technical and industrial processes to overwhelm our traditional humanistic values. It is the consequence of an ethical failure. Martin du Gard examines the problem from a somewhat different angle. In the first parts of his novel, he studies the evolution, under the impact of social and economic forces, of the French bourgeoisie as represented by two middle-class families. Du Gard's point of view seems close to that of a nonpolitically oriented pre-Marxist socialist. Until 1914, when the war breaks out, each character in his novel pursues his own existence within a changing social framework, on the assumption that nothing other than the normal accidents of individual living will disrupt his life. But the war bears down upon these characters from outside, an unexpected, unforeseen cataclysm flicking aside all their expectations, "stealing their future," as Sartre later would say. As one of the main characters, Antoine, a doctor, lies dying in a hospital, he makes a discovery which marks him as a precursor of what was to be the mid-century awareness: he had once thought that he could decide what he would do and be but he sees now that he was historically conditioned. He and his whole generation had erred in their failure actively to participate in the making of their own history.

Jules Romains constructed his entire novel to show that History was moving toward the creation of ever larger human communities, through the coming of age of new and ever larger groups acceding to ever broader forms of Western civilization. This process, inevitable in his eyes, called only for intelligence among leaders. His novel is a blueprint for a future which was not so soon to arrive, rudely superseded as it was by the overwhelming realities of World War II.

But whether a moralist like Duhamel, an historian like Martin du Gard, an engineer like Romains, all three writers take for granted the fact that there is no insoluble contradiction between the basic patterns of the history they observed and their traditional vision of human dignity. The future was to be a continuation of the best in the past, and the writer's task was to show the truth inherent in the situation and to weigh the right and wrong of it for the enlightenment of his readers. From his position outside and above events, the writer was to deal with History according to moral principles. He is to set it right.

But already Antoine, in Martin du Gard's novel, had realized that the process might not be automatic and had glimpsed the need of what Sartre was later to refer to as "commitment." As he returns home from the trenches, Jallez, one of the heroes of Romains' novel, has a flash of intuition going further, to the very heart of a new problem:

> "We must continue to live, mustn't we? If we are not going to die of disgust right where we are, we've got to react . . . and admit that humanity is also this: a mass of filthy little animals, multiplying too rapidly in the plains, and that the passage of an exterminating plague from time to time is something just about as natural as a storm. . . . But what is frightening is that once this idea has occurred to us, it can take us a long way . . . and in a direction in which I don't want to go. On the contrary . . . I try to cling to the idea that humanity is precious in all its texture, that a man's life is precious." [10]

[10] Jules Romains, *Men of Good Will*, Vol. XX: Quoted by Pierre-Henri Simon in his excellent book *L'Esprit et l'Histoire* (Paris, 1954), p. 64.

L. F. Céline in his *Journey to the End of the Night* (1932) had already traced a bitter epic of a humanity that Jallez cannot bring himself to contemplate. Our memories, refreshed by the Eichmann trial, need only recall the language of Hitler's Reich to see that this humanity, considered as the raw material for the achievement of political ends, was a legitimate prey for the strong. Cyclical views of history such as Spengler's, reinforcing a dangerously distorted Nietzschean "will to power," could easily be grafted upon a vision of humanity as no more than a species of planetary bacillus. There was nothing in this view that could counterbalance those "spots of blood" of which Scali spoke. Marxism in the thirties proposed to the French writer, in its theory at least, a future in which the dignity of human beings would be ultimately respected. Writers like Malraux and the former surrealist Aragon, and like the young Camus in Algeria, sought, for a few years, the answer to Scali's "spots of blood" in the double activity of participating in the violent struggles of the time and in searching for a "new literature" which would draw from these struggles their meaning. The writer, on the side of the masses, had a task: to strive for and to express "Man's hope."

The turning point in the debate is clearly manifest in the evolution of Malraux's work. If, as with the Marxists, History was considered the unique source of value, then human beings could be used for the achievement of political ends; the present human being could be, and frequently was, sacrificed in the name of a desirable but problematic future. To what, then, were the writers committed? Here, for a number of them, arose the conflict between the "comfortable belief" in the future—an intellectual pattern of thought—and the immediate experience with which the writer must deal. He could only conceive of himself as "guilty": guilty certainly in the eyes of the doctrinaire, whose faith he did not share; guilty in his own eyes when faced with those "spots of blood" for which he could see no justification; guilty towards his own involvement in an art which seemed futile.

The problem of elucidating the meaning of our history was

therefore soon superseded in Malraux's eyes by another question: What "gives History its limits," if not the idea, to which Romains' Jallez had tried to cling, that "a man's life is precious"? What concerned Malraux was the ease with which individual aspirations to violence, vengeance, or power could find their justification in a new mythical absolute, History. The "future" had disappeared from under Malraux's feet and with it the justification of a politically committed art. "Man's fate" as recorded by History seemed to be defined by humiliation, the submission to forces that expose the nothingness of what each individual holds dear. It was to another record of human activity, the history of art, that Malraux now turned.

In the history of art he saw what he called an "anti-destiny," because, recording as it does man's freedom to redefine his own experience in his own terms, to dominate and judge the forces that destroy him, it militates at all times against the evidences of men's nothingness to which everything in our present history seems to point.

"The greatest mystery," says one of the characters in Malraux's unfinished novel *The Walnut Trees of Altenburg,* "is not that we are thrown by chance between the profusion of matter and the profusion of the stars; it is that in our prison we can draw from ourselves images powerful enough to negate our nothingness." The artist is the man who, in the "images" he creates, whether in painting, sculpture, or literature, suggests the grandeur and beauty of the human adventure which the facts of man's history seem to negate. He proposes therefore to other men "images" of a humanity forever transcending its apparent limitations. Art is thus the concrete form of man's *"hope,"* as opposed to the evidences of his *"fate."* The "images" that Malraux considers are valid, however, not as art, with those values peculiar to art, but as quasi-religious, collective, and somehow sacred expressions of the mystery inherent in the species, man. They are the tangible signs of an orientation, a spiritual history transcending man's factual history. The task of the writer, one may surmise, should be to project certain mythical images of man, such as, perhaps Don Quixote, Don Juan, or Faust.

What Malraux suggests, without explicitly stating, is that we no longer have any image of man to put into circulation, no image which can stand up against those "spots of blood." It would seem that, in Malraux's eyes, our literature can do nothing that is more than insignificant until we produce a great new image, valid for all men today, to give our time a spiritual orientation.

Basing his thought on the anthropologist's distinction between civilization and culture, Malraux regards civilization as that which a large body of men share with each other—techniques and scientific knowledge, for example—and culture as that which allows each individual within a civilization to feel and express his own view of life, a prerequisite for the artist. "To express a powerful civilization," he declared at the Congress of Soviet writers in August 1934,

> does not necessarily mean to create a powerful literature, and here in Russia it will not be enough to photograph a great epoch in order to bring to birth a great literature. Art is not an act of submission, it is a victory. The victory of what? Of emotions and the means of expressing them. Over what?

The answer is over "indifference and logic," which fail to differentiate among individual men. The work of art is thus seen as a "conquest," a "struggle between the artist and his world." The first activity of the artist is "an accusation" launched against the "Gods," whatever they be, which hold humanity in servitude; then an appeal to men, to make them "conscious of the hidden greatness and dignity in themselves." But along this path Malraux abandoned literature, perhaps unable to find the "image" of which he spoke; he became a philosopher of art.

In the *Voices of Silence* (1951) and the *Metamorphosis of the Gods* he gives the most imperious and startling interpretation of the function of art as such. We may question it, as others have questioned it; nevertheless Malraux is saying something pressing and urgent. Our civilization in its techniques and patterns of living is today world-wide. Moreover, it is an agnostic civilization, and thus an entirely new phenomenon. All living civilizations have produced a living art—"In the world of art," he writes, "life always begins with the meaning of art." A living art is produced by a living culture creating its own universe within a civilization by ordering the elements of the world so that the civilization is oriented through its culture toward some essential part of man.

Since the end of the nineteenth century, our artists have step by step destroyed the "style" we inherited and with it the image of man that oriented the world for us. But our artists have not yet succeeded in "wrenching" from the past styles of art, which for the first time in history we have gathered from all times and all cultures, the new style, the new image of man that would give our civilization its human meaning. Implicit in all Malraux's thought is the idea that unless this be done, our civilization, like others before it, could be submerged for centuries by the overpowering force of nature and the barbaric myths of society, the myth of History among them.

Never perhaps has art been cast in so ambitious a role, nor the artist been so exalted as "master-creator," nor given so difficult a task. Malraux has transferred to him the powers that Hegel attributed to the "hero" and has made the "hero" dependent for his meaning upon the artist. But somehow, in the process, he has left the immediate, concrete realm of the individual writer and of literature far behind.

Putting aside all metaphysics, Sartre with characteristic determination set out in 1945 to make a complete examination of the immediate "situation of literature" and to define its function in our contemporary world. The 317 pages of his *Situations II* (1947) contain discussions—under the title *What Is Literature?*—which propose a program for a new orientation of literature. Sartre's point of view—simplified, of course—is a kind of synthesis of those of Alvear and Scali, and behind it the shades of Hegel and Marx.

Sartre wants to define writing as a useful profession. Each historical moment requires a new form of literature, the significance of which can be defined in social and historical terms, allowing us to differentiate clearly between literature that is valid and literature that is spurious. In a history seen as evolving according to Marxist dialectics, a valid literature states the case for that part of humanity which, moving out of oppression, is becoming conscious of its right to the freedom inherent in man. The writer who is "situated" in a nation, a class, an historic moment, errs if he thinks in terms of a timeless absolute. He must write for the immediate future in relation to an immediate political situation. Today he cannot be concerned with an individual "world of solitude" that militates against the leveling power of a civilization; he can be concerned only with the emergence of the collective civilization of tomorrow. The writer is he who prepares us for the social and political changes in the making.

In his 1947 discussions, however, Sartre segregated writing from all the other arts including poetry.[11] And as has often happened in his case, he had led himself into something of a trap. He found himself forced to reject whole blocks of literature, and, in particular, Proust's vast novel, which quite obviously did not fit his definition. He also found himself caught in a very personal dilemma. The writer, by what he chooses to write about, also chooses for himself and literature either an "authentic" or a "non-authentic" role. Either he speaks directly for those men who are assuming their freedom or he does not speak for them at all. Flaubert did not speak in favor of the insurgents at the time of the commune; therefore Faubert, in Sartrean terms, failed as a writer. According to Sartre's point of view, the proletariat in France is the only part of humanity acceding to freedom today—and that proletariat is represented by the Communist Party. Sartre, who was no Marxist, found himself obliged by the very force of his

[11] Sartre has lately seemed to be moving away from the positions he took in 1947.

own reasoning to speak at least temporarily in line with Marxist ideology—a curiously paradoxical outcome. He has thus moved, like Malraux, *out* of literature, or at least into a small corner of literature: social satire. The rest of his writing is marginal to literature, with the exception perhaps of his plays.

Unlike Sartre and Malraux, Camus, who belonged to the proletariat, attempted to think the problem through in somewhat different terms. First, he felt that today—as in certain other periods—the writer, along with his whole generation, has acquired a new sensitivity for which he must find a new form of expression, a sensitivity keener than ever before to the weight of the collective human misery in our world. The History he speaks of is not the metaphysical process to which Malraux refers, nor the preordained dialectic process implicit in the philosophies of History, Sartre's among them. It is our history as we experience it daily. "The object of the artist in history," wrote Camus in an article entitled *The Artist and His Time,*

> is . . . what he can see of history and suffer himself, directly or indirectly; it is the present in the strict sense of the word, that is to say, the men living today, not the relation between this present world and a future which cannot be foreseen by the living artist. What, in fact, characterizes our time is the violent impact of the masses and their miserable condition upon our sensitivity. We know they exist whereas there used to be a tendency to forget them. And if we know it, it is not because the élite—whether of the arts or not—have become better human beings, no; it is because the masses have become stronger and prevent others from forgetting them.

In other words, the writer is faced with a new dimension of human experience, the sense of immediate solidarity with millions of individuals. He must control this experience by ordering it according to his inner exigencies. It is not only the *substance* of his experience that has changed, but his sensitivity itself, the essential tool of the artist. His initial problem is therefore to find the themes, the vocabulary, and the forms that will corerspond to this new sensitivity. His is a quest for an expression which might transform "the community of suffering into a community of reconciliation."

The difficulty for the writer today, as Camus saw it, is that in the most acutely sensitive part of his being he is conscious that he is taking part in a collective adventure, and that he must take part in it fully, living it with his flesh and blood. He must accept fully his solidarity with the masses of men around him, a dangerous and exhausting task which, more likely than not, may lead to violent death in this "era of violence."

But he can write only if he is able to master this experience in order to give it form. He must have seized it in its entirety, rejecting no part of it before he sets up that "contestation" of reality—that disputation with reality—in which Camus saw the essence of the work of art. The artist must work in solitude, alone: this is a difficult task but it does bring him back to earth—to the specific problems of his craft—and literature once again comes into its own. "Perhaps," Camus concluded, "we here touch upon the greatness of art, in this perpetual tension between beauty and suffering, the love of human beings and the folly of creation, intolerable solitude and the harassing crowd, refusal and consent." [12]

In this respect the writer today faces a dilemma more arduous perhaps than any that confronted him in the past. The artist is a man who cannot accept reality in its fleeting, formless, and incomplete aspect. He intervenes to give form to his experience; but he cannot detach it from the reality that is the source of his emotion and that is therefore part of his creativity. Art creates its own order, which is neither metaphysical nor social. It cannot cater to the requirements of a society for which art is a luxury and it is unacceptable to a society which adheres to a collective dogmatic interpretation of reality. These two forms of conformism eliminate the artist. Camus does not claim for the artist any exalted position

[12] Albert Camus, *Speech of Acceptance upon the Award of the Nobel Prize for Literature,* Knopf, 1958.

in society, nor does he see him as one of the "mandarins." The artist is, in his eyes, fully responsible for his work and for the values it proposes and induces in those who may be led to appreciate it. Camus seems to have no trace of that sense of the "superiority" of the role of the artist as such, which both Malraux and (in spite of himself) Sartre seem to have inherited from their predecessors. But for Camus, the artist can fulfill his task only if he is left free to discern for himself the elements of his art and to function as artist, as best he can, within a given society. This very need makes it imperative that he fight any forces which impinge on this freedom, the same forces that violate or thwart it in any other man. This is the price he has to pay if he is to maintain his integrity; whence the quality of a work through which his experience can be shared and which thereby may, in some small measure "change the world."

> It seems to me that the writer must be fully aware of the dramas of his time and that he must take sides every time he can or knows how to do so. But he must also maintain or reserve from time to time a certain distance in relation to history. . . . The artist, if he must share the misfortune of his time, must also tear himself away in order to give it form. This continual shuffling, this tension that gradually becomes increasingly dangerous, is the task of the artist today. Perhaps this means that in a short time there will be no artists. And perhaps not. It is a question of time, of strength, of mastery, and also of chance.[13]

Art therefore embodies an esthetic form of ethical consciousness. Involving choice and will, art is in the last analysis directed toward the achievement of the higher individual development of those who come into contact with it.

Curiously enough this takes us back to Proust, who, in *Time Regained,* answered many of Sartre's arguments concerning art a quarter of a century before Sartre stated them and whom Camus,

[13] Albert Camus, *Resistance, Rebellion, and Death* (Knopf, 1960), p. 238.

in the chapter on "Revolt and Creation" in *The Rebel,* placed among the greatest writers. For Proust it mattered little what the content of the work of art was in fact; what mattered essentially was that it be the unique and complete substance of a man's experience, the artist's problem being to discover what was his authentically and how it could be shaped uniquely and thus communicated.

Though nothing could be more different than their two worlds, Marcel Proust and Albert Camus come singularly close to each other when they attempt to define that part of the artist's work which has to be evolved in solitude and which is tied to an individual effort and enterprise and the discovery of a unique relation with the world, sufficient unto itself:

> CAMUS: I know with certainty that a man's work is nothing but the long journey to recovery, through the detours of art, the two or three simple and great images that gained access to his heart.[14]
>
> PROUST: The grandeur of real art . . . is to rediscover, grasp again and lay before us that reality from which we live so far removed and from which we become more and more separated . . . and which is simply our life, life as it really is, life disclosed at last and made clear, consequently the only life that is really lived, that life which in one sense is to be found at every moment in every man, as well as in the artist. But men fail to see it because they do not try to get light on it. . . . Only by art can we get outside ourselves, know what another sees of his universe which is not the same as ours and the different views of which would otherwise have remained as unknown to us as those there may be on the moon. Thanks to art, instead of seeing only one world, our own, we see it under multiple forms, and as many as there are original artists, just so many worlds have we at our disposal, differing more widely from one another than those that roll through infinite space, and years after the glowing center from which they emanated has been extinguished, be it called Rembrandt or Vermeer, they continue to send us their own rays of light.[15]

[14] Albert Camus, Preface to *L'Envers et l'Endroit* (Paris: Gallimard, 1958), p. 33.
[15] Proust, *op. cit.,* II, 1013.

Proust does not really answer here the question raised by his narrator. But it is interesting to note, in conclusion, that when the writers I have so briefly examined speak to us of their art, when they attempt to explain or justify it, they employ the language in current use among their contemporaries. Proust often speaks in a vocabulary that recalls Bergson, or Croce perhaps even more, the vocabulary of contemplation, revelation, and vocation. Malraux, Sartre, and Camus echo the philosophies of History borne forward on the overwhelming events of our time: they speak in terms of action, of man's fate, of the dialectics of materialist determinism. But there is always a point at which the writer turns about and transforms the vocabulary he has used. He throws into the scales terms which qualify all his explanations: Proust speaks of hieroglyphs, vision, beauty, a world redesigned; Malraux of power, conquest, style, and anti-destiny; Camus of revolt, contestation, conciliation, and beauty. And all, including Sartre, speak of freedom.

What they speak of so confidently is something that critics do not necessarily experience in the same way. The fact remains that a writer can be a writer and literature can exist only where, as Hamlet's voice begins to flag, the spotlight falls inevitably on Fortinbras.

Literary Criticism: Poet, Poem, and Reader

CLEANTH BROOKS

THE CRITICAL ACTIVITY of the last forty years has created a sufficient stir. It has developed new methods for teaching literature; it has generated a new critical vocabulary, and, as might have been predicted, it has aroused a vigorous reaction. Undoubtedly there has been faddishness connected with some of its critical ideas and, like other kinds of faddishness, what is mere fad will die and will eventually be replaced, one supposes, by a newer fad. I dare say that aspects of recent criticism have been overpraised; but it is plain that other aspects have been overblamed. In any case the recent trend in criticism has been only partially understood even by some of its converts. The fact of misunderstanding helps account for the mechanization of certain of its critical "methods"—for example, heavy-handed and witless analyses of literary works, often pushed to absurd limits and sometimes becoming an extravagant "symbol-mongering."

These are general remarks. To become more specific: a typical misunderstanding interprets modern criticism as mere aestheticism. Our renewed interest in poetic form, in the eyes of some viewers, approaches dangerously near to a doctrine of art-for-art's sake in its apparent neglect of the great moral problems with which it is assumed that art ought to concern itself.

A few years ago, Professor Douglas Bush, in his presidential address to the Modern Language Association, put this case very forcibly. He scolded what he called the "new criticism" for its "preoccupation with technique, its aloof intellectuality, its fear of emotion and action, its avoidance of moral values, its dislike of 'impure' poetry (which includes," he went on to argue, "the greatest poetry we have)." He summed up the indictment of what he regards as "a timid aestheticism" by saying: "The common reader might go so far as to think that poetry deals with life, that for the serious poet life embraces morality and religion, and that it seems very strange for a serious critic to retreat into technical problems."

It may be amusing to reconsider, in the light of these strictures, the first great critical document of our Western tradition. Aristotle was certainly no timid aesthete. As a many-sided and healthy Greek of the great period, he took all knowledge to be his province. He was very much concerned with politics and morality as his *Nicomachean Ethics* and his treatise on politics testify. And what does he say about Greek tragedy? Does he praise Aeschylus for his profound insight into the human soul? Does he call attention to Sophocles' deep concern for moral problems? Well, hardly. Here is the sort of thing that Aristotle singles out for a comment in Sophocles' masterpiece, *Oedipus Rex:*

> A Peripety is the change of the kind described from one state of things within the play to its opposite . . . as it is for instance in *Oedipus*. . . . A Discovery is, as the very word implies, a change from ignorance to knowledge, and thus to either love or hate, in the personages marked for good or evil fortune. The finest form of Discovery is one attended by Peripeties, like that which goes with the Discovery in *Oedipus*.

Aristotle made plot the soul of the drama, and since plot is concerned with action, his discussion of plot might seem to promise a consideration of moral problems. But when we turn to the text of the *Poetics,* we find that Aristotle is again back to technicalities, writing: "We assume that, for the finest form of Tragedy, the Plot must be not simple but complex. . . ." If the author were other than Aristotle, the moralistic critic might be tempted to argue that the sentence was written for the delectation of a coterie of aesthetes and that the critic had forgotten that the great Greek tragedies were presented before flesh-and-blood auditors, interested in and oppressed by, grave moral problems and the issues of life and death.

The *Poetics,* in sum, does not discuss the lives of the dramatists, nor their deep human experiences, nor the way in which their plays reveal their personalities. Even when Aristotle addresses himself directly to the moral issues encountered in a work of art, he scarcely writes in a fashion to satisfy the determined moralist. When he faces the specific question of whether something said in a poem is "morally right or not," the critic hot for certainties might find him evasive, for Aristotle counsels us to consider "not only the intrinsic quality of the actual word or deed, but also the person who says or does it, the time, the means, and the motive of the agent." Instead of making a strict interpretation of a given code, Aristotle seems to appeal to something like a principle of dramatic propriety. In asking us to judge a statement or action in terms of the total dramatic context he sounds suspiciously like the so-called (and badly named) "new critics."

Now my purpose in dragging Aristotle into this discussion is not to claim that the *Poetics* is the be-all and end-all of criticism. It is not even to claim that recent criticism is markedly Aristotelian. My point is a more modest one: I invoke Aristotle's example simply to suggest that a man who has a proper interest in politics, history, and morals may still find it useful to concern himself with the structure of literary works and with defining the nature and limits of aesthetic judgment.

In view of such considerations, it is possible to restate the history of criticism in our time thus: We have been witnessing a strenuous attempt to focus attention upon the poem rather than upon the poet or upon the reader. Along with this stress upon the poem as a structure in its own right, has come the attempt to fix the boundaries and limits of poetry. Modern critics have tried to see what was meant when one considered the poem as an artistic document.

I. A. Richards, some thirty years ago, argued that for the sake of the health of literature, we needed a spell of purer poetry and of purer criticism. The attempt at a purer criticism has been made. But in my more pessimistic moments, I wonder whether there has been much real clarification of the critical problem. The popular critics—in *Time* magazine, for example, or in the great metropolitan newspapers—continue to print their literary chitchat, their gossip, and their human interest notes on the author of the latest best-seller. And often out of the other side of their mouths, they go on to talk about the novelist's politics, his moral asseverations, and his affirmation or lack of affirmation of "life." To such people, the discussion of literary *form* is bound to seem empty. Ingrained habits of thinking make it hard for them to conceive of form as anything other than an empty container. On the other hand, when a critic like Allen Tate makes the point that form is *meaning*, he deliberately rejects any notion of form as a mere envelope for some valuable ethical or psychological content. Indeed, he rejects the whole implied dualism of a form-content poetics. To understand modern criticism, it is necessary to grasp this point. Some typical misunderstandings of this point may be avoided by remembering the example of Aristotle. A universal thinker, not a mere aesthete, a man who believed that art "imitated" reality and that art could exert ethical and political pressure, could nevertheless find it profitable to deal with literature in formal terms on the assumption that it possessed a structure of a characteristic kind.

Poetry has a characteristic structure and yields a characteristic knowledge. It does not compete with, but exists alongside of, and complements scientific knowledge and historical knowledge. Since poetic knowledge is made available through poetic form, the attempt to assimilate poetic knowledge too directly and abruptly to other kinds of knowledge has its risks. We lose the value of poetic knowledge in losing the perspective that poetic form gives. It is surely quite proper to deal with Milton's *Paradise Lost,* for instance, as a reflection of a Puritan ethic. But we may learn more about its ethical content if we respect its own characteristic mode of statement as a poem and do not, in our anxiety to extract the ethical content, violate that mode.

My argument is not an esoteric one: it involves no mystical view of poetry. Rather it rests upon the evident fact that poetry does make use of certain characteristic devices and that if we ignore these devices we shall have badly misread the special kind of document that is the poem.

One of the simplest but surely the most essential of these devices is metaphor. (Robert Frost has made the point that poetry *is* fundamentally metaphor.) But the function of metaphor is often misconceived. Many readers still take its function to be that of mere illustration or decoration, with term A being "compared" to term B, or term B to term A. This misconception of metaphor as a kind of rhetorical glossing of the "facts" is one aspect of the form-content dualism which sees the poetic form as simply a superficial gilding of the content—not as something by which it is transformed. If, under the impression that we are somehow being "scientific" and thus more directly grasping reality, we do write off metaphor as mere decoration, we shall certainly lose what poetry has to give us. After all, we must not forget how much of our discovery of the truth—scientific as well as poetic—is gained through metaphor.

I confess that I once thought that the imagery in the second stanza of Wordsworth's "Solitary Reaper" was meant to be merely decorative, vaguely ennobling. Hence it is small wonder that I found the poem rather flat and dull. It was only when I stumbled upon the fact that the thinking of the poem was really being done through these images—that the poet had implicated a whole manifold of relations in associating the natural spontaneous songs of the nightingale and the cuckoo with the natural and spontaneous singing of the girl—it was only then that the poem came to be deeply meaningful to me. The Highland girl was not simply being complimented for the beauty of her song. Hers was presumably not a great voice; it was evidently an untrained voice—as "natural" as that of a bird. In effect, her song was wordless, for the girl was singing in an unknown tongue, Gaelic, as the nightingale sang in another unknown tongue, "nightingale." Like the birds, the girl was conscious of no audience and was singing for none, the song simply welling up out of the daily round of her activities, as the birds' welled up out of theirs. And like the birds, the girl sang "As if her song could have no ending." A work of art, Aristotle has told us, has a beginning, a middle, and an end; and the concert singer had better sing *her* song with a concern for its beginning, its middle, and its end. But the songs of the birds (and of the girl) are not the music of art, but of nature—they properly have no ending. In sum, through the two bird images—and only through these images—the hearer indicates the special significance of the solitary reaper's song. It is as if the traveler had been allowed, through the utterly unself-conscious song of the solitary girl bending to her task, to overhear the "still, sad music of humanity" rising from hidden depths, plaintive, sweet, artless. Thus, the bird comparisons cannot be dismissed as mere decoration: what the poem "says" is said primarily through the imagery.

To recur to a point made earlier: the attempt to assimilate poetic knowledge too directly to other kinds of knowledge is dangerous. If we ignore the poetic form, we may hopelessly distort the meaning. One can illustrate the danger from another lyric by Wordsworth, one of the celebrated Lucy poems.

> She dwelt among the untrodden ways
> Beside the springs of Dove,
> A Maid whom there were none to praise
> And very few to love:

A violet by a mossy stone
  Half hidden from the eye!
—Fair as a star, when only one
  Is shining in the sky.

She lived unknown, and few could know
  When Lucy ceased to be:
But she is in her grave, and, oh,
  The difference to me!

A few years ago a critic and literary scholar insisted upon using the poem to make a sociological point. Knowing that the young Wordsworth sympathized with the common man and had been strongly affected by the French Revolution, our scholar was bent on showing how much this simple love poem actually reflected a transitional age and foreshadowed the modern age to come. Indeed, he found in the poem a number of remarkable reflections of the changing nineteenth-century social scheme. For one thing, the speaker was revealed to be conscious of his moral isolation in his choice of a love object—someone who "dwelt among the untrodden ways." Moreover, Lucy herself turned out to be a young woman of neurotic personality—and the speaker "modern" in choosing a neurotic. You may wonder how our scholar detected Lucy's neurosis. The answer is simple. He interpreted the lines "A Maid whom there were none to praise/And very few to love" with painful literalness. One had always assumed that the lines meant that in her remote, rural situation, none of the few simple people who knew the maiden and loved her was capable of singing her praises; that is, Lucy lacked the poet that her loveliness deserved. One had also supposed that the second stanza praised Lucy's modesty ("A violet by a mossy stone") and her sweet serenity ("Fair as a star, when only one/Is shining in the sky.") But our critic was convinced that her shyness concealed what he called "an unpleasant rejection of other people." Few loved her, and of those that did, none could honestly say a good word for her! Granted that the example just cited is an extreme case, there are plenty of misreadings conducted under the same auspices which are only somewhat less absurd.

I once knew a sociologist who delivered his judgment to the effect that Shakespeare's Cleopatra was simply a maladjusted girl. I dare say that in some sense she was. But his remark makes sufficiently plain the fact that he had missed the meaning of the play. One can, to be sure, treat *Antony and Cleopatra* sociologically, psychologically, historically, morally, etc., but the play is, after all, a work of art, and if we consider it to be a work of art we shall find ourselves talking about it necessarily in terms appropriate to aesthetic structure—whether terms like Aristotle's *peripeteia* and *anagnōrisis,* or those of recent criticism like *tension* and *ironic reversal,* or in still other terms. To treat the play in terms of aesthetic structure does *not* mean that we are denying ethical problems. There can certainly be no objection to making use of terms that have to do with human interests, human motives, and human emotions. Indeed, how can we avoid such references if we are to talk about the play in terms of its pattern of tensions, complications, and resolutions? For these are the things that are patterned, balanced, and resolved. But whatever the terminology we use, we will do well to keep the ethical problems at one remove, seeing them, that is, in the perspective which aesthetic structure affords and which the fictional nature of the play actually enjoins. Otherwise we shall find that our study of this play with its "maladjusted girl" and its adultery and double suicide threatens to turn into a clinical study or a police court inquest.

One could illustrate nearly everything about poetic structure and its relation to politics and morality from this complex and brilliant play. But present purposes call for an example that is smaller and more readily manageable. For that, one might go back to "The Solitary Reaper," which in spite of its apparent simplicity can tell us a great deal about poetic form. But it may be better to illustrate from a longer and more complicated poem, "The Grassehopper," by Richard Lovelace, one of the Cavalier poets of the seventeenth century.

THE GRASSE-HOPPER

To my Noble Friend, Mr. Charles Cotton

ODE

I.

Oh thou that swing'st upon the waving haire
  Of some well-filled Oaten Beard,
Drunke ev'ry night with a Delicious teare
  Dropt thee from Heav'n, where now th'art reard.

II.

The Joyes of Earth and Ayre are thine intire,
  That with thy feet and wings dost hop and flye;
And when thy Poppy workes thou dost retire
  To thy Carv'd Acron-bed to lye.

III.

Up with the Day, the Sun thou welcomst then,
  Sportst in the guilt-plats of his Beames,
And all these merry dayes mak'st merry men,
  Thy selfe, and Melancholy streames.

IV.

But ah the Sickle! Golden Eares are Cropt;
  Ceres and *Bacchus* bid good night;
Sharpe frosty fingers all your Flowr's have topt,
  And what sithes spar'd, Winds shave off quite.

V.

Poore verdant foole! and now green Ice! thy Joys
  Large and as lasting, as thy Peirch of Grasse,
Bid us lay in 'gainst Winter Raine, and poize
  Their flouds, with an o'reflowing glasse.

VI.

Thou best of *Men* and *Friends!* we will create
A Genuine Summer in each others breast;
And spite of this cold Time and frosen Fate
Thaw us a warme seate to our rest.

VII.

Our sacred harthes shall burne eternally
As Vestal Flames, the North-wind, he
Shall strike his frost-stretch'd Winges, dissolve and flye
This *Ætna* in Epitome.

VIII.

Dropping *December* shall come weeping in,
Bewayle th'usurping of his Raigne;
But when in show'rs of old Greeke we beginne,
Shall crie, he hath his Crowne againe!

IX.

Night as cleare *Hesper* shall our Tapers whip
From the light Casements where we play,
And the darke Hagge from her black mantle strip,
And sticke there everlasting Day.

X.

Thus richer then untempted Kings are we,
That asking nothing, nothing need:
Though Lord of all what Seas imbrace; yet he
That wants himselfe, is poore indeed.

—*The Poems of Richard Lovelace,*
ed. C. H. Wilkinson (Oxford, 1925)

The poem is addressed by the poet "To my noble friend, Mr. Charles Cotton." It would be interesting to know more than we do about Lovelace's noble friend. The scholars do not agree as to his identity. C. H. Wilkinson thinks it was Charles Cotton, the son;

C. H. Hartmann, Charles Cotton, the father. But even if we do not know the identity of the noble friend, we still can enjoy the poem and understand it.

There are, I grant, poems which do depend for their basic meaning upon some knowledge of the historical characters mentioned in them. Marvell's "Horatian Ode upon Cromwell's Return from Ireland" would be hopelessly obscure to a reader who knew absolutely nothing about Oliver Cromwell. Yet we can and must make a distinction between a poem as a personal document and as a poetic structure. For example, it is conceivable, though highly improbable, that some day a scholar may come upon a set of seventeenth-century letters which would tell us that Mr. Charles Cotton had performed several great services for our poet, and that this little poem had been written by Lovelace in grave apprehension as he received news that his friend had been stricken with a serious illness. While we are using our imaginations, let us suppose further that the letters showed that this poem was written in the hope of cheering his friend by suggesting that they had many more years of fine companionship before them. Such letters might very well enhance for us the meaning of the poem as a personal document of Lovelace's life. But if we may thus enhance a poem at will by importing into it all sorts of associations and meaning, then we can theoretically turn an obscure poem into a clear poem —and a poor poem into a good poem. Even the verse from the newspaper agony column beginning "It is now a year and a day/ Since little Willie went away" might move us deeply if we actually knew little Willie and his sorrowing mother. But only the unwary would take the triggering of such an emotional response as proof of the goodness of the poem. In the hypothetical case just cited, the response comes not from the poem as poem but as personal document. What references and allusions are legitimate parts of a poem and what are merely adventitious associations? The distinction is not always obvious, and I do not care to try to fix here a doctrinaire limitation. But I think that we shall have to agree that some limits must exist.

The first part of Lovelace's poem derives from the Anacreontic poem "The Grasshopper." (I use Abraham Cowley's translation.)

> Happy *Insect* what can be
> In happiness compar'd to thee?
> Fed with nourishment divine,
> The dewy *Mornings* gentle *Wine!*
> *Nature* waits upon thee still,
> And thy verdant Cup does fill;
> 'Tis fill'd where ever thou does tread,
> *Natures* selfe's thy Ganimed.
> Thou does drink, and dance, and sing;
> Happier than the happiest King! . . .

Lovelace evidently began his poem as a free translation of the Greek poem; but he went on to develop out of it a thoroughly different poem—different in theme and different in tone. The little Anacreontic poem becomes merely a starting point of the poem that Lovelace actually writes. Whereas the Greek poet contents himself with giving a charming account of the insect's life, Lovelace uses the account of the grasshopper's life to set up the contrast between the spurious summer of nature and the genuine summer to which men have access. If we are interested in the way in which the poem was composed, we shall certainly want to know what sources Lovelace used, and there may be a special delight in seeing how he has reshaped his sources to his own purpose. But a mere round-up of the sources will never in itself tell us what the poet has done with them. A bad poem may assimilate Anacreon as well as a good poem. The value of a poem as a work of art is not to be determined by an account of its sources.

In the same way, the history of ideas might tell us a great deal about this poem. The historian can trace the development of such concepts as that of the actual considered to be a dim and limited reflection of the ideal—specifically, the summer of the grasshopper in the natural world of the seasons viewed as a mere shadow of the genuine summer which transcends the seasonal world of nature. The historians of ideas can trace for us the development of the concept of richness based not upon the possession of goods but upon one's freedom from wants—that is, the notion of richness as completeness. The ideas that Lovelace is using here are familiar to most readers and can be taken for granted; but I concede that the reader who is not familiar with these concepts might have serious trouble with the poem. Even so, criticism has to be distinguished from the scholarship of the history of ideas, for the obvious reason that the historian of ideas may find just as much to explain in a poor and unsuccessful poem as in a good poem.

It is the critic of moralistic bias, as we have already noted, who is most likely to object sharply to modern critical procedure. The serious moralist finds it hard not to become impatient with a critic who seems to ignore the moral problems, and to concern himself merely with "form" and technique. Nor will he necessarily be satisfied with the critic's concession that wisdom is certainly to be found in poetry. Lovelace's poem, for example, says, among other things, that happiness is not dependent upon external circumstances but is an inward quality. But the moralist argues that this is surely the doctrine that ought to be emphasized in any critical account of the poem. For it may appear to him that it is this moral truth that gives the poem its value.

But the sternest moralist will have to concede that many poems that contain admirable doctrine—Longfellow's "Psalm of Life," for example—are very poor poems. Furthermore, if one tries to save the case by stipulating that the doctrine must not only be true, but must be rendered clearly, acceptably, and persuasively, he will have come perilously close to reducing the poet's art to that of the mere rhetorician.

Moralists as diverse as Marxists and the later Van Wyck Brooks are all for making the Muse a rewrite girl. But the Muse is willful and stubborn: a thesis presented eloquently and persuasively is not necessarily the same thing as a poem. "The Grasshopper" is, among other things, a document in the personal history of Lovelace, testifying to his relation with Charles Cotton. It is an instance of Lovelace's regard for the classics; it incorporates an amalgam of ideas inherited from the Christian-classical tradition of Western thought; it is an admonition to find happiness within oneself. The point is that it could be all of these things and yet be a very poor poem. It could be all of these things and not be a poem at all. It could be, for example, a letter from Lovelace to Charles Cotton, or an entry in Lovelace's commonplace book.

It happens to be a poem and a rather fine one. But defense of this judgment, if it were questioned, would involve an examination of the structure of the poem as poem. And with this kind of examination the so-called "new criticism" is concerned. I should be happy to drop the adjective "new" and simply say: with this kind of judgment, literary criticism is concerned.

Lovelace's poem is a little masterpiece in the management of tone. Lovelace makes the life of the insect thoroughly Lucullan. The grasshopper is "drunk ev'ry night": Lovelace provides him with a carved bed in which to sleep off his debauch. But actually the grasshopper is up with the dawn, for his tipple is a natural distillation, the free gift of heaven. The joys to which he abandons himself are all innocent and natural, and his merrymaking makes men merry too.

The grasshopper's life, then, though described in terms that hint at the human world, is not used to symbolize a type of human experience to be avoided. We have here no fable of the ant and the grasshopper. Lovelace would not reform the little wastrel, but delights in him, so joyously and thoughtlessly at home in his world.

Stanzas V and VI define very delicately and precisely this attitude, one of humor and amusement, touched with the merest trace of pity. The grasshopper is happy because he cannot possibly foresee the harvest or the biting blasts of winter. "But ah the Sickle! Golden Eares are Cropt." Everything in the line conspires to place the emphasis upon the word *golden,* a word rich in every sort of association: wealth, ripeness, luxury, the Saturnian age of gold. But the full force of *golden* is perhaps not realized until we come to line 13: "Poore verdant foole! and now green Ice!" The clash of gold and green absorbs and carries within it the whole plight of the grasshopper. Green suggests not only the little insect's color but all that is growing, immature, unripe, and innocently simple. The oaten ears on which the grasshopper loves to swing change, by natural process, from green to gold; the grasshopper cannot change with them. The mature oaten ears may resemble the precious metal—one remembers Milton's "vegetable gold"—but greenness turned to something hard and stiff and cold—the sliver of green ice—is a pathetic absurdity.

I should not press the contrast so hard, had Lovelace not insisted on the color, and emphasized its connection with springing verdure by his phrase "Poore verdant foole!" And here it becomes proper to acknowledge the critic's debt to the lexicographer and to concede that my suggestion that *verdant* here means *gullible* has no specific dictionary warrant. The Oxford Dictionary's first entry for this sense of *verdant* is as late as 1824; the same dictionary, however, does indicate that *green* could carry these connotations as early as 1548. In the context of this poem, *verdant,* followed by the phrase "green ice," and associated as it is with "fool," must surely carry the meaning of inexperienced, thoughtless innocence.

The gentle and amused irony that suffuses "Poore verdant foole" continues through the lines that follow: the grasshopper's joys are measured by the instability of the insect's precarious perch—"Large and as lasting, as thy Peirch of Grasse." But the speaker soon turns from his contemplation of these ephemeral joys to man's perdurable joys—from the specious summer of nature to the genuine summer which he and his noble friend can create, each in the other's breast.

The poem pivots sharply in the fifth stanza, and the management of tone is so dextrous that we may be tempted to pass over the last half of the poem too easily. But these latter stanzas have their difficulties and if we want to understand the poem I think we shall want to find precisely what goes on. Moreover, these stanzas present their problem of tone also. The poem must not seem smug and sanctimonious; man's happiness must not seem too easily achieved. For if man rises superior to the animal kingdom, he is not, for all of that, a disembodied spirit. He is animal too, and he has to reckon with the "frost-stretch'd winges" of the North Wind and with the blackness of the winter night. Moreover, as man, he has his peculiar bugbears of a sort that the grasshopper does not have to contend with. There is at least a hint of this in the reference to "untempted kings."

As a general comment, suffice it to say that in this poem the flesh is given its due: the warm hearth, the lighted casements, and showers of old Greek wine fortify the friends against the winter night and give a sense of real gaiety and mirth. If there is high thinking, the living is not so plain as to be unconvincing. And the sentiment on which the poem closes is none the less serious because it comes out of festivity and has been warmed by wine. He who "wants himselfe"—who owns things but has not mastered himself—is poor indeed. It is this full possession of himself, this lack of dependence upon things, which makes him richer than "untempted Kings."

The last phrase, however, is curious. In this context, Lovelace ought to be writing to his friend: "since we are untempted by material possessions, we are actually richer than kings." The force of the contrast depends upon the fact that kings are more than most men tempted by material possessions. Why then *untempted* kings? The solution is probably to be sought in the source of the poem. In the Anacreontic "Grasshopper" the insect is referred to as a king—the Greek text has Βασιλεύς—and Abraham Cowley, Lovelace's contemporary, uses the word *king* in his translation. Lovelace, then, for his fit audience who knew the Greek poem, is saying: we are like the grasshopper, that rare specimen, an untempted king; but we are richer than he, since our joys do not end with the natural summer, but last on through the genuine (and unending) summer of the heart.

But it is Stanzas VIII and IX that cause the real trouble. As

C. H. Hartmann remarks: "Lovelace himself could on occasion become so involved as to be utterly incomprehensible even without the assistance of an eccentric printer." To deal first with Stanza IX: the drift of the argument is plain enough, but Lovelace's editor, Wilkinson, also confesses to difficulties here: the friends will whip night away from their casements. But what are we to make of the phrase "as clear Hesper"? Wilkinson writes "The meaning would seem to be that 'just as Hesperus shines clearer as the day draws to a close, so will our tapers whip night from the lighted casements of the room where we amuse ourselves. . . .'" But I fail to see the relevance of his argument that Hesper shines the brighter as the skies darken. Why not simply read "as clear Hesper" as an ellipsis for "as clear Hesper does"? Our tapers will whip away night as clear Hesper whips it away. Moreover, the poet chooses as the dispeller of gloom the modest light of the star just because it is modest. He is not claiming that he and his friend can abolish winter. "Dropping *December" shall* come weeping in. The friendly association with Cotton will not do away with the wintry night. What the human being can do is to rid the night of its horror—exorcise the hag—maintain a small circle of light amid the enveloping darkness. This is precisely what the evening star, clear Hesper, does, and all that he and his friend with their gleaming tapers propose to do. As with light, so with heat. Their hearth will be an Aetna, but an Aetna is epitome—a tiny volcano of heat. The poet is very careful not to claim too much.

Stanza VIII contains the most difficult passage in the poem, and Lovelace's editors have not supplied a note. "Dropping *December*" means *dripping*, or *rainy* December. But why will December lament the usurping of his reign? Does the warm fire and pleasant company maintained by the two friends constitute the usurpation against which he will protest? We may at first be inclined to think so, but the lines that follow make it plain that December is not crying out against, but rejoicing in, the two friends' festivities. Seeing them at their wine, December exclaims that he has "his Crowne againe." But what is December's crown? One looks for it throughout Greek and Roman mythology in vain.

We have here, I am convinced, a topical allusion. The crown of December is evidently the Christmas festivities, festivities actually more ancient than Christianity—the age-old feast of the winter solstice of which the Roman Saturnalia is an instance. December's crown is indeed a venerable one. And who has stolen December's crown—who has usurped his reign? The Puritans, by abolishing the celebration of Christmas. We remember that it is a Cavalier poet writing, and I suspect, if we care to venture at dating the poem, we shall have to put it at some time between the Puritan abolition of Christmas in 1642 and the publication of Lovelace's volume, *Lucasta,* in 1649. Line 23, then, "And spite of this cold Time and frosen Fate," is seen to refer to more than the mere winter season. It must allude to the Puritan domination—for Lovelace, a cold time and frozen fate indeed. I would not press the historical allusion. The poem is certainly not primarily an anti-Puritan poem. The basic contrast is made between animal life and the higher and more enduring joys to which man can attain. But a casual allusion to the troubled state of England would be a thoroughly natural one for the poet of "To Althea from Prison" to have written, and nowhere more appropriately than here, in a poem to a close friend.

The reader may not be convinced by this interpretation of the eighth stanza. Very frankly, my basic concern has been to read the poem, not to seek out historical allusions. But an honest concern with the text characterizes, or ought to characterize, the work of both scholar and critic. In view of the much advertised quarrel between scholarship and criticism, the point is worth stressing. The critic selects from scholarship those things which will help him understand the poem *qua* poem; in some matters the contribution of the scholar may be indispensable. Literary criticism and literary scholarship are therefore natural allies in their concern to understand the poem; they may at points coalesce. But if, because of unavoidable specialization, the scholar and critic cannot always be one and the same man, I think it a pity if, with short-sighted jealousy, they elbow each other as rivals and combatants.

Earlier in this paper, I said that recent criticism had attempted to focus attention on the poem rather than upon the poet or upon the reader. But there is no danger that people will cease to talk about the poet and his reader. Our basic human interest is most readily served when we talk about the reader's reactions—our own responses to the poem or the novel—the chill down our spine or perhaps it is the special sensation in the pit of the stomach that A. E. Housman claimed to experience when he encountered a genuine poem. Human interest may be almost as readily served if we talk about the personality of the author. Such talk may include everything from Lord Byron's amours to the possible effects of Keats's tuberculosis upon his personality—everything from Shakespeare's alleged Oedipus complex to Robert Frost's love for New Hampshire.

No one wants to forbid either the study of the author or the study of the reader. Both kinds of study are legitimate and have their own interest. In view of the present state of criticism, it may be somewhat more to the point to say a final word in justification of recent stress upon the poem as such.

A study of the reader's reactions may be most interesting and illuminating. But concentration on the reader's reactions tends to take us away from the work of art into the domain of reader-psychology. We ask why Keats's "Ode on a Grecian Urn" provokes the different responses that it does, and we find the answer in the differing psychological make-up of the various readers. Or we may ask why certain aspects of Shakespeare were praised in the eighteenth century and others in the nineteenth, and typically find our answer in the differing cultural climates of the two centuries. But even though a poem can be realized only through some reader's response to it, the proper study of the poem is the study of the poem.

A study of the poet's personality and intellectual background will almost certainly be rewarding. After all, the poem is an expression of the mind and sensibility of the man who wrote it, and may well reflect his cultural background and the time spirit of his age. Yet concentration upon these matters can also take us away from the poem—into author psychology or the history of ideas or cultural history. In any case, it is valuable to ponder the fact that we often know very little about the author's experience beyond what he has been able to catch and make permanent within the poem. We know, for example, very little about Richard Lovelace. About the greatest of our poets, Shakespeare, we know even less—if we exclude what we may surmise from the works themselves. Even where we know a great deal about the author's personality and ideas, *we rarely know as much as the poem itself can tell us about itself;* for the poem is no mere effusion of a personality. It is a construct—an articulation of ideas and emotions—a dramatization. It is not a slice of raw experience but a product of the poet's imagination—not merely something suffered by him but the result of his creative activity. As a work of art, it calls for a reciprocal imaginative activity on our part; and that involves seeing it for what it *is.*

Toward a Definition of Romanticism

CALVIN S. BROWN

PAUL VALÉRY once remarked that only a man who had lost all sense of precision would attempt to define romanticism.[1] If this be true, such loss seems to be epidemic, for there has been a terrible proliferation of definitions. A generation ago, a Belgian scholar gathered a hundred and fifty of them,[2] and this number has probably at least doubled during the past thirty-five years. Under these circumstances, it may be argued that to offer another definition reveals a loss not merely of all sense of precision but of all consideration for one's fellow men.

Nevertheless, I am about to offer another definition, and a brief defense of this act may serve to indicate the general direction which this discussion will take. In the first place, there will be no "definition" in the sense of a pat formula or epigram, no description like "the renascence of wonder," or "strangeness added

[1] Quoted by Paul Van Tieghem, *Le Romantisme dans la littérature européenne* (Paris, 1948), p. 6.
[2] *Ibid.*, p. 7.

to beauty." Romanticism will be considered (as it often has been in the past) as a general state of mind conspicuously present in a good deal of the world's literature at various times and places, but reaching its most obvious climax in the early part of the nineteenth century. It will be approached, not directly from the point of view of its characteristic subjects, statements, or even attitudes, but from the point of view of the literary type—the *genre*—which is its most characteristic expression, and the other type which is its normal antithesis. By dealing with types rather than movements or schools, we shall be able to see that we do not have simple dichotomies, like classicism and romanticism, but more complicated relationships: another possible antithesis is romanticism against naturalism, but classicism and naturalism can also be set off against each other.

This approach will increase the impossibility of accurate definition, for we shall be driven to discuss romanticism in terms of lyric and satire, terms which are themselves notoriously slippery.[3] To a strictly logical methodologist, the use of undefinable terms is indefensible. To any practical thinker in general fields, it is inescapable. If a doctor chooses to define medical progress in terms of the saving of lives, we do not demand that he first give air-tight philosophical definitions of *progress* and *life*. To do so would be to forbid him ever to discuss his own field. We "know what he means," even though we might think up embarrassing distinctions and quibbles. Similarly, as long as we can all agree that the "Ode to the West Wind" is a lyric and not a satire, and that *Candide* is a satire and not a lyric, we must "know what we mean" to a considerable extent, even though we might argue about whether Robinson's "Mr. Flood's Party" is either, neither, or both. As we proceed, we shall be working towards a definition of the three concepts *romanticism, lyric,* and *satire* in terms of each other, in the hope that each will help to throw light on the other two.

[3] The numerous attempts to legislate against satire have been failures because of the impossibility of adequate definition. It is impossible to make any legally tenable statement as to just what is being forbidden.

Many general literary types have a remarkably continuous history, going on for age after age in about the same quantity and quality, in spite of changes in approach and emphasis. Others are sporadic or intermittent. One pair, however, offers what is probably a unique case of complementary distribution. As a very broad generalization, it may be said that a great age in the lyric is a poor age in satire, and that a great satirical age does not produce lyric poetry of the highest quality, or produce even mediocre lyrics in any great abundance. Like all such generalizations, this one can easily be challenged by individual exceptions, but in the long run it stands up to inspection remarkably well. Without being exhaustive—which would require a complete history of literature—we may glance at three periods in the cycle of alternation in order to illustrate the general principle.

If we look at Latin poetry, we find that the first century before Christ is primarily an age of the lyric, beginning with Catullus and continuing with his elegiac followers (not always inferior to their master), Tibullus and Propertius. By the end of the century the lyrical vein seems to have played out. (Since we are here concerned only with writers who are primarily either lyricists or satirists, Vergil and Ovid are left out of account, though both incline more to the lyrical than to the satiric.) The first two centuries of the Christian era show a shift to a great school of satire in verse and prose, in both Latin and Greek. Here we find the erudite satirical verse of Persius, the realistic prose of Petronius (in which vulgarity is allowed to display itself in its full flower), the savage epigrams of Martial, the impassioned indignation of Juvenal, and the satirical whimsy of Lucian. But there are no lyric poets worth remembering. In this account, one man has been deliberately omitted. His inclusion, in his proper place, clinches the argument. Horace is the turning point, contemporary with the lyrical group (he was eleven when Catullus, the earliest of them, died), but outliving them all. As a transitional figure, he belongs in both camps, but is entirely at home in neither. He is the least ecstatic of the great lyric poets, and the gentlest of the great satirists.

To take another period, if we look at the literature of the first half of the sixteenth century, we find a flourishing spirit of satire. Rabelais and Erasmus are too familiar to call for any special comment. Their contemporaries include Pietro Aretino, who brought satire perilously close to blackmail (to say the least); Sebastian Brant, whose *Narrenschiff* or *Ship of Fools* is almost an encyclopedia of that human folly which Erasmus had ironically praised; and John Skelton, who converted doggerel into a deadly weapon. But this half century gives place to a great burst of lyric poetry, with the Pléiade in France and the singing choir of the great Elizabethans following close after. It may be worth noting here that such generalizations cannot be absolute. The Elizabethans, dutifully following classical precedent, wrote a good deal of satire, but it was not their main, or best, or natural form of expression. After all, Joseph Hall and Marston are not the great names of the period, and of the principal writers only Ben Jonson is a really significant satirist.

For the third and closest period little discussion is necessary, so familiar are the names and so obvious is the distinction. The century of Butler's *Hudibras,* of Molière and Boileau, of Dryden, Pope, Swift, Defoe, and Addison, of Lesage and Voltaire, is obviously an age of satire. Its lyric poetry is remarkably slight, both in bulk and in value. But it gives place to the century of Goethe, Hölderlin, Wordsworth, Shelley, Keats, Lamartine, Hugo, Musset, Baudelaire, Tennyson, Mörike, Leopardi, Pushkin, Lermontov—the list could be continued indefinitely. Here again, of course, there are anomalies. Byron was a distinguished satirist as well as a lyric poet, and the same is true of Heine. But there is no question that the age was an age of lyricism. Since I am pleading for my own theory, it may be worth while to support it from disinterested sources. From many witnesses, I select only two, both authorities on satire. James Sutherland remarks, "It is significant that, apart from Byron, the English Romantic poets leave satire alone, or else, like Shelley, make very poor work of it." [4] And David Worcester

[4] James Sutherland, *English Satire* (Cambridge, 1958), p. 15.

tells why this is so. "The romantic poets were capable of an occasional invective piece, thrown off in the heat of generous indignation, but preoccupation with self prevented them from taking the attitude of ironic detachment." [5]

If there is anything to the idea of the spirit of an age, the complementary distribution of lyric and satire must mean that the two forms are opposite, or at least incompatible, in spirit. Now, if we look back over the history of literature, we find that the greatest lyrical periods—the twelfth and thirteenth centuries, for example, the Renaissance in France and England, the Romantic Period generally—have always been periods during which the outlook called romantic has dominated literature; and the great ages of satire have never seen life from the romantic standpoint.

This observation leads to my central thesis, which may be concisely stated as follows: Romanticism is that set of mind (or literary mode) of which the lyric is the characteristic expression, and of which satire is the antithesis.

We can now ask some basic questions about the lyric and satire in general. Who is speaking, and to whom? Why? About what? What basic assumptions do the speaker and his audience share? And how does the speaker go about achieving his purpose? If the distinction between lyric and satire as incompatible modes is valid, these questions ought to have valid and different answers for the two; and the answers about the lyric ought to tell what romanticism is, just as the answers about satire ought to tell what romanticism can never be.

Our first question, then, is: Who is the speaker? We shall expect to find that the speaker in the lyric is an entirely different person from the speaker in a satire. Furthermore, we shall be prepared to find that almost every poem, no matter what its character, assumes a different speaker; but if the distinction between lyric and satire has any meaning, each will represent a different genus of speaker containing a large number of different species. It is essential to recognize from the beginning that the speaker is

[5] David Worcester, *The Art of Satire* (New York, 1960), p. 164.

not the poet himself as an actual person, but rather an assumed role—a *persona,* or mask. This is obvious enough in forms like the dramatic monologue, where the speaker is not Browning but Fra Lippo Lippi, or not Tennyson but Ulysses. But it is actually true of all poetry. We shall have occasion to refer to wish-fulfillment later, but it is worth remarking here that the speaker is seldom a pure fiction, just as he is seldom the actual man writing the poem. Usually, he is a blend of the poet himself with the poet's ideal of what he would like to be (or to appear to be), plus a further addition of some characteristics deliberately adopted as appropriate to the speaker of the particular poem in question.

By examining the fictional self-portrait of a satirist and comparing it with the similar picture of a lyricist, we may be able to see what characteristics are appropriate to the speaker of each of these literary types.

In the "Epistle to Dr. Arbuthnot," Pope represents himself in a conversation behind closed doors with an intimate friend. The general topic is the occupational hazards of a poet, ranging all the way from scheming scribblers and false friends to scheming slanderers and real enemies. The self-portrait is scattered throughout the poem, wherever it is appropriate to the matter in hand, but the essential parts of it can be collected into a passage of about fifty lines.

> Oh let me live my own, and die so too!
> (To live and die is all I have to do:)
> Maintain a poet's dignity and ease,
> And see what friends, and read what books I please:
> Above a patron, though I condescend 265
> Sometimes to call a minister my friend.
> I was not born for courts or great affairs:
> I pay my debts, believe, and say my prayers;
> Can sleep without a poem in my head,
> Nor know if Dennis be alive or dead. . . . 270

Cursed be the verse, how well soe'er it flow,
That tends to make one worthy man my foe,
Give Virtue scandal, Innocence a fear, 285
Or from the soft-eyed virgin steal a tear!
But he who hurts a harmless neighbor's peace,
Insults fall'n worth, or beauty in distress,
Who loves a lie, lame slander helps about,
Who writes a libel, or who copies out;
That fop, whose pride affects a patron's name, 290
Yet absent, wounds an author's honest fame; . . .

Who reads, but with a lust to misapply, 301
Makes satire a lampoon, and fiction lie;
A lash like mine no honest man shall dread,
But all such babbling blockheads in his stead. . . .

Not Fortune's worshipper, nor Fashion's fool,
Not Lucre's madman, nor Ambition's tool, 335
Not proud, nor servile; be one poet's praise,
That, if he pleased, he pleased by manly ways:
That flattery, even to kings, he held a shame,
And thought a lie in verse or prose the same;
That not in Fancy's maze he wander'd long, 340
But stoop'd to Truth, and moralised his song:
That not for Fame, but Virtue's better end,
He stood the furious foe, the timid friend,
The damning critic, half-approving wit,
The coxcomb hit, or fearing to be hit; 345
Laughed at the loss of friends he never had,
The dull, the proud, the wicked, and the mad;
The distant threats of vengeance on his head,
The blow unfelt, the tear he never shed;
The tale revived, the lie so oft o'erthrown, 350
The imputed trash, and dulness not his own;
The morals blacken'd when the writings 'scape,
The libell'd person, and the pictured shape;
Abuse, on all he loved, or loved him, spread,

> A friend in exile, or a father dead; 355
> The whisper, that to greatness still too near,
> Perhaps yet vibrates on his sovereign's ear—
> Welcome for thee, fair Virtue! all the past:
> For thee, fair Virtue! welcome even the last!

From this we learn that the satirical poet is, above all, an ordinary man, like other men except that he is considerably more virtuous. He can sleep without a poem in his head: poetry is a profession (like medicine or the law), but it is not an obsession and does not set a man apart. Though he is a satirist, no worthy man need fear him, for he is on the side of virtue, innocence, virginity—and doubtless motherhood as well. His satire is both a defense of the right and an art. In fact, prominent among those who need castigation is the man who writes and spreads libels, or who so far distorts things as to make satire (a literary art) into a lampoon (a crude personal attack), or to refuse to distinguish between fiction and lying. The satirist is independent, manly, and tolerant. When he is the innocent victim of all sorts of vicious attacks, he is simply a martyr bearing witness for the moral and social virtues of his calling, and to his own high principles. Virtue is always persecuted. But with all his virtues and principles, he is above all a normal, ordinary, social and sociable man. One critic has pointed out that in his satires Pope has three principal roles and speaks with the different voices of "the *naïf*, the *vir bonus*, and the hero." [6] In our passage he seems to be all three, not by turns, but at once. In Pope's portrait the satirical poet—like the tippler of the contemporary song—lives as he ought to live and dies a right good fellow.

In "Adonais," Shelley gives a portrait of himself (that is, his *persona*) under very different circumstances. The mourners assembled to pay tribute to Keats (Adonais) range from the Muse Urania through such abstractions as Desires and Adorations to poetical versions of contemporary figures like Byron ("the Par-

[6] Maynard Mack, "The Muse of Satire," *Yale Review*, XLI (1951–1952), 91.

thian of the age") and Shelley himself. Here is the idealized character which Shelley sees fit to attribute to himself in this poem.

31. Midst others of less note, came one frail Form
A phantom among men; companionless
As the last cloud of an expiring storm
Whose thunder is its knell; he, as I guess,
Had gazed on Nature's naked loveliness,
Actaeon-like, and now he fled astray
With feeble steps o'er the world's wilderness,
And his own thoughts, along that rugged way,
Pursued, like raging hounds, their father and their prey.

32. A pardlike Spirit beautiful and swift—
A Love in desolation masked;—a Power
Girt round with weakness;—it can scarce uplift
The weight of the superincumbent hour;
It is a dying lamp, a falling shower,
A breaking billow;—even whilst we speak
Is it not broken? On the withering flower
The killing sun smiles brightly: on a cheek
The life can burn in blood, even while the heart may break

33. His head was bound with pansies overblown,
And faded violets, white, and pied, and blue;
And a light spear topped with a cypress cone,
Round whose rude shaft dark ivy-tresses grew
Yet dripping with the forest's noon-day dew,
Vibrated, as the ever-beating heart
Shook the weak hand that grasped it; of that crew
He came the last, neglected and apart;
A herd-abandoned deer, struck by the hunter's dart.

34. All stood aloof, and at his partial moan
Smiled through their tears; well knew that gentle band
Who in another's fate now wept his own,

> As, in the accents of an unknown land,
> He sung new sorrow; sad Urania scanned
> The Stranger's mien, and murmured: "Who art thou?"
> He answered not, but with a sudden hand
> Made bare his branded and ensanguined brow,
> Which was like Cain's or Christ's—Oh! that it should be so!

The satirist bent every effort to show himself as a man among men. He could not conceivably have assumed the role of "a phantom among men," and if some lampooner had called him that, he would have considered it a foul blow. Yet the romantic lyricist develops at length the idea that the poet is "frail . . . a phantom . . . companionless . . . with feeble steps . . . girt round with weakness . . . dying . . . falling . . . breaking . . . neglected and apart." This is indeed a pitiable picture—for pity is precisely the effect at which the description aims. The *persona* here assumed is as different from ordinary men as the satirist is like them. Both may suffer, but the satirist strives to show that he can rise above his griefs, while the lyric poet boasts that his pain is greater than he can bear. The final revelation of "his branded and ensanguined brow, which was like Cain's or Christ's" sums up the whole position. The satirist is proud of lashing the guilty, for in his world right and wrong are clear, basic, and immutable. But the lyricist refuses to "moralize his song." His brow is marked by and for pain. Guilt and innocence are so irrelevant that slayer and savior can be lumped together without distinction, for both suffer, and it is the suffering itself that really matters. Feeling is supreme.

Of the many other contrasts inherent in the two portraits, only one can be briefly mentioned here. The worlds in which the satirist and the lyricist move are totally different, and neither could survive in the other's realm. The satirist typically lives in the everyday contemporary world. If he wants privacy, he tells a servant to shut the door, and he shares his privacy with a friend. The lyricist lives in a dream-world outside time and space, a world where Urania, Dreams, Splendors, and Leigh Hunt can meet on an equal footing, where the feelings of the everyday world are refined and intensified, and from which its social norms and daily trivialities are forever barred. (Let no one protest that trivialities sometimes enter this world, for they are admitted only when they cease to be considered trivial.)

Our next question concerns the poet's audience. To whom is he speaking? Here the answers are relatively simple. The satirist speaks to an audience like himself, or at least like the *persona* he has assumed. It is an audience which is in agreement on all fundamentals, an audience that hates folly and knavery, and agrees with the writer both as to who the fools and knaves are and as to the desirability—in fact, the necessity—of publicly exposing them. The satirist's best trick for winning his audience to his own point of view is to assume that the audience is already won. The whole matter may be briefly summed up by saying that satire is addressed to an audience which more obvious polemicists address as "all right-thinking people." The true satirist, however, is too skilful and devious to give himself away by using such an obviously loaded term; hence he does not state it, but simply takes it for granted.

One other restriction limits his audience. Because of the indirection of satire, it is not enough for the reader to be right-thinking; he must also be intelligent. Dryden, one of the greatest of satirists, stated the point once and for all: "Satire is a poem of a difficult nature in itself, and is not written to vulgar readers."[7]

At first sight it seems difficult to define the audience of a lyric poet because of the fiction that no audience exists. In a context that clearly labels satire as a form of eloquence and the lyric as the purest sort of poetry, John Stuart Mill remarks that "eloquence is *heard;* poetry is *over*heard. Eloquence supposes an audience. The peculiarity of poetry appears to us to lie in the poet's utter

[7] "A Discourse Concerning the Original and Progress of Satire," *Essays of John Dryden*, ed. W. P. Ker (Oxford, 1926), II, 74.

unconsciousness of a listener. Poetry is feeling confessing itself to itself. . . ."[8] Northrop Frye, commenting on this passage, points out that "The lyric poet normally pretends to be talking to himself or to someone else: a spirit of Nature, a Muse . . . , a personal friend [this is a favorite device of satirists, too], a lover, a god, a personified abstraction, or a natural object. The lyric is . . . to *epos,* rhetorically, as prayer is to sermon."[9] Keeping this figure, then, we may ask for what sort of congregation the lyric is uttered. And this question can be answered in only one way. It is not any *sort* of person (as the assumed audience of satire is), but any person of any sort whatsoever who is in sympathy with the prayer —in short, anyone who is interested in the poet's feeling. The satirist and his audience share social norms, a respect for wit, a moral, ethical and social code; the lyricist and his audience share an interest in individual feeling. And just as the satirist's audience must be intelligent, the lyricist's audience must be sensitive.

The lyric poet is sometimes accused of conceit because he seems to assume that all the world cares how he feels about things. If—as sometimes happens—he assumes that the world will care because the feelings are *his,* the charge is well founded; but the true poet simply assumes that the world cares about human feelings, and uses his own because they are the most available and real to him. The fact that he may occasionally write a lyric for an assumed person or type—Browning's "Cavalier Tunes," for example—without being any the less a lyric poet is adequate proof on this point.

We may sum up the distinction as to audience, then, by saying that the satirist speaks to all right-thinking men, whereas the lyric poet speaks to anyone or no one for the benefit of all sensitive and perceptive men.

Why does either of them bother to speak at all? The satirist's traditional self-defense is that, by exposing fools and scoundrels,

[8] In "Thoughts on Poetry and its Varieties" (1833). Mill, *Dissertations and Discussions: Political, Philosophical, and Historical* (New York, 1882), I, 91.

[9] Northrop Frye, *Anatomy of Criticism: Four Essays* (Princeton, 1957), p. 249.

he protects and defends intelligence and human decency. In short, satire, as a primarily social art, has thought up a social usefulness for itself. Of course, as has been pointed out, if the function of satire is to correct the evils it attacks, then a satire can live as a literary work only when it has been a social failure. If Molière's *Tartuffe* had put an end to religious hypocrisy, the play would be so "dated" now that no one could be interested in it. Satire can survive only when the evils it attacks are still rampant, and any reader of Juvenal on imperial Rome is amazed to find how many of his strictures apply with equal force to Hollywooden America. Actually, the claim of social utility is usually a part of the satirist's *persona* rather than a personal belief. Faith in exposure as a corrective still flourishes among newspaper editors and Congressional committees, but hardly among writers sophisticated enough to be satirists. Juvenal's *difficile est saturam non scribere* and *facit indignatio versum* [10] seem to give a much simpler and more honest account of the satirist's reason for writing: when one looks about him and sees what is going on in the world, it is hard *not* to write satire, and indignation makes the verse. Dryden (speaking of Juvenal) completes the account by adding the reaction of the reader: "[Juvenal's] spleen is raised, and he raises mine." [11]

The lyric writer's purpose is harder to assess, partly because it is more complex and variable, and partly because it is so generally taken for granted that the lyricist has seldom been under the satirist's necessity to justify himself. Northrop Frye calls "the poetry of the isolated individual" a lyric, as opposed to the "poetry of the social spokesman," which, of course, includes satire.[12] Sir Francis Bacon seems to have been the first man to define poetry as a process of wish-fulfillment:

> The use of this feigned History [poetry] hath been to give some shadow of satisfaction to the mind of man in those points wherein

[10] *Satires,* I, 30 and 79.
[11] Dryden, *op. cit.,* II, 84.
[12] Frye, *op. cit.,* p. 54.

> the nature of things doth deny it. . . . And therefore it was ever thought to have some participation of divineness, because it doth raise and erect the mind, by submitting the shows of things to the desires of the mind; whereas reason doth buckle and bow the mind unto the nature of things.[13]

In a remarkable book devoted primarily to an elaboration of this thesis, F. C. Prescott comments:

> Poetry is written always in a mood of dissatisfaction. The lover, separated from his mistress, who falls to scribbling verses, is typical of all poets; as, if he dreams of her, he is typical of all dreamers. The poetic desire may be a mere personal want of this kind, or it may rise to the highest aspiration of which the mind is capable, like that, for example, which inspired the vision of St. John's Apocalypse.[14]

These comments of Bacon and Prescott identify *all* poetry as a kind of wish-fulfilling dream. What, then, is peculiar to the lyric? Schematic though it may sound, I believe that we can at least make a simple distinction between lyric and satire in these terms: the lyric arises from dissatisfaction caused by the absence of some desirable thing, but satire arises from dissatisfaction caused by the presence of some undesirable thing.

From what has just been said, it is obvious that no absolute distinction can be made between the subjects of lyric and satire. It is a matter of personal taste, depending on what one desires and what one abhors. If Bunyan had been a lyric poet, he might well have waxed lyrical over Sir Hudibras, and in that case Sir Hudibras would have been presented in a light very different from that of Samuel Butler's inspired doggerel. Even at the same period, the roles may be reversed on different levels of sophistication. Fielding satirized the calculating sentimentality of Richardson's hero-

[13] In *The Advancement of Learning. The Philosophical Works of Francis Bacon*, ed. J. M. Robertson (London, n.d.), p. 88.

[14] Prescott, *The Poetic Mind* (Ithaca, 1959), p. 128.—First published in 1922.

ines. Similarly, the values of the lyrics of popular songs of the twenties—and the songs themselves—are among the targets of T. S. Eliot's satire. Nevertheless, there is a certain stability in human tastes which enables us to say that, statistically, nightingales, gazelles, and beauteous virgins are more likely to appear in lyrics than in satires, and that the reverse is true of vultures, swine, and bedizened madams. We can add to these generalizations the fact that, because of the nature of satire, anything which is primarily thought of in its broad social relationships (such as status-seeking) is a likely theme for satirical treatment, and anything which is usually considered an individual matter or relationship (such as kissing in the moonlight) is a more likely candidate for the lyric. Nevertheless, the fact remains that anything whatsoever *can* be a subject of either lyric or satire, though in the two treatments it will no longer seem to be the same thing.

In any form of communication, certain things are simply taken for granted, while others must be explicit. What does the satirist take for granted, and what the lyric poet? The satirist's chief assumption is the existence of norms for thought and conduct, together with personal responsibility for deviation from these norms. (Our sociologists are strong on norms, but they generally reject the concept of personal responsibility; hence they cannot write and do not approve satire.) One writer has summed up the assumptions of satire in a single sentence: "In the world it offers us, madness and blindness are usually the emblems of vice and folly, evil and good are clearly distinguishable, criminals and fools are invariably responsible (therefore censurable), and standards of judgment are indubitable." [15] The reader is assumed to share these assumptions with the writer. He is also assumed, as we have seen, to be no "vulgar reader"—that is, to share the writer's delight in parry, riposte, and all the delicate techniques which satire demands.

The assumptions of the lyric poet are not nearly so definite.

[15] Mack, *op. cit.*, p. 85.

We have already seen that the fulfillment of wishes has been recognized as one of the chief functions, if not the only function, of poetry, and that this function is differently oriented in the satire and the lyric. We now find that romanticism, of which we have found the lyric to be the typical form, has been viewed specifically as a dream world. F. L. Lucas describes romantic literature as "a dream-picture of life, providing sustenance and fulfillment for impulses cramped by society or reality." [16] (Note, in passing, that the satirist is one of the agents of this social cramping.) In another passage, he describes it as "a liberation of the less conscious levels of the mind." [17] Since dream worlds and the activities of the unconscious mind follow individual trains of desire and association, we shall expect archetypes to appear frequently, but we can really make no assumptions for the lyric writer like those of the stable order and social responsibility made by the satirist. The primary assumption of the lyricist, then, is that there are no assumptions beyond the validity and interest of individual dream and sensation —that it is legitimate to lump Cain and Christ together as sufferers without any concern for the rights and wrongs of the cases—or, more accurately, that it is legitimate to lump them together if you think of them together. The great characteristic of the dream world and of lyric poetry is that they have a logic and morality of their own, differing in every case, but they refuse to submit to the censorship of conventional logic or morality.

In their techniques, satire and lyric are as different as in their assumptions. Perhaps the best delimitation of the province of satire is that of Northrop Frye.

> As a tone or attitude, then, two things are essential to satire. One is wit or humor, the other an object of attack. Attack without humor, or pure denunciation, thus forms one of the boundaries

[16] F. L. Lucas, *The Decline and Fall of the Romantic Ideal* (New York, 1937), pp. 35–36.
[17] *Ibid.*, p. 277.

> of satire; humor without attack, the humor of pure gaiety or exuberance, is the other.[18]

This separation between satire and sheer invective has always been recognized. Dryden, for example, insists that "the nicest and most delicate touches of satire consist in fine raillery." He goes on to explain that this playfulness—serious though it may be—is the thing that takes away the personal affront of satire even while it gives the literary work its edge. "Neither is it true, that this fineness of raillery is offensive. A witty man is tickled when he is hurt in this manner, and a fool feels it not. The occasion of an offense may possibly be given, but he cannot take it."[19] Pope developed the fool's incomprehension of satire further:

> You think this cruel? Take it for a rule,
> No creature smarts so little as a fool.
> Let peals of laughter, Codrus! round thee break,
> Thou unconcerned canst hear the mighty crack:
> Pit, box, and gallery in convulsions hurl'd,
> Thou stand'st unshook amidst a bursting world.[20]

The essential of raillery—the thing which the fool cannot grasp—is that a man can make a serious attack in a playful manner. "The satirist is most devastating when he appears to be most completely disengaged."[21] These passages give the essential of the satirical technique: it attacks *as if* in play, thereby securing both the effect of the attack and an assumption of superiority to the thing attacked. By attacking, the satirist assumes that something is evil; by laughing, he assumes that it is also ineffectual. I can laugh at a rat-terrier bearing down threateningly on my car, but not at a

[18] Frye, "The Nature of Satire," *University of Toronto Quarterly*, XIV (1944–1945), 76.
[19] Dryden, *op. cit.*, II, 92 and 93.
[20] "Epistle to Dr. Arbuthnot," lines 83–88.
[21] Sutherland, *op. cit.*, p. 72.

locomotive doing the same thing. The combination of hostility and disengagement is, of course, contempt, which, when it is combined with wit, may be considered the basic attitude of satire.

The techniques of satire are many, but all involve a certain indirection simply because direct attack cannot be disengaged. And this is why satire is not for the vulgar, who are baffled and irritated when a man does not come out and "say what he means." Some of the more obvious devices include *reductio ad absurdum* (Voltaire, *Candide*), *naïve* reporting with no grasp of real significance (Swift, through Gulliver), overstatement of the opposing side (Defoe, *The Shortest Way with Dissenters*), and sheer burlesque of things that take themselves seriously (Butler, *Hudibras*). But as long as the basic combination of attack and disengagement is kept, the shadings and approaches are almost infinite and are constantly shifted and recombined. A good fighter always varies his attacks.

The lyric also has manifold approaches and techniques which can be suggested by some of the phrases that turn up in statements about its nature: "the record and communication of ecstasys," [22] "the poetry of the isolated individual," "feeling confessing itself to itself." The definition of romanticism as "a withdrawal from outer experience to concentrate on inner experience" [23] now appears to be a justification of the position that the lyric is the typical romantic literary form. We can go further and see why satire is its antithesis. Almost the only approach utterly incompatible with the lyric is the attitude of ironic detachment towards the external world. The lyric poet may, as Donne often does, view *himself* with this sort of detachment, in an attempt to view inner experience objectively—or to give the appearance of so doing. But the lyric presents personal experience, and things outside the poet cannot become personal experience strong or inter-

[22] John Drinkwater, *The Lyric* ("The Art and Craft of Letters," No. 5; London, n.d.), pp. 14–15.

[23] Lascelles Abercrombie, as quoted by Lucas, *op. cit.*, p. 13.

esting enough for poetic recording *unless he becomes engaged with them.* It is impossible for Wordsworth to write a lyric about a Highland lass reaping a field and singing in Gaelic, but he can write a fine one about *his experience* of such a scene. Wit also is, if not outlawed entirely, at least much restricted in the lyric, except, of course, in the special case of "metaphysical wit" (which is much like the symbolism of dreams); for we do not break jests over the insubstantial stuff of our visions.

One other difference between the techniques of lyric and satire is worth noting. Satire is usually written on a rather large scale. The lyric is essentially a short poem, and small productions are typical of romanticism in general. It is a commonplace of criticism that the Romantic Period is rich in works like *Kubla Khan* and *Endymion*—ambitious projects which were never finished. Some lyricists, like Poe, even made their own limitations into a dogma, and developed the theory that a true poem must be short. In this respect also, then, the lyric is the typical romantic form; and satire, which is usually a larger work, is the negation of romanticism. The difference goes back to the nature of the works, for the dream-world is essentially one of flashes and insights, not of large designs consistently executed. Satire, which requires an intellectual approach and some personal detachment, can be planned and carried through on a large scale. Furthermore, its indirection makes it difficult to control except at some length: a very short satire is likely to become an epigram, which is something else.

If the general thesis of this essay is valid, what can we infer about our literary future? Since the great lyric age of the Romantic Period began over a century and a half ago, we have had no great satirical period, in spite of a fair number of such works as Laforgue's *Moralités légendaires,* Lewis' *Main Street,* and Huxley's *Brave New World.* (Orwell's *1984* is, of course, not satire at all, but an apocalypse with a dash of science fiction.) There is no question that the lyrical vein has been thinning for some time now, that we should be moving into a cycle of satire again. The declining sense of individualism, the increasing worship of conformity, the constantly tightening social controls—all the signs point in the same direction.

But this time there is a complication. The present-day satirist faces three formidable obstacles: one sociological, one psychological, and one fashionable. Our general social theories do not quite commit themselves to complete determinism, but in practice they certainly assume that, whatever a person is or does, someone else is always to blame. If the chronic liar is the product of faulty upbringing, then the satirist who wants to attack him must shift the attack to his parents; but as soon as he does so, their responsibility shifts to *their* parents—or the community—or the economic system. Satire must assume the moral and intellectual responsibility of its victims; otherwise it loses its target and becomes an infinite wild-goose chase.

The psychological hazard is the author's own risk. A few months ago, a writer on American satire inquired, "Has Freud exerted such an influence on our subconscious mind that we are over-anxious about criticism out of some exaggerated guilt feeling of our own?" [24] Personally, I don't think the satirist feels any such anxiety: he comes of a tough and self-confident breed. But I believe that Freud has increased the hazards of satirical writing and destroyed a large part of its potential audience. Satire demands an intellectual audience, and the intellectual readers today are precisely the ones who are likely to take satire, not as a valid form of art, but as a revelation of anxieties and insecurities in the satirist. And there is certainly no incentive to produce works of art which are sure to be misread as damaging clinical revelations.

The merely fashionable hazard is the slogan of positive thinking. Negative thinking about evil things used to be all right—eight of the Ten Commandments are negative. But even in antiquity some seem to have condemned it. Plutarch tells us that the inhabitants of Asia became slaves because of their inability to

[24] Jean B. Kern, "American Satire, the Elusive Muse," *Western Humanities Review,* XIV (1960), 201.

utter the word *No!* They were evidently positive thinkers. Satire is, on the surface at least, a form of negative thinking, and it can hardly flourish until this fashion plays out.

These sociological, psychological, and fashionable obstacles to a revival of satire are clearly interrelated, each gathering support from the other two. It may be that they will be able to prevent the rise of a period of satire, in spite of all the forces working for it. If they do, their success will be simple self-preservation, for if satire does come back, they will certainly be its first and juiciest game.

The Three Revolutions of Modern Poetry

STANLEY BURNSHAW

ANYONE WHO PRESUMES to deal with the three revolutions of modern Western poetry must take care to define his terms, and especially "modern." I use it historically, to enclose a block of time and to suggest the cultural-philosophic climate decisive for the poets of the period. For no matter how deeply we believe a literary work to be a "linguistic system" or a "self-sustaining object" immune to time's erosions, we also know that the man who created it lived during a specific age and breathed its specific air. In the last few decades critics have given too little attention to the experiences that writers of an epoch have had in common; each author has been separated and studied as a more or less unique phenomenon. As a consequence a reader underrates the importance of the possessions and deprivations they held in common, even when these cry out to be seen and explored.

Owen Barfield, in discussing a lyric by one of the Elizabethans, observes that

> part of my aesthetic experience I owe to the individual genius of the poet [and] part is due to something which I will call its "Elizabethan-ness." Needless to say, the phenomenon is not peculiar to the Elizabethan lyric. It is true of other times and places, of the poetry of the Greek Anthology, for example, of the French Pléiade, of the English Metaphysicals, or the Cavalier lyric, and it has been well named by some critic "joint-stock poetry." It arises whenever different poets work together in a kind of coterie or come under the same contemporary influence. . . .[1]

In a very broad sense, the poets whom I call modern exemplify this phenomenon of "joint-stock poetry," even though they are widely spread out in time. For the period begins with the outbreak of the Industrial Revolution and ends with the close of World War II. This is a huge block of time compared with the little ages of the Pléiade or the English Metaphysicals, and yet all the poets whom I regard as modern lived under essentially the same influence of a civilization that had declared war on Nature in a contest that would stop at nothing short of unconditional surrender.

This war was, of course, inevitable, man being what he is: a maker of tools and bent on mastery. Actually he had always been moving toward an open declaration, from the ancient moment when he developed the hand axe and the flint in his struggle for food and survival. The intervening preparatory stages can be traced by anyone who studies the evolution of science and technology down through what we call the Age of Reason. By that time, of course, the intellectual élite of England had ceased to be intimidated by the forces of Nature. Nature was less a mystery than a machine. But it was not until animal power had been displaced by waterpower and steampower that the war began in earnest. From that point on it was simply a question of time, one thing leading to another until the discovery and use of atomic power. The war against Nature had been confidently waged and

[1] *Poetic Diction* (Faber and Faber, 1952), p. 51.

won; and we post-moderns, of 1945-and-after, breathe the spirit of a different epoch, and we have a different terror on our minds: Now that man is victorious, how shall he stay alive?

The attitude toward the Deity shows a complementary evolution, immediately before and during the war for mastering Nature. The all-powerful Western God of the Middle Ages ceaselessly drew men's eyes from earth to heaven, and it was not till the advent of Renaissance Humanism that men could look upon their dwelling place, earth, with a certain curiosity and with growing confidence in their own capacities. The notion that men might cope with Nature without God's help became so solid that, as everyone knows, by the eighteenth century He could be looked upon as the proverbial Divine Mechanic of the Great Machine. But with the Industrial Revolution even this function was removed; He was merely to stand aside, above the battle, and to watch or urge men on to grander achievements. Max Weber made this tellingly clear in his essay on the "Protestant Ethic," tracing the development of Luther's idea of "the calling" to Calvinism's elevation of a "this-worldly asceticism" into an ideal of conduct for the godly man—"More specifically, this-worldly asceticism tended to identify spiritual salvation with business success, and so created the capitalistic spirit, which . . . retained its vitality even after its religious sources had evaporated." [2] God might be invoked by name and worshipped on Sundays, but as a reality, as an everliving spiritual presence in the everyday life of Western Industrial Man, He had all but disappeared. The "operational" objects for worship were things, things.

But not for everyone—especially not for the poet. The more the people around him concentrated on external reality, the more he turned inward. Industrial man was making noisome advances in his conquest of Nature; he was building more and more factories, producing more and more goods—these were the things

[2] Hans Speier, in *Encyclopaedia of the Social Sciences* (Macmillan, 1935), XV, p. 388.

that really mattered! [3] To the poet, what mattered was his inner self: a limitless world for private exploration. As a paradigm of rejection, this is almost too tempting to be ignored by anyone with a Freudian cast of mind. But whether or not poets acted out of defensiveness, because they could not cope with their age, is irrelevant. What interests us is what happened in literature, and what happened there has unmistakable import.

Everything that the poet now experiences in this swiftly industrializing world is significant only in terms of his private reaction: this alone is worth expressing. After years of virtual absence, the first person singular returns to poetry—but with a now magisterial force and with a new assertiveness quite different from anything heard at an earlier time. Moreover, with vanguard Romantics in Germany and France, it involves something in addition to the ordinary subjective self: the subliminal mind enters literature as a necessary part of the creative intelligence. Jean Paul registered this change in a sentence that looms as a landmark in modern culture: "Our measurements of the rich territory of the Me are far too small or narrow when we omit the immense realm of the *Unconscious,* this real interior Africa in every sense."

The modern age of poetry, then, begins with these two "differences," and the greatest part of its achievement can be traced to this twofold source. For the two are really one: (1) a commitment to a subjective self (2) that is now vastly, even infinitely, expanded. Look synoptically at Western cultural history of the last hundred and fifty years, and the picture seems almost too neat to be credible—on the one hand, the province of society at large: the external reality of the whole of Nature; on the other, the province of the poet: the internal reality of the whole psyche; and both

[3] Poets were reacting and would continue to react to the concomitant effects of the Industrial Revolution more than to the Revolution itself—to changed attitudes, values, personal relations, social institutions, etc. From such alienation a few sought refuge in religion, but a great many more in the Unconscious, no doubt, in some instances, as a substitute for the divine.

opened up for endless exploration and exploitation.[4] The same cannot be said of the novel or the drama, but we are speaking of poetry. And we are looking down from our late point in time, from which this mainstream course of the poem is grossly clear.

Once we come close, to be sure, we encounter complexities—of date, location, temperament, for this is Western Europe and also America. The cross-currents of uneven development call to mind the painting of the Renaissance, which moved from Italy to France to the Low Countries, blooming in each place at a different period and always with characteristic change. After Romanticism burst upon France, Germany, and England, its energies centered in Paris, where it broadened and deepened into something seemingly different. But French Symbolism was merely a matured growth of Romanticism; indeed it was latent in a number of Romantic writers from the start.[5] Wordsworth's "The Simplon Pass," though published in 1845, had been written at least forty-one years earlier. The twenty-line poem ends by declaring that the woods, waterfalls, winds, rocks, crags, skies, darkness, and light

> Were all like workings of one mind, the features
> Of the same face, blossoms upon one tree,
> Characters of the great Apocalypse, 18
> The types and symbols of Eternity,
> Of first, and last, and midst, and without end.

Nobody refers to the 18th and 19th lines as "British Symbolist verse," yet how near they bring us to the heritage of Swedenborg, whose importance to French Symbolism cannot be overstated. And how far is it from Wordsworth's "types and symbols of Eternity" to Baudelaire's, in

[4] Is it necessary to state that poets had one attitude toward nature and that society at large had quite another? or that the use of nature by Romantic poets is a typical example of internalization?

[5] E.g., in Shelley, and in Blake. (See Louis Cazamian, *Symbolisme et Poésie,* and Henri Peyre, *Shelley et la France,* 1935.)

> La nature est un temple où de vivants piliers
> Laissent parfois sortir de confuses paroles;
> L'homme y passe à travers des forêts de symboles
> Qui l'observent avec des regards familiers. . . .

(Nature is a temple where living pillars / Sometimes allow confused words to escape; / There man passes through forests of symbols / That watch him with familiar [intimate] glances. . . .)

Though it aroused little attention when it first appeared (1857), "Correspondances" came to exert a greater impact on modern literature than any other single poem, for it epitomizes the Symbolist view that the external event is a sign of an event taking place elsewhere—the so-called vertical correspondences between the event visible to human beings and its corresponding event in the invisible world. If then, the invisible and the visible exist in a one-to-one correspondence, the poet through his symbols can make the invisible reality available to himself and to his readers. He is no longer just a maker of rimes: he is an explorer and a wielder of vast, unsuspected powers, whose discoveries can literally bring heaven down to earth. This is not simply to paraphrase Swedenborg, but to epitomize the attitude of the typical poets of the period (including the German Goethe and the American Emerson), to whom symbols stood for profoundly important "somethings," to whom external reality was a surface to be seen through and explored for the greater reality of the truths that lie in wait there.

As for words, individual words, who could say what they might not mean and what they might not do? As components of a metaphor—which is to say, the verbalization of the symbol—they possessed more than the evocative force of which earlier poets were aware. As vehicles of the new method of discovery, they had the power to recreate reality. No wonder the Symbolist explored their suggestiveness and their reverberations—or that the successors of Symbolism would pant after pluralistic meanings. No wonder that a poet like Rimbaud tried to create a new language, or that a later poet like Mallarmé went so far as to break up ordinary relations among words in order to replace them with a new syntax of larger meanings.

And if words were to be explored for unsuspected significations and powers, the Unconscious itself would be the vastest of all possible sources. The most obvious approach was taken, of course, by Rimbaud, in his deliberate cultivation of hallucinatory states. But note the stress upon language in the closing phrase: "Then I would explain my magic sophistries with the hallucination of words." And the no-less-famous journey toward self-alienation, which succeeded at last with his victorious "Je est un autre [I is another]." But this is still relatively tame. Greater audacity was on the way—in the effort to overcome mortal limitations and to exercise superhuman power. Such so-called "angelism" was soon attempted by Rimbaud and later by others, including Mallarmé, with his infatuation with the Absolute and Nothingness; by Saint-Pol Roux, who wanted to replace the God above with the God within; by the Surrealists, who tried to transform and remake the very objects in nature. Angelism is a very far cry from Jean Paul's almost gentle fascination with the "interior Africa" of the Unconscious, but how was anyone to know what might happen when poets, in an ever more desperately rushing world of Industrialism, drove deeper and deeper into their private selves?

So much for the first two stages of modernism—Romantic and Symbolist; what of the poets who came later? French critics refer to "Three Generations of Symbolists" and suggest that Surrealism, contemporaneous with the third, was an alternate Symbolist development. When one looks at the names that distinguish these "generations," a question arises: Why label them "Symbolist"? Baudelaire and Rimbaud, as the initiators, cannot be questioned; but Mallarmé, as emblem for the second generation? and Valéry, as emblem for the third? Are these two poets legitimate exponents of Symbolism? Decidedly not in the Swedenborgian sense in which Baudelaire could take reality. But decidedly yes when one considers how Mallarmé extended the psychological and linguistic exploits of his predecessors; and how Valéry went further, with the "detached referents," the *leitmotif* use of symbols, and the concern to fathom the nature of the human mind. One has to guard against oversimple notions that inhere in the "Symbolist" label. It spreads confusion—yet it also can serve to make clear the central role of the poets of France in fostering and conditioning the poetry of the modern Western world.

The twentieth century is the French century to the extent that virtually every important Western poet was affected by Symbolist or Surrealist practices (need one point to Rilke, Yeats, Eliot, Lorca, Montale, Ungaretti, Seferis, Blok?). And the nineteenth century? The second half was also the century of France, both directly (because of the amount of excellent poetry contributed by the French) and to the extent that poets who worked independently—and even earlier (Hölderlin, Leopardi) [6]—wrote in a spirit congenial to its spirit. Certain Victorians may seem to stand apart, but like their peers they were also the creatures of Romanticism and, in any case, neither England nor the United States produced significant poets who consistently celebrated the values of the Industrial Age; on the contrary. There were marginal movements, of course—from the now-silent cannonading of Marinetti's "Futurists" to the sometimes memorable outcries of the socially conscious thirties and forties. But the mainstream of modern poetry is a continuous flow from the Romantic and Symbolist source, threading through not a few nations but the Western world.[7]

[6] As his translator, Michael Hamburger, points out, the development in Hölderlin's poetry between 1797 and 1803 "in many ways prefigures the development of all European poetry in the next century and a half" (*Hölderlin*, Penguin Books, 1961, p. xxi). Leopardi's case is more complex. What he referred to as *noia* (spleen, tedium) appears again and again in nineteenth-century European poetry—in the *ennui* of Baudelaire, for example. Sainte-Beuve's substantial essay on Leopardi's poetry appeared in the *Revue des Deux Mondes* in September 1844, and Luciano Rebay raises the question: "Is it reasonable to assume that Baudelaire could have been unaware of this essay and of all it had to tell him?"

[7] To distinguish as "modern" the period from the beginning of Romanticism to our own time is justifiable not only in poetry. See, for example, Jacques Barzun, *Darwin, Marx, Wagner,* 2nd ed., Doubleday Anchor Books, pp. 322–338 *passim.*

I

Let us look at the "revolutions," beginning with a brief characterization of each so as to review them later in terms of a new direction. From the handful of adducible examples, I take three: the first labeled somewhat approximately "syntax."

We start with Hölderlin's late hymns and fragments. Though in time of composition contemporary with the *Lyrical Ballads,* this poetry could hardly be farther away from Wordsworth's in syntax. As Michael Hamburger points out, "it combines the directness of common speech with the most daring use of ellipse and inversion, not for rhetorical, but for imaginative ends," and he cites Hölderlin's own explanation of one aspect:

> It is common practice to have inversions of word order within the period. But clearly much greater effects can be obtained by the inversion of the periods themselves. The logical order of periods, in which the basis (the basic period) is followed by its development, the development by its culmination, the culmination by its purpose, and the subsidiary clauses are merely appended to the main clauses to which they primarily apply—all this can only very rarely serve the poet's ends.[8]

A half century later we come upon a second and no less startling violation of what Webster defines as "the due arrangement of word forms to show their mutual relations in a sentence." Mallarmé's syntax issues from a different system of relations, as exemplified in the following poem, "Sainte":

A la fenêtre recélant
Le santal vieux qui se dédore
De sa viole étincelant
Jadis avec flûte ou mandore,

Est la Sainte pâle, étalant
Le livre vieux qui se déplie
Du Magnificat ruisselant
Jadis selon vêpre et complie:

[8] *Hölderlin* (Penguin Books, 1961), p. xxiv.

A ce vitrage d'ostensoir
Que frôle une harpe par l'Ange
Formée avec son vol du soir
Pour la délicate phalange

Du doigt que, sans le vieux santal
Ni le vieux livre, elle balance
Sur le plumage instrumental,
Musicienne du silence.

(At the window secretly hiding/ The old sandalwood shedding its gilt/ Of her viol shining/ Formerly [once] with flute or mandore [mandolin],

Is the pale Saint, spreading out/ The ancient book that unfolds/ Of the Magnificat streaming/ Formerly according to [once in] vespers and complin [nightsong]:

At this monstrance [stained-glass] window/ Which is touched by a harp shaped by the Angel with his evening flight / For the delicate phalanx [bone]

Of the finger that, without the old sandalwood/ Or the old book, she holds poised/ Upon the instrumental plumage,/ Musician of silence.)

Sixteen lines of eight syllables each—all one sentence, with five commas, one colon. No simple series of stages: beginning, middle, end. One thing runs into another, but not always the next. To get at this poem, one must read and read—and then, if one doesn't resist, certain elements may take on sudden importance. The structure is made of "presences," similar to the images bodied forth in a dream; for ordinary connectives—words like *but, because,* and other signs of relationship—are absent from a dream. Yet a dream communicates, often with memorable residue; and a poem of Mallarmean syntax may also be able to communicate, for the relations are held together by a logic of their own. Mallarmé's word order is often bewildering, with inversions, appositions, and what seem to be capricious displacements. But the main difficulties come from the lack of terms to denote the relations among the parts. He removed these with a will, as he removed other clues to his intention. It would be up to the reader to supply not only the morphemes and the normal word order but even an occasional verb. For Mallarmé was writing according to his new theory: "To paint, not the thing, but the effect it produces."

So far as we know, Emily Dickinson was not following any such theory when she wrote this poem, which in its own way is as nonsyntactical as "Sainte":

Further in Summer than the Birds—
Pathetic from the Grass
A minor Nation celebrates
Its unobtrusive Mass—
No Ordinance be seen—
So gradual the Grace
A gentle Custom it becomes—
Enlarging loneliness.

Antiquest felt at Noon
When August burning low
Arise this Spectral Canticle
Repose to typify—
Remit as yet no Grace—
No furrow on the Glow—
But a Druidic difference
Enhances Nature now—[9]

Charles Anderson finds this to be "her finest poem on the theme of the year going down to death and the relation of this to a belief in immortality."[10] Wherein lies the difficulty? One has to know what she is talking about; and this fact has now been supplied: the poem is called "My Cricket," for the insect that symbolized for her the mysterious moment of the year's transition from autumn into winter. Aware of this meaning, we may still find the poem as a whole indecipherable, until we surrender ourselves and are lucky enough to begin to perceive its "presences."

But revolutionary syntax does not necessarily produce difficulty. On the contrary, some of Cummings' most popular poems play havoc with the reader's expectations while communicating not with losses but with gains. Here are two familiar fragments:

(1) my father moved through dooms of love
through sames of am through haves of give,
singing each morning out of each night
my father moved through depths of height . . . .

[9] Reprinted by permission of the publishers from *The Poems of Emily Dickinson*, edited by Thomas H. Johnson, The Belknap Press of Harvard University Press, copyright 1951, 1955, The President and Fellows of Harvard College, Cambridge, Massachusetts.

[10] *Emily Dickinson's Poetry* (Holt, Rinehart and Winston, 1960), pp. 151 *f.*

My father moved through theys of we, . . .[11]

(2) what if a much of a which of a wind
gives the truth to summer's lie; . . .

what if a keen of a lean wind flays
screaming hills with sleet and snow:
strangles valleys by ropes of thing
and stifles forests in white ago? . . .[12]

Cummings typically "makes" words by derivation: changing parts of speech; adding prefixes or suffixes; converting verbs, pronouns, adverbs, adjectives, and conjunctions into nouns. These coinages, instantly understood, provide a strange yet natural pleasure as they extend the usual meanings of the words. But the reader may be also led into complex discovering, which comes on slowly, and especially so when the word order demands reconstruction:

to stand(alone)in some

autumnal afternoon:
breathing a fatal
stillness;while

enormous this how

patient creature(who's
never by never robbed of
day)puts always on by always

dream,is to

taste
not(beyond
death and

life)imaginable mysteries[13]

[11] Copyright, 1940, by E. E. Cummings. Reprinted from *Poems 1923–1954* by E. E. Cummings by permission of Harcourt, Brace & World, Inc.
[12] *Ibid.*
[13] Copyright, 1958, by E. E. Cummings. Reprinted from *Ninety-Five Poems* by E. E. Cummings by permission of Harcourt, Brace & World, Inc.

A fourth example, from the Spanish, can make its point despite the language barrier, for its violation is of a kind we no longer notice. As in Mallarmé and Dickinson, the words themselves are ordinary:

Without eyes, without voice,
  without shadow.
Now, without shadow.
Invisible to the world,
To everyone.
	Sin ojos, sin vos, sin
	  sombra.
	Ya, sin sombra.
	Invisible para el mundo,
	para nadie.

And you, sea, And you, fire, And you, Hastened wind of my dream.	Y tú, mar, y tú, fuego, y tú, acelerado aire de mi sueño.

"In his shorter lines," says the translator, C. M. Bowra, "Rafael Alberti often uses a highly impressionistic method of putting down the vital words without forming them into grammatical units."[14] Note: the vital words. Here lies one clue to the unriddling of poems that violate the expected pattern in the reader's mind. When one concentrates on these vital elements, the poem can begin to emerge. For there is nothing sacred or even superior in the rules of syntax; like grammar and usage, it is enthroned by custom and acceptance. Its way is not the only way of effective communication; in fact it is plainly a block in certain contexts.

II

The second revolution—in prosody—can be traced to French Symbolism, though it was never an article of its faith. Baudelaire and Mallarmé felt no need to rebel against the rigidities of French versification, with its fixed number of syllables per line, placement of caesura, perfect rime, and so on. They were fond of the prose poem, and Baudelaire could even rhapsodize about it—"musical

[14] *The Creative Experiment* (Grove, n.d.), p. 226.

without rhythm or rime, supple and bold enough to adapt itself to the lyric movements of the soul, to the undulations of reverie, to the somersaults of the consciousness"—but of free verse he would have none.

It was Rimbaud who violated the canons of prosody, and timidly, it seems to us today. In 1886 the first *vers libre* poem (written before 1873) was published; then a second, also by Rimbaud; then some appeared by three other poets, among them Laforgue. Finally (1889) Viélé-Griffin prefaced a book of his own with the declaration "Le vers est libre." The statement was premature; controversies continued to rage between advocates of *vers libre* and the vast majority, who upheld the classic rules. But in time the *vers librists* succeeded in establishing their claims—and in the last sixty years their successors have done almost everything imaginable to the once inviolable classic line.

Readers trained only in English may marvel at the fury of this French revolution, having already known free verse in Milton, Arnold, and Whitman. But our language is tonic; every polysyllabic word has at least one fixed stress. A line of English verse is always held together to some extent by a pattern of strong and weak syllables. In ordinary French discourse, however, each syllable is about equally strong; hence, it was believed that the only way to keep a line of verse from falling apart was by constructing it with a fixed number of syllables and by tying it to another line of the same "length" by rime. *Vers librists* had therefore to show that a line could also be held together by a different pattern—by an accent of meaning. To this extent the revolution in French prosody introduced an external force. By contrast, the revolution in English prosody, if there was to be one, would have to come from within—as in fact it did with Gerard Manley Hopkins.

The impact of his new departures can hardly be exaggerated. It is apparent not only in the influence of his "sprung rhythm" upon the general sound of contemporary English verse but also in the elaboration of internal rime, assonance, and alliteration, for example. Such devices had of course been used for centuries, but

Hopkins' especial way of using them has had much to do with the confidence with which twentieth-century poets have altered the basic iambic. Alongside Hopkins', the innovations of Owen and of Auden seem marginal, though they too are part of the general revolution in prosody—as was Imagist free verse and the short-lived "polyphonic prose"—as are also the yet unchristened devices in the poems of the latest magazines. We have now become so accustomed to experiments in versification that we no longer stop to appreciate that it was not always so. Yet fifty years ago they were scattered and few. One has only to compare the look of the page in anthologies of 1900 and 1960—in English, French, German, Spanish, Italian—to see how much the revolution in prosody has achieved.

Examples are scarcely needed: they are our monthly and quarterly fare. Let us look instead at some evidences of departures from the basic tradition itself, and first at the attempt to move verse in the direction of prose, which is part of a larger fascination with the blurring of distinctions among literary forms. The following stanzas come toward the close of "Poème à l'Étrangère":

> Mais ce soir de grand âge et de grande patience, dans l'Été lourd d'opiates et d'obscures laitances, pour délivrer à fond d'abîme le peuple de vos lampes, ayant, homme très seul, pris par ce haut quartier de Fondations d'aveugles, de Réservoirs mis au linceul et de vallons en cage pour les morts, longeant les grilles et les lawns et tous ces beaux jardins à l'Italienne
>
> dont les maîtres un soir s'en furent épouvantés d'un parfum de sépulcre, . . .

The poet is Saint-John Perse. Paul Claudel might also serve as an example, but not Robinson Jeffers, for all his range and sonal complexity. Perhaps the French language lends itself particularly to the verse paragraph. Not that such structures are entirely absent from English, but that they tend to appear more readily in fiction and as passages rather than as works complete in themselves. Yet what one might call "prose-directed verse" is by no means lacking in English. It can be noted in the general sound of such a passage as the following by Auden, on Sigmund Freud:

> And if something of the autocratic pose,
> The paternal strictness he distrusted, still
> Clung to his utterance and features,
> It was a protective imitation
>
> For one who lived among enemies so long;
> If often he was wrong and at times absurd,
> To us he is no more a person
> Now but a whole climate of opinion. . . .[15]

One can disregard the line-breaks and read this as prose—and it is prose of a kind till the line-breaks insist and one is back again in verse. The experience differs with the work of Marianne Moore, whose poems can be scanned if not by stress then by syllable. Such verse has uniqueness of sound because it has appropriated some of the muscularities of prose:

> I, too, dislike it: there are things that are important
> beyond all this fiddle.
> Reading it, however, with a perfect contempt for it, one discovers in it, after all, a place for the genuine.
> Hands that can grasp, eyes
> that can dilate, hair that can rise
> if it must, these things are important not because a
>
> high-sounding interpretation can be put upon them but because they are useful. When they become so derivative as to become unintelligible, the same thing may be said for all of us, that we
> do not admire what
> we cannot understand: . . .[16]

[15] Copyright, 1940, by W. H. Auden. Reprinted from *The Collected Poetry of W. H. Auden* by permission of Random House, Inc.

[16] Copyright, 1935, by Marianne Moore. Reprinted from *Collected Poems* by Marianne Moore, by permission of The Macmillan Company.

A quite contrary phenomenon in the general revolution can be traced to the popular song. Modern French is especially rich with examples—from Verlaine and Corbière to Apollinaire and Aragon—and instances can also be found in English, but most often in passages used for ironic effect. Entire poems are rare, except, of course, for the proletarian satires of Kenneth Fearing, with their heavily syncopated rhythms:

> But just the same, baby, and never forget,
> it takes a neat, smart, fast, good, sweet doublecross
> to doublecross the gentleman who doublecrossed the gentleman
> who doublecrossed
> your doublecrossing, doublecrossing, doublecross friend.

Or:

> And wow he died as wow he lived,
> going whop to the office and blooie home to sleep and biff
> got married and bam had children and oof got fired,
> zowie did he live and zowie did he die . . .

From such jazz versification to *Un Coup de Dés* is as far as sound can ever get from sight, and yet Mallarmé's final poem was part of the same revolution, no doubt the most drastic attempt of all. Whether or not we try to read it only with the silent ear, the white spaces, indentations, italics, capitals all demand to be "heard." Mallarmé read the poem to him, said Valéry, in a low, even voice—which seems entirely opposed to the theory expounded in the preface by the poet. As Wallace Fowlie remarks:

> By the appearance of the poem, the thought reveals its very life; its hesitations, prolongations, designs, disappearances. Such and such a word [demands] large print and a whole page for itself. Each word, each space, each silence has to be apprehended.[17]

An English-speaking reader who looks at *Un Coup de Dés* inevitably relates it to the typographical arrangements frequent in

[17] *Mallarmé* (Univ. of Chicago Press, 1953), pp. 219–220 *passim.*

Cummings' poetry. But, as Norman Friedman makes clear, Cummings does not use typographic devices as part of an *attempt to equal* things, actions, feelings, or ideas. In the grasshopper poem that begins:

r-p-o-p-h-e-s-s-a-g-r
who
a)s w(e loo)k
upnowgath
PPEGORHRASS

"it is rather that the spacing is governed by the disruption and blending of syllables and the pause and emphasis of meaning which produce a figurative equivalent for the subject of the poem, as the reader reads in time." [18]

Thinking over the last few pages, a reader may object that the "what" has been omitted from discussions of the "how"—and of course *as the poem* the two are one. But must it always be declaimed that neither "form" nor "content" can exist except as terms, terms to denote ways of abstracting? Only in such an imagined sense can a poem be said to have structures of sound, syntax, and the like, for the poem is not a verbal amalgam which analysis takes apart. If critics seem to assume the contrary, it is only because they look and try to know at separated times and from separated stances. To experience a poem is a quite different action, in which critical knowing plays no part.

III

Approaching our third revolution, we face the fiercest of controversies, for this is the upheaval in poetic communication as a whole and specifically in its referents. Here we meet the end-result of the poets' decision to turn inward, to reject the world at large for their private worlds. And since the poet writes of his

[18] *e.e. cummings* (Johns Hopkins Press, 1960), p. 123.

purely private universe, its points of reference—its objects and experiences—must inevitably be obscure, if not meaningless, to those outside. Now, poetry has to some degree always been clouded with allusions to matters of private import to the writer; nevertheless people assume that in the decent days of yore poets felt honor-bound to be understandable whereas modern poets delight to "mean" only to themselves. Readers wishing to penetrate the obscurity may try, but the poet will not help them. He writes whatever he pleases, never caring whether his referents mean something or nothing to anyone but himself.

The charge is of course not new. Ben Jonson sneered: "Nothing is fashionable till it be deform'd; and this is to write like a gentleman." Chapman, himself no "easy" poet, had little patience with contrived obscurity, but he was careful to declare that where obscurity "shroudeth itself in the heart of the subject, uttered with fitness of figure, and expressive epithets; with that darkness will I still labour to be shadowed"—(a statement that Perse might have cited today in his Nobel Prize speech of acceptance). Samuel Johnson offered a typically sane distinction: ". . . words are only hard to those who do not understand them, and the critic ought always to enquire whether he is incommoded by the fault of the writer or by his own." And he added: "Every author does not write for every reader." This remark could have served excellently a century later in France, if poets had been willing to own up to what they were doing. But of course they were not—and they counter-attacked. "The profane multitude I hate," Chapman had said. Mallarmé preferred to use the colder word "disdain."

But is there occasion for such fire or ice? Is it not rather that a gap must grow between the vanguard and those in the rear, till the space can narrow or close? How else explain that the very same poems once thought of as "hard" can be taken as "easy" today? Not that a reader could be blamed for finding them once impossible to enter. The poems were obscure because the poet had made them so—but not out of wilful desire to be hermetic. For a writer of verse is often faced with an irreducible choice between "clarity" and "truth": he can retain one at the sacrifice of the other. Dare he allow the "understandable" statement to remain when it is not what he feels he must say? If, faced with such a choice, he decided to keep the obscure version, it is only because the clear statement is unacceptable as untrue. The literature of the past is overladen with such troubled choices, and the responsibility all too often can be traced to the limits of language itself.

Although comprehensibility is essentially a matter of such "choice," it is so only to a degree. Certain statements that are difficult for another person to follow may nevertheless continue to feel right to the poet; to alter them is to falsify. A writer of verse is likely to be compelled to let such an obscure passage stand, for poetry is feeling, and a poet, like everyone else in an uncertain situation, will act out of faith. Trusting his feelings, he must take the consequences: that his unaltered words will mean very little to most people or evoke even hostility and contempt. It is time that this much-argued problem were recognized in its context of struggle. In the last analysis, obscurity involves purely moral problems that only the poet can decide.[19]

Turning now to specific instances, we distinguish three main sources of "difficulty" whose results are visible everywhere in Western verse today. The gaps are still large, although narrower than they were at one time. But whether they will ever quite close, who would dare to predict?

The first of the three sub-revolutions was—paradoxical as it sounds—a deliberate attempt to enrich the communicative content of language by expunging the unessential words. Such removal of connectives gave rise to baffling images, yet these same images carried a new type of content in accordance with a new set of communicative principles sponsored by the high-priest Mallarmé. "To *name* an object is to do away with three-quarters of the enjoyment of the poem, which is derived from the satisfaction of guessing little by little; to *suggest* it, to *evoke* it—this is what

[19] This paragraph and the four sentences that precede it first appeared in my *Early and Late Testament* (Dial Press, 1952), pp. vi–vii.

charms the imagination," this is the ideal. Now, the difference between naming and suggesting is the difference between communicating to the reader and offering him something to unriddle. So far as Mallarmé is concerned, the poem ought to be "a mystery to which the reader will hunt the key," and his emphasis is upon the mystery; for poets who "take the thing just as it is and put it before us . . . are consequently deficient in mystery: they deprive the mind of the delicious joy of believing that it is creating." One can give the mind such joy by removing the clues, by deliberately stripping away the words that would present the thing "just as it is."

Which is precisely what Mallarmé continued to do, and with dedication unsurpassed in the history of art. He presented words and phrases as entities, almost wholly detached from other words and phrases. Words were no longer to serve as names for objects; they were to be objects in themselves. And existing as objects within the poem, they would develop new interrelations and therefore give rise to new and unpredictable reverberations—and to new meanings, of which the poet himself would not be aware as he watched them interacting, displaying a life of their own. This was creative writing of an altogether new kind; the poet as proverbial "maker" was now making something that had never been made before: he was disposing live materials. And these live materials produced different messages when arranged in different sequences. No wonder Mallarmé could regard them with a certain reverence. They were creations that would speak to him: as he rearranged them in the line, they would say different things, reveal new meanings, unclear and multiple, inexhaustible and ever elusive. Mallarmé had suddenly acquired a power analogous to God's, with each poem a new universe of his own making. This was angelism *par excellence;* and Mallarmé never stopped exploring its possibilities, drawing on typography, blank spaces, and everything else he could think of, as his final act of angelism bears witness in *Un Coup de Dés.*

For readers the end-results of this type of creativity are usually too bewildering to draw them in. Mallarmé might be concerned with producing "an orphic explanation of the Earth," but readers are interested only in poems that will speak to them, which is what Mallarmé's most extreme experiments quite fail to do. When faced, for example, with his sonnet "A la nue accablante tu," they must either apply themselves with immense and patient labor or throw up their hands. For the fourteen lines at first glance defy unriddling, with the subject (sepulchral shipwreck) delayed till line 5 and the main verb (abolishes) till line 8.[20] And even after studying the explications, they may flounder forever in uncertainties. Despite the fascination of the artistry and its strangeness, readers will doubt that the game was worth the striving. It is the sort of poem that may offer no future for poetry as a whole: the beginning and the end of its own tradition.

But its legacy is very much alive, having been adapted and refined by the disciple Valéry. Not the angelism, of course, but the enrichment of communicative content by detaching the image from its referent. A good example is the first quatrain of "L'Abeille":

> Quelle, et si fine, et si mortelle,
> Que soit ta pointe, blonde abeille,
> Je n'ai, sur ma tendre corbeille,
> Jeté qu'un songe de dentelle.

(However, so sharp and so deadly,/ Be your point, blond bee,/ I have, upon my tender basket,/ Thrown only a dream of lace.)

To what does "tendre corbeille" (tender basket) refer? It is not tied to anything, it floats free in the sentence: what can it mean? This depends on the reader, on what he chooses to attach to it: only he can do the attaching. Valéry has not done it; he has left it carefully unanchored. Possibilities come to mind at once—roundness, flesh, soft curve of the body, fruit, ripeness, garden—but

[20] Fowlie, *op. cit.*, pp. 216 *f.*

these are speculations, and *the* meaning remains obscure. But it is obscurity of a special kind, for the very indefiniteness of relation between image and referent sets up multiple reverberations. This vagueness thus contributes a special type of poetic pleasure which is further enriched by the resonances of such other words in the stanza as "fine," "mortelle," "blonde," "songe," "dentelle" (sharp, deadly, blond, dream, lace). One encounters such potentialities wherever indefiniteness is cultivated as an end in itself: toward enrichment. Hence we find ourselves making a paradoxical remark about this stanza, as we should about Valéry's "La Jeune Parque," whose emotionally colored words often can be taken to refer to a number of different objects at once: we say that if the images and the referents were more definite, the poetry would diminish in richness.

We have traveled a long way from Pre-Symbolist communication, in which at least one clear tie can be adduced between image and referent. We are in a new universe of relations among the parts in a poem, where ties are merely suggested by images that condense a variety of meanings and hold them suspended upon others. A world in which the poet assumes that his readers will look for the meanings because they feel they are there, both beneath and within the words, and therefore also between.

This Symbolist development calls to mind other modes of compression, exemplified in such lines as Allen Tate's "We are the eyelids of defeated caves"; César Vallejo's "Poetry of the purple cheek bone/ between saying and not saying"; Rilke's figure of Night, the "tender disillusioning," who is "painfully there." [21] Our best-known example is Hart Crane's "At Melville's Tomb," with its opening statement: "Often beneath the wave, wide from this ledge/ The dice of drowned men's bones he saw bequeath/ An embassy," and his own explanation:

[21] Vallejo: "Poesia del pómulo morado, entre el decirlo/ y el callarlo." Rilke: "sanft enttäuschende," "mühsam bevorsteht"—sometimes given in English as "mild enchantress," "wearily" (or "laboriously") "present" (or, more literally, "impending").

Dice bequeath an embassy, in the first place, by being ground (in this connection only, of course) in little cubes from the bones of drowned men by the action of the sea, and are finally thrown up on the sand, having "numbers" but no identification. These being the bones of dead men who never completed their voyage, it seems legitimate to refer to them as the only surviving evidence of certain messages undelivered, mute evidence of certain things, experiences that the dead mariners might have had to deliver. Dice as a symbol of chance and circumstance is also implied.

Alongside the verse of earlier periods, the modern varieties are spectacularly condensed, but not only as a result of such means as we have been noting. Certain poems are arrays of discrete details, no more conjoined than a series of cinema stills. Others come from the page with the seemingly simultaneous impact of dream, as a *Gestalt* of "presences." How classify so simple a poem as Quasimodo's "Antico Inverno"?

Desiderio delle tue mani chiare
nella penombra della fiamma:
sapevano di rovere e di rose;
di morte. Antico inverno.

Cercavano il miglio gli uccelli
ed erano subito di neve;
così le parole.
Un po' di sole, una raggera d'angelo,
e poi la nebbia; e gli alberi,
e noi fatti d'aria al mattino.[22]

(The desire for [of] your hands, transparent / in the penumbra of the flame:/ they had the fragrance of oak and of roses;/ of death. Ancient winter.

The birds were looking for millet / and they were suddenly of snow;/ so [with] words./ A little sun, an angel's halo,/ and then the mist; and the trees,/ and ourselves made of air at morning.)

[22] Reprinted from *Ed E' Subito Sera* by permission of Arnoldo Mondadori Editore, copyright 1942.

Largely because of the bewildering varieties of compression, critics have been busily explicating poems—sometimes to the surprise of their authors, occasionally to their dismay. But one might wonder where readers would be without such help.

Our second sub-revolution can also be traced to France, specifically to a member of the Romantic generation. As early as 1837, Gérard de Nerval spoke of his desire "to compress years of anguish, dreams, and projects into a sentence, a word," but it was not till the end of his career that he succeeded—with a handful of incomparably beautiful and cryptic sonnets. Their difficulty comes not from missing links but from symbols and allusions that cannot possibly be understood without recourse to the poet's autobiographical prose writings and related materials. Take, for example, the opening of "El Desdichado." The Spanish title means "The Unfortunate One" or "The Outcast," and for some critics these meanings epitomize the poem. For others, however, the title means "The Disinherited," coming supposedly from the inscription on the shield of the mysterious knight in *Ivanhoe*. Thus a reader begins with two different keys, and his choice will affect the first line in particular:

> Je suis le Ténébreux,—le Veuf,—l'Inconsolé,
> Le Prince d'Aquitaine à la Tour abolie:
> Ma seule *Étoile* est morte,—et mon luth constellé
> Porte le Soleil noir de la *Mélancolie*.

(I am the Dark [the Shadow], the Widowed, the Unconsoled,/ The Prince of Aquitania of the ruined tower:/ My only *Star* is dead—and my starred lute/ Bears the black Sun of *Melancholy*.)

Line 2 can be explained by Nerval's claim of descent from an old southern family whose titles of nobility were abolished in the Revolution and whose coat of arms bore Three Towers Argent. But Nerval was supposedly born under the sign of Plutus; hence "El Desdichado" is an incarnation of Plutus and the "ruined tower" can be taken to be the "castle of Plutus" or number XVI of Court de Gébelin's tarot cards, which represents a tower full of gold and falling in ruins. And so it goes—with the Star, the constellated lute, the black Sun of Melancholy: readers have more than they can manage before they reach line 5. They must ultimately depend on their own imaginative interpretations, of course, for a poem is much more than the sum of its symbols and allusions even when these can be looked up in the poet's private code-book. Nerval was writing a poem to be experienced by others as a poem. No wonder, then, that each reader becomes his own authority, once he has listened to all the scholars.

Such composition by private symbols calls to mind the case of Yeats's *A Vision*. Unlike Nerval, who could allude to myth and to public and private events simultaneously, Yeats organized a complicated system of symbols into twenty-eight "phases," comprehending the individual, history, and the universe. To what extent he thought it essential to read his poems in terms of this system, we may doubt; and in any case his work can be read without such help. But not entirely: a few symbols recur, and the poetry enlarges once they are understood. But no less important are references to persons, places, and events which have nothing to do with a code-book. Other allusions explain themselves—"Byzantium" becomes both an actual city and a symbol peculiar to this poet. On the other hand, the recurring "gyre" grows in the mind of the reader once he appreciates its symbolic force in Yeats's work as a whole.

Every artist makes use of personal symbols to the extent that he creates his own cosmology in which certain images accumulate heightened meanings. They reveal themselves in their almost obsessive recurrence, as though the artist could never quite encompass all that they stand for. Such symbols, though personal, are nevertheless public, in being accessible to anyone who reads the poetry; whereas private symbols, such as those of Nerval and Yeats, must be illuminated from outside the verse. How many devoted readers of Rilke could have grasped the import of his "Angels" and "Night" and "Narcissus," for example, without the comments of scholars?

The same question may be asked in regard to our last sub-revolution, which gives rise to a poetry of "appropriated effects." Its most famous example is found of course in *The Waste Land.* Forster dubbed the conclusion a "scrap-heap of quotation," and, as everyone knows, the last eleven lines are made up entirely of original passages transplanted from five different languages. Poets have always referred to materials in the storehouse of literature, myth, and religion, but Keats's Ruth who "stood in tears amid the alien corn" and Tennyson's "Now lies the Earth all Danaë to the stars" are allusions: they are not quotations from other men's writings. Mark Van Doren takes a line from *King Lear* to entitle a poem "Down from the Waist They Are Centaurs." MacLeish goes earlier, to Villon, for "L'an trentiesme de mon aage." As J. Isaacs points out. Edith Sitwell places "O Ile leape up to my God," from *Faustus,* in her poem "Still Falls the Rain" as Marlowe himself had done with a line from Ovid ("O lente, lente currite, noctis equi!"). Whether or not he learned it from Dante, Eliot, says Isaacs,

> has taught modern poets . . . that method of incorporating a line from some other poet, or some other language, deftly converted, deftly conveyed, its license-plates so altered that its own proprietor would hardly recognise it. It is a device used not for mere decoration, or even wit, but to produce reverberations of meaning, and above all of feeling.[23]

Like the other two sub-revolutions in referents, this third one gives rise to obscurities; but these can be clarified easily, by telling the reader where he can find the originals. Such acknowledgment is accepted practice in scholarly prose; why not use it for scholarly poetry as well? For how else should a reader know, for example, that Eliot's "To purify the dialect of the tribe" (*Little Gidding*) refers to Mallarmé's "Donner un sens plus pur aux mots de la tribu" ("Le Tombeau d'Edgar Poe")? How expect a reader to respond as he should to the secondary effect unless he can experi-

[23] *The Background of Modern Poetry* (Dutton, 1958), pp. 64–69 *passim.*

ence the primary source in its context? A poet may shrink in horror from the notion of footnotes, but this would be an odd kind of delicacy in one who appropriates the effects of others to produce his own. And much as he might like to believe such passages to be self-sufficing, he knows what they owe to the original context from which they were lifted—as he knows that reproducing them is less a matter of creating than of editing.

IV

To speak in a few pages of a century and a half of poetry is to slight some figures and omit a great many others. We could point to angelism, for example, in at least one poem by Frost ("I Could Give All to Time"), perhaps in others; to appropriated effects in Stevens; to popular songs in Brecht; to floating images in Montale; to private symbols in Alberti—we can add case after case after case, but where do we stop? [24] And except by remarking the most striking shifts of the course, how keep track of the mainstream and its meanings?

What was once the menacing wildness of the few subsides into norms for the many. And hindsight shows why this had to happen: that an upheaval in one area would cause upheavals in others; that once a revolution had built up enough momentum, it would run its full course regardless of what it might overwhelm as it ran. Once he knew his direction, Mallarmé strove for greater and greater allusiveness and concision—compare the early (1864) and final (1887) versions of "Le Pitre Châtié"! Others in this age of discovery that was always just starting would take advantage of virtually anything novel—that something had never been done

[24] Example, regarding prosody: we have said nothing of such notable matters as the "trans-sense" experiments of the Russians (*zaumni*); the study of physiological mimicry, through the body's muscles, as a series of rhythmic metaphors; the views of T. S. Eliot on the way a poem or a passage "may tend to realise itself first as a particular rhythm before it reaches expression in words" in relation to Shelley's practice (as noted by Isaacs, *op. cit.*, p. 102); the "versets" of Claudel, Whitman, and others.

before was itself sure proof of its value. Apollinaire, at the last moment, deleted all punctuation from the proofs of *Alcools* (the verse had been punctuated in the manuscript given to the printer), with results as "new" as those he later sought by expunging all verbal connectives. No wonder he came to regard Baudelaire as limited. He was indeed, compared to his literary grandchildren—the Surrealists, for example, who tried to produce incongruous images and succeeded. What had begun as fascinated concern with multiple latent meanings could in time dispense with all notions of "primary" and "secondary," so that with Jarry all the meanings are on one plane: simultaneous, whole. We are now at the end of the line, where every meaning is equally important and true.

Such a point was bound to be reached, once the Unconscious had been opened up to dazzle all eyes with its treasures. "I believe only in what I do not see, and solely in what I feel," said Gustave Moreau. "Only inner mood seems to me eternal and undeniably sure." If undeniably sure, then all it contains must be sacred and all its productions equally true and important. Better yet: if totally laid bare and used with absolute courage, the Unconscious might bring in a new and greater reality, through the fusion of waking reality with dream.

To achieve this super-reality was, of course, the aim of the Surrealist poets gathered around André Breton, whose 1924 manifesto makes the direction appear to be quite unprecedented. But viewed historically, Surrealism was actually the last of the three stages of Unconscious exploring, begun by the Romantics and broadened by the Symbolists. Even some of its particulars had already emerged—in *Ubu Roi* (1896), in Apollinaire's startling verbal combinations (he had even used the term "surrealism" in his text for *Parade*). Dream and reality might be fused into a sur-reality by means of images bringing together the most far-fetched elements; the more they were unrelated, the greater their power in combination—such as Breton's "Eternity is searching for a wrist watch/ A little before midnight by the waterfront" or "This morning the daughter of the mountain is holding upon her knees an accordion of white bats" or Eluard's "Along the walls furnished with decrepit orchestras/ Darting their ears of lead toward the daylight/ On guard for a caress mingled with the thunderbolt." Aragon, as one of its exponents, could refer to Surrealism as a "trial of language," but this is a very special kind of "trial." "Through the word," says Anna Balakian,

> the impossible is made possible, nature can be endowed with metaphysical properties, sensuality takes on new proportions: visions dispersed on the face of the earth, going a-begging, undiscerned in their individual solitudes, are drawn to a new linguistic magnet and brought together into a new synthesis of imagery which in turn creates a new synthesis of existence. . . . language creates, it makes concrete the ineffable dream, it establishes the promised land, it enables man to discover the absolute. . . .[25]

But not just by reading, for a Surrealist poem demands active creativity on the part of the reader: he must bring to the poet's images his own thoughts, collaborating in its fulfilment. Hence the extremely compressed language and the absence of evident meaning, all within conventional syntax.

After ten years of heady activity, the movement broke up and the members went their separate ways. Was it a premature victim of menacing war and fascism in the middle thirties? or had Surrealism, after making its contribution to the later work of Eluard, Aragon, and others, quite exhausted its power for good and entered history? Today there is something incredible in its stance, particularly in the bedazzlement of some of its poets as they contemplated the Unconscious. Actually not much time was needed before scales could fall from the eyes, so that they could see that this vastest of sources was, like all human thinking, a mixture of everything that enters through the fallible organs of

[25] *Surrealism: the road to the absolute* (Noonday Press, 1959), p. 137.

sense: wisdom and foolishness; truth, half-truth, and deception. One could explore and exploit it in countlessly different ways—to open and lay bare was hardly enough. Writing at the time Surrealism had begun, Claudel insisted, in regard to one of its ancestors, that "The aim of poetry is not, as Baudelaire says, to plunge 'to the depths of the Infinite in quest of something new,' but rather to the depths of the definite to find the inexhaustible." Not many years later Wallace Stevens could declare that "the essential fault of Surrealism is that it invents without discovering," a distinction applicable to other movements as well.[26]

But if poetry began to retreat from its extreme position in regard to the Unconscious, it was only as a means for making a new advance: of another type, with the help of increased knowledge, and with undefensive awareness that what has been learned thus far may be only a beginning.[27] A beginning that traces its descent from earlier views of the relation of the self to the world outside, attitudes concerned less with exploring than with joining. They differ basically from notions of a physical merging with the infinite through death (as reported of Shelley and the sea), for the fusion is wholly an extension of living awareness. The wall between man and the world disappears, as in moments of mystical ecstasy, but without such union with God as the mystics avow. The "secular" quality comes through in Mallarmé's "Ma pensée se pense" (My thought thinks itself) and in Baudelaire's "What a delight to drown one's gaze in the immensity of the sky and sea . . . all those things think through me, or I through them (for in the vastness of revery, the I quickly loses itself). . . ." Roger Shattuck calls this

[26] It is as easy to mistake Surrealism's will to innovate as merely an effort to be original as it is to undervalue its achievements as a catalytic agent in twentieth-century writing: to ignore its extremely enriching effect upon writers outside the movement.

[27] E.g., *Hermès,* the journal published in France from 1933–1939, which is to be revived; also such a work as *Connaissances par les Gouffres* (Paris, 1961), by Henri Michaux.

> one of Baudelaire's most lucid moments, a purely self-reflexive perception. Henri Michaux, a poet writing eighty years later, disciplines himself to abdicate his personality and attains the same reversal of consciousness, the same simultaneous attunement: "One no longer dreams, one is dreamed." [28]

This is not the same thing as Rilke's

> Durch alle Wesen reicht der *eine* Raum:
> Weltinnenraum. Die Vögel fliegen still
> durch uns hindurch. O, der ich wachsen will,
> ich seh hinaus, und *in* mir wächst der Baum. . . .

> (Through all things that exist [all beings] the *single* space spreads [reaches, stretches]:/ World Inner Space. The birds silently fly/ right through us. Oh, I who would [wants to] grow,/ I look outside, and *within* me the tree grows. . . .)

for Rilke believes that external phenomena "Want us to change them entirely, within our invisible hearts,/ Into—oh endlessly—into ourselves! whosoever we may be after all." [29] Yet in terms of poetry, the basic belief in the continuity of the self and the world outside is the same. Baudelaire prefigured it when he called the modern conception of pure art "a suggestive magic which contains both the subject and the object, the external world and the artist himself." It has also come to be the view of philosophers and scientists for whom "subject-and-object" are no longer valid distinctions and common-sense notions of time no longer true. The West has taken centuries to arrive at this awareness, and yet it has always suffused the act of poetic creation with a "feeling-knowledge" too large to need to be stated. Perhaps it is also found, at least in embryo, in well-known pronouncements by Romantic poets on the unity in diversity and the kinships underlying even

[28] *The Banquet Years* (Anchor Books edition, 1961), pp. 350 ff.
[29] Wollen, wir sollen sie ganz im unsichtbaren Herzen verwandeln / in—o unendlich!—in uns! Wer wir am Ende auch seien.

the most recondite phenomena—except that now both the disparate and the perceiver are also one.

What happens next? What will be the course of the poetry of the post-modern period already begun? If one is not obliged to announce which grains will grow and which will not, he can dare to look into the seeds of time and timidly mutter that revolutions have often seemed to turn into their opposites. A not impossible direction, after all that has been done in the last hundred and fifty years, for what is there left to try that hasn't been tried? Little, perhaps—or perhaps a tremendous amount. But whatever the attempt, post-modern poets will not be able to reject the world at large, unless they learn ways to escape from a Nature that may be annihilated. A dozen years ago an age of anxiety gave way to an age of responsibility: its poetry cannot avert the central drive—toward a confrontation of the self that fulfills its power or dies. Poems of such general direction can be found in the books of the last century and a half, and we post-moderns begin with this heritage, one whose huge variety and complex richness are yet to be spread out and comprehended—and not by means of an essay of thirty possibly arbitrary pages.

How to Read Dante

JOHN CIARDI

IN THE OPENING allegory of *The Divine Comedy,* Dante finds himself lost and in darkness:

> Midway in our life's journey, I went astray
> from the straight road and woke to find myself
> alone in a dark wood.

These are familiar allegorical devices and no sensitive reader will fail to understand that "the straight road" has something to do with rectitude ("the straight and narrow"), that "the dark wood" has something to do with error/sinfulness/loss of purpose, and—by extension—that the proper course must lie in finding the light.

Having "something to do with" is not close enough, however. Dante demands more careful reading. Because of that demand, because of the immense and minute scholarship that has been expended upon Dante, and because too few English readers have been pointed in the right direction to him, Dante has acquired a reputation as an immensely difficult poet.

It is true that Dante writes in depth. Though his language is normally simple, his thought is normally complex. But if the gold of Dante runs deep, it also runs right up to the surface. A lifetime of devoted scholarship will not mine all that gold; yet enough lies on the surface—or just an inch below—to make a first reading a bonanza in itself. All one really needs is some first instruction in what to look for. Thereafter he need only follow the vein as it goes deeper and deeper into the core of things.

The instruction may properly begin with those opening lines. "Midway in our life's journey," writes Dante. The reader must understand that Dante is not tossing off a poetic generalization. "Our life's journey" means specifically the "three score years and ten" of the Biblically allotted life span. "Midway," therefore, means that Dante was thirty-five years old at the time of which he writes. Since he was born in 1265, it follows that the poem opens in the year 1300. And from a number of statements that can be culled from the poem, the careful reader can learn that the exact time is just before dawn of Good Friday.

By culling certain other statements, most of which are made at once, the reader may further learn that the sun is at the vernal equinox, that it is in the sign of Aries (the zodiacal sign in which God placed it at the Creation), and that the moon is full. These elements, added to the fact that it is the hour of the dawn and the season of Easter, clearly compound a massive symbol of rebirth. All things are at their regenerative peak when the lost soul realizes it has gone astray, for that realization is itself the beginning of the soul's rebirth.

Scholars have since shown that there was no Friday in the year 1300 on which all these conditions obtained. Dante, moreover, was a close student of astronomy and astrology. He knew that no such conjunction of sun, moon, zodiacal sign, and Easter season had taken place. He invented that conjunction as a full-swelling introductory theme in what amounts to a symphonic structure. The poem sounds its first chords with first light striking through darkness. In what follows, the darkness must grow more and more absolute to the very depth of dark (Hell); the light must then begin to overcome the darkness (Purgatory); and finally the "music" must mount from light to light to the ultimate indescribable glory or the all-blazing presence of God at the peak of Heaven.

As soon as Dante recognizes that he is lost and in darkness, he looks up and sees the first light of the new day glowing on the shoulders of a little hill. Throughout *The Divine Comedy,* the sun ("that planet/whose virtue leads men straight on every road") is a symbol for God, for Divine Illumination. In "Purgatorio," for example, souls may climb only in the light of the sun: once it has set, it is possible for them to descend, but they lack the power to move upward even so much as an inch. Only in the light of God may one ascend that road, for that is the light to which the soul must win.

Another allegorical theme begins immediately. Dante, in his passion to reach the light (God), races straight up the hill to it. He uses a grand and typical synecdoche to describe his speed, saying that he raced up that slope at such a pace "that the fixed foot was ever the lower."

Synecdoche is that figure of speech in which a part is taken to represent the whole. A less certain writer might have reached for all sorts of great metaphors to describe the speed of his climb. Dante focuses on a single detail that does for all. If the feet of a man climbing a steep slope move in such a way that the moving foot is forever above the one that is pausing, it follows that the climb must be taking place at a blurring speed—in fact, at an impossible rate, whereby hyperbole must be added to synecdoche as a reinforcement of the poetic effect. The point for the reader to remember is that it will not do to slide over Dante's details. They will take thinking about because they took thought to find.

There is perhaps nothing so entirely impressive about *The Divine Comedy* as its power of mind. The true mark of any writer is in the choices he makes. Having written three words, he must choose a fourth. Having written four, he must choose a fifth.

Nothing happens into a good poem; everything must be chosen into it. A poem may be thought of as a construction for making choices, and it is in the quality of his choices that Dante makes his greatness known. His language and his prosody can be rough and awkward. Anyone who reads the original will wonder at times if this is really "poetry." Very well, then, let it be prose, if one insists on folly. But if it is prose, it is prose of a previously unknown order, for the depth and multiplicity of mind that seem to function at every choice have not been matched in any piece of Western writing.

Meanwhile, back at the narrative, Dante is racing up the slope to what would be immediate salvation, could he manage to reach that light. The sinner has realized he is in darkness, he has seen the light, he ardently desires it, and he races to be received by it. But salvation is not to be had that easily: Dante finds his way blocked by three beasts. There is a She-wolf that represents the sins of Incontinence, a Lion that represents the sins of Violence and Bestiality, and a Leopard that represents Fraud. The beasts themselves are derived from Jeremiah; the three categories of sin are derived from Aristotle. Into these three categories fall all the sins of the world. The Three Beasts therefore, represent the total blindness of which the world is capable. Symphonically, they also foreshadow the three divisions of Hell through which Dante must journey. In the Hell of the She-wolf are punished the sins of excessive animal appetite. In the lower Hell, the Hell of the Lion, are punished the sins of bestial violence. In the lowest Hell, the Hell of the Leopard, are punished the sins of fraud, worse than the sins of bestiality because they involve the perversion of the higher gift of intellect—a beast, that is to say, can murder; but only a rational being, by perverting the gift of rationality, can commit a fraudulent act.

These three beasts drive Dante back into the darkness, blocking the direct and easy way to that light. In that darkness, when all seems to have been lost, and when Dante can find no way around those beasts of worldliness, there appears to him the figure of Virgil.

Virgil is a complex figure, combining within himself, among other things, the classical heritage, genius, magic powers, and Dante's personal devotion. On the first level, however, it will do to take him as representing Human Reason in its best development. More subtly, he may be taken as Esthetic Wisdom, the knowledge of the true poet. For present purposes let him be taken simply as representing Human Reason. In that role, he points out that there is no such express road to God as Dante had imagined in racing up the hill: "He must go by another way who would escape/this wilderness."

The other way—the long way round—is the total journey into ultimate darkness and out again to ultimate light. Such is the arduous road of *The Divine Comedy*. It is the painful descent into Hell—to the recognition of sin. It is the difficult ascent of Purgatory—to the renunciation of sin. Then only may Dante begin the soaring flight into Paradise, to the rapturous presence of God. God, that is to say, may be found only the other side of the total self-searching experience of a zealous life. There are no short cuts to that totally encompassing experience. Salvation must grow out of understanding, total understanding can follow only from total experience, and experience must be won by the laborious discipline of shaping one's absolute attention. The object is to achieve God, and Dante's God exists in no state of childlike innocence: He is total knowledge and only those who have truly experienced knowledge can begin to approach Him.

Virgil, as Human Reason, is the first guide to that ultimate knowledge, but Virgil cannot guide Dante all the way. Reason is finite and God is infinite. The greater guide, in the medieval concept, was Faith. Reason was merely the handmaiden of Faith. Virgil can guide Dante to the recognition of sin and to its renunciation, which is to say, through Hell and to the top of Purgatory. But once at that summit, the soul has achieved purity. It has risen beyond Reason. It is ready to enter the Divine Mysteries. And there Beatrice (call her Divine Love) must take over.

It was in her infinite compassion as Divine Love that Beatrice sent Reason to the man's soul in his hour of darkness, that Reason might serve as his guide to bring him into her higher presence. One may not simply wish himself into that higher presence. That presence must be won to by devout labor.

That devout labor is what might be called the basic plot and the basic journey of *The Divine Comedy*. All that follows, once the journey has begun, is an amplification of themes that have already been established. That much understood, the writing itself will best explain itself as it unfolds—always, of course, with the help of those indispensable footnotes.

When, however, one has read all the way through the poem and has returned to reread these first Cantos, he will find many other themes rooted in them. There are four such themes that any beginning reader will do well to grasp as particularly able to enrich his first experience.

The first has to do with Dante's sinfulness. What sin was it that had brought him into the dark wood of Error? Dante was expelled from Florence on charges of having been a grafter, and some commentators have tried to identify his guilt in that charge. In "Purgatorio" Dante himself recognizes that he is guilty of Pride, and to some extent of Wrath. He has both those offenses to pay for when he returns to Purgatory after his death. But the charges against Dante were certainly trumped up by his political enemies, and no specific act of Pride or Wrath can be cited to account for Dante's opening mood. His offense was, rather, Acedia. Let it serve to label this first theme.

The Seven Deadly Sins for which souls suffer in Puragtory are —in ascending order—Pride, Envy, Wrath, Acedia, Avarice, Gluttony, and Lust. Acedia is the central one, and it may well be the sin the twentieth century lost track of. Acedia is generally translated as Sloth. But that term in English tends to connote not much more than laziness and physical slovenliness. For Dante, Acedia was a central spiritual failure. It was the failure to be sufficiently active in the pursuit of the recognized Good. It was to acknowledge Good, but without fervor.

The spiritual awakening to which Dante comes in the Dark Wood—the enormous rebirth—is the awareness of the fact that he has not been sufficiently zealous in his pursuit of the Good. *The Divine Comedy* is the zealous journey from the man's recognized spiritual torpor (neglect of God) to the active pursuit of his soul's good (love of God). Every step of that journey may simultaneously be understood as the man's active embrace of his Godly experience, as the soul's active pursuit of the love of Good, and as the artist's active pursuit of form.

The second theme—perhaps it is not so much a theme as a method—is inseparable from the others. Call it the Five Levels. In a letter to his patron, Can Grande della Scala, Dante explicitly names four levels of meaning that he intends all the way through *The Divine Comedy*—*narrative, allegorical, moral,* and *anagogical.* That letter may, as many scholars contend, be a forgery. Whether genuine or not, what it states explicitly is clearly implicit in the writing. And to those four stated levels may be added a fifth: the journey seen as a *progress of the soul.*

Dante was a parochial man. He was persuaded that the One Truth had been revealed to him, and he was intolerant of all non-Catholic views. He refused, for example, to think of Mohammed as a religious leader but dismissed him as a schismatic and heretic and assigned to him a particularly grotesque punishment in Hell.

But if the man was parochial, the artist was universal as only art can be. *The Divine Comedy* is a triumph of art over creed. And that triumph—to paraphrase terms that Dante himself might have used—arises from the force of the Esthetic Mysteries, which is to say, the power of form in the interplay of its structures and its levels of meaning.

The first obvious level, for example, is narrative: a travelogue. But that journey is through a country populated by second meanings. On one level Dante writes of Hell as a literal place of sin and punishment. The damned are there because they offended a theological system that enforces certain consequences of suffering. But part of that theological system has also decreed that salvation was available to all men. Christ in his ransom had procured endless mercy. One need only wish to be saved, need only surrender his soul to God in a last gasp of contrition, and he will be saved. He may have to suffer at length in Purgatory, but, once there, his place is reserved in Heaven and he will in time arrive there. Purgatory is like our modern colleges: no one can flunk out of them.

It follows, then, that the only way to get into Hell is to insist upon it. One must deliberately exclude himself from grace by hardening his heart against it. Hell is what the damned have actively and insistently wished for.

Thus, allegorically, Hell is the true goal of the damned. On the surface the state of the sinners is described in terms of sin. The wonder and the universality of it is that a reader who does not care for those terms may restate them in terms of behavior, and the "Inferno" remains entirely coherent as a dramatic treatise on self-destructive behavior. Like addicts, the damned both hate and love their self-destruction. "They yearn for what they fear," says Dante.

Thus Hell is not only a specific place but a moral and anagogical allegory of the guilty conscience of the damned. It is the projection into a physical reality of the inner state of the damned. As Purgatory is such a projection of the inner state of those who suffer toward grace. As Heaven is such another projection of the inner state of those who have achieved grace. Each environment is an allegory and a moral and anagogical commentary on the essential nature of the souls one finds in each. Hell exists from within.

In a detailed discussion in the "Purgatorio," Dante reinforces these levels of meaning by pointing out that though mortal man may deceive by hiding his true nature under false semblances, the dead, by the very nature of their aerial bodies, can only appear to be exactly what they are. The dead cannot dissemble. *What* they appear to be and *where* they appear, they are.

The third theme—let it be called the Moral Universe or the Sentient Universe—is the vast, overriding concept of the total universe that makes *The Divine Comedy* the massive vehicle it is. Every artist seeks the vehicle that will best engage all his possibilities, just as every actor seeks the perfect role for himself. So, any actor would rather play Hamlet than Uncle Tom. Hamlet gives him more chances to act.

Dante's vehicle is nothing less than the total universe. Where in all poetry is there an equivalent subject-structure? Dante not only draws a map of his universe; he walks it from end to end. But his map is both of a physical geography and of a structure of values. That universe exists on all five levels of meaning.

For Dante, as for classical man, there was no real distinction between moral and physical law; between, say, the moral law against incest and the physical law of gravity. All of matter was a projection of God's will, and what we call physical law and what we call moral law derived equally from that will. When Oedipus, though unknowingly, transgressed moral law by killing his father and marrying his mother, a plague descended upon Thebes. It would not have occurred to the Greeks that to think of a flight of locusts as a consequence of what happened in the king's bedroom was to cross categories.

Dante's physical universe is Ptolemaic. It consists of nine concentric circles (spheres) with the earth as the center. In ascending order those spheres are: the Moon, Mercury, Venus, the Sun, Mars, Jupiter, Saturn, the Fixed Stars, and the Primum Mobile. Beyond the Primum Mobile lies the Empyrean, which is the dwelling and presence of God. God is an essence that entirely surrounds and contains creation.

If God is the circumference of this nine-layered sphere, the center is the greatest distance one can travel from God. That center is the earth, and the center of that center is the bottom of

Hell. Inevitably, it is there, at the Ultimate bottom of the universe, that Dante places Satan.

Satan is a powerful symbol. He is described as an unholy reverse-Trinity with three foul heads and three pairs of wings. He has been flung from Heaven to the farthest distance one can go from God. To his dark center drain all the waters of the earth, bearing the filthy sediment of all sin and uncleanliness. Satan's six wings beat madly in his efforts to escape from that foul lake but they succeed only in whipping up a freezing gale that turns all to ice, fixing him ever more securely in the bottom ice-tray. From the top of Purgatory, moreover, there flow down to him the waters of Lethe, in which the finally purified souls bathe and are washed clean of every memory of sin. That memory, too, is frozen into the filthy ice about Satan.

Thus that center is the center of all weight, of all sin, of all darkness, and of all cold. And to it flows all the filth of time. Weight, sin, dark, cold, and filth are, of course, the five things farthest from God. And thus the universe becomes a scale of precise values: the closer a thing is to the center, the lower it is on that scale; the closer a thing is to the circumference, the higher it is.

The existence of that scale makes possible an enormous economy in Dante's writing. Dante need only place his finger on that map and say what he saw there. The very act of placement becomes the value judgment.

That economy is further assisted by the firm laws of the other world. As one sins, so is he punished; as he strove for grace, so is he rewarded. In Hell, then, each punishment is a symbolic analysis of the nature of the sin and of the state of the sinner's soul. The reader need only be told, for example, that the punishment of the Lustful is highest in the Infernal scale, and that it consists of being buffeted eternally round and round by a dark whirlwind. The reader knows at once that this sin, though sufficient for damnation, is the least weighty of all the sins of Hell proper, and that the nature of the sin is to allow one's soul to be buffeted round and round by the dark winds of immoderate passion. Love is a sweet human state, but by excessive physical love these sinners shut their souls from God, surrendering "reason to their appetites."

Dante's Cantos average about 140 lines. As a general thing he requires no more than twenty or thirty lines to identify the sinner and to describe the punishment. Since the value judgment is already established by the map, and since the punishment is a symbolic analysis of the sin, these essential matters are settled in short order, and Dante has the rest of his Canto available for all sorts of matters that attract his ranging mind.

Dante had once set out to be an encyclopedist. His "Il Convivio"—never finished—was an effort to set down in Italian all human "science." There is nothing that does not interest him. As a poet, moreover, he would naturally look for chances to use his dramatic, lyric, and didactic powers. So, with his structure firmly determined by its basic economy, Dante is free to range at will, packing every rift with those fascinating details that add so much to his poem. He has time for gossip, for prophecies, for marvelous dramatic interplays, for treatises on history, for analyzing the French monarchy, the corruption of the Church, the decay of Italian politics. He has time for all sorts of metaphysical treatises on such matters as the nature of the generative principle, literary criticism, meteorology—in short, for his whole unfinished encyclopedia. And he still has time to invent a death for Ulysses, to engage in a metamorphic contest with Ovid, to make side remarks to his friends. He can give full rein to his powers because he has found the inexhaustible vehicle.

The fourth principal theme will inevitably reveal itself to the careful reader, but he will lose nothing by having it in mind from the start. Call it the Architectonics. *The Divine Comedy* has often been compared to a cathedral, and, whether or not the comparison is finally apt, it is certainly true that Dante's details keep acquiring significance as one goes on and learns to look back at them from some corresponding point in the later structure. The structure, that is to say, produces a *back-illumination.*

Charon, for example, is the boatman of the damned, ferrying them across Acheron into Hell proper. He is a memorable figure. Later, one meets the Angel-Pilot who ferries souls to Purgatory. He, too, is a memorable figure. But no reasonably careful reader can fail to see that one ferryman stands in meaningful relation to the other. Thus, the Angel is not only himself, but an opposite figure to Charon, and Charon seen backwards from the figure of the Angel acquires a dimension he did not have as an isolated figure. The development of these structural correspondences—of an endless number of them—is an everlasting and ever-enlarging source of the power of *The Divine Comedy.*

The supreme art of poetry is not to *assert* meaning but to *release* it by the juxtaposition of poetic elements. Form, in its interrelations, is the most speaking element. Because in any extended poetic structure these juxtapositions will fall into different perspectives when looked at from different points of vantage, that release of meaning is subject to endless meaningful reinterpretation. The inexhaustibility of *The Divine Comedy* is a consequence of this structural quality. It is for that reason that no one can ever finish reading it. There will always be a new way of viewing the elements. But if no man can finish the poem, any man may begin it and be the richer for having begun. The present imperfect gloss—skimming though it be—is really about all one needs to start with. And, having started, all he needs is to pay attention. The poem itself is the rest of the way, and the way is marked.

Moby-Dick: An Hamitic Dream

EDWARD DAHLBERG

> "I never wish to meddle with names that are sacred, unless when they stand in the way of things that are more sacred."
>
> —William Hazlitt

> ". . . but from the horror of infernall deepes, my poore afflicted ghost comes here to plain it."
>
> —Samuel Daniel

Nobody can deceive a man so well as he can gull himself, and I do not blame anybody else for my own folly. My thought is to spare others, although I know that there is hardly a man in the earth who will take advice unless he is certain that it is positively bad. As for myself, I am not homesick for the fusty books I worshipped as a youth; I am no victim of that most scurrile of all ruses, nostalgia. Let me guard what is sacred, and raze to the ground the stupid, indolent Thebaid of my past because I know Pindar's house will yet remain. I have changed my mind about Herman Melville, for I once loved this Cyclops whose father is Oceanus.

It is natural that we should have a wizened, intellectual literature—and who would want to empty our little Hippocrene—but it is malignant to feign that we are the new Attica of literature. When poeticules assert that Philip Freneau is a bard or that the pages of Charles Brockden Brown are not hellebore to the reader, they are establishing a republic of letters for solemn apes. How much noise is made for a drumbling poetaster or a Thersites of scatological fiction! Let a man, as Rabelais writes, "chew ordure" in twenty novels, and for such coprology he is wreathed in tamarisk as though he were a god instead of a sweeper of privies. We worship size and bulk and the surest way to be accounted a genius is to write the same big, ignorant book many times.

Herman Melville, who died in 1891, had been interred by the currish literati. This hapless shade is now the object of the unmuzzled barking of the same Cerberus; this beagle with the gravelled throat always stands at the gates of Hades and bays the moon whenever he scents carrion, dead works.

Canting, stuffed praise of writers is a sort of starved malice; whenever a critic tells such falsehoods about our past he shows his hunger and envy, and instead of providing us with a more opulent Parnassus, he parches the American Elysium. He carries, as Ben Jonson writes, "a commonwealth of paper in his hose. . . ."

Is it necessary to declare that there was not one erudite versifier or prose stylist in nineteenth-century America except Thoreau to compare with those geniuses who flourished when London was the fairest Hellas? There was no Mermaid Inn in New York where one could savor a beaker of ale with learned poets; the sepulchral Spouter Inn of New Bedford, whose proprietor is Peter Coffin, was no substitute for the coffee-houses and the chocolate shops in which one might find a Will Congreve, Swift, Pope, Dryden or Wycherley to be a whetstone for his own faculties. Dio Chrysostom said that the father of Achilles selected Phoenix to teach his son the arts of discourse. No matter how charitable we are to Hawthorne, Whitman or to Poe, of what advantage could they be to poor, torn Herman Melville? Ruth could glean more barley in Boaz's field after it had been reaped than Melville could have culled from Poe's *Marginalia* or Whitman's *Democratic Vistas*. Boaz was far more prodigal, but kindness, the father of good thoughts, does not permeate *belles lettres* in the United States.

Herman Melville was as separated from a civilized literature as the lost Atlantis was said to have been from the great peoples of the earth. Allen Tate, in his oracular poem, "The Mediterranean," has comprehended the sorrows that lie beyond the Pillars and the Sea of Darkness:

> What country shall we conquer, what fair land
> Unman our conquest and locate our blood?
> We've cracked the hemispheres with careless hand!
> Now, from the Gates of Hercules we flood
>
> Westward, westward till the barbarous brine
> Whelms us to the tired land . . . .

Let nobody imagine that I am unmindful of Herman Melville's scorifying deprivations; he burnt in Puritan ice, but not in woman; God shrive his shade, and may we sin less, for all flesh is error. Our best writers, Thoreau, Whitman, Melville, Hawthorne, Emily Dickinson and Poe, produced frigid works: ". . . admire and model thyself after the whale! Do thou, too, remain warm among ice," is the admonition of a man whose sorest affliction was that his vitals froze in all latitudes. However, I am concerned with Zeus Asklepios, the healing powers of a god-like book upon the American polity.

There was a dearth of those masculine fiery particles in the Puritan. Aristophanes averred: "By Jupiter, testicles are capital things." The nineteenth-century American was still the vassal of that Puritanic Beelzebub, Cotton Mather, the father of the Christian homosexual. What else could be the result of Thoreau's celibacy, Hawthorne's inclement identity, Whitman's ambiguous bachelordom, or Poe's and Melville's misogyny but the contemporary Pauline invert? Not one of these unusual men could produce a seminal poem or a great confession like St. Augustine's. Born to sin because we have genital organs, we live to confess our faults, and that is scripture and literature.

Man is a tragic animal because he has a teleological impulse to prove that he is reasonable though he knows he is not. Nothing can be proved, and the need to assert that the Archangels Gabriel and Uriel exist is the valor and cosmic energy in the human race. Agamemnon reproaches Calchas for never having prophesied good fortune for him. We would have the right to blame the universe for all our faults did not such a feeble attitude bring us greater woes. One assails a poet who does not feign well. We expect an author whose life has been foolish, stupid and full of misfortunes to be clever, sage and quick in his books; otherwise poems betray us as much as life does.

The Word is the Logos, which is the domestic white Cock, and the phallus that impregnates the body and the soul. One of the heresiarchs claimed that the Logos was the offspring of Mercury, but the Word in New England literature never became flesh. What congealed works came from those savants! Style is the absolute limit of a man's character and bad writing shows a lack of love; its most malignant symptom is delay. Henry James postponed his periods as long as he could, and Melville deferred action until the last few pages of *Moby-Dick.* Of the 131 chapters, only the last three before the Epilogue are about the pursuit of Moby-Dick, and the *Pequod* is always in the calms. The whaling-craft is similar to Zeno's paradoxical arrow, which, though hurled through space, is at rest in different places. There is no motion in this novel, without which there cannot be any positive affection or heat in the mind.

A good remark uttered in cumbersome words feebly put together is evil. Not one wise thought can be told without great energy. When the will languishes the demons are triumphant. Whatever one knows comes from the motions of the will. We know ourselves by our acts. Velleity is the principal reason for human perversity.

Sick books beget far more ailing ones just as potently as Abraham begat Isaac, and Isaac Jacob. Moreover, Melville's solitude was, in part, wilful. As Sir Francis Bacon explains: ". . . those that want friends to open themselves unto, are cannibals of their own hearts." We have been Ishmaels of letters since the republic was established, banished by society. Although poems are composed in sepulchral rooms, for writing is as private as dying, a healthful song is a hymn to the sun, and not as Melville felt, "a dismal stave of psalmody." Seneca's advice is: "It is every man's duty to make himself profitable to mankind." But when the imagination of the writers is ill and distempered, the social corpus is also cankered. Melville's separation from the human race was as deranged as Bartleby's. Melville refers to the seafarers in the *Pequod* as *Isolatoes* who did not acknowledge "the common continent of men." Ishmael, who has "a damp, drizzly November" in his watery soul, is as boreal as the first Void and as much of a beggar in the winds as Lazarus.

Epictetus, who had all the fortitude of the Stoic, had quite a different view from the author of *Moby-Dick:* "Miserable man, is there any one that maintains himself? Only the universe does that." How many people, who have known the acute pangs of solitude, go abroad to tell everybody that their utmost felicity is in being absolutely alone, a rapture easily attained by simply dying? A nation that is just and strong is a commonweal of kinsmen, and a volume unimpaired by diseased organs and a morose heart is an equatorial friend. "Call me Ishmael," the opening line of the novel, is prophetic, and I doubt that anybody ever composed as true a one. But we cannot forget that in Scripture the hand of Ishmael, a wild ass of affliction, is against every man's, and every man's against his. Montesquieu wrote, "Men born for society are born to please one another."

Moby-Dick, a verbose, tractarian fable on whaling, is a book of monotonous and unrelenting gloom. Rozanov once said that he did not care for Jesus because He never smiled; in this respect Jesus and Melville have similar dispositions. Melville is more dour than King Saul and there is no harper in the book to assuage his implacable melancholia. Nobody can endure such absolute and unrelieved misery of the spirit and duodenum except the wailing shades by the banks of the Cocytus. What pierces us is not *Moby-*

Dick, but the woe in Melville, "the wild, watery loneliness of his life."

It has been told many times that Herman Melville had an equinoctial identity but that Hawthorne was a wintry prig from Salem. Both were hibernal stylists. Of the two Melville, perhaps, deceived himself the more and on rare occasions to our advantage, as in the line: ". . . the currents carry ye to those sweet Antilles where the beaches are only beat with water-lilies." However, the soft climes that had made his flesh drowsy had turned his thoughts not to Epicurus but to the anthropophagi. The Tahitian experience had not made him averse to the delights of a cannibal gourmet. Let not the Sirens, who praise Melville for the few lovely lines he composed, take you to the isles already white with the bones of a whole generation of admirers of *Moby-Dick.*

Prometheus stole the fires of Zeus to warm the human race; Ahab's sole purpose is to thaw those frosts within him. How astonished he was when he remarked: ". . . the blood of a Polar whale is warmer than that of a Borneo negro in summer." Hawthorne had disclosed that human coldness is the worst of all afflictions. Giordano Bruno said that not even the snows of the Alps could cool him, but how seldom are April and May in unverdured, mizzling Melville.

"Can one warm his blue hands by holding them up to the northern lights? Would he not far rather lay him down lengthwise along the line of the equator?" asks Melville. "Would he not be moored to one of the Moluccas?" But this North American Lazarus is lodged, not in Abraham's Bosom, but at the Spouter Inn. His bed-companion for the night is not a buxom tavern wench, but a cannibal, Queequeg, "a jolly good bedfellow."

The malady common to both Ishmael and Ahab is unrelieved, warping coldness. Ahab, named after the wicked king who ruled lascivious Samaria, represents a nation that had been bled to death in colonial America, the *terra incognita* of the Pilgrim Lotophagi. Stendhal, mentioning the Americans, thought that "the source of sensibility is dried up in this people."

Moby-Dick is gigantology, a tract about a gibbous whale, and fifteen or more lawless seamen, who are alone, by choice, though they are together. Ahab is Adam, Cain, Ham and Nimrod; he is the incarnation of all turpitudes, just as Leviathan is the demiurge and the Pacific is the forest of Nôd; Cain had a beast in the forehead, and Melville writes that Ahab, though evil, has a "crucifixion in his face." In the same wayward vein he claims that the sea is a domestic household at times, and that the sailor experiences a "filial, confident, land-like feeling towards the sea"; Ishmael believes that his bed-mate, Queequeg, furnishes him with ease and connubial comfort.

Melville seems to have taken his revenge against the characters in his book as a reprisal for his own solitude. These seafarers have private, mouldy hearts; at the conclusion of this heavy dirge, Ishmael is as alone as he was in the opening pages of *Moby-Dick.* Sir Thomas Browne, whom Melville read avidly, was of the mind that "there is no man alone, because every man is a microcosm."

The characters are scarcely limned at all, except gaunt, miserly Bildad "who . . . sat and never leaned, and this to save his coat tails." When Bildad is considering how small the wages of Ishmael should be, Peleg, fearing he might offer him a few pennies too much, tells him to be wary: ". . . thy conscience may be drawing ten inches of water." Melville abhors both Bildad and Peleg—each is a "magnified species of mouse."

The unmothered, mongrel crew is made up of Nantucketers, sailors from Martha's Vineyard, and the Cape, and whalemen from the lands of Asia Minor and of Hamitic Africa. Aside from Starbuck, Stubb and Flask, the Nantucketers, exsanguious, castaway Cains, who had fished for "crabs and quohogs" on New England's coast, the other main characters, save one Indian from the Vineyard, are Persians, Africans and Polynesians, those hot men at whose hearth Melville could warm himself.

Stubb, a Capeman, is "neither craven nor valiant." This is the rudest paraphrasis of *Revelations:* ". . . because thou art lukewarm, and neither cold nor hot, I will spue thee out of my mouth."

Starbuck, of Nantucket, is a "long, earnest man"; Flask is "short, ruddy, and young." However, Melville cribs the Polynesian, Indian, Parsee and the imperial African in his crusty heart. Tashtego, Indian from Gay Head, is the "inheritor of the unvitiated blood of those proud warrior hunters"; Daggoo is a gigantic, Negro Ahasuerus; Fedallah, the Parsee, is a mystic. Melville moans over "black little Pip," "poor Alabama boy." Contradicting himself, he also asserts that "Starbuck, Stubb, and Flask were momentous men." We never find out why. The Carpenter is described as having a "ramifying heartlessness," and is a "stript abstract; an unfractioned integral; uncompromised as a new-born babe." Bulkington, who, as his appellation implies, should have dramatic weight, disappears from the book not long after he enters it, and for no tangible cause. Obviously Melville forgot him altogether. Flagitious Ahab is dear to Melville; he is evil, but, his author believed, washed in the blood of the lamb. Ahab nods for over half a century of pages. He is wearying because his sorrow is picturesque rather than active; like Milton's Satan, to borrow from Hazlitt, Ahab's deformity is in the depravity of his will.

Melville took the sea, not fire, the house, the orchard, or the earth, as his element. "With a philosophical flourish Cato throws himself upon his sword; I quietly take to the ship." Marcus Aurelius said, "Always remember the saying of Heraclitus, that the death of earth is to become water." Heraclitus also reported, "a dry soul is the wisest." Thales said water is the original element and the end. The ancients feared drowning more than any other disaster; there would be no quiet for the deceased in those inscrutable, voracious deeps.

This is a Doomsday book about water. The sea is the foe of Odysseus, and the *Odyssey* is the Orphic battle to overcome this moist element or passion. According to Porphyry, Odysseus desired to "appease his natal daemon with a suppliant branch" of the olive tree of Minerva. Homer, as well as the Greeks, who feared the Ocean, which is the cause of Odysseus' desolation, intends to absolve Odysseus in the end so that he can be with earth-born people "who ne'er knew salt, or heard the billows roar." But Melville is the acolyte of Poseidon and not Minerva. "I am, by a flood, borne back to that wondrous period . . . Here Saturn's grey chaos rolls over me."

The Void made God miserable, and He was unquiet until the Waters had receded. The Ocean is too close to Primal Nothing, and neither the Cherubim nor men have composure in water, which is the corrupt kindred of nihilism. In the second book of Esdras, Enoch, who is said to be good, is the ruler over dry ground, and Leviathan over the drowned parts of the globe. Adamah, in Hebrew, is virgin red clay, or as Stanley Burnshaw, the poet, says:

> All thought is clay
> And withered song.

Go to the sea, ye who seek the solace of that immense empty Bosom, the Ocean, and ye shall lament for the teats, for the pleasant fields, for the fruitful vine. "Do you know that there is not . . . a tree in de Sade?" is an observation in the *Goncourt Journals.*

Water is a Babel and a confusion in *Moby-Dick;* otherwise, how can we account for Melville's allusions to "sea-pastures," "watery prairies," "Potters' Fields of all four continents," or comprehend "those fabled undulations of the Ephesian sod?" Yet the Deluge is his passion, and he only wrote *justly* when he dealt with the great flood of Noah or Deucalion or the pelagic contents of the universe. The Flood was also for him, as for all early peoples, a punitive disaster.

A plethora of water in the spirit destroys filial affection; Cyclops, who is a son of Neptune and always found on the coast, sins because he cares for nobody, neither the gods nor his parents, save himself, and Euripides considers this his most foul infamy. Whoever sees Cyclops with a wife, children or a brother? Giants are parricides, and if they have a mother or any kin they are utterly dead to them. The Cyclopian sea-ruffians in the *Pequod* never mention their progenitors. *Moby-Dick* is a feral and unfilial book, and the words thereof are the children in Sheol.

Theophrastus was of the mind that moisture in people was the cause of their stupidity. Tertullian, having no regard for the pagan god of the seas, accepts the ancient claim that the dolphins vomit forth in honor of Neptune. In *Moby-Dick* water is less a natural element than a biblical, allegorical substance. Of the four powers of nature, Melville selected the one that grieved his spirit the most. According to an Egyptian ideograph, water signifies deprivation; the Chinese regarded it as a negative element, and Virgil thought it a deceitful one. Homer said that Oceanus was sterile; Ceres cannot sow wheat here, nor can we find the parsley and the Orphic meadow-land surrounding Calypso's Cave in *Moby-Dick*. Had Melville been an Hippocrates he would have related that sea-water maddens the intellect, makes men splenetic, pituitous and costive, weakens the large, benevolent organs we have inherited from the Angels who lusted after the fair daughters of men, and gives them instead the hopeless aches of androgynes and eunuchs who are governed by Aquarius. The hermaphrodite rarely laughs, for such boisterous noise is pocketed in that bountiful Adamic sac, the testes. In Scripture it is written: "Let the waters be gathered to one place, and let dry land appear." But Melville never departed from the seas to return to the earth.

Melville imagined he had taken the paschal lamb of Christ and covered it with the coat of Leviathan. He cringed when he thought of the "universal cannibalism of the ocean, or unverdured seas," and yet most of his volumes are salt-water folios. A hydromaniac, there was very much more of liquid properties than flesh in his prose style. It was in vain that he heaved forth his pain: "Though in many of its aspects this visible world seems formed in love, the invisible spheres were formed in fright."

What is important is not brit, squid, ambergris, or the chapter on Cetology, but Ham's vice, which is the cry of all waters in man. This is the portent of water in *Moby-Dick*. "Yea, foolish mortals,

Noah's flood is not yet subsided." God drowned the earth as a judgment of man, for, is it not written in *Psalms,* "The Lord sat at the Flood"?

The human race perished in the Great Inundation, according to Talmudic Cabalists, because of the intellectual and sexual perversions of mankind. When the Body is false unto itself, the intellect is a liar. *Moby-Dick* is an Hamitic dream; water and meditation are forever married, says the author, and nocturnal visions are damp.

The making of the book took a year; Melville made no corrections, and never rewrote any moiety of it. A novel of over 500 pages is a great hulking hull. The *Canticles of Solomon* are short, the *Book of Ecclesiastes* and the *Song of Songs* a few pages, and how many Hebrew scribes composed and mended these sage and amorous ballads no one will ever know. Who can know all of his errors? Is everything that falls out of the mouth a divine truth? If so, the gabbling women who chase the geese of Camelot are sibyls and canting trimmers are prophets.

In a book of a half a millennium of pages, the adjectives alone are heavy enough to sink the Theban Towers, or to borrow from Swinburne: ". . . the eyes which keep open through the perusal of six consecutive pages must never hope to find rest but in the grave." There is more sorrow in his epithets than in the characters, and moreover the adjectives are made to suffer alike on all occasions, for he had a pelting memory and repeated the same desiccated, gothic descriptions frequently.

Only the insane wish to be misologists, and, assuming that one can, at least, read with a tolerable amount of reasonableness, I find no other way of showing how shabbily written *Moby-Dick* is than by adducing the evidence which is always the "windmills in the brain." What have we of the nature of Ahab but repetitious phrases about his head and mind, which at first may fetch the ear, but later are no more than the specious Elizabethan thunder of a very weary Zeus. The stage roar only deafens us so that all we hear is the monotonous din of surging pages that commenced to roll before the time of Adam, and which do not cease until the readers themselves are drowned in the great Deluge.

At the risk of being a burden of Tyre to the auditor I quote the following: Ahab, the ocean, Moby-Dick, and even the *Pequod*, are "moody," "mad," "demonic," "mystic," "brooding," "crazy," "lunatic," "insane," and "malicious." Ahab is stricken, mad or moody on any page that he is mentioned, and this prolix refrain is likely to send a reader to Bedlam solely to hear a raving inmate declare that he is sane. The brows of Moby-Dick and Ahab are baked in the same kiln of Moloch. Melville had no understanding of heroical size in literature, and tried to achieve the epic by hurling hoaxing, hot phrases at the reader: "Give me Vesuvius' crater for an inkstand!" He attempted to convey the impression that he had large, passionate organs. "Hyperbole is the most frigid of all forms of speech," says Aristotle.

Melville was as luckless with his metaphors, that are nearly always awry and have little connection with the thought in the sentence, as he was with his characters. Had he washed his similes in the Pool of Bethesda they would still be lame and palsied. One might say of Melville what Swinburne said of Byron: "Much of the poem is written throughout in falsetto . . ."

His solecisms and hyperboles are mock, dead lava. Ahab's nature is gorged, Homeric fury and is of the lineage of the fabled python of the deep: "the delta of his forehead's veins," "burnt-out crater of his brain," "Ahab's brow . . . gaunt and ribbed," "globular and ponderous heart," "my splintered heart," "the last gasp of his earthquake life," "he burst his hot heart's shell," "the wondrous cistern in the whale's huge head," "his broad milky forehead," "the whale's huge head," "his pleated head," "his pleated forehead," "his oblong, white head." Ahab and the sperm whale are malevolent monomaniacs: "The white whale . . . as the monomaniac incarnation of all those malicious agencies," "Moby-Dick, with that malicious intelligence," "monomaniac old man," "monomaniac Ahab." Ahab, the Parsee and Leviathan are mystagogues: "the mystic-marked whale" and the Parsee's "mystic watch."

I have told you all there is to know about the characters: Melville discloses in fifty phrases, more or less, that Ahab is a monomaniac. This is scenic diabolism; there is more of Ahab in one line of *Hamlet* than in the entire supernatural allegory: Hamlet speaks, ". . . to define true madness, what is't but to be nothing else but mad"; "I am but mad north-north-west; when the wind is southerly, I know a hawk from a handsaw." Moreover, the tragical writers do not repeatedly say how desolate and broken their heroes are.

This huffing tract is glutted with a conflagration Melville could not create: "the whole grim aspect of Ahab," "he was a raving lunatic," "moody stricken Ahab," "his delirium," "the old man's delirium," "Ahab's full lunacy," "madness sat brooding on his brow," "the whale's direful wrath," "all the subtle demonism of life," "the demoniac waves."

Melville's jadish vocabulary is swollen into the Three Furies, and we flee from them as Ben Jonson in his *Poetaster* took flight from "furibund," "magnificate," "lubrical," "fatuate," "turgidous," "ventosity." For those who are reluctant to believe that such dross is not the customary aliment in this novel, the best advice I can offer is, "Read it yourself, and see."

The atrabilious Ahab is only wicked in the sluttish, supine words with which the author depicts him. Evil is energetic and must accomplish its ends that are just as essential to the Kosmos as the work that good must do. Nobody should resolve to be vile: "See! Moby-Dick seeks thee not. It is thou, thou that madly seekest him!" What is bad will fall out of the soul anyway. Who looks everywhere for trouble? In *Proverbs* it is stated: "A prudent man seeth evil, and hideth himself."

There is no voyage, and there are no more hints of the characters themselves than were given in the beginning of the book. We see Ahab either lying in a hammock when the *Pequod* skirts the howling, wet shingle of Patagonia, or standing close to the mizzen-shrouds, or upon the quarter-deck leaning on the taff-rail. "But in the cautious comprehensiveness and unloitering vigilance

. . . Ahab threw his brooding soul into this unfaltering hunt. . . ." Ulysses is a wise, crafty freebooter, but the *Iliad* is a regal poem of action, and the poet justly ascribes "to Ulysses, a thousand generous deeds."

Ahab is no less opaque at the conclusion of the tome than he is at its inception; if, as Shakespeare says in *Lear*, "Ripeness is all," then one can say that in *Moby-Dick*, "Ripeness is nothing." Moreover, we are drinking the waters of Lethe, for Melville did not remember whether he was describing the ocean, the *Pequod*, Ahab or Leviathan. "The Pequod gored the dark waves in her madness," "great demon of the seas," "all the swift madness of the demoniac waves."

Moby-Dick is a rabble of words which could not have been excreted without much travail. Moreover, does one go to a novel to apprentice himself to a mariner? If this is true, one will be as much a pauper after acquiring the nautical information in *Moby-Dick* as the Greeks were when they returned home following their Trojan victory.

A good deal of bombast has come from the noddles of our intelligentsia about Melville's knowledge of the food and properties of the whale. Contrary to his usual garrulous habits there are only penurious references to these oceanic viands: "Squid . . . is a vast pulpy mass, furlongs in length . . . twisting like a nest of anacondas," "we fell in with vast meadows of brit, the minute, yellow substance, upon which the Right Whale largely feeds," "ambergris is soft, waxy, and so highly fragrant and spicy, that it is largely used in perfumery, in pastiles, precious candles, hair-powders, and pomatum." Ambergris, according to Melville is "supposed to be the cause . . . of the dyspepsia in the whale."

I should mention a few of the chapter titles and charitably refer to them as a bill of lading of a clerkly Triton sitting in a shipping office on lower Wall Street: "The Chart," "The Try-Works," "The Battering Ram," "The Affidavit," "The Quadrant," "The

Monkey-Rope," "Whales in Paint," "The Line," "The Dart," "Pitch-Poling," "Fast Fish and Loose Fish."

There is not the scanticst humdrum minutia omitted: "A belaying pin is found too large to be easily inserted into its hole," "The line . . . used in the fishery was of the best hemp," ". . . while the one tackle is peeling and hoisting a second strip from the whale, the other is slowly slackened away." Demetrius rebukes those clodpates on Mt. Ida who "press home every detail as though your hearer were a fool," and Webster writes: "A fantastical scholar, like such who study to know how many knots was in Hercules' club, or what colour Achilles' beard was." Milton reminds us: "What a stupidness is it, then, that we should deject ourselves to such a sluggish, underfoot philosophy."

Do you want natural history? Then let Aristotle, Pliny, Theophrastus, Dioscorides, Buffon, Darwin or Humboldt be your masters. Melville's cetology, the science of whales, is borrowed from a hundred books and *Moby-Dick* is only the lees of other men's marine lore. Most of his knowledge came from natural historians, and, like the waterwagtail, who pursues the gull until he drops the dung that is the wagtail's principal food, Melville filled himself with the droppings of many volumes on whaling.

We do not study Homer for his nautical information: besides, he knew, perhaps, as little of the sea as Melville did about whaling. One reads Montaigne, Anacreon, Diodorus, Strabo, La Bruyère for pleasure and the intellectual viaticum in wise books. But are chapters on hemp, the pots in which the "hissing masses of blubber" are scalded and recondite nonsense about old Bible prints of Jonah, a whaling Cabala?

When I want to take a voyage, I don't go to *Moby-Dick,* any more than I read Sir John Mandeville's *Travels*—he wrote about the Holy Land and the ancient world without ever having left England. Mandeville's book is a cento of Pliny, Strabo, Marco Polo, and the refuse of sundry Apocryphal Christian works. If you would travel, then go to the Voyages compiled by Hakluyt, or wander through the marvelous pages collected by Purchas, or take rough Drake, or Pigafetta's Magellan as your guide.

However, so many of the borrowed facts about the habits of whales are of no unusual significance, anyway, in a novel or a work of the imagination. I am unable to enumerate the piscatory errors in Izaak Walton's *The Compleat Angler,* but I read him for his style, which is another name for perception or wisdom. The thoughts we have are only the words we use. Melville's sentences, however, are always to the windward, so that the reader is worn out by the heavy, ululant blasts of his fraudulent blank verse. Form is the real food of the imagination; facts are the stepdaughters of the Muses.

Melville writes: "The previous chapter gave account of an immense body or herd of Sperm Whales," which is gawkish advice to his auditors who, he imagines, could not even recollect a single chapter fifteen minutes after reading it. But how often we reprove others for our own faults. Hesiod thought that Zeus lay with Mnemosyne, who is Memory and the Mother of Muses, for nine days and nine nights without interruption; and it requires that much Olympian, not whale, sperm to fecundate the intellect. Melville had never gone to Delphi to comprehend the best of admonitions: "Know thyself." A novelist, he had almost no knowledge of people. What we call knowledge of others is what we know about ourselves.

How much more fortunate is his short, but renowned chapter, "The Whiteness of the Whale"? There is the same melancholia in it as in the rest of the novel. Though Moby-Dick is priapic Jupiter, the snow-white bull, white represents death. The Albatross in those "exiled waters" is a portentous wraith, and "the White Mountains of New Hampshire" are "a gigantic ghostliness" that hangs over his gray, hulled soul. ". . . the White Sea exerts such a spectralness over the fancy." "Witness the white bear of the poles, and the white shark of the tropics . . . transcendent horrors they are." St. John the Evangelist rides on his pallid horse and the fierce-fanged tiger wears the same mortuary vesture, and Lima, a lepry city of sin "has taken the white veil." ". . . all deified Nature absolutely paints like the harlot, whose allurements cover nothing but the charnel-house within." Melville concludes this white Golgotha with: "And of all these things the Albino whale was the symbol. Wonder ye then at the fiery hunt?" Of course, he is again paraphrasing *Revelations:* "And I looked, and behold a pale horse: and his name that sat on him was Death."

Compare this with Rabelais, who, grounded in ancient lore, reminds us that the Thracians and Greeks marked their "good, propitious and fortunate days with white stones." Gargantua wears Jovean, white slops trimmed with blue, which contain 1105 ells of phallus, bacon, tripes, roasted thrushes basted with hen-scum and wine. Paris was formerly called, Rabelais avers, Leucotia, in honor of the white thighs of the women there.

When the Archangel Raphael appears before Tobit, the latter announces that there is nothing so good and comforting as Light, which is the raiment of the Cherubim. Allen Tate writes that for Dante "Light is Beatrice; light is her *smile* . . ." Alba, the sacred first town in Latium, was founded by Aeneas where the white sow sat down to rest. Such a legend signifies gestation, the keeping-room and the house, but who breeds porkers or reaps wheat in the Pacific?

Malvolio, one of the scholiasts on *Moby-Dick,* furnishes us with Melville's Notes, which are no less baneful than the brackish sea-water in *Moby Dick:* "In Sperm-whalemen with any considerable quantity of oil on board, it is a regular semi-weekly duty to conduct a hose into the hold." In *Moby-Dick* Melville discloses: "But if the doctrine of Fast-Fish be pretty generally applicable, the kindred doctrine of Loose-Fish is still more widely so."

The following citations are culled from the narrative:

> . . . this strange uncompromisedness in him involved a sort of unintelligence . . .

To insure the greatest efficiency in the dart, the harpooneers of this world must start to their feet from out of idleness . . .

[The Carpenter] was singularly efficient in those thousand nameless mechanical emergencies continually recurring in a large ship . . .

. . . this omni-tooled, open-and-shut carpenter . . .

. . . these spiritual throes in him heaved his being up from its base, and a chasm seemed opening in him, from which forked flames and lightnings shot up . . .

. . . crazy Ahab, the scheming, unappeasedly steadfast hunter of the white whale; this Ahab . . . had gone to his hammock . . .

Here be it said, that this pertinacious pursuit of one particular whale, continued through day into night, and through night into day . . .

. . . little Flask bobbed up and down like an empty vial.

He was like one of those unreasoning but still highly useful, *multum in parvo,* Sheffield contrivances . . .

. . . this half-horrible stolidity in him, involving, too, as it appeared, an all-ramifying heartlessness;—yet was it oddly dashed at times, with an old, crutch-like, antediluvian, wheezing humorousness, not unstreaked now and then with a certain grizzled wittiness . . .

. . . however promissory of life and passion in the end, it is above all things requisite that temporary interests and employments should intervene and hold them healthily suspended for the final dash.

There are some enterprises in which a careful disorderliness is the true method.

Is this the "honest manna of literature"?

However, may nobody believe that I would conceal the chants of a man who had enough genius to sing on occasion, but not sufficient strength to write an epical novel. A good sentence or emotion will come as dear as the cost of dove's dung at the time of the famine in Samaria. Here are some of Melville's canorous lines:

> I leave a white and turbid wake; pale waters, paler cheeks, where'er I sail. The envious billows sidelong swell to whelm my track; let them; but first I pass.
>
> Yonder, by the ever-brimming goblet's rim, the warm waves blush like wine. The gold brow plumbs the blue.
>
> But it is a mild, mild wind, and a mild looking sky; and the air smells now, as if it blew from a far-away meadow; they have been making hay somewhere under the slopes of the Andes, Starbuck, and the mowers are sleeping among the new-mown hay. Sleeping? Aye, toil we how we may, we all sleep at last on the field. Sleep? Aye, and rust amid greenness; as last year's scythes flung down, and left in the half-cut swaths . . .
>
> . . . let me look into a human eye; it is better than to gaze into sea or sky; better than to gaze upon God. By the green land; by the bright hearth-stone! this is the magic glass . . .
>
> There is a wisdom that is woe; but there is a woe that is madness. And there is a Catskill eagle in some souls . . .
>
> Oh, grassy glades! oh, ever vernal endless landscapes in the soul; in ye,—though long parched by the dead drought of the earthly life, —in ye, men yet may roll, like young horses in new morning clover. . . . Would to God these blessed calms would last.

American literature is exceedingly poor in victuals and in amours. Nobody has been adequately fed or loved in an American novel throughout a hundred and twenty-five years. The sailors on the *Pequod* seem as content with biscuit and ship's beef as Cyclops, a part-time vegetarian monster, is with curds and cow's milk. But the Colossus of Euripides prefers a roasted stag, a lion on the spit or gobbets of human flesh. A heathen's collation on the *Pequod* consists of large gammons of whale-blubber. These mariners have the gloomy, Phrygian throats of Bacchanal nymphs who milked a lioness and made cheese of the milk. Melville knew no subtler delicacy of the table than strawberries swimming in the milk of the sperm whale. The author thought that "brains of a small Sperm Whale are accounted a fine dish." "The casket of the skull is broken into with an axe, and the two plump, whitish lobes being withdrawn (precisely resembling two large puddings), they are then mixed with flour, and cooked into a most delectable mess." "The imagination is wounded long before the conscience" is a wise thought from Henry David Thoreau.

What wry joy does this descendant of Ham and Polyphemus, perverse in all of his appetites, take in telling the reader of those profane, Polynesian meals of human flesh: the barbecued heads that had been decapitated by cannibals in Tahiti "were placed in great wooden trenchers, and garnished round like a pilau, with breadfruit and cocoanuts; and with some parsley in their mouths." Aristotle advises the poet that not everything can be divulged, or offered for public view "lest Medea murder her children in front of the audience, or impious Atreus cook human flesh in public."

Whose gorge is not qualmish as he witnesses Stubb eating his "spermaceti supper" as "thousands on thousands of sharks" are swarming round the dead whale roped to the *Pequod.* What froward humor there is in Melville when he places before the reader "a meat pie nearly one hundred feet long" made of the innards of a whale. The Psalmist declares that Leviathan will "be broken into pieces, and given as meat to the people inhabiting the wilderness." So much blubber gives one indigestion for "the rest of his reading days."

There is no doxy, trollop or trull in any of Melville's volumes. He had no likerish palate; even chaste Spenser would allow the desolate tribe of males the solace of "Her snowy breast was bare to greedy spoil." Moreover, who, after such an incubus, does not pine to hear the sound of her petticoats, the sweet, nourishing sight of her licentious skirts. After considering the intricate intestines of a sperm whale, as Melville advises us to do, I am as ready as Holofernes to swoon when I behold Judith's sandals.

Samuel Daniel pined for Delia, Swift wrote memorable epistles to Stella, and the singers in Israel were pierced by those maids who had eyes like the fishpools of Heshbon, but Melville lays bare the beams, the joists, the sinews of a whale. Montesquieu told his friends that the only reason he wrote was to seek favor with the Venuses at court. Herman Melville at the age of thirty, when he should have been an amorist, was as gloomy as John Donne who sat in his shroud after he had passed his fiftieth year.

None can misdoubt Melville's misogyny. The hatred of women is the pederastic nausea that comes from the mention of the womb. Robert Burton, in *The Anatomy of Melancholy,* says that a Muscovite Duke vomited when he saw a woman. Melville, Whitman, Poe, and Thoreau loathed the female, and the first three sages suffered from sodomy of the heart. No more than three generations separate us from Thoreau, Whitman, Poe and Melville; little wonder then that we are now in the age of ice, and that one man in every ten craves to burn in the fires of Sodom and Gomorrah.

Instead of all those spermal ablutions for the pathic, in which Melville said the male should wash his heart, give me the Restoration wit of: "Two years' marriage has debauched my five senses. Everything I see, everything I hear, everything I feel, everything I smell, and everything I taste, methinks has wife in it." "Methinks my body is but the lees of my better being," declares Melville, whose prose was almost disembodied. At Sais the peplum of Isis was never lifted, and in sixteen volumes by Melville no woman is bedded, seduced or gulled, and, by heaven, that is gross deception.

Perversity is the black angel of our century, and the hatred of the clan of females, so deep in Melville, Poe, Whitman and Thoreau, is our Atlean inheritance which we must understand or perish. Eros is the source of masculine life and wit; what there is of gaiety in American letters is either puerile or those few parched, sly conceits in *Moby-Dick* and *Bartleby the Scrivener.*

Melville's "If ye touch at the islands, Mr. Flask, beware of fornication," is a wry imitation of Paul's admonition to the *Colossians:* "avoid fornication, impurity, lust, evil concupiscence." Melville's line is likely to produce a pewed smile, but far better and more jovial is Rabelais' Bumpkin who keeps the Psalter in his codpiece.

Who wants to chase a Sperm Whale for over five hundred pages when he can pursue a Shulamite, a Cressid, a dowdy or a shake-bag? Had Herman Melville never been moved by amorous ballads? Can a dolphin, a chine of blubber or the white hump of a whale take the place of the thighs of Aspasia or the rump of Lais of Corinth? This is Melville's phallic song: "Other poets have warbled . . . the soft eyes of the antelope . . . less celestial, I celebrate a tail [of Leviathan]."

Melville composed amorous canticles to an oceanic brute, and the sea was his hymeneal bed. Leviathan is a "luxurious Ottoman," with "all the solaces and endearments of the harem"; the Sperm Whale has a "beautiful and chaste-looking mouth . . . glossy as bridal satins." The pelagic brutes are "unprincipled young rakes"; Leviathan is a "Lothario, like pious Solomon among his thousand concubines."

What else are "the submarine bridal chambers of Leviathan," and all those spermal remedies that he said Paracelsus advised the ill to take to allay their wrath, than epithalamiums. Though Melville could not reject the old Hebrew law of retribution, he had little of that masculine fire in him; Empedokles believed that "in its warmer part the womb brings forth males."

Ahab's solipsism comes from the pride of Narcissus, and there is no hemlock so pernicious as the arts of self-love. Ahab represents moisture, and in the *Psalms* it is "the proud water." "Blind is the man who does not hate self-love," said the author of the *Pensées.* What reason has Narcissus to regard a woman when he finds so much satisfaction in contemplating his own face?

Woman is still the imperial booty of the races, and men will sack towns, capture cities to furnish their courtesans with money to purchase cosmetics and soap, or rape the Sabine virgins when they cannot obtain wives otherwise. Plato knew that nothing was so acute as the pleasures of the body, without which men will hanker for a whale, a dog, a cat, and go stark mad to be like "that lecher that carneled with a statue." Origen horrified the Christian Fathers by castrating himself although they were intellectual wethers themselves. Men suffer either because they have testes or because they have none.

Rather than dissecting the body of one woman, which Balzac advises the novice in amours to do, before he selects a wife, Melville offers the American the anatomy of Leviathan. Here is the cause of Melville's woe, and ours. He wrote a book for men, or, at least, hermaphrodites and spados. I would just as lief reread *Moby-Dick* as live in a volume or a world without any females in it.

Woman is a perfidious creature in *Moby-Dick,* and he cannot refer to Judith or a Cleopatra without giving the impression that it was not Holofernes nor Antony who was betrayed but Herman Melville. In an allusion that has no reasonable connection with the sentence or the chapter he speaks of the gory head of Holofernes hanging from the girdle of Judith. "Towards noon whales were raised . . . they turned and fled . . . a disordered flight, as of Cleopatra's barges from Actium." When Melville writes of Jupiter abducting Europa, his sole interest is in the "lovely, leering eyes" of Zeus; of Europa he says nothing. "By Jupiter, I must not fear a woman," say Beaumont and Fletcher in *The Philaster.*

Melville believed Sir Thomas Browne who wrote that woman is . . . "the rib and the crooked piece of Man," and that "man is the whole world, and the breath of God," which, if true, indicates that there is something amiss in the Lord's respiration. The mariners of the *Pequod,* like Adam, must have been "born without a navel," for none appears to have a mother; all are either unwived or unsocial, despite the few reluctant allusions to those "far-away domestic memories" that afflict Ahab, a "houseless, familyless, old man."

After the blubber-pots and the love-scenes of these corrugated, mammoth Don Juans of the sea, what virile male reader does not yearn for the witty bouts between a smell-smock and a flirt or a sweet bosom that would set Ilium on fire. Whatever Sir John Brute is aching for it is not the Ephesian dugs of a whale, the matrix of a porpoise, or the oceanic marriage-bed of Leviathan. Wycherley's Dorilant has enough wit to penetrate the most amiable feminine heart: "A mistress should be like a little country retreat near the town; not to dwell in constantly, but only for a night and away, to taste the town the better when a man returns."

The Roman virgin sat on the image of the phallus; in Egypt at the time of Philadelphus Ptolemy there was a festival in which the matrons carried Priapus who was a hundred and twenty-five cubits in length, and that is as long as a seminal book should be. Now that we are prepared to hawk this divine god, Priapus, let us announce that what we are willing to sell, barter, or even give away is, *For Women Only.*

What nature makes us we are; contend with this absolute force at the risk of your sanity. A virile male craves his opposite, and that is nature and habit which are the parents of morals. The wise Rabbins said that the contemporaries of Noah were defiant sinners, and drove the Shekinah away from the world.

At the risk of sowing dragon's teeth, and acquiring another legion of foes whom I have never seen, I must impugn *Moby-Dick* as human literature. What kind of a moral novel is this? Alas, the word, moral, has been the shibboleth of the Philister. That gentle genius, Herbert Read, mislikes this word, and prefers justice in the place of it, but what will prevent the academic Presbyters of literature from preempting this word, too.

Who worships vice, arrogance, or a brute of the salty deep? Since the beasts and demons are within man, what need is there to pursue them? Jesus goes into the wilderness to withstand temptation, but the *Gospels* are gray, plain truths. Moreover, who wants to be worse than he already is? And who would not care to obey Ben Jonson's maxim, "He that for love of goodness hateth ill."

Goodness did not tempt Melville sorely. Pascal says that "Milton is well aware that Nature is corrupt and that men are hostile to morality." Melville, a Pauline invert, remarks: "Bethink thee of that saying of St. Paul in *Corinthians,* about corruption and incorruption; how that we are sown in dishonor, but raised in glory."

We only recognize men's virtues when they benefit us. Moreover, morals which do not come from a concupiscent nature are a cold wind upon the frail, reedy spirit. He who is in agony because he is not hot hankers for the fabled Apples of Sodom.

Melville was unable to understand St. Paul because he himself was the prey of corrosive velleity. The work of the moth and rust had deprived him of energy, without which morality is a basilisk. "For the flesh lusteth against the Spirit, and the Spirit against the flesh." No one can avoid this battle, whether he be a hedonist or have strong ascetic inclinations, lest he be a viper to his brother and detest everybody for no other reason than his reluctance to overcome his faults. One who has tepid or cold privities can never pardon anybody, especially those whom he has harmed. Worse, he regards the human race as his foe though in his secret soul he knows the real adversary is himself.

It is told that Paul fought with the beasts at Ephesus; but with what sort of clandestine lust was Herman Melville concerned in *Moby-Dick?* What turpitude does he wish to drown in the great Deluge?

Nobody really perceives how vile he is, and the most depraved is he who asserts that he knows he is vicious. A bad person cannot comprehend his on vitiated nature because when the will languishes, the mind rots. Says Seneca: "A man may dispute, cite great authorities, talk learnedly, huff it out, and yet be rotten at heart." But who does not talk as though his heart were not decayed. St. Paul and Pascal spoke simply, never failing to understand that they suffered because they were obsessed by foul imaginings, a truth that Herman Melville never understood.

We are not dealing with Melville's torn, empirical life, but with his imagination, which is the truest experience. Men reveal themselves most when they dream, and Moby-Dick is the Titanic sodomite serpent that crept into his dark, blighted heart, never to quit that lair in which the most abominable passions lurk, as we see in his last, homosexual, work, *Billy Budd.*

Though he has been somewhat touched by that dreariest of screeds, the perfectability of man, "immaculate manliness" is what Melville calls it, one can look in vain for a piacular sentence in *Moby-Dick.* So much of our lives is given over to the consideration of our imperfections that there is no time to improve our imaginary virtues. The truth is we only perfect our vices, and man is a worse creature when he dies than he was when he was born: ". . . and Jesus said, Why callest thou me good? None is good." Men cocker their vices, and whatever they do that is good is the consequence of vanity, and thoughtlessness: he is born stupid and dies depraved. Christ sent his lambs to go among the wolves, and Moby-Dick is no lamb.

Ahab does not seek glory but scrapes the bottom of Tartarus and all obscure depths for infamy. The Puritan is a clandestine lecher, and dreams are beasts that come in the night; *Moby-Dick* is the vision of the noctambulist and a furtive, dark trance. Ishmael, Ahab, Daggoo, Queequeg, Pip, Fedallah, Tashtego, the detritus of Tartary and Asia Minor, are symbols of nocturnal orgies. Moby-Dick is a primordial animal, and his watery home is the Pacific, which is an Asiatic ocean, for the first peoples came to the new world over this vasty stream. Leviathan is one of the Minotaurs, Sphinxes, and Centaurs, which Plutarch thought were the products of the monstrous, incestuous, and ungovernable lusts of man.

Melville abhorred nature, and thought that God was not the peer of the demiurge, who, as one of the Ante-Nicene Fathers held, was the cause of corruption and death. The Gnostics also referred to Sophia as the Spirit and the "Demiurge" as the "Devil." The suffering atheists, or self-gnawing agnostics, who composed the *Book of Job,* had the same conception. Who can accept that spurious and pusillanimous addendum to the *Book of Job*? Though it is good to endeavor to be virtuous, had Job had any other guerdon for his sorrows save the muck-heap? The pedantic gnomes always prevail over the poet whose only Petrine rock is his doubt: How can man, the worm, know whether God exists or not?

The author of the *Zohar* said that before Noah there were only three just men in the earth, Methuselah, Enoch and Jared, and who can forget that Noah is the father of the first sodomite, Ham? Moreover, who has not the most acute compassion for Herman Melville's ontological pain? Had not the prophet Jeremiah also cried out in anguish: "O Lord, Thou hast deceived us," and does not Jesus in a rueful, gnostical mood lament: "Your Father is a murderer from the beginning"? What concerns us is that Melville was a perverted Christian, and that the tawdry writing in *Moby-Dick* is to some extent wilful self-hatred. Is there a genius in Christendom whose holy screed is not: "In the beginning was the Word"?

Herman Melville had committed sodomy, as it is meant in the *Old Testament;* in his mind he had had connection with a beast of the deep. Take woman from man and he will yearn for an angel, a porpoise, a whale. This starveling became a hunter for profane and nether flesh, dolphins, sharks, leviathan and man, whatever could ease those clinkered, lava lusts. Unable to be consumed in the flames of Troy for Helen, he was cindered in the fires of Sodom and Gomorrah.

The only real marriage in the book is between Queequeg and Ishmael. "He pressed his forehead against mine, clasped me round the waist, and said that henceforth we were married." "No place like a bed for confidential disclosures," and this is as close to the bed of Venus as he ever comes.

Melville's Christ is "soft, curled, hermaphroditical," "negative" and "feminine." Give us a pagan Christ, in part Apis and Mnevis! Why does Jesus wear a loin cloth? The women at Pompeii substituted the cross for the image of the phallus they had worn around their necks. The crucifix hangs against the fertile paps of the Catholic virgin, and what natural woman carries the image of a man close to her carnal bosom without sensual pangs? We must cast out such diabolical conceptions of goodness, as the Lord himself "opens the kingdoms of heaven to eunuchs," and "it remains, that they who have wives so be as if they have not" or there will be a universal Sodom and Gomorrah.

Though Melville abhorred Christianity, he wrote Puritan gospels in Tophet.

Melville is an Ophite and his supernatural whale, "the starry Cetus," is a species of Dagon, the fish-like deity of the Philistines. The whale, though a mammal, was a great fish and a serpent to the ancient fabulists, and Christ is a moist star—Jesus is Pisces.

Leviathan in the *Zohar* is feminine. The Leviathan, the oldest foe of man, is called Rahab by Isaiah and the Psalmist—the Dragon and the serpent. "Thou hast broken Rahab in pieces," and "Art thou it that hath cut Rahab and wounded the dragon," both of which come from Isaiah and refer to a feminine creature, and is not Rahab also the whore of Jericho? Elohim, too, is often feminine in the *Cabala* and in Gnostic theology. Proclus in the *Timaeus* believed that "Nature is suspended from the back of the vivifying goddess." The female part of God was known as the Shekinah to the cabalistical thinkers. Clement of Alexandria writes that the symbol of the Bacchic orgies is a consecrated reptile and also that the name Hevia, or Eve, signifies a female serpent.

But for Melville, a superstitious scientist, or a Talmudic one, the pelagic Demiurge is masculine. His mammoth, in part, is one of the "monsters of Rahab" of the olden Rabbins; Leviathan is Tiamat of the Gilgamesh epic, the dragon of Isaiah, the Psalmist, Job and Enoch. *Moby-Dick* is a hybrid of Scripture and zoology, and this brute of the sea is the product of the "half-foetal suggestions of supernatural agencies." Thomas Traherne wrote that "to call things preternatural Natural is Monstrous."

Osiris, the personification of the generative organs of man to the Egyptians, was second in importance to Isis, the begetter. She is the Ancient One just as God is known as the Ancient of Days in the *Book of Daniel.* It is Isis, the goddess, and not the aboriginal hermaphrodite, masculine in front, but feminine in the hinder parts, who is searching all the waters of the Nile for the genitals of her consort. Did she find them, or are we men with only a tithe of a prepuce?

However, it is the spermal deity Melville worships, not the Generatrix, as is apparent in one of Melville's extraordinary raptures: "In thoughts of the visions of the night, I saw long rows of angels in paradise, each with his hands in a jar of spermaceti." Of the sperm Melville writes: "I washed my hands and my heart [in] it."

Spite of the fact that the novel is a doxology of a wicked beast of the seas, Melville believed in punishment, for the *Pequod* is a "whited sepulchre" on the outside, but full of "dead men's bones within." Furthermore, in the *Cabala* it is explained that the human race perished, save Noah and his family, by drowning. But why was homosexual Ham spared, and does not Melville follow the same parable since all die by water save Ishmael, who is really Ham? And the universal Hamite is grum, aqueous and froward.

Moby-Dick is Christian zoolatry, a Puritanical bestiary, and in some respects, not dissimilar to the Egyptian *Book of the Dead.* Philo Judeaus had rebuked the Egyptians for their idolatry of crocodiles, dogs, the ibis, and cats. In olden Cairo superannuated cats were fed in charity hospitals. One cat in a house is a sign of loneliness, two of barrenness, and three of sodomy. *Moby-Dick* is the bestial *Bible* of modern Ham.

The dark races awakened his concupiscence: is not Ham the Father of Africa. Melville called his seafarers mermen. Only dark or olive flesh stirred in him the ashes of Borsippa, Ur and Canaan.

Ham is also the father of Canaan who is the primal forebear of the Canaanites who were destroyed because of their terrible wantonness. The "imperial" Negro Daggoo was his phallic idol, and the name was obviously derived from Dagon, a god with the tail of a fish. There were Tashtego, black Pip whom he fondles, and Fedallah the Parsee who is the only one before whom Ahab stands in awe. Water is vice, retribution and Ham, and the spermal whale is Priapus who has deprived Ahab of his phallical leg. As Fedallah is drowning, Ahab, for no overt cause, moans for the "unforgiven ghosts of Gomorrah." The words in the soul rise to the lips on a sudden, because no lust can sink them. Ay, it is a dry, dry book in which a man can drown all his sins.

These are seafaring Nimrods; Nimrod is the hunter whose iniquity is his pride, and the *Pequod* is a Babel, as Melville shows in the chapter "Midnight, Forecastle"; it is the Tower of Hubris on the watery plains of Shinar.

Since we are as bad as our dreams, and our books are no better, it was inevitable that Melville should have had Cyclops' anthropophagous palate, and that after *Moby-Dick* he should have written *Pierre,* a novel about incest. Those meager sentences that are supposed to be cetology in *Moby-Dick* are very close to quack erudition because there is a failure in sensibility and a drought of the organs of the body. We can only write well about our sins because it is too difficult to recall a virtuous act or even whether it was the result of good or evil motives, or just an accidental deed.

There is now a pederastic hagiography composed of people who prefer the bad to the good, who like excrements instead of pondapples, sumach, dogwood, or hyacinths, and who choose men rather than women to be their paramours. Intellectual sodomy, which comes from the refusal to be simple about plain matters, is as gross and abundant today as sexual perversion and they are nowise different from one another. This kind of pathic in literature has wan, epicene affections. A misologist, he takes ophidian pleasure in the misuse of words, and his sacerdotal gibberish sounds more like the cries of animals than the holy Logos or the alphabet of the god Thoth. Specious rebels, they are the advocates of the rabble arts.

The martyrology of the sodomite consists of Saint Ordure, Saint Incest and Saint Matricide. The inverted Christian eremite nowadays has a matricidal heart, and is either totally separated from his parents, or utterly detests them. How feeble is the image of the father in nineteenth-century American literature; had Poe any parents at all? What do we know of Melville's male progenitor, or Whitman's, and was the great savant, Thoreau, born of stocks and stones? The misogamist spawns the homosexual, and *Moby-Dick* is the worship of the male sperm. Phallic idolatry is the concern of women, and no literature can be bawdy, human and sage unless men love women; no nation can survive, not Hellas nor Jerusalem, when the stews for males are substituted for the hetira and the olive-complexioned damsels who were the solace of the harper and his son, the Amorist Solomon.

The Equívoco[1] of *Don Quixote*

ÁNGEL DEL RÍO

I

THE NEW LITERARY GENRE that Cervantes created in *Don Quixote* (later to be called "the modern novel") arose out of a changed situation of man in history, one in which incongruities between individual intentions and individual capacity for realizing them became apparent, and in which truth became a problem—not in the abstract nor in relation to transcendental forces but relative to man's own existence. After the formalist criticism of the eighteenth century, the Romantics were able to perceive for the first time the deeply human and poetic significance of the history of the strange knight; yet they failed to give sufficient emphasis to the meaning of the novel as a whole. This meaning is rooted in

[1] "Equívoco" has been retained in the title because the nearest English translation, "ambiguity," has become closely associated with language, and the ambiguity with which this essay deals is a matter of broader literary and philosophic meanings. The author hoped that his use of "ambiguity" for "equívoco" would be taken in this emphasis and of course without any taint of the pejorative—S.B.

the conflict between the hero and his environment, between the character and its circumstances, and out of it develops that "ambiguity" which Ortega y Gasset pointed to in his *Meditaciones del Quijote:*

> Let us be sincere: *Don Quixote* is an ambiguity [*equívoco*]. All the dithyrambs of national eloquence have served for nothing. All the learned research into the life of Cervantes has not clarified one corner of the colossal ambiguity. Is Cervantes laughing? And what is he laughing at? Far off, alone on the broad plain of La Mancha, the long figure of Don Quixote curves into a question mark . . . . What is this poor tax collector laughing at from the dark depths of a dungeon? And what does it mean to laugh? Is the laughter necessarily a negation?

Since the publication of these remarks, Américo Castro, Casella, Casalduero, Hatzfeld, and a host of other scholars, philosophers, critics, poets, and even plain enthusiastic readers have continued to provide us with keys for entering, with ever greater awareness, the uncertain universe that Cervantes conceived. But it was Ortega, employing strict philosophical rigor, who penetrated and explored the novel's artistic significance, and who best understood that what Cervantes had done was to give poetic expression to a rich vision of a problematical reality. From this vision arises the problematical character of the work itself, its *equívoco,* a term which the Spanish dictionary defines as "that which can be understood in various ways or occasion various judgments." [2]

Ever since Fielding, *Don Quixote* has been subjected to varying and at times contradictory interpretations, particularly among the eighteenth-century rationalists who tried to discover in it a meaning beyond merely the joyfulness of the narration of merry adventures. Is the story of this grotesque, sublime madman an

[2] lo que puede entenderse o interpretarse en varios sentidos o dar ocasión a juicios diversos.

affirmation of faith, an exaltation of idealism, or is it rather the skeptical derision of all ideal aspirations? Do we have here the finest expression of the activist impulse in the Spanish character, or is it an undeceived critique exposing the decadence of that impulse? Does Cervantes save the heroic illusions of his youth by transferring them to the domain of creative fantasy, or is he laughing at them with a laughter that can at times approach cruelty? Does *Don Quixote* destroy the spirit of chivalry, or does it raise it to its final apotheosis? Is this, as Byron said, the great book that killed a great people, or have we here a great epic which immortalizes in the world of art the daring and deluded image of that people? And, on another level, is Cervantes a rationalist, or is he a Catholic reactionary expressing the ideals of the Counter-Reformation? And what of his art, is it a summation of the Renaissance, or a perfect utterance of the spirit of the Baroque? Et cetera, et cetera. All these interpretations seem to have equal validity . . . and yet we may never be able to give a satisfactory answer to Ortega's "Is Cervantes laughing?" and "What is he laughing at?"

This situation seems to me to have no parallel among the great books of humanity. Innumerable commentaries have been composed about the epics of Homer, Greek tragedy, Dante, Shakespeare, Goethe, the French and English classics, but in all these cases, criticism evinces a certain continuity: each new observer proceeds from the discoveries of his predecessors. With *Don Quixote,* however, once we have left behind the scholarly, formalistic criticism of the eighteenth century for the criticism of meaning, which followed, we find ourselves forced to penetrate to the very root of the author's intention, and, finally, to examine his achievement from a point of view that is, in great measure, personal.

Granted the legitimacy, even the necessity, of such an approach, I should like to comment upon several episodes of Part II, where the ambiguity that Ortega recognized probably exists in its most extreme form. But before doing so, it may be prudent to remind the reader that the basic operating principle of the entire work consists of a constant tension or, better, a prodigiously maintained equilibrium between radical opposites: be—seem, reality—fantasy, madness—sanity, drama—comedy, sublime—grotesque, et al.

Although critics unanimously mention this quite evident polarity, they have not always given the necessary weight to two no less apparent facts: that the fundamental quality of Cervantes' mind is humor, and that the work reveals an astonishing artistic consciousness.

From their combination derives the essentially humorous game that Cervantes plays in every episode, every sentence, every line. It is a game that seems intent on robbing a delightful story of any transcendental implications: the comic follows upon the serious; the most anguished passages dissolve into the ridiculous; elevated language stands side by side with colloquialisms; and into scenes of the most exquisite poetry burst characters or objects of crassest materiality. But it is a game which only seems untranscendental, for Cervantes, now mocking, now quite serious, comes face to face with the problem of the meaning of life, or rather, with the problem of existence rooted in uncertainty. What is especially characteristic of Cervantes is that opposites do not so much oppose each other or harmonize as operate side by side and act inseparably.

Now, if this is already apparent in Part I, in Part II it reaches depths and significance where the opposition of reality and fantasy becomes complicated into visions of the extra-real and of the unconscious.

Cervantes prepares the reader for this in the Prologue and the first few chapters of Part II, with quite deliberate emphasis. It is clear that he was touched to the quick by the feigned scorn of the scholars of his day, so loath to recognize the novelty and importance of his work and the artistic conscience of its creator. Hence the story of the madman who blew up a dog and then gives forth with: "Does your worship think it is an easy thing to write a book?" (468).[3] And there follow several other tales of madmen intended to show that the hero's peculiar madness has far greater significance than the happy reader suspects, that it is indeed the hub around which the entire work revolves. The double idea—artistic effort and the transcendence of Quixotic madness—is riveted together in the last paragraph of the Prologue: ". . . Suffice it that an honest man has told the story of his amusing follies, and has no wish to take the subject up again" (470).

As the narrative begins in Part II, we are informed that almost a month has elapsed since the priest and the barber have seen their neighbor, Don Quixote: in other words, since the knight returned home in a cage, a fact whose full significance is not perceived until we realize that one of the most important themes of Part II—and it is in great measure a new theme—is the relativity of time. We are no longer to be concerned with physical or historical time, but with psychic, existential time. Hardly has the dialogue begun when the barber tells another story of madmen. Don Quixote immediately grasps his meaning and angrily retorts: "O, Master Shaver, Master Shaver, how blind is he who cannot see through a hair-sieve! Is it possible that your worship does not know that comparisons between wit and wit, valour and valour, beauty and beauty, birth and birth, are always odious and resented?" (476–7). He might have added madness and madness, for Cervantes has been insisting from the very outset that his hero's strange madness belongs to a species never before seen. The inference is quite clear: it is not so much a pathological state as a way of being and acting in the world.

From the beginning of Part II, it is patent that Cervantes almost imperceptibly has taken the reader into a climate very dif-

[3] All quotations have been taken from the translation of J. M. Cohen, published by The Penguin Classics. The page number is indicated in parentheses at the end of each quotation.

ferent from that which characterizes Part I. The problem of the reality that man perceives begins to take a twist hardly even suggested in the earlier exploits of the knight.

In Chapter 2, following his plan of putting into the novel a great variety of forms of being and existing, Cervantes takes an unprecedented aesthetic leap. It seems that in the short span of a single month in the internal chronology of the story—and let us not forget this—the exploits of Don Quixote and Sancho Panza are already to be found within the covers of a book. Fiction within fiction. Both Miguel de Unamuno and Américo Castro have written illuminating pages on this phenomenon, but here we are interested only in distinguishing some of its consequences. The good Alonso Quixano and the simple peasant who shares his destiny have already attained the kind of reality that the throng of wandering knights whom Don Quixote proposed to imitate had possessed in his sick mind. Now the relation of these two companions with the rest of the characters is not to be so simple. For between this extravagant old man with the ridiculous bearing and the no less ridiculous peasant who accompanies him, and the people they meet on the way, the poetic image created by the author interposes itself. Before, the relation was uncomplicated: one was in the presence of two fools who acted in unusual ways. Each person they met reacted to their folly in accordance with his own nature. Their friends followed after them in order to bring them back home again. Others listened to them with astonishment. Still others beat them or merely amused themselves at their expense. Now, however, it is no longer only a question of a nobleman named Quexana or Quixada, or whatever it is, who goes about the countryside acting strangely. It is now a question—strictly speaking, authentically, in terms of the psychological situation—of a knight, mad of course, but nonetheless quite real, and quite true insofar as he acts as a knight, as Don Quixote de La Mancha.

When the Bachelor Sampson Carrasco—one of the many mockers who will end by being himself mocked—rushes into his neighbor Don Quixote's house, he throws himself at his feet and says: "Give me your hands, Your Mightiness, Don Quixote de La Mancha," (486) he is actually kneeling before the hero invented by Cervantes, and not before his neighbor Alonso, whose identity both the novelist and the reader seem to have forgotten and which they will not recognize until the end of the story. It will be the same with the Duke and Duchess, Don Antonio Moreno, and with all the others who have learned of the existence of this new righter of wrongs.

After the appearance of the Bachelor, Cervantes feels it necessary to enlighten the reader as to the meaning of what he is creating and going to create, but without, of course, ever giving up the humorous game. Chapter 3 is dedicated to this end, and in accordance with the design of disguising the most serious intentions in comic language, it is entitled: "Of the ridiculous Conversation which passed between Don Quixote, Sancho Panza and the Bachelor Sampson Carrasco." Note that in the preceding chapter, as soon as he had mentioned that the story of Don Quixote was in print, the author had made Sancho say that he was wonderfully astonished and even frightened at how the writer could have come to know the things he had put into the book. To which Don Quixote had replied: "You may be certain, Sancho, that the author of our history is some sage enchanter" (484). Thus prepared, we enter into the ridiculous conversation, which turns out to be a marvelous game of ambiguities. We are told, in the first place, not to expect any *truth* whatsoever, "for he could hope for no truth from the Moors [Cide Hamete], since they are all cheats, forgers and schemers" (485). The author then announces and proclaims the moral qualities which his mad hero represents: ". . . gallantry . . . great courage in confronting perils . . . patience in adversity . . . fortitude . . . in misfortune and wounds and the chastity and continence of the most platonic loves . . ." (487). And, realizing what the reactions of his future readers will be when confronted with the misfortunes of this poor, sublime madman, he anticipates their objections:

> . . . some who have read your history say that they would have been glad if the authors had left out a few of the countless beatings which Don Quixote received in various encounters.
>
> That's where the *truth of the story* comes in, (487–8)

Sancho points out. And the Bachelor makes it even clearer: "That is true . . . but it is one thing to write as a poet, and another as a historian. The poet can relate and sing things, not as they were but as they should have been, without in any way affecting the truth of the matter" (488).

Castro, Toffanín, Casella, and other critics have pointed out the significance of the concepts of poetry and history in this passage in relation with Renaissance literary theory. Cervantes sets the poetic universal in the sphere of the historical particular, in a permanent dynamic polarity. But apart from this, he does something particularly Cervantesque: he shows that poetry and history, idea and reality, go hand in hand in life because both are an integral part of man's relation to the universe.

In our passages from the Prologue and the first few chapters of Part II the word *truth* occurs several times. What is truth? This is the question that our frolicsome author who was "more versed in misery than in verses" keeps asking himself. Cervantes makes no attempt to answer, probably because he knows that the question does not have an answer. But with wonderful inventiveness and penetrating humor, he comes perhaps as near as anyone ever has come—now jestingly, now quite seriously—not to solving the awful riddle but to extracting from it the utmost in artistic and vital consequences.

The whole of Chapter 3 is charged with especial meaning. It is both a lesson in self-criticism and a complete exposition of the aesthetic motives at the base of the whole work. Cervantes seems to guess the objections of his future readers and to take pleasure in meeting them in advance. Ideally we should quote and comment in entirety, for every sentence is filled with intention and significance. But for our purposes, it will suffice to call attention to the alternating movement and the resulting ambiguity. When Cervantes seems to be saying one thing, he is actually saying something else; when he seems to be speaking seriously, he is really joking, and it is when he is jesting that he tries to reveal to us the secrets of his art. Either the author is a master craftsman from whom nothing is hidden, or he is a fool, an ignorant charlatan who works without purpose, at random. Either the story will have to be thoroughly glossed in order to be understood, or it is so clear that children will have no difficulty comprehending it. What we have here is a constant affirmation and negation, a continuous yes and no, the ambiguity centered upon man's incapacity to draw a distinct line between what is true and what is not true, between what is and what is not.

II

Ten years elapsed between the publication of the first and the second parts of *Don Quixote*. During that time, Cervantes meditated upon the possibilities and consequences of his invention, *i.e.*, of having engendered the very highest of ideal aspirations in the sick mind of a madman who is moreover weak and ailing, and whose sole strength lies in heroic will. The contradiction inherent in this conception cannot be resolved by saying, as has so often been said, that the hero merely intends to revive anachronistically the ideals of the Gothic in the world of the Baroque—that is, the ideals of an already dead past which have no significance for the present. Such a theory is applicable only to an exposition of the literary elements and an understanding of the artistic composition; it is scarcely of use in clarifying the ambiguities which the author put into his creation. For the truth of the matter is that Don Quixote's ideals are equally valid for every age. Of course, the fabulous monsters, the giants, the sorcerers, and the knights who bide in woods for the happening of vague adventures belong to the poetic world of the Gothic. But to defend maidens, to right wrongs, to protect the helpless against abuse by the powerful; in a word, to strive for justice and the liberty to be and to act as one likes—for perfect love and courtesy—these are human aspirations good at any time. It is Don Quixote's *means* which are anachronistic, not his ends. And his madness lies not in his desires but in his inability to see that he lacks the powers to fulfil them.

Cervantes meditated also on the nature of illusion and the delusiveness of reality, a reality which man must attempt to see clearly, for his life consists of acting in or within that reality. The outcome of these meditations is the second part of *Don Quixote,* which is organized around three central and converging questions stated or suggested in the Prologue and the first few chapters: (1) the significance of madness; (2) truth in its double plane of poetry and history, from whose conjunction results Cervantesque truth, which is the existential, vital truth each individual, mad or sane, must live, according to his circumstances; and finally (3) the evasive character of reality, which is now seen to exist on a multiplicity of levels. In Part II many of these levels are introduced for the first time.

Although the unity of the novel as a whole seems undeniable, Cervantes was obviously working differently in 1615 when completing Part II. Ten years earlier the rhythm had been rapid: by the opening of Chapter 2, the hero was already in the field. But in Part II six chapters elapse before any action begins. Conversation follows conversation, and with the third sally (Chapter 8), Don Quixote makes no mention of being pleased or delighted. The enamored gentleman sets out for El Toboso to find Dulcinea, in the hope of strengthening his faith, which has already begun to weaken. Now only Sancho is delighted, for he is infected with the love of the freedom of the road and with his master's madness. Things do not happen in the sanguine light of dawn, nor does Apollo show his golden face on the horizon. An air of melancholy descends on the scene. Night is falling for Don Quixote. The knight and the squire converse about—and it does not seem fortuitous—bringing a dead man back to life.

The relation with the real world begins to deepen, and from this point on, the sense of death, of mystery, and of disillusionment will never abandon the reader. The entrance into El Toboso—"It was on the stroke of midnight"—with the shadows of the humble dwellings which our hero takes to be castles falling on the silent streets, and the voice of the peasant singing a ballad of foreboding—is an hallucinatory scene. But though all is bathed in the light of dream, Cervantes does not allow himself to be bemused for long by the poetical. With a sure hand he precipitates the reader into the grotesque, with the encounter of the uncivil village women, one of whom Sancho maliciously turns, by enchantment, into none other than Dulcinea.

The components of the vision of reality undergo an unusual transformation. In Part I, and especially in the first adventures, the formula was relatively simple. Indeed, it might have become merely a mechanical contrivance, but the author's inexhaustible inventiveness never allowed this to happen. A madman proceeds through the lonely countryside and transforms the objects of the sensible world—windmills, flocks, the noise of looms, lights—into images which have existence solely in his perturbed imagination. Impelled by the force of his illusion, he attacks the imaginary object he himself has created, with results to be expected of all error of vision.

In Part II, the transformation no longer takes place in the mind of Don Quixote, for most of the time objects present themselves to him already changed into fantastic images through the ingenuity and industry of those intending to mock him (primarily Sancho) or through the sorcery of the author himself. In the episode of the enchantment of Dulcinea, referred to above, Don Quixote does not behold a peasant whom his own deluded will has turned into a princess; he stands before a princess created by Sancho's malicious imagination, while to him, Don Quixote, she is still a crude country girl. In a later episode—the encounter with the Knight of the Mirrors (Chapters 12 and 13)—his challenger appears to him as a real knight, after which Dulcinea's sorrowful lover "saw . . . the very face, the very physiognomy, the very image, the very picture of the Bachelor Sampson Carrasco" (558).

Enchantment now operates inversely, flowing not from the real to the fantastic, but vice versa. In other words, it does not arise from a deluded, fascinated subject; rather the subject passively receives the fantastic image.

Almost every episode in Part I is based on an encounter with persons and objects belonging to an ordinary reality: inns, muleteers, a barber, Yanguesans, windmills. In Part II, almost everything encountered belongs to forms of existence not usually found in everyday life—lions, Camacho's wedding, an enchanted bark —to the world of pure representation, of theatre: the chariot of death, the dance of love and interest, Master Peter's puppet show, a prophesying ape. No wonder the unfortunate knight, after the adventure of the enchanted ship, cries out "I can do no more," for the world around him has been so transformed that things have lost their recognizable identity.

At this point Cervantes has put himself into a position from which a deep exploration of imaginative invention becomes possible. And he goes all the way, beyond the limits of material objects and historical events. He submerges his hero in visions of pure imagination, of the unconscious, and of dream. In the two episodes that reveal the artist's ultimate design—the cave of Montesinos and Clavileño's flight—and in their consequences, we come to the heart of the great ambiguity: What is true, what is false? Note how the descent into the dark cave is prepared for: "Don Quixote asked the skilful licentiate to give him a guide to lead him to the cave of Montesinos, for he had a great desire to explore it and see with his own eyes whether the marvels related about it thereabouts were true" (609).

The licentiate is a humanist by profession, and he intends to achieve fame by composing a treatise in which he will give a minute description of all the types of livery, 703 of them, to be precise. He also proposes to write a "Metamorphosis" or "Spanish

Ovid," and a "Supplement to Polydore Virgil" in which he will elucidate in an elegant style matters of great importance omitted by Polydore, such as "who was the first man to have catarrh." All these points are to be set out with the utmost precision on the testimony of twenty-five authorities.

The absurdity is immediately remarked by the squire and the knight. Cervantes will now resort to a technique frequently used throughout the whole work to link contrasting themes: a theme is presented to the reader from one point of view, then transposed to a different plane. In Part I we moved from real goatherds to poetic shepherds (Chrysostom and Marcela); from lust (Rocinante and the mares, and Maritormes and the carrier) to a complicated series of love stories (Don Ferdinand-Dorothea, Cardenio-Lucinda, the Tale of Foolish Curiosity, the Captive and Zoraida). Here Cervantes takes us from the world of barren erudition, whose findings are not worth a farthing, to drop us with his hero into an abyss of imaginative delirium. In other words, from absurd erudition (supposed truth) into absurd fantasy (supposed falsehood).

Commending his soul to God and Dulcinea, Don Quixote proceeds to drive off the small birds, ravens, and jackdaws that guard the secrets of the cave in a tangle of vegetation. He enters with intrepid heart. Some time later he is brought out, apparently unconscious. When, shaken by his companions, he recovers his senses, it is "as if waking from a deep sleep." And the first thing he says is

> God pardon you, my friends, for you have robbed me of the sweetest existence and most delightful vision any human being ever enjoyed or beheld. Now, indeed, I positively know that the pleasures of this life pass like a shadow and a dream, and wither like the flowers of the field (614).

As Casalduero points out, what Don Quixote has been dreaming about is the meaning of life: dreams teach us, when we are once more awake, that all is fleeting and passes away like a shadow.

The theme recurs from remotest antiquity down to Calderón, but what is peculiarly Cervantesque is to convert the dream itself into a problem of cognition and to make its content an essential question in the rest of the novel: whether what Don Quixote has seen in the darkness of the cave is true or untrue, real or unreal.

The following chapter (23) begins with the setting of the exact time—"It was about four in the afternoon"—and the knightly explorer of the mysteries of the cave begins to recount his adventures in equally precise words—"about eighteen or twenty feet down in the depths of this dungeon." Then he informs his astonished auditors that he was overcome with a deep sleep, from which he awoke to find himself

> in the middle of the most beautiful, pleasant and delightful meadow nature could create or the liveliest human imagination conceive. I opened and rubbed my eyes, and saw that I was not asleep but really awake. For all that, I felt my head and my bosom to make certain whether it was my very self who was there, or some empty and counterfeit phantom; but touch, feeling and the coherent argument I held with myself assured me that I was there then just as I am here now (615).

Note that he "was really awake"—awake within the very dream itself. The proof leaves no room for doubt. Touch, feeling, and reason all establish the subject's reality and consequently his capacity to give a true account of what he has seen.

It is not necessary to recall in detail all the visions in the cave. Cervantes allows his "rare inventor's" pen delightful free reign with castles, meadows, Montesinos, Durandarte, Belerma, Merlin, processions of lovely damsels and enchanted knights, and Dulcinea, enchanted also, leaping and frisking in her peasant dress in those pleasant fields.

We are in the domain of unfettered imagination, but the material is treated quite differently here in Part II from the manner of its employment in Part I. There the themes characteristic of the Renaissance were presented in stylized fashion: Pastoral,

Epic, Moresque, or Amorous. In the cave of Montesinos, although the characters are taken from *romances* and ballads issuing from books of chivalry, all has the aspect of pure fantasy without order or sense, as in an oneiromantic vision. How well Cervantes understands its nature is shown by the juxtaposition of incoherent images—out of the dreamer's unconscious the idealized figure of Dulcinea rises—or he makes a sudden sharp turn toward vulgarity, with Durandarte's "patience and shuffle the cards," with the rings under the eyes or the sickly color of Belerma; with those half-dozen *reals* that Dulcinea wishes to borrow from Don Quixote.

As Sancho observes, his master's account is nothing but a string of absurdities. They are fundamentally of the same order as the nonsensical discoveries of the licentiate, but they have more meaning. For the truths, based on authorities, which concern the licentiate do not have interest for anyone else, while the absurd creations of the imagination and the unconscious—as a reflection of human desires—hold one of the very greatest of mysteries: Is what man creates, dreams, imagines, or thinks, awake or asleep, true? And, what kind of truth is it?

Cervantes realizes quite well the transcendental nature of this problem. He knows that imagining and dreaming are human functions as real as any other—as eating, for instance. Real and specific, but of a different order of being, for they occur in a different kind of time—in unmeasurable, psychic time. He states the problem clearly: "I do not know, Don Quixote . . . how your worship could have seen so many things and heard and said so much in the short space of time you were down below" (620).

It is Sancho into whose mouth the author now puts the most acute and valid judgments and who gives the appropriate solution: "perhaps what seems to us an hour may seem three days and nights down there." (*ibid.*) And Don Quixote confirms that all he has recounted he had seen with his own eyes and touched with his own hands. The appeal to the senses is often repeated with meaningful insistence.

At the conclusion of the episode, there comes a qualifying observation:

> The translator of this great history from the original written by its first author, Cide Hamete Benengeli, says that when he reached the chapter relating the adventure of Montesinos' cave he found written in the margin in the hand of this same Hamete these words:
>
> "I cannot persuade myself that all that is written in the previous chapter literally happened to the valorous Don Quixote. The reason is that all the adventures till now have been feasible and probable, but this one of the cave I can find no way of accepting as true, for it exceeds all reasonable bounds" (624).

The story has left the pathways of the possible and the "verisimilar," a concept which Cervantes himself explains, in his *Persiles,* as a narrative which, "notwithstanding and in spite of the lie that creates a dissonance in the understanding, should form a true harmony." If Cide Hamete rejects the authenticity of his hero's visions, it is because they "exceed all *reasonable* bounds" (my italics). (In addition to being opposed to nature, they are opposed to what is reasonable, to Reason which the men of the seventeenth century were to rediscover as the fountainhead of certainty.) By this time the whole question posed by Don Quixote's report of his visions now seems to be clear, but it is not clear, for Cervantes carries it further. Indeed the truth or untruth of the visions of the cave becomes the vital thread running throughout the remainder of the novel.

In Chapter 41 we come to an episode which in many ways parallels the one of the cave: the flight of Clavileño, where the dark sky is an inverted image of the cave. Here it is Sancho who lets his imagination run free through the heavens, clearly pitting his inventiveness against that of his master in the past. When the squire returns to earth, Don Quixote feels it necessary to tell him: "Sancho, if you want me to believe what you saw in the sky, I wish you to accept my account of what I saw in the Cave of Montesinos. I say no more" (735).

How far we are now from the relatively elementary opposition of objective reality with the reality formed in the sick brain of Don Quixote in the first adventures. There are no sorcerers any more. The question is whether one is to believe or not to believe in the fantasies invented by the imagination without relation to any real object.

Does Don Quixote believe? Does he doubt? He believes and doubts at the same time. The dilemma will stay with him throughout the long process of his disillusionment, throughout the second stage of his fortunes, a phase in which he seems to walk like a somnambulist in a long dream whose ineluctable end, we know from the first chapters, is the awakening of death. In contrast to the gay impetuosity of the first departures, he now obeys an inexorable destiny. "A knight I am and a knight I shall die," he had said at the beginning. "I can do no more," he says after the adventure of the enchanted bark. "I do not know what I am conquering by the force of my labours," he will later exclaim sadly when he meets the images of the saints. He goes on, that is, in search of certainty which will give him life in the fog of his madness. He seeks a certainty which had never concerned him before because he was sure of himself and of the truthfulness of the books of chivalry. And Cervantes attains one of the great heights of his irony when he makes the arbiter of the doubts which assail the knight, once the symbol of shining faith, Master Peter's prophesying ape. Thus the ape becomes the definer of the perennial ambiguity.

Sancho, who is always incredulous, suggests the consultation:

> I wish, sir, that you'd ask Master Peter to ask his ape whether it's true what happened to you in Montesinos' cave. For it's my opinion, begging your worship's pardon, that it was all fraud and fictions, or at least that you dreamt it (637).

Don Quixote replies with incredible humility: "Everything is possible. . . I will do as you advise, though I have certain scruples about it." The ape's verdict is that "part of what your worship saw or experienced in the said cave is false and part true." And Sancho exclaims: "Didn't I say you'd never make me believe all you told us about the happenings in that cave, or even a half of it?" Don Quixote answers: "Events will show, Sancho, . . . for time, which reveals all things, leaves nothing that it does not drag into the light of day, even things hidden in the bosom of the earth." Thus the final proof is consigned to the future, the court of last appeal for every illusion.

Almost at the very end, the doubt still persists, and Don Quixote consults the enchanted head in the house of Don Antonio Moreno. The reply is equally sibylline:

> Tell me, . . . was it truth or a dream, the account I gave of my experiences in the cave of Montesinos?
>
> As for the matter of the cave, . . . there is much to say: it has something in it of both (874).

Unamuno made the following comment about the visions of the cave in *The Life of Don Quixote and Sancho:*

> If he [Don Quixote] had already accomplished these and so many other no less astonishing exploits, he may very well have seen in the cave of Montesinos whatsoever it occurred to him to see in it. And if he did see those things, which we have no reason to doubt, what shall we say of the reality of his visions? If life be a dream, then why should we be obstinate in denying that dreams are also life? And everything which is life is true. What we call reality, is it anything else than an illusion which makes us act and produces actions? Its practical effect is the only true standard by which to judge the veracity of any vision, whatever it may be.

I suspect that Cervantes' solution is not so simple as this other Don Miguel would have it in his anxious seeking after certainty.

For Unamuno forgets something essential: that the knight he so much admires scarcely acts at all after he comes out of the cave. He becomes almost passive, an object of the mockery of others. He is adrift until the moment he returns to his village to die.

III

Don Quixote was written at the opening of a period in which man, discovering his inner self, began to blur the line which divides reality from illusion. Finding himself in a world of antimonies, he sought a firm basic position from which to differentiate among them and to try to learn what is true.

But what is Cervantes' solution? Not to give a solution, like the prophesying ape. Of all that we do, of all that we live, of all that we dream, part is true and part is not true. Or, to change the paradox a little, one might say that "In this Life Everything is Truth and Everything is a Lie," which is the title of a play by Calderón. The crux of the matter resides in the fact that the ape does not say which of Don Quixote's visions are false and which are true. The doubt remains to the end. Here we have at least one of the essential parts of the colossal ambiguity of *Don Quixote,* which so disturbed Ortega. Cervantes succeeded, almost without resorting to any abstractions, in putting into *Don Quixote* the ambiguity of human existence itself. Or, in other words, he discovered how to make poetry out of the radical uncertainty of life. No work of literary art is clearer or more natural. The ambiguity is not in the novel but in the life which the novel so faithfully mirrors.

At a critical turning point in the history of Western culture—from the Renaissance, still held by a transcendental, Platonistic conception of the world, to Rationalism, which destroyed all possibility of such a philosophy—Cervantes intuitively perceived that the destiny of man, be he mad or sane, in a universe which is in its very nature uncertain, is acted out not so much among shadows and appearances as among a multiplicity of realities. Some of these are perceptible, some dreamed, and upon being interpreted in the light of human aspirations—of hopes, desires, appetites, ideas, and ideals—they produce unlooked-for effects. The question is not, as it were, perspectivism but a kind of superperspectivism. My perspective is true as mine, but living entails a conflict between my point of view and those of others. And it is not always possible to say who is mad and who is sane. Thus at the very center of the story of the noble knight of La Mancha is the problem which became basic for post-Renaissance man: What is true? What is the truth? Cervantes does not suggest a definite solution. He merely writes a novel about the search for truth which the ambiguity of life involves. *Don Quixote* is a novel of doubt: not rational, Cartesian doubt, but rather what we should call today existential doubt.

Cervantes stands midway between the two extremes of seventeenth-century thinking: Rationalism and the Baroque. He sees that the utopias constructed by Rationalism as valid at all times and in all places give neither a satisfactory explanation of nor a meaning to life. Yet he cannot accept the totality of the ascetic doctrine of the Baroque, in which this world is but a dream, a lie, a fiction, a way-station on the journey to the reality of eternity, a here which is nothing as opposed to a hereafter which is everything. Nevertheless, this negative doctrine contains several important ideas which Cervantes shares. Calderón insisted upon the necessity of accepting fiction as if it were true, of acting in the theatre of the world because that is what God has created us for and has given us our role for: "What counts is to work well, and do good works,/ in case all this be true, because it is;/ and if it be not true, then to win friends/ to help us at the hour when we awaken."

Francisco Quevedo (1580–1645) held the world to be a terrifying nightmare in which all is chaos. Fortune takes delight in making sport of man. But man, according to the wise judgment of Jove, should have no complaint against a Fortune which distributes things indifferently and without malice. "Let each one receive whatsoever she may apportion him, since neither her scorn nor her favor is in itself evil; for the first being suffered and the second disdained, they are as useful one as the other." The moralist Baltazar Gracián (1601–1658) expresses himself on the subject in a series of negative metaphors: "Fountainhead of Deceptions"; "Charms of Falsehood"; and finally "Cave of Nothingness." Man is shipwrecked on the seas of illusion; but he can nevertheless reach the shores of the isles of immortality if he works and acts prudently and uses human means as though they were divine.

What is common to these Spaniards of the Baroque is that they proclaim the necessity of living, of acting. It is an affirmative credo which paradoxically contradicts the belief that all that surrounds us is illusion, dream, nothing. For despite this, one must live, and live according to certain rules. But the author of *Don Quixote* goes much farther. Besides, he mocks. And he discovers the great palliative of anxiety, laughter. But his laughter is not sarcastic, like Quevedo's: it is full of understanding and humanity. He works the miracle of saving untarnished all the values he is laughing at, including the very highest, the dignity of man, and of making his poor mad hero, Don Quixote, its paradigm.

It is clear that Cervantes, especially in Part II, propels his extraordinary pair between the two great metaphors of the Baroque: "all the World's a stage," and "life is but appearance, illusion, dream." Yet I would not subscribe unreservedly to the thesis that *Don Quixote* is typically Baroque, as are, for example, the works of Calderón, the *Dreams* of Quevedo, or the doctrine of disillusionment of the ascetic writers of seventeenth-century Spain. Many of Cervantes' themes are indubitably Baroque; the composition of the novel takes the form of a balance of contrasts; and even the language, with its characteristic juxtapositions, could be placed in the Baroque tradition. But the conceits and witticisms that abound in Quevedo and Gracián appear only seldom in Cervantes, and as for the moral philosophy that sustains the style, never. That moral philosophy affirmed the inanity of life as a fleeting transition between the cradle and the grave and it underlined the difference between the temporal and the eternal. Cervantes, on the contrary, suggested, when he did not actually make, an affirmation of the value of individual human existence hemmed in by the great ambiguity.

Perhaps we can now answer Ortega's second question: What is Cervantes laughing at? He is laughing at everything and he is laughing at nothing. He is laughing at the knight who lives by ideals and at the squire who dreams of isles and the life of ease. He is laughing, too, at those who laugh and mock. He is laughing especially at all pretention to certainty, at all who claim to know what is true, for, as he says somewhere, "a lie runs ever hard behind the truth," and man can never hope to possess it. Life is an ambiguity, a constant yes and no, an unending series of contradictions, among which he sees each individual existence hurtling toward sanctity and heroism, or toward stupidity and madness, each according to his circumstances.

The French critic Ramon Fernandez has said that "with the triple reaction of Montaigne, Shakespeare, and Cervantes to a world in which truth is not distinguished from image, we enter into the modern age of European literature." The statement would seem to be true, so long as we keep in mind that, for Cervantes at least, the image, as a creation of the human mind and of human intentions, is also part of the truth.

Cervantes' hero, like any individual who is a person and not an automaton, travels toward death among truths and images, among realities and appearances. The end is suggested from the beginning of Part II, where the meaning of the whole book is to be found: "I was born . . . to live dying," Don Quixote proclaims in a melancholy moment.

The final proof of the author's intentions remains to be given. In the shadow of death, when he is about to descend into another cave which has many similarities with that of Montesinos—the cave of the real secret, of the hereafter—our madman recovers his reason: "My judgment is now clear and free from the misty shadows of ignorance. . . . Congratulate me, good sirs, for I am Don Quixote de La Mancha no longer, but Alonso Quixano, called for my way of life the good" (935–936). He abjures his past in order to enter into the dream of eternity as a good Christian. In his disillusionment, he has discovered what is truly true, in accordance with the ideas of Baroque asceticism. He would like to dedicate himself now to the reading of books which will enlighten his soul. He prepares for a good death, cursing his follies.

The nature of the ambiguity might now seem to be clear, and indeed many critics have thus interpreted it. But, to me, it is not quite so simple. For in the midst of these solemn thoughts, the other half of Don Quixote interposes itself: his squire and his spiritual heir, the sensible Sancho, abruptly cries out:

> Oh, don't die, dear master! . . . take my advice and live many years. For the maddest thing a man can do in this life is to let himself die just like that, without anybody killing him, but just finished off by his own melancholy. Don't be lazy, look you, but get out of bed, and let's go out into the fields dressed as shepherds, as we decided to. Perhaps we shall find the lady Dulcinea behind some hedge, disenchanted . . . (937).

Later, when the visionary knight is already dead, "his niece ate, his housekeeper drank, and Sancho Panza [who had but lately been weeping] was cheerful" (938). The curtain falls. But life, the performance, the ambiguity, does not end, and everyone will go on living among truths and non-truths, according to his nature.

If there is any lesson to be learned from *Don Quixote*, it is that one must live as one can, with no other certainty than that which derives from one's self and from being true to one's destiny, whose ultimate purpose we shall never be able completely to understand. "A knight I was born, and a knight I shall die," Don Quixote had once declared. The sentiment was corroborated by his squire Sancho in an admirable passage, when the Duchess reproached him for his simplicity in following Don Quixote although he had long since been convinced of his master's madness:

> . . . that was my luck and my ill-luck. I can do nothing else; I have to follow him; we're of the same village; I've eaten his bread; I love him dearly; I'm grateful to him; he gave me his ass-colts; and, what is more, I'm faithful; and so it's impossible for anything to part us except the man with the pick and the shovel (687).

. . . To be faithful to one's self until death, throughout this ambiguous dream which is life, without ever being able to have any certainty outside that which constitutes one's own person. One must live one's life within its own circumstances, and he who thinks he possesses the secret of the world is as mad as he who believes he can transform it to suit his ravings. For perhaps it is neither possible nor good for man to have certainty—"don't go about looking for a cat with three legs" (178). Or, as Don Quixote says to the Duchess when she expresses doubt as to the existence of Dulcinea: "There is much to say on that score. . . . God knows whether Dulcinea exists on earth or no, or whether she is fantastic or not fantastic. These are not matters whose verification can be carried out to the full" (680).

Let us accept what is. How is it possible for us to laugh at this poor madman and this fool who accompanies him, when both of them can constantly give lessons in discretion, in goodness, and in honesty to those who mock them? Mockery becomes truth. Yes-and-no; it is a constant contradiction from the first word until the last.

The miracle of Cervantes is that he gave artistic life to this contradiction, and with the greatest naturalness, concealing or overcoming every artifice. He has thus been able to exemplify in his characters the most profound knowledge, stripped of all solemnity, pedantry, or aestheticism. He has succeeded in suggesting the most universal ideas and problems in the manner of one who is joking, who is telling an entertaining story. And for this he had to create—and it is his greatest feat—a style so apparently easy, simple, direct, and natural as to be capable of containing the ambiguity of life itself in a complete representation of humanity concentrated for a moment on the bare stage of the plain of La Mancha and the arid Spanish roads between Toboso and Barcelona.

The extraordinary thing about *Don Quixote* is the enormous variety of forms of life and of art which are represented within the simple scheme of the novel. That variety, combined with the contradictory character of the reality which the novel reflects, has made it possible for each epoch to interpret it in its own way, according to its own tastes and preferences, perhaps more so than any other work of similar stature. Thus today we can find our concerns reflected there, as the men of the seventeenth century, the Romantics and the Realists, found in it their respective problems and literary forms. That is why it is not out of bounds to speak of Cervantes' perspectivism. One might say also, and with good reason, that *Don Quixote* is above all an existentialist novel, although its existentialism is not of the anxious, pessimistic variety in vogue today. Like the modern existentialists, Cervantes feels that there can be no rational certainty. But he feels, and in this he is profoundly Spanish, that the lack of certainty does not remove from life the necessity implicit in it of its being lived with all its possibilities and in all its forms; that it can contain madness and sanity, rogue and saint, and all the varieties of human stupidity, but also, and let us never forget it, the noble aspirations of the spirit. That is why *Don Quixote* is anything except a pessimistic book. If absolute certainty is not attainable, if man's fate is to live in uncertainty, he can nevertheless give meaning to his life by remaining faithful to his individual self and without taking himself too seriously, or trying to impose his views on anyone else. Everyone, if he has enough imagination and faith, can live and create his own truth, his reason for being and existing in the grand ambiguity of life, the sum of all truth and all illusion, though it may cost him not a few defeats and falls, like those of the Knight of La Mancha. In him and in his faithful companion,

Cervantes created the lasting model for all genuine heroes of novels, whose essential characteristic, in contrast to the epic hero of antiquity, seems to be progressively to discover through experience and through the collision of illusion and reality which is an inescapable law of human life, a destiny which is in itself uncertain.

(Translated by Arthur Armstrong)

How to Read *The Sound and the Fury*

LEON EDEL

I

The opening pages of *The Sound and the Fury* take us into a bewildering world, as if we were traversing without pause the ages of man—and in the wrong order. The seasons merge and blur; disembodied voices speak to us; we participate in a choreography of the senses. Old sensations are evoked: the brightness of certain days, dancing sunlight and firelight, the smell of damp leaves, the hard, cold frostiness of winter. It is April, bright grass and green; and the next moment it is Christmas. There are caddies on a golf course, and there is a girl named Caddy. Benjy is thirty-three, but he is also three, or thirteen. Certain pages remind us of Joyce's artist-as-a-baby and the moocow coming down the road. The click of Benjy's sensory memory seems to be accompanied by the click of the linotype: long passages are given in alternation, first in roman type and then in italic. The editors of the Modern Library rightly feared that frustrated readers might hurl the book away in anger; but when they asked Faulkner to write an explicatory preface, he wrote an Appendix instead. So much for publishers who want artists to explain their art! If we read this Appendix, where one usually reads the preface, we enter the book so to speak by a back door. And Faulkner's genealogy of the Compson family only increases our confusion. But to explain technique and discuss the form of the novel is foreign to Faulkner and his intuitive art. Moreover, it would have involved telling the reader what he must, in the end, discover for himself. And what he must discover, above all, in such a book as *The Sound and the Fury*, is a new way of reading fiction.

A new way of reading fiction. For obviously, when the material is offered to the reader not in the old, neat, ordered, narrated form, packaged, so to speak, chapter by chapter, but comes to him higgledy-piggledy, it is at this scrambled story that he must look—unless he starts to refashion the book. Indeed such a thing has happened: two teachers in California, gathering round them their little flock of seminar students, did try to take the Benjy section of this novel apart and re-assemble it in a traditional way. They drew a map of the terrain; they numbered the "levels" of narration both alphabetically and numerically, and concluded that this section "was consciously constructed as a puzzle or a mystery story, or both combined." Otherwise, they said (with the assurance of the clockmaker looking at all the parts of his clock on the worktable), "otherwise it would seem impossible that the scattered and often brief units could be conclusively placed in the whole structure." A little sober thought suggests that the method of the clockmaker is not applicable here. Faulkner may have enjoyed mystifying the reader; novelists usually are supposed to do that; but he was not constructing a wilful puzzle. It is not in his nature, for one thing, to build labyrinths: in this he differs markedly from Joyce. Moreover, a close scrutiny of the text itself, and the author's design which it reveals, makes it amply clear that the "brief units" need not necessarily be consistent with the whole structure. We are concerned here, after all, with consciousness, and with the portrayal of consciousness;

moreover, it is the consciousness of an idiot, a man of thirty-three, whose faculties were arrested before he was three—if one can speak here of his having "faculties." And consciousness, even in persons of sanity, for all its brave attempts to find order in the world, is a great confusion of moments of experience, unsorted memories, an intricate organ-board of sensory impressions, with occasional areas of clarity and lucidity.

The first problem, therefore, which must be solved in contemplating this novel is how to cope with the scrambled materials. They *are* scrambled, beyond a doubt; and any hope of recovering whole eggs from the omelette must be set aside at once. Our new way of reading invites us to accept the material in its unsorted unchronological heterogeneous state: it stipulates that we must not try, like the energetic California teachers, to impose conventional order upon it; our obligation is rather to perceive it *in its disorder,* as Faulkner placed it before us.

The material of Benjy's consciousness is given to us, it is clear if we patiently read our text, in terms of his own perceptions—as they come to him. He smells things and people; he often experiences visual objects as if they were odors; he bellows when the unfamiliar crosses his path. We are dealing, in other words, with a three-year-old for whom the world is a safe and neat place only when the *known* things of existence are encountered; otherwise there is discomfort and often anxiety and terror. His world is the world of stimulus and response: and when certain things happen which have happened before, these melt together: each memory recalls another and enfolds it, probably to "trigger" still another. Benjy snags his clothes on the nail at the golf course in April, when he is with Luster: presently we learn that he snagged them also at some long-ago Christmastime when he was with Caddy. One happening piles upon the other. In the timeless world of Benjy, past and present become one, this moment, and no other. It is Christmas, it is Easter, they are all one. He is thirteen on one page and thirty-three on the next. It is possible to set down a rough chronology if one wishes: but to what purpose?

The story is supposed to come to us as it happens to Benjy. This is what Faulkner intended.

Indeed, when an author elects to tell us a story in this fashion, it would seem logical to follow him in his premises and not to construct new ones. In accepting the material in its scrambled state and seeking to understand it, we are invited by Faulkner to place ourselves within the angle of vision or perception of Benjy; we are involved with what critics of fiction like to call the *point of view*. We are maneuvered by the novelist into taking over all of Benjy's senses: not only do his eyes become our eyes, but his sense of smell is ours and his unique experience of the world around him is our experience for the duration of the book. We are, so to speak, on the inside of an idiot—looking out—even though we retain, at the same time, our own reason and our own awareness. A peculiar empathy is asked of us.

> The room went away, but I didn't hush, and the room came back and Dilsey came and sat on the bed, looking at me.

In Benjy's world rooms come to him and go away; the lawn approaches and he walks; the bowl comes up to his mouth and he eats. It is he who is the center of the universe. And when the horse and buggy drives to the left of the statue, instead of to the right, as he is accustomed, everything suddenly is not in its Benjy-ordered place: façade and cornice, doorway and window, post and tree, are completely reversed, they flow from right to left. Terror seizes him and he sets up a howl that reverberates through the square. Then, when Jason restores his usual world to him and drives the buggy to the right of the statue, buildings and objects resume their familiar aspect, and Benjy, clutching his broken narcissus, can subside into his staring quiet. Everything now flows from left to right, "each in its ordered place." [1]

[1] "We have attempted to work out why things should be flowing in that special direction and have failed to determine why," say the searchers for the egg-in-the-omelette, in their article in *American Literature* (Vol. XXIX; No. 4, January 1958), "unless [they add] the author is speaking in cryptic terms about his book itself and the smooth flow of type from left to right?"

"Each in its ordered place." Exegetes of the Benjy section have for years made much of this "order"—but the order which Faulkner invokes here is simply the compulsive idiot order of Benjy's world, which is a world of innocence and childishness, of someone who, as Faulkner has said, was mindless from birth, as blank and blind as the empty eyes of the Confederate soldier in the square in Jefferson, round which Luster had driven the horse and buggy the wrong way. The "order," in other words, is the order of Benjy's familiar blind world and we will never understand it if we introduce into it a new kind of order, the order of our own perceiving world.

What Faulkner has achieved in this section has been a significant change in novel-dimension. I refer not only to the technique, nor to the poetry: it is his assimilation, in a remarkably intuitive fashion, of the lesson of Joyce and of the French Symbolists: for he shows us how a novelist, or a poet, can use language to evoke more perceptions and feelings than unilinear prose has been hitherto accustomed to doing. We can perhaps make a useful analogy with what the impressionist painters and the abstractionists have achieved in our time. They have given us a new way of looking at impressions and abstractions, substituting their vision for the familiar representation of the things we see. With painting or sculpture, as Lessing long ago observed, we are capable of grasping visually—and continuing to observe—what is before our eyes. With words, as with music, we are involved in the double-process of remembering as well as grasping, since a page of printed symbols can never be a picture, or an image. It can only evoke images; it is a way of stimulating our own sensory apparatus.

The new way of reading, then, in prose fiction, is much more complex than the new ways of looking at plastic art. Not only must we take our bearings among the scrambled data, and experience them in terms of our own sensory world, while trying to imagine ourselves into the world of Benjy, but we must in the end deduce story and character, aspect and scene, from the information given us in this disordered fashion. That information has included the words spoken to the character by other characters, and the occasional aid given by the intrusive author. We have, in effect, been thrown bodily into scene and into narrative; the author has withdrawn, as in a play, to allow us to figure things out for ourselves. He has placed us neither in a labyrinth nor a puzzle: we are merely in an unfamiliar landscape, as if we had journeyed to a foreign country, and we are asked to use our eyes and ears and nose, indeed all our senses, so as to enable us to determine where we are.

Writing, word by word and sentence by sentence, yet no longer in the old neat chronological order of traditional novelists, Faulkner achieves in the Benjy section an unusual act of "extrapolation." Neither he nor anyone has ever been inside the consciousness of an idiot; somehow—perhaps by observation of the behavior of half-wits, by deduction and inference, and his own experience of states of childhood—the novelist has been able to create for us the illusion of what the idiot state might be, the helpless, baffled world of pleasant and unpleasant sounds and smells and color impressions, the calm and the terror which the idiot himself can articulate only in animal sound, for Benjy lives in a wordless world. It is Faulkner who supplies the words. He is the scribe-poet-interpreter. And with patience, and the use of our own sensory imagination, we can gradually begin to feel Benjy's world as we become aware that we are reading an exquisite bit of poetic imagining.

> Father went to the door and looked at us again. Then the dark came back, and he stood black in the door, and then the door turned black again. Caddy held me and I could hear us all, and the darkness, and something I could smell. And then I could see the windows, where the trees were buzzing. Then the dark began to go in smooth, bright shapes, like it always does, even when Caddy says that I have been asleep.

This *sounds* as if Benjy really comprehends. But it is Faulkner who is putting this world into words. A voice is given (as I have elsewhere observed) to the voiceless.

II

In the foregoing, we have by no means exhausted the complexity of the process involved in this new way of reading. We know that we are concerned with scrambled data and point of view. Step by step, as we determine what happens in accepting this unsorted, disarranged world and the given angle of vision, we are forced to recognize that certain other things are occurring. The language may be set down word-by-word and paragraph-by-paragraph, but Faulkner is busily creating an illusion of simultaneity: we are hearing, smelling, seeing *at the same time,* as in life. The effect he achieves resembles that of movie-montage where the rapidity of the images, and the sequence in which they come before the eyes, create a multiple activity of the senses and an illusion of things occurring at the same time. It is much simpler to do this with pictures than with words. The effect of simultaneity in a novel can be achieved only by the way in which words are grouped and verbal images juxtaposed. Flaubert did this originally in the celebrated fair scene in *Madame Bovary;* Joyce, emulating Flaubert, achieved certain spectacular effects by his verbal audacities in *Ulysses.*[2] Faulkner follows the example of these masters with extraordinary skill. The helpful voice chimes in at the moment Benjy watches the firelight or captures a smell. And the other simultaneities operate as a further scrambling process. We experience the sights and sounds and smells together, as they come to us in life, and not in the rearranged way of conventional prose fiction. At times the illusion, the nearness, that is, to experience, can be almost too close for comfort.

In the attempt to give us a sense of simultaneity, resides the author's awareness that he is working in a changed time-dimension. In fiction we have usually found ourselves in the past, listening to an historical narrative; we learn of something which

[2] As when he takes us with Stephen Dedalus to the beach and we look at the "ineluctable modality of the visible" while at the same time we hear the crunch of seashells under Stephen's boots.

occurred "once upon a time." The devices employed in *The Sound and the Fury* are designed, on the other hand, to convey the immediate: it is here, it is now. Time in such novels may be described as being vertical instead of horizontal. To be sure, Faulkner has dated each section and it is always a specific day in the past. His labels are those of clock and calendar time. Yet when we read, we have the illusion that we are inside his personages, thinking their thoughts, having their perceptual experiences, *at the very moment that these occur,* and these moments are moments of psychological or human time. We all know the difference between the clock and that individual timepiece which exists within us. The clock is, as Faulkner calls it, an "arbitrary dial." It is arbitrary because our inner clock is even more arbitrary: the latter can make a moment seem like a day, or a day a moment; it sometimes makes our winters seem long and our summers short. An hour spent in a traffic jam can seem longer than a whole day on a ski-slope. We can find endless examples of the difference between what our wristwatch tells us and how we feel about the passage of time on any given day. In *The Sound and the Fury,* Faulkner is concerned at every turn with this difference. And with keeping us in the present, a continuous present: we think the thoughts of the character at the moment that they emerge into his consciousness; and into this present come memories out of the past, which then fall back into the hidden part of the character where all the old impressions are gathered and stored, to be reawakened in some future present, often in an involuntary fashion, as Proust reawakened Combray within himself at the taste of the cake dipped in the cup of tea. We are in April 7, 1928, when Benjy and Luster are at the golf course, as the label at the beginning tells us; and Luster makes us aware of the immediate in his search for the twenty-five cent piece which will take him, if he finds it, to the circus. For Benjy, on the other hand, the date-label is meaningless. In his mindlessness, neither timepiece nor calendar exist; only that dumb period of childhood when we have our first primitive encounters with sensation, upon which a curtain of knowledge sooner or later descends—never to be fully raised again. The curtain is never dropped for Benjy. The only love and understanding he can discover is that of his sister Caddy and his relation to her is that of a dumb animal to a human.

In the second section of the novel we are with Benjy's brother at Harvard. It is June 2, 1910, eighteen years *before* the first section; and we follow Quentin Compson from the moment he awakens on the day he has decided to kill himself and tears the hands from his father's watch in an attempt to forget time. He cannot, however, escape its continuing tick. He wants to escape. For him his sister has been not an object of mute dependency, like Benjy, but an object of passion and his imaginings of incest are so terrifying that he must obliterate his guilt. We live with him through his private hell of the advancing hours; the shadows lengthen, and he finds his oblivion from the handless family timepiece in the river Charles.

Finally, in the third section, dated April 6, 1928 (the day *before* the Benjy section) we run the little rat-maze of the third brother's life, and experience the sordid and mean world of Jason Compson—up and down his three or four city blocks in Jefferson, Mississippi. For him, Caddy has always been an object of hatred. His world is a world of fury. His life is driven by a consuming rage.

Thus during three different days, the first two in Easter week of 1928 and the third almost two decades earlier, Faulkner has confined us (not trapped us, for at any moment the book can be hurled into a corner of the room and we can escape) in the consciousness of each of three members of the Compson family. Through them we have come to know the parents, the sister Caddy, who strangely holds them together in love and hate, her daughter Quentin (named after the Harvard student who died in 1910), and sundry other personages. We have come to know the family as three of its members experienced it and always through their individual perceptions. It is only in the fourth section, dated April 8, 1928 (the day *after* Benjy snagged himself beside the golf course), that the reader emerges from the inner vision of the three brothers into the light of external day. Instead of listening to the monologue of the personages, as we have been doing, we are listening to the voice of the narrator who has finally arrived upon the scene. At last we are concerned with objective, as distinct from subjective, reality: Dilsey's Easter morning.

III

In our daily lives we are confined—from beginning to end—within a single consciousness, our own. We can never find our way into the consciousness of another. We may obtain fitful glimpses into it, but that is all: we have only the barest sense of someone else's experience. We can never know the thoughts of another, save as he tells them to us, or as we deduce them. He may describe them in the sentence-by-sentence way in which we communicate with one another; or we may guess from the expression on his face or the gesture, or other tell-tale signs. But we seldom can be aware of more than this. It is impossible to capture fully the complex, chromatic, radiation of image, sound, fantasy, memory, association, sensation, within our own selves, let alone within another. We employ a loose and picturesque phrase, William James's metaphor, *stream of consciousness,* and remember that he described the attempt to capture some part of this swiftly flowing stream as "turning on the gaslight" to see what the darkness looks like. And yet in *The Sound and the Fury,* by Faulkner's method of telling his story, we have been taken into regions of experience not otherwise visitable: we have been inside the thought-flow or sentience of three persons other than ourselves, and one of them an idiot. It is all illusion, of course: but we have paid our visit through the empathy, artistic sensibility, imaginative construction, and the use of verbal imagery, with which Faulkner imparts life to his interior vision. This is the remarkable achievement of this book.

To accomplish this we have, to be sure, assumed a strenuous task but a challenging one: that challenge which Virginia Woolf expressed when she asked novelists to set down for us not mere "story," but the "shower of innumerable atoms," in our daily lives: to reveal the simultaneities of experience contained within any moment of a day, with peripheral awareness (as we listen, say, to what is being said to us, but suddenly are aware that we are hearing also the flutter of a window-blind and the low murmur of traffic, and several other voices, and the cough of a motor) even while we are attentively following the reasoning of the speaker, and evaluating what he is saying. If we are capable of this, we must recognize that we may be capable of as much or more in the very act of reading: that it is possible to deal *actively* with narrative material presented to us, rather than merely to listen to a story, as the old authors encouraged us to do. It is true that the richness of their voices and the witchery of their tale-telling quite sufficed. Faulkner's witchery consists in providing the ground and setting the stage for an unusual act of collaboration with the reader. He does a great deal of "arranging" and it requires unusual technical resources. His book is a supreme example of a work of art in which technique and substance are one.

The active reading which Faulkner asks of us involves, as I have suggested, our determining for ourselves what the people in this novel are like. The old novelists never left us in doubt; as each character came on the scene he was introduced, pictured, described; and then, in the light of this given knowledge, we could watch him act himself out. In the subjective novels of Joyce, Faulkner, Virginia Woolf, or in a novel such as H. D.'s *Palimpsest* or Conrad Aiken's *Blue Voyage*, the characters reveal themselves by their thoughts and by what they say; we learn to know them as we know people in our daily lives—through observation on our side, and self-revelation on theirs.

When we have read *The Sound and the Fury* we have thus been given a picture of the consciousness of three members of a family, and by this process a picture of the family itself—a declining family in a decaying South. But the picture is wholly subjective and seen in a series of mirrors. At the end, therefore, Faulkner decided to intervene to complete the story for us in such a manner as would make it possible for us to verify our observations. He accordingly gives us his account of Dilsey, the Negro housekeeper in the Compson family, and it is rendered wholly from the outside. We are never in her thoughts. We see her merely going about her work, knowing her affairs, and helping to link together the lost Southern family. Dilsey knows what time it is. The Negro in the South can ill afford to forget the clock. The Compson clock chimes a certain hour, but she always adds three hours to arrive at exact clock-time. It is indeed later than the Compsons know. Benjy's world, as we have seen, is timeless. Quentin's time is "out of joint." Jason is too busy rushing about, propelled by his rage, to have any true relation with the timed world in which he moves. Dilsey knows the time of the day and therefore she alone is truly in touch with the real and the immediate. In this way Faulkner symbolizes not only the decay of the Southern gentry, but the fantasy-world of the South for which only the past has had reality. Quentin indeed cannot go on living because what is real to him is a dream of incest in adolescence springing from love for his sister, which has no relation to his adult life. The burden of his imagined guilt springs, as Faulkner observes in his Appendix, from the fact that Quentin "loved not the idea of the incest which he could not commit, but some presbyterian concept of its eternal punishment: he, not God, could by that means cast himself and his sister both into hell, where he could guard her forever and keep her forevermore intact amid the eternal fires." Jason, on his side, is a clumsy, bumbling, sordid and cunning individual, living by his wits, but always so cunning as to outwit himself. He is the embodiment of a kind of instinctual evil.

Innocence, guilt, evil—each Compson brother in his own way symbolizes the moral world of Southern Calvinism; but he also symbolizes the way in which family tension and social tension mould an individual. The slowly crumbling gentry, selling their land and cultivating a gentility no longer in tune with their world, can end only by divesting themselves of their patrimony and destroying themselves, either literally, as Quentin did, or through a gradual process of self-undermining, as in the case of Jason. The whining helpless mother, the charming but futile resignedly-philosophical father, are the victims of a stagnation they cannot overcome. Their idiot son, in his eerie world, epitomizes the futility of all their lives. *The Sound and the Fury* as a novel expresses all the mortal frustration and questioning of Shakespeare's mighty soliloquy which gives the book its title. It is indeed a tale—a tale of great intensity—told by an idiot, and in the end signifying nothing, motion without purpose. The sound of Benjy and the fury of Jason, the innocence, guilt, and evil in this family and in their private world, is set by Faulkner into Easter week, where all is expiated and washed clean, and man may hope for some resurrection and recovery. In this world Dilsey alone has her task and her bearings. She alone knows how to speak to Jason, and to soothe Benjy, and she will take the idiot to the Easter service believing that some Divine illumination will enter his uncomprehending body and penetrate his timeless being.

Such a novel is well described as a Symbolist novel, because the entire work is made to symbolize for us a vision of the South: in giving us the imaged memories and the tortured inner life of a family Faulkner has given us the tortured inner life of a society which this family represents; and in using language evocatively, Faulkner has been able to make that language convey intensities of feeling and states of consciousness which words can never begin to *describe*. The world of William Faulkner in this novel is not a world of reason or intelligence or rational order. Faulkner proclaims neither order nor disorder. Certainly the "order" of Benjy is hardly rational. The novelist's concern is with feeling. The very title implies it. The sound is anguish and the fury is a manifestation of a kind of primordial animal rage: and this book is about the anguish of the innocent and the fury of the frustrated and the damned. These are the larger meanings we can read in this fiction when we have mastered its difficulties. And it is only through such complexities that Faulkner conveys to us the chaos of the Compson world in a fashion closer to human experience than any mere recital of the Compson's family history. We come to know it because we have been confronted by intensities of feeling rather than recitals of fact.

IV

There exists a short story about the Compson family, written some time after the novel, which throws a retrospective light on the book. It is called "That Evening Sun Go Down" and it is a tale of childish innocence playing itself out on the margin of adult terror. In this story we see Quentin, Jason, and Caddy when they are children. Their personalities are formed: little Quentin is the uncertain and sentient being we will meet at Harvard; Caddy is compassion and empathy; and Jason, a mere toddler, is already a little tale-telling rat. The story deals with Nancy, who has been temporarily replacing Dilsey in the Compson kitchen. She has been raped by a white man and is to have a child. Her husband has vowed that he will kill her and leave her body in the ditch near their hut. As each day's sun goes down Nancy fears the worst; and in the episode narrated in the tale she entices the children to her hut and plays games with them to fend off the terrible moment when she must face the night and the prospect of her doom. In the midst of this the children go about their games aware that Nancy acts strangely, but preoccupied with their world and the assertion of their diminutive egos. They are oblivious of the adult drama, and we never know whether Nancy was killed and left in a ditch for the vultures, as she feared. The story is concerned with the children, and with her terror, not her death. But in *The Sound and the Fury* there are several allusions to Nancy's bones lying in that ditch. We learn, however, that Roskus shot a crippled mare named Nancy on that spot and that the children thought the vultures had stripped the horse's flesh from the bones. The egg-and-omelette critics have accused Faulkner of creating "additional obfuscation" by having two Nancies, one horse and one woman. This again represents a failure to grasp the very nature of this book. In life, animals and humans often have the same names; and what Faulkner is recording is the process of association: that ditch and the name Nancy (whether of woman or horse) are forever linked in the memories of the Compsons with death and decay and with that night of Nancy's strange terror. This is particularly significant in that the common memory of the Compson children in *The Sound and the Fury* centers around what occurred in the house at the time of their grandmother's death. The short story, although wholly separate from the novel, embodies within it the novel's central theme: in both tale and novel Faulkner is seeking to show childhood innocence, unaware of an adult world which it will come to know in its own measured time: the world of suffering and death, and bigotry and hatred and atrophy—and sound and fury.

Faulkner has himself illuminated this theme in one of the most ingratiating portions of the literary seminar conducted by him in Japan in 1955. The transcript of the Nagano [3] meetings contains his reply to questions about his intention in *The Sound and the Fury* and the difficulty of the Benjy passages. This reply does not wholly help us with the novel's technical problems, which can be resolved only by attentive reading; but it has value as a post-factum account by an author of his creative thinking.

The Sound and the Fury, he tells us, began as a short story, a story without a plot, of some children being sent away from the house during the grandmother's funeral. They were too young to be told of death, and they saw things only "incidentally to the childish games they were playing." Faulkner continues:

[3] *Faulkner at Nagano* (Tokyo, 1956), pp. 102 *et seq.*

> . . . and then the idea struck me to see how much more I could have got out of the idea of the blind, self-centeredness of innocence, typified by children, if one of those children had been truly innocent, that is, an idiot. So the idiot was born and then I became interested in the relationship of the idiot to the world that he was in but would never be able to cope with and just where could he get the tenderness, the help, to shield him in his innocence . . . And so the character of his sister began to emerge, then the brother, who, that Jason, (who to me represented complete evil. He's the most vicious character in my opinion I ever thought of). . . . Then it needs the protagonist, someone to tell the story, so Quentin appeared. By that time I found out I couldn't possibly tell that in a short story. And so I told the idiot's experience of that day, and that was incomprehensible, even I could not have told what was going on then, so I had to write another chapter. Then I decided to let Quentin tell his version of that same day, or that same occasion, so he told it. Then there had to be the counterpoint, which was the other brother, Jason. By that time it was completely confusing. I knew that it was not anywhere near finished and then I had to write another section from the outside with an outsider, which was the writer, to tell what had happened on that particular day [or occasion]. And that's how the book grew. That is, I wrote that same story four times. None of them were right, but I had anguished so much that I could not throw any of it away and start over, so I printed it in the four sections. That was not a deliberate *tour de force* at all, the book just grew that way. That I was still trying to tell one story which moved me very much and each time I failed, but I had put so much anguish into it that I couldn't throw it away, like the mother that had four bad children, that she would have been better off if they all had been eliminated, but she couldn't relinquish any of them. And that's the reason I have the most tenderness for that book, because it failed four times.

The book just grew that way. We could have no finer statement than this of Faulkner's intuition in his *anguishing* to convey the state of innocence of childhood. He ultimately achieved what he was looking for: long after the novel he wrote his short story of the children and their unawareness in "That Evening Sun Go Down." But the search for that story led him to the writing of a novel he rightfully cherishes above his other works, even though he clothes it with the garments of "failure." It is failure if the reader reads it as the California teachers did, under the assumption that fictional narrative is fixed for all time and may never be scrambled or experimented with: that all fiction must be chronological and also have clarity for the lowest intelligence reading the book. We must turn our backs on such approaches to literature and recognize that as a novel of subjectivity, and as a novel of "point of view," *The Sound and the Fury* is perhaps the most remarkable of contemporary American novels. By its technical resources and symbolic strength Faulkner was enabled to perform in a work of art a great act of compassion—and of humanity.

Oresteia:

Dramatic Form and Vision

JOHN GASSNER

COMPARATIVE STUDIES may serve different purposes. It is my present intention to illustrate the close relationship that exists in a play between "dramatic form" and the "vision" or point of view it embodies. We might describe this relationship as the connection that can be found, without especial straining for subtlety or thoroughness, between the inner form of a dramatic work and its manifest content of ideas and attitudes. Even the term "inner form" is intended here in a limited sense—that of the choice, treatment, and arrangement of the events and other dramatic elements—in contrast to the external form determined by the conventions of a period that distinguish a classic Greek tragedy, for example, from a Japanese Noh play, an Elizabethan drama, or a modern realistic play.

I have selected three well-known treatments of a famous dramatic theme—the Oresteian, which culminates first in the murder of the Homeric king Agamemnon by his unfaithful wife Clytemnestra and, many years later, in the vengeance of his children—

the high point of which is the murder of the queen by her son Orestes. Many writers from Aeschylus and Sophocles to Giraudoux and Sartre have treated the theme with significant differences. In order to limit the inquiry as narrowly as possible, I have selected three extant works from the same period. Three distinctly different treatments were made, by Aeschylus, Sophocles, Euripides, expressing markedly divergent points of view and producing more or less different species of dramatic literature—the epic, the tragic, and the nontragic realistic—within the compass of the same dramatic and theatrical conventions. The plays are the *Oresteia* trilogy by Aeschylus and the *Electra* plays by Sophocles and Euripides.

A few introductory remarks are in order. The plays of Sophocles and Euripides appeared almost a half century after the production of Aeschylus' trilogy in 458 B.C. They were produced during the declining years of the Athenian democracy, whereas the Oresteian trilogy was written when Athens was the supreme Greek state, enjoyed unrivaled prestige, and was without question the one important outpost of Western civilization. Since the Greek tragedians were expected to deal exclusively with legendary and mythical matter, there was no question of imitation when Sophocles and Euripides took up the same theme. Moreover, they drew upon the same storehouse of literary material, which even for the Greeks of the fifth century was not always strictly distinguishable from history. The events are set in dimly dated Homeric times and concern a famous dynasty.

A vaguely defined curse rests upon the family in question; a strong feeling of fate (*moira*) hovers over its history of multiplying error, infatuation, and crime (*ate*) which leads, in one way or another, to retribution (*nemesis*). Tantalus, the mythical ancestor, had offended the gods by offering them the flesh of his own child: he was cast into the infernal regions of Tartarus, there to be tortured with thirst and hunger. His son Pelops, after successfully wooing the daughter of a king by winning a chariot race, ungratefully threw the charioteer who had helped him gain the victory into the sea. The dying Myrtilus cursed Pelops and his race for this treachery, and his curse was said to be responsible for the subsequent misfortunes of the family. The evil disposition, or hereditary guilt, was compounded in the next generation when the two brothers Atreus and Thyestes became mortal enemies: Thyestes had seduced Atreus' wife. Pretending to forgive Thyestes and inviting him to a feast of reconciliation, Atreus slew two of his brother's children and fed him their flesh. Escaping with another child, Aegisthus, Thyestes nursed a vengeance that attained fruition in the next generation when Aegisthus seduced Clytemnestra, the wife of his cousin Agamemnon. Agamemnon had sacrificed his daughter Iphigenia to enable the Greek expedition under his command to set sail for Troy; in revenge for this action, as well as in furtherance of her adulterous lust, Clytemnestra, with the help of Aegisthus, murders Agamemnon upon his return from the war. The family vendetta is carried yet one step further when Agamemnon's son Orestes, upon arriving at manhood, murders Aegisthus.

I

Aeschylus gives the legendary story a full-scale treatment, whereas his successors deal solely with the vengeance of Orestes and his sister Electra. He devotes separate plays to the murder of Agamemnon, the death of Clytemnestra at the hands of her son Orestes, and the sufferings and final release of Orestes. This treatment constitutes the trilogy, and only a trilogy could have projected his ruling idea, which concerns the development of private and public morality in the Greek world. As in most of his other extant work, Aeschylus is here concerned with the evolution of beliefs, principles, and institutions.

The first part of the trilogy, the *Agamemnon,* is on the simplest level a domestic tragedy, but it introduces the main theme and carries it forward. Vengeance is a prime *motif* since Aegisthus, who has won Clytemnestra and helps her in her project of murdering Agamemnon, is simply carrying on his father's (Thyestes') feud with Agamemnon's father (Atreus). There is a further parallel between the past conflict and the present: just as Thyestes seduced his brother Atreus' wife, so his son Aegisthus has possessed himself of the wife of Atreus' son, Agamemnon. Moreover, Clytemnestra claims to have turned against her husband only after his sacrifice of their daughter Iphigenia to his military ambitions. To justify her calculated murder of her husband, she maintains that she is simply avenging that death. Other possible motivations are subordinated, if not indeed suppressed, in the *Agamemnon.* Although love or sexual attraction for Aegisthus and aversion to Agamemnon must have played a part in her adulterous conduct, the romantic interest a modern reader might expect is simply nonexistent in Aeschylus' play. Although she resents Agamemnon's bringing home a concubine and kills her after slaying Agamemnon, jealousy is not presented as a motive in the betrayal and murder of the king. Clytemnestra's adultery, hinted at by the Watchman who appears in the Prologue and by the Chorus early in the play, had occurred long before Agamemnon's return home. Her private complexities and inner struggles do not concern the playwright either; it is enough for his purpose to portray her as strong-willed and resourceful—and unscrupulous. If Clytemnestra is to be considered an instrument of justice and of Zeus, then (as so often happens) a criminal character has been chosen to serve their ends and she is in no moral sense vindicated. Aeschylus does not ignore the compounding of evil by human beings and the punishment of crime by agents of Justice (*dikê*) who incriminate themselves by their very actions in the service of divine purpose.

Criminal psychology does not concern Aeschylus beyond the service that the particular character renders to the governing ideas of his work. The returning Agamemnon, too, is given only as much character-dimension as is needed for the drama's argument, and no more. He evinces a certain arrogance in bringing his concubine home and casually telling Clytemnestra to take good care of her, although we should note that concubinage and the bringing home of a captive woman from a successfully waged war do not seem the least unusual to the Chorus. Later he exhibits a conventional fear of committing the sin of pride (*hybris*) lest he offend the jealous gods, but he allows Clytemnestra to play on his vanity and inveigle him into walking into the palace on a purple carpet. He questions her about Aegisthus, for he has heard the news that his cousin has been received by her as a guest. But he does not press the question, because Clytemnestra distracts him; and here it is especially apparent that Aeschylus is disinclined to turn his play into a tragedy of jealousy. We go on, instead, to the main action—to the murder of Agamemnon—and to the prophetic allusions of the captive priestess-princess Cassandra, who recalls the long chain of guilt antecedent to the impending murder and foretells the continuance of retribution in the sorry history of the "house of Atreus." Cassandra, in accordance with a curse laid on her by the god Apollo, is unable to prevent the murder and, therefore, steeling herself to the inevitability of her own death, she goes into the palace, which she had previously refused to enter at Clytemnestra's urging. In killing her, Clytemnestra adds another sin to her criminal record, just as Agamemnon had enlarged his own by taking the virgin Trojan priestess for his mistress.

In one respect or another we are always made aware of an old disposition to evil that renews itself in the present action of the characters; we are never allowed to forget that even the historic, heroic actions that form the background of the immediate action have been steeped in guilt. Through the choral odes that bring the past into the present in a manner no less dramatic than poetic, we observe the sinfulness of both the abduction of Helen and the ensuing war led by Agamemnon. The latter is actually, according to the Chorus, punished *in advance* for the crimes he will commit in the conquest of Troy, since he is "compelled" before sailing to Troy to sacrifice his daughter. The war itself is strongly disapproved by the Chorus; it was apparently regarded as a mistake from the beginning. Not only does evil beget evil; it gives rise to complex questions as to the hereditary nature of sinfulness and the circuitous course of punishment, which itself engages evil agents (such as Agamemnon and Clytemnestra) as its executants.

The vendetta theme of private or tribal justice is clearly presented as the hurdle to be overcome by humanity in its progress toward civilization. At the end of the play, Clytemnestra, standing over the corpses of Agamemnon and Cassandra, claims the deed for her own and urges the justice of her action in accordance with the principles of private vengeance. Aegisthus, who arrives on the scene after the murder and is roundly denounced by the Elders as a lecher and coward, justifies himself by crisply reciting the details of the feud between his father and Agamemnon's father. Ignoring his love for Clytemnestra (and we must assume that he loves her), he, too, stresses only the claims of justice—that is, the privilege of the blood feud. The Elders do not actually know how to refute this claim, for as yet there is no alternative to the primitive right of retribution, which will now, of course, pass on to the murdered Agamemnon's next of kin.

How then can this endless round of vengeance come to a halt? In the second play of the trilogy, *The Libation Bearers* (*Choephoroi*), the blood feud is carried to its ultimate horror. If the obligation of taking revenge devolves upon the next of kin, Agamemnon's son, Orestes, now grown to manhood, must kill his own mother. Apollo himself, at his Delphic shrine, orders Orestes to carry primitive law to this dreadful but inevitable conclusion. Moreover, there is no honorable or even safe alternative as yet for the unfortunate son. The case becomes clear when presented in terms of primitive belief: if he had refused to avenge his father, he would have been subject to punishment by the Furies arising automatically from his father's blood. Orestes is, as it were, trapped between his father's and his mother's Furies.

We first encounter Orestes as a character in literature when Homer refers to him a number of times in the *Odyssey* as a heroic young man who performed a meritorious deed. There are no dire consequences for Orestes in this early report; on the contrary,

Pallas Athena holds him up as an example to Telemachus, Odysseus' son: "Haven't you heard what a great name Orestes made for himself in the world, the fine young fellow, when he killed the traitor Aegisthus who had murdered his famous father?" (Book I). And in Book III, the wise Nestor includes Clytemnestra's fate in his report, saying, "When Orestes killed him [Aegisthus], he gave a funeral feast to the people over his hateful mother and Aegisthus the coward." [1] Moreover, Sophocles, long after the Homeric period, also elected to present the matricide without following it with retribution. Can we doubt that Aeschylus was bent upon undermining the primitive institution of the vendetta by devoting the second play of his trilogy to a major crisis in moral history?

Despite the static quality of its opening, *The Libation Bearers* makes an extremely moving experience out of the crisis. Seven years have elapsed since the murder of Agamemnon when Orestes returns. Retribution comes even though Clytemnestra took the primitive precaution of mutilating the king's corpse before burying it, apparently in order to render her victim's spirit powerless. And vengeance falls even though, warned by a frightening dream that she has given birth to a viper that draws blood from her breast, she sends her servants with libations for the tomb of Agamemnon in the hope of placating his angry ghost. Aeschylus spares no effort to make the rule of Clytemnestra and Aegisthus abominable. Clytemnestra's daughter Electra, who had entrusted young Orestes to relatives in the distant city of Phocis some time before Agamemnon's death, has now been degraded by Aegisthus and Clytemnestra. The common people have apparently been oppressed, and the foreign serving-women or slaves who make up the Chorus of *The Libation Bearers* are so resentful that they have become the natural allies of Agamemnon's children.

Electra and the slave women pray for vengeance against their oppressors; and another round of prayers in the form of a great choral lyric follows once Orestes has revealed himself to his sister.

[1] Rouse translation, except for a slight change in the spelling of "Aegisthus" in order to keep it uniform in the present essay.

He also reveals that he has been commanded by Apollo's oracle to perform the deed, and he prays for guidance to Zeus, the supreme god. At what we could consider the cost of much delay, the groundwork is laid for the vengeance that falls swiftly when it finally falls: Aegisthus and Clytemnestra are slain. Most of the delay is caused by the preliminaries to this action, which apparently must give every possible sanction for Orestes' deed—a god has ordered it; supplications have been made at the murdered king's tomb, where his spirit is supposed to reside; the avengers themselves have been greatly wronged; there is collective approval from the Chorus; and as the Chorus reminds us, "It is but Law that when the red drops have been spilled upon the ground they cry aloud for fresh blood" (Lattimore's translation). Also, the young avengers—the new agents of the old law—are a breed different from Clytemnestra and Aegisthus: they are pure of heart. And Orestes is by no means an unfeeling killer when he confronts his mother—as he cries out "What shall I do?" he has to be strengthened in his resolve by his hitherto silent companion Pylades, who warns him to heed the oracle and not to make an enemy of the gods.

Nevertheless the consequences are dreadful, and it is plain that Aeschylus would have it so. He prepares for the impact of his indictment of the old order of justice by raising the scene of the murder to an acute pitch of human drama. The excitement produced by the rhapsodic manner in which the avengers work themselves up to their task is followed by a scene which, although hardly sympathetic to Clytemnestra, stresses the appeal she makes to her long-absent son. Her appeal is so strong that it weakens his resolution until he is reminded to obey the god. As if this were not enough, the outrageousness of the deed is climaxed by the conclusion. Orestes justifies himself effectively before the populace in another highly dramatic scene, when he displays the robe in which Clytemnestra had cunningly entangled Agamemnon preparatory to slaying him. But his reasoning is of no avail; Orestes' mind begins to wander, terror overcomes him, and he runs away pursued by the Furies, the vengeful spirits whom he alone notices. The result of his unnatural act is madness, human nature having been brought to the breaking point by the inflexible operation of the law of the vendetta. Significantly enough, Electra has no role in this last scene despite her importance in the earlier action, nor does she appear in the last play. For all her sufferings, she is not directly involved in the evolutionary drama of *dikê*. It is Orestes in his public role of avenger, not Electra in her private role of sufferer, who is important to the central question of Aeschylus' trilogy.

Its resolution is the theme of *The Eumenides,* the concluding play, which now introduces some interesting changes. For one thing, the Furies are entirely objectified. They are first seen in all their repulsiveness in the sanctuary of the Delphic Oracle as they surround Orestes, who has taken shelter at the altar. They have been put to sleep by Apollo, who sends Orestes away to Athens under the guidance of his brother-god Hermes. We next see them awakened by the enraged ghost of Clytemnestra, who expects to be avenged by them even against her own son. On finding themselves robbed of their prey, the Furies protest bitterly that the upstart Olympian god has deprived them, the elder powers, of their rights. Apollo drives them out of his temple scornfully; but, undeterred by his contempt and claiming their ancient prerogatives, they run off in pursuit of Orestes, intent upon tracing him by his mother's blood. Apollo, in turn, declares that he will continue to assist *his suppliant,*—whence the shift in emphasis in the trilogy. What was up to this point a conflict between human beings has now been transformed into a conflict between supernatural forces; or, in the familiar terms of Hegelian dialectics, into "a conflict of two rights." The moral position of the old goddesses of retribution, the Furies, is clear enough: they are avenging a horrible, unnatural crime. As for Apollo's position, although it is morally admissible in a patriarchal society and especially in a world in which revenge by the nearest of kin is lawful, it has its weaknesses—not only because its consequence has been the horrendous crime of matricide but also because the Furies have every right to make themselves the mother's avenger if vengeance for the father is justified.

In the next part of the play, Apollo will argue quite explicitly for a patriarchal point of view, but it is doubtful that he could convince any audience, ancient or modern, with his contention that the mother does not create the child but merely carries it. Aeschylus obviously sees little merit in Apollo's argument: it is not successfully pleaded and it fails to win an acquittal for Orestes. Moreover, Apollo's last speech to the Furies in the first part of *The Eumenides* implies a shift in his own position. He does not exculpate Orestes; he declares, instead, that he intends to assist and try to save a *suppliant*. Apollo's words are important not simply because it is noble for a god to help those who appeal to him for protection but also because it is only such an act of grace—in Christian terms, the mercy of God, and in the *Oresteia*, as we shall see, Pallas Athena's vote—that can redeem a guilty man.

In the *Oresteia*, however, redemption is not a religious mystery and Pallas Athena's mercy is tendered only after she has instituted the legal machinery of a trial, presumably the very first, in Athens. The trial that takes place is political, in being an act of the "*polis*," or Greek city-state. Due process of law, as administered by the specially created court of the Areopagus, takes the place of private retribution. The great event in the final play of the trilogy is the institutionalization of *dikê* as a function of the *polis*. And this comes to pass in the City of Reason, the city of Athens presided over by the goddess of wisdom and the paragon of reasonableness, a virtue she displays abundantly throughout the second half of *The Eumenides*. Mercy, reason, and reasonableness form, as it were, a triad which ensures social evolution. It is both reasonable and merciful to keep retribution within bounds. Where reason prevails, retribution ceases to be blind, automatic, and without term.

Time is an important factor in the resolution of the *Oresteia*, and the last play of the trilogy, *The Eumenides,* is that rare thing, a Greek tragedy that violates the so-called unity of place. The scene shifts from Delphi to Athens; considerable time is supposed to elapse before Orestes succeeds in reaching Athens. The development of a new type of justice—the new *dikê* of the *polis*—is a historical process, and it is the product of "knowledge won by suffering," as the elders of Argos in the *Agamemnon* put it. The passage of time, moreover, is associated with simultaneous processes of punishment by the matricide's conscience, which cannot in all decency be brief, and of the healing or the recovery of reason, which cannot be effected in a moment. When Apollo put the Furies to sleep and told Orestes to make his escape, he did not tell him that the way to "Pallas' citadel," or, if you will, the City of Reason, was going to be easy or short. The "repulsive goddesses," says Apollo, "will track you down . . . and your driven feet forever pound the earth, on across the main water and the circle-washed cities" (Lattimore translation). Declaring, "I have been beaten and been taught," Orestes later tells Pallas Athena that he has come to request her favor "blunted at last, and worn and battered on the outland habitations and the beaten ways of men" (Lattimore). Moreover, after the performance of lustral rites at Apollo's hearth, he is no longer an unpurged suppliant whose very presence brought pollution, and he is confident that the stain of blood on his hand is fading. Facing the Furies who have caught up with him in Athens, he proves himself once again sound of mind by his freedom of spirit and by the rationality of his behavior.

Nevertheless, the playwright's prime concern here is not with the individual but with the generations of men. Athena's course consists of *two* significant actions: she establishes a court for trying cases of homicide, apparently for the first time in history, and she casts a vote for acquittal, which proves decisive when the votes of the jury, made up of the worthiest citizens of Athens, are counted. In the first instance, she takes the administration of justice out of the hands of individuals, families, and tribes when she establishes the court on the Hill of Ares (the Areopagus) that shall henceforth try all cases of homicide in Athens. This is tantamount to creating the true City of Man, a viable political union of rival interests. Significantly enough, one of the "moral teachings" of the play is its explicit denunciation of *civil war*, which is followed by the assurance that Athens shall forever escape this calamity.

Athena's second decision is, as previously noted, truly an act of grace. The reason she gives for favoring Orestes at the trial is of course casuistical—having been born of no mother but of the brain of Zeus, she confesses herself a partisan of the male against the female. Such reasoning may have had considerably more force in fifth-century Athens than in twentieth-century New York, since the Athenians associated their success as a political unit with the substitution of a hard-won patriarchal society for a primitive matriarchal one. Nevertheless Athena's vote transcends any narrow sexual bias in the context of the humanistic character of the trilogy; what is important is that with her vote for an acquittal the patron goddess of Athens puts an end to blind vindictiveness and primitive retribution.

One thing remains: what to do with the Furies. A determination must be made after Orestes departs for Argos to assume the throne of Agamemnon. The reasonable Athena resorts to her great gift of persuasion, the civilized alternative to violence which is an indispensable instrument of the democratic *polis*. She succeeds in pacifying the Furies by offering them a hillside sanctuary in the city and converts them into spirits of benevolence—henceforth they will be known no longer as the "Erinyes" (Furies) but as the "Eumenides": the Kindly Ones. Their new benevolence, however, emanates from their old function as punitive goddesses; they are the representatives of conscience, without which civic order and civilization can be neither attained nor preserved. *The Eumenides* concludes with a torchlight procession of citizens conducting the mollified goddesses to their sacred habitation in the *polis*. Aeschylus' dialectical thinking ends in a "synthesis" of the conflicting forces represented by the bright, essentially amoral, young Olympian gods (especially by Apollo) and the primitively exacting earth-goddesses of retribution.

So ends the *Oresteian* trilogy of Aeschylus, one of the profoundest and most majestic works of literature. The more we ponder it the profounder it grows, and the grander it also grows; the visual components of stage action and spectacle—the varied and striking use of ceremonial acts, processions, choral recitation, and song—may well stagger the imagination of anyone but an expert in Wagnerian opera. We have said almost nothing about the theatrical qualities of the trilogy, though they are in fact commensurate with the impressive governing idea of the work.

There is no loss of dramatic power in the work as a result of Aeschylus' moral and philosophical intention. When the trilogy ceases to be a drama of persons and becomes a conflict of forces the action rises to new peaks of suspense and intensity. This is evident in the passages of moral fervor throughout the trilogy. It is also apparent in *The Eumenides,* first in the argument between the Furies and Apollo at Delphi, then in the suspense-laden trial, and finally in the scenes in which Athena placates the enraged Furies after Orestes' acquittal.

Each of the three plays, we must observe further, is a complete dramatic work and has a unique character, revealed in part by its structure. The *Agamemnon* is a great lyrical tragedy in which a crucial action in the present is enveloped in dramatic recitatives that fuse the past, present, and future. *The Libation Bearers* verges on character drama in the last two scenes, when Orestes kills his mother and is overcome with terror. *The Eumenides* veers toward the earliest form of Greek drama, in which the Chorus was the main actor.

In the *Agamemnon,* the Chorus of the Argive Elders, although it speaks with superb excitement, is primarily reflective; it fails to act while Agamemnon is being slain and makes a vain show of action only toward the end, when Aegisthus arrives to gloat over the death of the king. In *The Libation Bearers,* the Chorus of foreign slave women, sympathetic to Electra, is privy to the design against Clytemnestra and even prevails upon the old Nurse to mislead Aegisthus so that he will come to the palace unattended; the action, however, belongs not to the Chorus, but to an individual—to Orestes. In *The Eumenides* the action, except for a few minutes when Orestes speaks, is carried by the Chorus of Furies, with which Apollo and Athena have to contend; Athena's moral importance is great indeed, but even her role is dramatically secondary, because the Chorus is the aggressor. There is also a second choral group in *The Eumenides,* consisting of the Athenian citizens who act as judges at the trial and later make up the torchlight procession that accompanies the Furies to their shrine.

The Eumenides culminates as a fundamentally collective drama relating the private fate of the house of Atreus to the larger realities of moral law. The "people" have been on the stage in the first two parts of the trilogy; and the "people" and the gods take over entirely in the third play. A work that Richmond Lattimore has aptly called "a grand parable of progress" could have no other effect than that of a collective issue and action, and this was bound to be especially evident in a work permeated by an imagination that is not only moral and political, but, be it noted, *religious.*

The Oresteia is the work of a poet and thinker steeped in the mystery cults of classical antiquity. The trilogy is anagogical, so to speak, although in a fundamentally Greek sense, in which human reason and divine mystery—the "City of Man" and the "City of God"—are neither polarized nor even distinguished sharply. It is hard to avoid the thought that whereas the *Agamemnon* and *The Libation Bearers* are human tragedies, the trilogy as a whole is a sort of Divine Comedy. The outcome is a happy one and it bespeaks the operations of some dimly discernible divine plan associated with the Father-God Zeus. Apollo and the other gods, including of course the Athenian goddess of wisdom, are partial realizations of this All-God Zeus, who is the underlying creative and moral force of the world. Moreover, since it is an *evolving* force, Apollo may be described as a manifestation of Zeus at *one* evolutionary stage and Pallas Athena at *another, more advanced,* stage. The Furies distinguish themselves from the Olympian gods, but their conflict is not with Zeus himself. Everything that happens seems to occur through his will or with his permission as part of a divine plan identifiable perhaps with a spiritualized concept of the Destiny which, according to the Greeks, ruled gods and men alike. Zeus is fundamentally undefinable by men. "Zeus, whatever he be, if this name suits him" (Lattimore translation) is how he is invoked by the Chorus of Elders in the *Agamemnon.* But he reveals himself partially again and again, in specific events and in the overall course of *dikê;* present at the decisive trial of Orestes, says Athena, is "the luminous evidence of Zeus."

II

The distinctly narrower vision in the Oresteian dramas of Aeschylus' immediate successors, Sophocles and Euripides, produces narrower plays (just as the later treatments, including O'Neill's *Mourning Becomes Electra* and Sartre's *The Flies,* are narrower). Sophocles attains dramatic perfection in his *Electra* at the cost of a marked limitation of scope, imagination, and perhaps even sensibility. He seems to have gone out of his way to avoid moral complexities and theological commitments. He seems impervious to the outrageous character of Orestes' deed, so that the work invites the charge of moral callousness on the author's part. (An attempt has been made to explain this seeming detachment in regard to the murder on the grounds that Sophocles had set out to write an archaic heroic drama. Another explanation maintains that he presented his *Electra* as a corrective to Euripides' version, presumably written before Sophocles' play. These explanations, whether right or wrong, can have no particular bearing on our analysis, which is concerned solely with the effect of the play.) Euripides, on the other hand, unmistakably wants us to be outraged by the murder of Clytemnestra, but except for one speech that informs us that a common man can possess noble traits, he virtually exhausts his moral and intellectual (though not his dramatic) content with his explicit denunciation of the murder. There is no particular profundity in the work, although it can be praised for possessing other qualities. Sophocles gives us a heroic, Euripides an antiheroic drama. Sophocles creates character-drama, whereas Euripides, carrying realism to naturalistic extremes, offers pathology and melodrama.

When Orestes in *The Libation Bearers* addresses the people of Argos in self-justification, he declares brokenly "I have won; but my victory is soiled, and has no pride" (Lattimore's translation). Then he perceives the Furies and, crying out to the Chorus "You cannot see them, but I see them," he runs, presumably mad, out of the city he should be ruling. Sophocles' Orestes, on the contrary, is not at all overwhelmed with a sense of defilement and guilt. There are simply no postmortems, recriminations, or complications in Sophocles' *Electra.* Evil has been put down and the city freed from its tyrants; the play is, in effect, a heroic drama of liberation. (It is perhaps noteworthy that in a later treatment of Orestes' deed as an act of liberation, in Sartre's existentialist drama *The Flies,* Orestes is also in full control of his faculties and devoid of feelings of guilt; the liberation from the sense of guilt is, in fact, a principal theme and the resolution of Sartre's play.) The subject of *dikê* presents no particular problem to this younger representative of the post-Aeschylean "Enlightenment," the Periclean Age: Sophocles takes the rise of the well-ordered *polis* as a matter of course rather than as a hard-won victory for civilization. His sole concern appears to be with the individuals who became involved in an historic situation that taxed their human resources and tested their spirit or virtue (their *aretê*). "*Electra*" is the best possible name for this play since it is concerned chiefly with her character. Her suffering is of long standing, her situation is the desperate one, her endurance is tested in the extreme, and she is contrasted with more easy-going, opportunistic, humanity in the person of a sister, Chrysothemis, who does not appear in the plays of Aeschylus and Euripides. Sophocles invented this unheroic character apparently to help create a tragically isolated *heroic* Electra. His tragic vision focuses on the question of how integrity can be maintained and at what price.

Electra's sense of wrong disintegrates her essential womanliness, turning her into the virago of the later part of the play who stands guard outside the palace while her brother, Orestes, kills her mother inside; who calls out to him to strike her again, and then urges him to despatch Aegisthus, too, and throw his body to the dogs. The most tragic element in the play lies *within* the character of Electra, where nobility (*aretê*) and femininity are in conflict. That the womanliness is there is carefully established in the so-called recognition scene between Electra and Orestes, to which Sophocles assigns more weight than either Aeschylus or Euripides. Electra's happiness at recovering a long-absent brother, her clinging to him at the risk of endangering their plot, and the total humanization of this scene contrast vividly with what the embittered woman has been throughout the long years of waiting and what she will be soon again in the moment of vengeance. The dramatic design of the work is masterly in its simplicity as a result of Sophocles' dramatic tact and simplification of issues. The only complexity is complexity of character. Sophocles' play is not epic but individual tragedy; moral and religious, let alone metaphysical, problems have no place in it.

His *Electra* ends with a sense that a serious wrong has been righted, and with only a natural recoil by the son and daughter to save the action from melodrama. Serenity of a considerable degree is secured for the young Orestes, who arrives at dawn (a dawn full of singing birds) in the company of a wise tutor, the Paidagogos. Orestes is in all respects the composed and confident young aristocrat, and this is particularly evident in his superior bearing toward Aegisthus before he kills him. Electra is a more troubled character indeed, but she remains well within the bounds of sanity even when desperate. She manifests nobility rather than madness or some obsessional neurosis when she resolves to enact vengeance with her own hands on being told that Orestes is dead.

Sophocles, who limits the action to strictly human dimensions (he never brings the gods on stage, for instance, and avoids all supernatural manifestations), also limits the extent of his protagonists' disturbance before, during, and after the deed. If his Electra suffers from "tragic excess," it is an excess of spirit. Her so-called tragic flaw is that she cannot live at peace with her father's murderers, cannot accept her mother's sensuality, and cannot endure seeing Aegisthus sitting on her father's throne and wearing her father's royal robes. She readily admits to the sympathetic Chorus of Mycenean women that she has let life slip by her and that she has invited the harsh treatment she has received. Unable to accept their advice to live moderately, "neither forgetting nor hating too much," she can only affirm her sense of obligation not to rest until she has avenged her father's death. She is plainly modeled after Sophocles' earlier heroine Antigone, to whom he also assigned an unheroic foil in the person of a compromising sister (Ismene).

III

Electra, we may conclude, is (like Antigone and Oedipus) one more character Sophocles has forced to the limit of endurance in order to dignify humanity rather than to degrade or reprove it. He has transmuted tragic excess into tragic victory in this tragedy with a nontragic conclusion. His *Electra* reflects all that was both splendid and contracted about the culture associated with the short-lived Periclean period.

Sophocles' younger contemporary, Euripides, was one of the most persistent of the challengers of Athenian society when it started to deteriorate, and his readiness to question conventional values and expose heroic characters to realistic scrutiny is abundantly evident in his *Electra.* The contrast with Sophocles' tragedy is all the more apparent because Euripides too makes Electra the central character, though he gives Orestes a greater share in her anguish. Like Aeschylus, he totally deplores the murder of Clytemnestra. But his dramatic focus is no less, and perhaps even more, contracted than Sophocles'. Euripides' treatment of the Oresteian theme does not take any evolutionary view of humanity's moral history and institutions. He dwells upon the religious problem in attributing to Apollo's orders the murder of Clytemnestra by her children, and is concerned only with showing what crimes are committed in the name of religion. There is no prophetic inspiration in his treatment of the moral impasse that arises when a son is required to execute his mother as his father's slayer. In the *deus ex machina* epilogue of Euripides' *Electra* one may find, it is true, a wisp of Aeschylean evolutionary thought. Since the young gods Castor and Pollux, who come down to earth to assist Electra and Orestes in their blackest hour, deplore not only the murder but also Apollo's part in the crime, we may conclude that a more humane dispensation is somehow taking hold in heaven. But Euripides is not engaged by this subject; he does not develop it.

Euripides concerns himself, as does Sophocles, with the *agents* of the action; and toward the action itself he brings neither religious nor political vision, but a distinctly disdainful and anti-heroic (as it were, "debunking") attitude. His approach is comparable to that of a liberal newspaper reporter covering an especially repulsive murder case, writing a realistic and somewhat lurid account—except that Euripides happens to be a dramatist of genius writing poetic drama for a theatre that has formal and ritualistic features. And this of course makes quite a difference; it is the difference between poetic drama (even when deliberately stripped of poetry so far as the murderers are concerned) and yellow journalism. Realism—within the framework of formal and poetic drama—dominates Euripides' *Electra;* it is visible in every significant aspect of the work up to the epilogue. The speeches are unelevated, though at the same time so shaped to fit the characters and their feelings as not to remain on a dead level of insensibility or mediocrity. Euripides also draws a sharp contrast between a commoner, the small farmer Electra was forced to marry, and the royal children of Agamemnon. Electra's husband respects her person and is the superior of any aristocrat in the play. As to the details of the murder, they are made especially repulsive: they reflect no glory whatever on the avengers. In this respect, Euripides works on us largely as a naturalistic writer, establishing an inglorious Orestes and a self-pitying, neurotic Electra, who does not exhibit a single attractive feature.

Euripides' Orestes, unlike his Sophoclean counterpart, is a nervous youth whose heroism is extremely doubtful. As if bent upon degrading him altogether, Euripides assigns him a rather dastardly and repulsive action. Aegisthus, playing the gracious host, has invited Orestes to partake of a sacrifice of a bull to the Nymphs. He offers him a knife or cleaver with which to perform the ceremony. As Aegisthus bends over the sacrificial animal in order to examine the entrails, Orestes assaults him with his butcher's instrument, breaking his spine and leaving him to die in agony. Aegisthus is hacked down like an animal in the midst of religious observances, and this rather sacrilegious action stands in sharp contrast to Orestes' dignified conduct in Sophocles' *Electra*. As for Euripides' Electra, her role is no less contemptible. Euripides actually evinces sympathy not for her, as Sophocles does, but for her victim, Clytemnestra. Electra traps her mother, who is portrayed as a remorseful middle-aged woman, by sending word that she has given birth to a child and calling upon Clytemnestra to perform the necessary rites. At the end, Electra is further implicated in the murder by Euripides. Not only has she bullied the hesitant Orestes into killing his mother but, as we now learn, she actually pushed Orestes' sword toward her mother's breast when he drew back from the deed. That both Electra and Orestes should later be appalled at what they have done is completely believable.

Moses Hadas does not speak too strongly for our modern sensibility when he calls Electra "a self-pitying slattern obsessed with sex" and Orestes "a timorous young ruffian." [2] Euripides' Electra and Orestes are caught in a web of destiny—or, if you prefer, of circumstances and "conditioning"—worse than any that Clytemnestra wove for their father, but one cannot be stirred by these characters. Their situation, which is melancholy at the start of the play, remains depressing throughout. The action no doubt becomes dramatically intensified but it is hardly elevated as Electra reveals her pathology and Orestes his inadequacy for heroic action. A great deal of powerful *drama* but very little *tragedy* results from Euripides' naturalistic undercutting of the old Oresteian saga. There is much that is pathetic or subtragic in this essentially modern play. Indeed, we may well wonder whether such a work agrees with the formalistic nature of classic tragedy; whether, as it were, the "inner form" of the play harmonizes with its external choral, and more or less lyrical, structure. I am not disturbed by this disharmony, which actually contributes to the tension of the work, because here the "inner form" —the weave of the style, the characterizations, and the incidents —powerfully realizes Euripides' evident intention of showing what conventional heroism amounts to when observed closely.

One structural feature may be cited as additional evidence of Euripides' procedure in the service of his objective: In the sequence of events in *The Libation Bearers*, Aegisthus is killed *before* Clytemnestra: Aeschylus forces the appalling act of matricide into the foreground. Sophocles reverses the sequence, so that the action of his play comes to a climax with the slaying of the tyrannical usurper of the throne, Aegisthus, by the legitimate heir, an act that the Athenian audience could approve unreservedly. Euripides adopts the sequence followed by Aeschylus and con-

[2] *Ten Plays by Euripides,* Bantam Books, pp. x–xi.

cludes with the death of Clytemnestra. After the climactic matricide, the epilogue, with its condemnation of Apollo and its compassion for misguided humanity, is entirely appropriate.

In spite of critical animadversions against Euripides—the most famous and fatuous appear in August Wilhelm Schlegel's *Lectures on Dramatic Art and Literature*—we may wonder indeed who works with greater skill toward a particular end by means of tone, characterization, and structure, Sophocles or Euripides. Concerning Sophocles' *Electra,* the British scholar A. J. A. Waldock exclaims with admiration, "How a horror can be sapped of its strength, how a crime can be so drained of its power to shock that we are left in full sympathy with the criminals, how an offence against nature can be smothered and we can be led to accept an atrocity—this is the technical lesson of the *Electra.*" True enough! But how horror can be magnified, how a crime can be made repugnant even when committed in the name of justice, so that we are left utterly dismayed by the experience—this is the technical lesson of Euripides' *Electra.*

Euripides also reflects an attitude expressive of his times, which happened to be Sophocles' times as well. His play is not a mere *tour de force* of realistic denigration, but a radical writer's protest against vengefulness and hysteria in the midst of the deteriorating morale of Athens. Both Sophocles and Euripides produced their Electra plays toward the end of the twenty-seven-year-long Peloponnesian War, a war that Athens was to lose once and for all in 404 B.C., at about the time when both playwrights died, the older in the fullness of years and honors in Athens, the younger in self-imposed and apparently expedient exile in distant Macedonia. Sophocles, who had reached manhood in the high noon of Athenian culture under the leadership of Pericles, could draw upon reserves of humanistic faith, confidence, and balance. Euripides had no such reserves to draw upon, and the heroic tradition of the Greeks lost much of its glamor for him when the war between Athens and Sparta was senselessly protracted. (We know that Euripides became a member of the Athenian peace party that endeavored to put an end to the conflict.) The older man celebrated traditional heroism, the younger looked askance at it; the former achieved exultation, the latter pathos. Aristotle, we may recall, considered Euripides "the most tragic of poets on the stage"; he was certainly the master of pathos. Euripides achieved it in his *Electra,* as in several other plays, despite his realistic characterizations; it was for humanity as a whole that he had compassion—for the guilt-laden Clytemnestra as well as her appalling children. Like his scepticism, his critical spirit, and his fondness for disputation, Euripides' "humanitarian" and "liberal" sentiments belong to the twilight of the Athenian state, not to its high noon. But his less "classic" and more "modern" disposition attained authority and integrity in the plays, such as his *Electra,* in which he successfully translated pity into passion and argument into human experience.

An effective agreement between means and ends, moreover, is apparent in the *Electra* even if one adopts a radically different interpretation, which holds that "there is no focus of sympathy" left in the play, "only a pervasive bad taste which leads to disgust with all forms of violence," and that Euripides simply demonstrates here that "justice can be as ugly as crime," or that his sole, if brilliantly accomplished, objective has been to alienate us from the conventionally regarded "right side." [3] It is hard to believe, besides, that the playwright who invites this alternate interpretation has not actually introduced humanitarian and liberal principles into his work and demonstrated compassion, no matter how bleakly, for bedevilled humanity. Even the *deus ex machina* epilogue strengthens agreement between form and content, for it is only proper that the young gods be brought onstage to deplore the conduct that an older god sanctioned and to mitigate its consequences for the misguided avengers. Having first resorted to naturalism in depicting gross human action, Euripides has gone

[3] Emily Townsend Vermeule, "Introduction to *Electra,*" *The Complete Greek Tragedies,* ed. David Grene and Richmond Lattimore (University of Chicago Press, 1959), IV, pp. 390–94.

on to challenge its religious basis with a suitable epiphany; both the naturalistic and poetic elements serve the same end—the work is "structured," as it were, by its ruling idea. Dramatic form and dramatic vision, then, are interdependent in Euripides' drama just as they are in the parallel tragedies by Aeschylus and Sophocles.

Rebirth of a Classic: *Celestina*

STEPHEN GILMAN

IN THE LAST few years, the *Celestina*, a fifteenth-century Spanish dialogue novel, has shown signs of undergoing an international revival. There have been three new translations in English,[1] a revision in five acts of the classic Mabbe rendering, as well as new translations in French, German, and Russian. Scholars in a number of countries and languages have shown increased interest in the text, the author, and the artistry, and performances have been attempted with increasing frequency, particularly in French. The *Celestina* has long been a classic, second only to the *Quixote*, in its own language, but in view of its return to the international exchange of literary values, it is appropriate to estimate anew the nature of its importance. Perhaps, this may also illuminate from within something of the *Celestina*'s appeal to our time.

A provisional spectrograph of the importance of the *Celestina* divides it into three areas or aspects. It is, in the first place, a

[1] By Mack Singleton, (Madison, Wis., 1958), L. B. Simpson, (Berkeley, Cal., 1955), and P. Hartnell, (London, 1959).

central landmark in the history of Western literature. In it we can see, as perhaps in no other work, not merely how the novel and drama began but also what they had to overcome in order to begin. At the frontier between the didactic and allegorical forms of the Middle Ages and the modern genres, the *Celestina* is a triumph of literary discovery as startling and in its own way as important as any geographical or technological discovery. To think of its author—a man not so much forgotten as never yet remembered—as a literary Gutenberg or Columbus may seem farfetched, but that is exactly what he is. In the second place, the *Celestina* is a masterpiece in its own right, which is to say that it evaluates human life in a way that is lastingly significant. Its vision of man at home, in society, and in the universe, of the individual in perilous encounter with himself, with others, and with the dimensions of time and space, has increased in relevance over the centuries. Finally, in the area of imaginative creation, it presents not so much a literary experience as direct immersion in an acid bath of life. The over-used word of book reviewers, "unforgettable," is misleading for the *Celestina.* Indelible would be better. Knowing Celestina herself as intimately as the reader comes to know her is something more than unsettling; the shock waves can penetrate far beneath the surface of mind and habit.

When the first reader opened to the first page of the *Celestina* in 1499 (or possibly the year before) [2] and began to read the summary put at the beginning by the printers (these "arguments" were the jacket blurbs of the time),[3] he was probably somewhat disappointed. Here was a commonplace plot of love and seduction, one used in the Middle Ages and based on types inherited

[2] The first known edition is dated 1499, and there has been much speculation about lost earlier editions. Internal evidence recently uncovered indicates 1497 as the earliest possible date of composition.

[3] The first printers, the author himself tells us, added a summary of the whole as individual summaries for each act—the standard practice of the time for the printing of dialogue.

from Roman comedy. Calisto, a hot-blooded young gentleman, badly advised by his corrupt servants, employs Celestina, a professional go-between, to seduce Melibea, whom he had met by accident and with whom he had fallen violently in love. Gentleman, servants, and go-between all succeed in doing what they want to do. And then, by way of retribution for their immorality and imprudence, they all meet sudden and violent deaths. So far there was nothing to surprise that first reader, yet when he began to leaf through his new purchase, he was surely disconcerted. The outward sign of the inner uniqueness and originality of the *Celestina* was its twenty-one acts of unbroken dialogue. A book looking like this had never been printed or seen before. The familiar story had been strangely reshaped. And it is with an examination of this reshaping into dialogue that we may best begin.

Dialogue had, of course, been used before. Boethius in his *Consolations* had left a model of didactic and exemplary dialogue which had been imitated by countless mediaeval writers. In the face of anarchy, the anarchical surging forth of raw human life, the Middle Ages took refuge in order and doctrine. And debates in dialogue—between philosophy and the self, water and wine, the soul and the body, and so many others—were favorite devices for explaining order and teaching doctrine. Whatever illusion of speech the dialogue could give served (like the brilliant colors of church windows) as a pleasant coating around a less tasty core of moral instruction. Even when mediaeval readers encountered such a delightful and often playfully cynical playwright as Terence, they worked hard to convince themselves of his strict moral intentions, as is demonstrated by the elaborately annotated editions which were printed over and over again in the time of the *Celestina*. As for the mystery and miracle plays, their speeches were mostly spoken doctrine embedded in traditional characterizations and rôles. There were a few exceptions, of course. There were moments of tense face-to-face encounter in some of the epic poems and, above all, in a few of the most moving episodes of the *Divine Comedy*.[4] But before the *Celestina* there had been no systematic use of dialogue for its own sake, nothing resembling the two major dialogue forms today so taken for granted, the drama and the novel. Mediaeval writers, in other words, could not produce, or were not interested in producing, sustained interchange between individuals each speaking to the other from his own point of view and from within his own life.[5]

The *Celestina* in one stroke changed all this. After the *Celestina,* literature was to be of a sort more familiar to us; before, it was much more alien. Not that all dialogue as we know it today stems from the *Celestina,* but that in its pages dialogue was perfected and used systematically. For the first time in centuries a work had been written in which an "I" from inside himself speaks to a "you" whom he hopes to sway in thought, action, or feeling. For the first time we can hear [6] lives impinging on each other, living together and struggling with each other in sustained oral interchange. Once this is achieved, of course, the creation of full characters (as distinct from types who serve only to entertain, to reach and make the story-teller's point) becomes a possibility. Even more, that mysterious living independence, that capacity for breaking away from the author, which is the privilege of liter-

[4] Characteristically Dante's dialogue is based on a static situation, to which the principal speaker is irrevocably chained and which he explains *after the fact.* The *Celestina*'s dialogue, on the other hand, moves with the "action" of a series of constantly changing situations. In this sense it is much more dramatic than narrative.

[5] The *Decameron* and the *Libro de buen amor* (the *Conde Lucanor* is an even more extreme example) show a relative lack of interest in dialogue despite their utilization of spoken language. The narrator's rôle is paramount. This is much less true of the Chaucer of the *Troilus,* but, taken as a whole and excepting the oral epics, I believe my generalization to be valid.

[6] The first "editor" of the text (a humanist named Alonso de Proaza) appended to the 1500 edition some closing stanzas. In them, among other things, he indicates that the *Celestina* was written for reading aloud with appropriate mimicry. The work represents a moment of transition in reading habits. The introduction of the printing press was also an introduction to a new world of silent reading. But the *Celestina* had not yet fully entered this world and often needs actual declamation for its full comprehension.

ature's great character creations is aided by mastery of dialogue. Specifically the *Celestina* furnished Cervantes with the dialogue tradition he used in the *Don Quixote,* the first true novel precisely because of its conversations between knight and squire. It lay also—just as decisively—at the headwaters of the drama, providing a flow of dialogue which was still running strong in Spanish theaters when Lope de Vega (a fervent admirer of the *Celestina*) perfected his definitive formula. Writers, it is more fashionable to admit in our day than it was in that of our grandparents, don't create out of whole cloth. They work with and in a tradition, and the *Celestina* is a central root of the European tradition of dialogue.[7]

As I suggested previously, it is interesting to note that dialogue was for the first time consciously discovered and explored during the same decade that America was given the same treatment. This may or may not be coincidental, but it does at least indicate another suggestive coincidence. When Columbus came from Italy to Spain, as is well known, he Hispanicized himself and severed all connections with his past. He even gave up his own language for another. It was an indication of the shift of the creative center of history at the end of the fifteenth century from Italy to Spain, where it was to rest until it swerved northward in the second half of the sixteenth. And in a similar way, the new interest in the inner life of the individual, so audible in the dialogue of the *Celestina,* seems to have emigrated from Italy to Spain. Preoccupation with inwardness, self-conscious exploration of one's own psyche, found its first concentrated literary expression in Petrarch's lyrics and its first extensive exposition (after Saint Augustine) in his Latin treatises. It was these latter that

[7] Such claims are, of course, dangerous, but "defenders" of Spanish literature see the novel both in France and England as stemming from the *Don Quixote.* With respect to the theater, they point with pride to the Spanish origins of *Le Menteur* and *Le Cid.* Surely the French would have mastered dialogue without these Spanish examples (just as the English developed their own theater), but these are nonetheless facts of literary history.

influenced the *Celestina* so strongly. In them Petrarch, using and renovating the educational dialogue of his time, revives the Stoic notion of man's inwardness besieged from without by both temptations and misfortunes. Man is a subject, "sub-jected," that is to say the target of all the slings and arrows that are launched at it—the *-jected* is, of course, from *jactare*—from the objective world. We are most immediately and vividly familiar with this sense of consciousness as a state of warfare (besieged consciousness) from our experience of Shakespeare. And if the Italians think of it in Petrarchist terms, the French know it from Montaigne. The *Celestina* is very different from the works of any of the three (it is not tragic, not lyrical, and certainly not essayistic) but, nonetheless, the same Neo-Stoicism is present in almost its every speech and scene. Its version of Stoic warfare is primarily verbal, an incessant oral aggression of one life against another both in argument and appeal. This is the built-in advantage of the *Celestina*. Precisely because collision of lives in dialogue is all that happens in it, it can show consciousness at work without killing or freezing it, not only in depth but at length as well.

What was found in the *Celestina*'s initial sounding of this queer and enormous place? The question is best answered by reading the text, but it is my business here to give at least a schematic reply. Luis Vives, the Spanish philosopher, humanist, and professor at Oxford (while in semi-exile), says in his *De anima et vita* (1538):

> It does not now concern us to know *what* the soul is but rather *how* it is and what are its operations . . . and it is impossible to define in an absolute way everything relative to its operations, because they make themselves manifest to our intelligence little by little, in bits and pieces.[8]

This is precisely the way the *Celestina* presents its souls. It is unconcerned with the "what" of their virtues or vices. Instead it pursues the "how," the change of each soul as it adapts to ever

[8] From *Liber primis* (p. 39, first edition).

new circumstances, its dynamic advance and retreat in spoken warfare with other souls. Through dialogue we see the soul alive in time, changing from one vital situation to another, remembering backwards, proposing forwards, and constantly forgetting—as life goes on.[9]

The formal model for the dialogue of the *Celestina* was Roman comedy, a genre which was being "reborn"—that is to say, being re-read in a somewhat inappropriate way—in the latter half of the fifteenth century. One can sense the presence of Terence and to a less extent of Plautus in both the names and the plot. But whereas their comedies used dialogue for amusing interchange and verbal display of theatrical types, the *Celestina,* in the tradition of Petrarch, converts it into a means for the expression of inwardness. Let us put sources and their combination into parentheses and sum matters up in this way: by focussing intensely not on the "I" in a state of immobile isolation but on the "I" talking to the "you," engaged in a process of conscious verbal living. The *Celestina* gave the first major literary answer to Luis Vives' fearfully simple question, "How does life work?" Each of its sentences is devoted to only one thing: communication of the transitory inwardness of the moment. We are used to this now. Ever since the *Celestina,* this has been the New World of the greatest author-explorers, that is to say, the novelists and dramatists of after centuries. But then, we also are used to living in America.[10]

[9] Unique in its age is the *Celestina's* systematic attention to remembering and forgetting. Events are witnessed and told again from memory with imaginary embellishment; reminiscence from the long past is observed clinically; and the forgetfulness of old age is contrasted with the significant mental lapses of younger minds (e.g., Alisa's forgetting of Celestina in Act IV).

[10] The reader should not be fooled by the unfamiliar and seemingly artificial rhetoric of some of the speeches. Rojas knew how to use it for dialogue purposes. Just as Shakespeare preserved and used the "high astounding terms" of Marlowe's monologue in his own intense dialogue, so too features of past language remain in the *Celestina.* But read rightly—with awareness of what each character has to reveal and wants to convey—the text contains hardly a word (after the apprenticeship of Act I is completed) that does not find its *raison d'être* in the new art of dialogue.

What kind of a man undertook this literary expedition into the unknown? It would be unsuitable to discuss here the incredibly complex arguments regarding the *Celestina's* authorship. In any case, more and more of us are coming to believe what is stated in the prologue material: [11] that the long first act was by an unknown writer and that the other twenty were completed in two successive stages by a law student at Salamanca. His name, Fernando de Rojas, was revealed in a strange and awkward way, in the initial letters of verses appended to the second edition (1500). But why this acrostic and why the caution and hesitancy which an acrostic would seem to imply? Here we are helped by certain documents turned up in recent years, especially the record of the trial of Rojas' father-in-law before the Inquisition. The author of the *Celestina* belonged to that numerous class of converted Jews which was so intellectually and creatively active throughout the whole of the sixteenth century and so frequently victims of the Inquisition. Only in recent years [12] have we begun to realize fully the enormous contribution to Spanish culture made by these forced converts. Not only were there Rojas and that same Luis Vives whose remarks on the "soul" are significant for the *Celestina,* but also a whole roster of the greatest writers, jurists, theologians, humanists, and even Saints. It is not tactful to mention this in today's Spain, but new documents have appeared establishing beyond doubt that St. Teresa of Avila herself was of a distinguished family of "conversos." [13]

[11] I refer to the introductory "letter to a friend" and verses, first included in the sixteen-act edition of 1500, as well as the prologue which was added to the twenty-one-act edition of 1502.

[12] The first person to see the full significance of the converted Jews to Spain's peculiar history was Américo Castro in his epoch-making *España en su historia* (Buenos Aires, 1948). Later discoveries have abundantly confirmed his insight. An English translation in revised form, *The Structure of Spanish History* (Princeton, N. J.), appeared in 1954. An expanded Spanish edition is in preparation.

[13] This is not said with the idea of provoking doubts as to the saint's saintliness. Saint Teresa remains herself, but this new knowledge of her background helps explain aspects of her fundamental differences with the society of her time (however much she came to be accepted by it afterwards). As for race, many "con-

The point to be made in the case of Rojas is a simple one. He belonged not to a class but to a caste [14] which was at once a functioning element of society (it would be very close to the truth to say *the* functioning element) and at the same time was excluded from it, looked upon with suspicion and dislike. He and others of his kind were at once in and out, at once fully aware of everything that went on in the social structure—hypocrisies, intrigues, power mechanisms, corruptions—yet, at the same time, removed from them, at an intellectual distance. Moreover, having abandoned one faith and not yet (in many cases) fully gained another, the "converso" found it hard to share the structure of beliefs which a fully accepted member of society could use to render harmless all awareness of social injustice or failure. He lived on the margin: he observed from without; he had a perspective and a capacity for cynical evaluation of motives that were unlikely in persons born to full membership in their society.

I would, in other words, relate the caustic irony of the *Celestina* and its refusal to accept face values to the ambiguous "converso" existence of its author. On one level the work can be thought of as a kind of confidential exposé, an "inside" story. As a worthy forerunner of the novel, it shows us what went on inside a Spanish town—or as Fielding phrased it, scandal from the "holes and corners of the world." But this is not all. Rojas' mental aggressiveness and axiological nihilism went so far as to deny everything that everyone around him believed was important, even the great epic event of his age, that climax to Spain's mediaeval history, the conquest of Granada. All is subject to time, all is eroded or swept away in its flow. As Sempronio says:

---

versos" were only remotely Jewish. It is much more a question of a variety of acute and often fecund consciousness of self in relation to society than of inherited characteristics or even of an ideological climate. In this sense the Inquisition, representing mass opinion, may be thought of as an instrument for provoking individual self-awareness in addition to repressing ideas and eliminating lineages.

[14] This fundamental distinction was introduced by Castro.

> Good and evil, prosperity and adversity, glory and grief, all lose the strength they start out with. Wondrous events awaited with high hopes are forgotten as soon as they're over with. Every day we see new things happen or hear about them, and then we pass them by and leave them behind. Time makes them small, even makes them doubtful. Would you be so awestruck if you were told there had been an earthquake or something like that, that you would not soon forget it? I mean things like the river is frozen over, the blind man can see again, your father just died, a lightning bolt has struck, Granada has been taken, the king is coming today, he has won a battle against the Turks, the bridge has been washed away, so and so has become a bishop, Pedro has been robbed, Inés has hanged herself, Cristóbal got drunk. You can't tell me that three days later or the second time he hears about it, anyone will still be amazed. Everything is like that; everything passes on in the same way; everything is forgotten; everything stays behind as we go on.[15]

The precaution of the acrostic and this half-gleeful elegy to the fragility of meaning combine in a single pattern, the pattern formed or set by thc consciousness of a man exiled in his own country.

But time does not merely pass externally in the *Celestina.* It is not satisfied with washing away with its days and years all that men care about in the world around them. It also flows ceaselessly within the soul. Rojas does not bring to his examination of his characters' minds any sort of psychological theory or method. Rather, through dialogue, he allows the characters themselves to betray ironically the contrast between their pretenses and rationalizations and what we judge from our reading to be the truth. He has a perverse and resentful urge to touch root motivations and, beneath them that subsoil of the soul, time. His characters pretend to fixed purposes and virtues; they attempt fixed characterizations for each other's benefit. But as Luis Vives knew, they really have no essence, no "whatness" at all. They exist in a

[15] Translation by Edmund L. King; others are my own.

series of states changing and shifting all along the temporal course of the dialogue and for each of which the question "how?" is the only appropriate one. Thus each character has a succession not of masks but of masked faces, selves and projected selves, each dependent on the situation of the moment. The most obvious example is Calisto, who thinks of himself as an ideal, true lover and yet has no scruples in using or even in worshipping Celestina, "the oldest whore of them all who has rubbed her back in the dirt of every brothel in the land." In general the characters can go from good to bad, from virtuous to vicious, and back again, without being troubled by the inconsistency. Like the things they hold to be important, they are true creatures of time.

Rojas was, thus, a man engaged in a corrosive assessment of life at every level. Yet he was not a satirist—at least in terms of John Middleton Murry's standard definition, as condemning "society by reference to an ideal." [16] For just as Rojas had no base for his life, so his "criticism" had no ideal basis. He was an anatomist engaged in an autopsy of human life, or, perhaps it would be better to say, a vivisectionist probing man in his innermost intimacy, in his social self-projection, and ultimately in his helpless relation to the cosmos.

What I have just done is to paraphrase what I believe to be the theme of the *Celestina*. Ostensibly I have tried to relate its peculiar presentation of man in the world to a possible biography of the presenter, Fernando de Rojas. But we know so little about him that such a relationship is imaginary. I believe in what I have said about Rojas, and at the same time I recognize that, instead of explaining the book in terms of the author's life (as does the biographical critic), I have reversed the usual direction and imagined the life as the book suggests it might have been. As a result, all that has been said about the life of Fernando de Rojas

[16] *The Problem of Style* (London, 1922). Murry points out that if the writer of comedy chastises deviation from a social norm, the satirist makes more radical demands. But Rojas, proposing neither norm nor ideal, goes beyond this venture at classification.

as a converted Jew can be considered as a kind of illustrative device for getting at the theme of the *Celestina.* In any delineation of a thematic vision, the critic can be helped a great deal by reconstructing (or even imagining) the existence and outlook of the viewer. On this level, biographical criticism cannot be dispensed with. But it is now time to abandon this device and plunge directly into the *Celestina,* the only place where the theme and vision are important or can really be said to exist.

The basic situation of life in the *Celestina* is domesticity. Life is lived at home in close company. The principal action takes place in three houses: Calisto's bachelor household, with its over-familiar servants; Melibea's family residence; and Celestina's home, brothel, and infernal warehouse "half falling down at the edge of the city near the tanneries along the river bank." Each of these domestic establishments is conceived as a kind of cell of human intimacy. But as we read, we quickly discover that the loyalty of the servants to Calisto is either shaky or feigned, and their affection hypocritical. As for Melibea and her mother, the secret adolescent meditations of the one and the superficial social preoccupations of the other (how well Rojas arranges for Alisa to betray herself in a few short sentences as a heedless bourgeoise!) prevent real communication between them. Only Celestina and her companion, Elicia, exhibit any sort of domestic harmony (in this Rojas displays the full bite of his irony), a weird and violent harmony which is maintained cynically by both of them.[17] Domesticity, then, is not only a series of deceits but also a situation of pseudo-companionship. The individual is without company yet never alone. Petty intramural wars and bickerings, ignorance of the state of mind of the nearest and dearest, characterize the daily solitude of all who live within walls. And when Melibea at long last pours out her inwardness to her father, it is from a tower where she stands alone, connected with him only by

[17] See the two brief homecoming scenes at the ends of Acts VII and XI. There is also a fourth house, in which Areusa lives alone and attempts to maintain a sterile and often desperate rebellion against domesticity as well as society.

a fragile bridge of words. She leaps, and he, in his turn, is left alone. Throughout this last scene the word "solo" occurs and recurs as a kind of final résumé of the theme of domesticity. If human life is only an inner flow, only the time of its own consciousness, a true touching of another person is brief and cannot be taken for granted. And domesticity is precisely this taking companionship for granted.

As far as that larger company called society is concerned, there is no direct criticism or satire.[18] Instead of social observation and indignation, we are given insight into the total moral corruption of the community. All the inhabitants pretend to despise and fear Celestina, yet all go to her secretly. She is the mayoress of a counter-society of sensuality, what Mann in *Felix Krull* calls "the hot inarticulate realm of nature" organized by cosmetics, glances, exclamations, gestures, beneath the covering of the "lukewarm" words of social intercourse. Celestina is, in fact, the only person in town who can bring these antithetical kinds of dialogue together. It is not that Rojas is a moralist who thinks of erotic compulsion as evil (although he pretends to in parts of the prologue material). Rather he observes with unremitting irony the spectacle of human beings living together in society, living together as falsely and unauthentically and artificially as they live at home.

Although the concept of social class as it appears in the realistic novels of the nineteenth century or in the sociological textbooks of the twentieth is misleading for the *Celestina*, there are at least two social categories in the cast. On the one hand: the masters and mistresses, Calisto, Melibea, and the latter's family, who are wealthy, well mannered and dressed, and of high lineage. On the other: all the rest who, possessing none of these advantages, live lives which are at times brutal but more often inept or bitter caricatures of the lives of their betters. Sempronio's reflected passion for Melibea or the banquet scene in Act IX are

[18] Exceptions: the usual mediaeval attacks on cosmetics and on the promiscuous behavior of the clergy. There are also one or two veiled and bitter references to Inquisitional justice.

only two of many examples. There is a kind of sardonic humor in the documenting of such parallel but deviant behavior. But when all is said and done, the two so-called classes really amount to the same thing. Manners and money are realities which channel human relationships in special ways. They may even result in a very special variety and level of rationalization (as in the case of Melibea's surrender to Celestina in Act X). Nevertheless the problems of all members of the cast are not different in kind, and their solutions to them no more dignified or important in the one case than in the other. They all—Celestina excepted—invariably choose the easiest way out. As for love, in spite of all the elevated language and special mutual awareness of Calisto and Melibea, its requirement and its practice are as unashamedly physical for them as for their servants. Rojas' social mathematics always returns to the same negative equation: there is no essential difference between categories of people. It is a notion which in this case has nothing to do with democratic ideas or the dignity of man. Calisto and Sempronio are equal in their indignity, as is so corrosively manifested in Calisto's soliloquy in Act XIV—a revelation of moral cowardice as despicable as Sempronio's physical cowardice in Act XII. Read carefully, the *Celestina* betrays as much scorn for class pretensions as it does for social pretense—that is to say, the organized hypocrisy of society taken as a whole.

It is, to be sure, not in society but face to face with the cosmos that the inhabitants of the *Celestina* discover the full extent of their insignificance, their vulnerability, and their loneliness. Rojas stresses such pessimism explicitly in Pleberio's final soliloquy, a kind of thematic epilogue and résumé. But for all the historical interest of this bitter *planctus* (so revealing of Rojas' feelings as a "converso"), most readers have been more interested in the *Celestina*'s expression of the human condition in the course of its dialogue. As readers we are less concerned with pessimistic ideas than with their representation in the flesh and blood of life. But in such a statement there is an assumption which should be turned around. The notion that ideas are put into literature, first thought out and then shaped poetically, is a misleading one for a work as profound and enduring as the *Celestina*. Rather, pessimistic ideas emerge at the end as a kind of self-conscious conclusion, a final flat schematization of a tragic sense or vision of life which was previously an inseparable element in the creative act.

What is this tragic sense or vision? Specifically, the *Celestina* is a work in which all the major characters die suddenly, first Celestina, then Parmeno and Sempronio, and finally Calisto and Melibea. Even Alisa, Melibea's mother, it is hinted, dies of grief in the last scene. Furthermore, at the moment of death, there is an instant of consciousness, of recognition that they like all mortals are about to encounter the cosmos head on. How does this come about? I think it is worthy of surprised remark that four of these five deaths are the result of falls. All throughout the preceding acts physical space is a determining factor in the characters' existence. They are barred from fulfilling their desires by doors and walls. They see each other approach and depart down long perspectives of vacant streets. They listen to each other's conversations at a safe distance, as in Act XII. They worry continually about tripping in haste or in the dark. And at the end their situation in space proves fatal to them; they are killed by space and in space. Melibea, a moment before her fatal leap from the tower, notices ships and a river stretching out to the horizon as in a Renaissance painting. The only landscape in the work, it accentuates the pathos of her death just as Breughel's immense sea, far promontories, and setting sun set off spatially the fall of Icarus.

What has happened is that the traditional and allegorical fall of Fortune is here presented as an actual fall in space purely by chance. The usual reenactment of this fundamental mediaeval myth—perhaps it would be better to call it a pattern of expectation and comprehension—is that reflected in the proverbial "pride goeth before a fall." A being of high estate, merchant, prince, pope, or angel, becomes proud and heedless and is tumbled down and destroyed—to the delight and moral improvement of all about him. But in the *Celestina* there is no suggestion of moral retribution or even of malicious fatality. Man lives in space (the work has all the verticality of the Gothic art of its time but lacks the closed arch of faith). Man is accident prone. Nothing more. A chance misstep from a ladder or a miscalculation of height in the dark and his brains are splattered on the cobble stones. The universe, like Melibea's seascape or that more elaborate picture of height and sea painted verbally in *King Lear* by Edgar for his blind father, may be beautiful but it is careless of human concerns. The air around man is *ajeno y estraño* (alien and strange), Rojas tells us in his preliminary verses, and in it we are exposed to destruction. Instead of the covered and vaulted-over mediaeval world, where man was cared for if he kept to his rôle of creature, the world of the *Celestina* is one of exposure and moment-to-moment danger. It is characterized by that rooflessness or shelterlessness which Lukacs sees as the basic situation of the modern novel.[19] Or as Camus puts it in *The Rebel,* in referring to Lucretius, "Already the great problem of modern times arises, the discovery that to rescue man from destiny is to deliver him to chance."

Actually I don't believe that Rojas was an intellectual rebel in Camus' Promethian sense or that he proposed to rescue man from anything. In the text of the *Celestina* there exist hints of a coming fall of Fortune, implicit promises of retribution, and other sorts of moral foreboding. But by the time the characters have unwound their lives, Rojas has created a world in which sheer space takes the place of fortune. The initial moral and exemplary intentions have been absorbed into an artistic organism of a more complex and less comforting significance. Rojas was not a rebel but an ironist, an ironist outside the realm of accepted values and explanations, who watched his characters from a distance and allowed them to betray their own rationalizations and corruptions. Fortune, as it were, was changed into space by being por-

[19] His word is *Obdachlosigkeit.* See his *Die Theorie des Romans* (Berlin, 1920).

trayed in a world viewed with astringent irony. Rojas, in creating, followed out his own non-conformism not to an idealogical but to a vital conclusion, which is to say to the point of death. And when he did so he saw Fortune in a new and unfamiliar way. In other words, Rojas did not change or revise the traditional and moral fall of Fortune any more than he interfered with the commonplaces on virtue or friendship as mouthed by his characters. What he did was to dig a pit under them, to portray them in an unexpected and disconcerting state of surrounding vacancy.

Wolfgang Kayser has defined the world of the grotesque as "our world—and at the same time not our world. Horror mixed with amusement has its basis in the experience that our trustworthy and familiarly ordered world has become alien in the face of the abyss and its powers." [20] And if we accept his definition, what we have just said about the *Celestina* classifies it as a masterpiece of the grotesque. Indeed I would maintain that it is the masterpiece, the epic of the grotesque, and precisely because it avoids the spooky, the caricaturesque, and the distorted. In it in an almost pure form, dimensions themselves, the newly perceived dimensions of time and space, are applied to a traditional moral universe. We can suddenly see under, through, and around that universe and seeing thus, we perceive the one thing society and culture itself want us least of all to perceive: that our highest aspirations and our meanest absurdities, our horrors and our amusements, are as close as the two sides of a coin, that they are in fact aspects of each other. It is this that is grotesque, and it is this that Cervantes meant when he said that the *Celestina* would have been a "divine" book if it had only known better how "to veil the human."

We in our time are hardly in a position to be as demanding as Cervantes. We can only admire Rojas for discovering so well how to balance the sublime and the ridiculous in close and complex cohabitation, not as polar possibilities of existence. For by doing

[20] *Das Groteske* (Oldenburg, 1957), p. 38. My translation is not literal, but it represents fairly Kayser's interpretation of the grotesque.

so, he brought together inwardness and outwardness, seeing in one light the characters' sharp consciousness of self and the great mindless dimensionality to which they (and we) are all exposed. Separating the sublime from the ridiculous confines a character to a representative and exemplary posture from which he cannot change: "I am ridiculous" or "I am sublime." Putting them together creates a problem of self (what I pretend to be contradicting what I am) surrounded, diminished, more aware, and in the end destroyed in its struggle with the newly recognized nonself.[21] By portraying our weaknesses and chronicling our helpless struggles, Rojas was surely the first to express the full dilemma of man in modern times: existence in a world drained of meaning. Thus, when Melibea commits suicide, there is no mention whatsoever of the mortal sin for which she must answer. The nature of the deed isn't even referred to in Pleberio's lament. Nor does he seem to imply that time has passed, shrinking the importance of such a major event as the conquest of Granada and such a minor one as the prophetic "Inés hanged herself." What is involved in Melibea's uncensured deed against herself is a tacit assertion that we are unjudged. Or even worse, as Pleberio (like Gloucester with his "wanton boys" and "flies") implies at the end, we may have been put here to be tormented.

The third aspect of the *Celestina*'s importance is that of imaginary creation, its power to immerse the reader in what I called an "acid bath of life." But the word "life," with its novelistic overtones, is misleading. The *Celestina* gives us less a portrait of Spanish (or human) life in the novelistic sense than it does of a series of interwoven lives, a texture of lives of which the warp

[21] Perhaps it would help at this point to think of King Lear, Tom, and the Fool in the storm, surely the finest grotesque scene in literature. There with extreme poetic intensity a limitless and raging universe (Kayser's "abgründige Mächte") is brought to bear on three variant combinations of human ridiculousness and sublimity. Rojas is prosaic and sardonic (rather than poetic and pathetic), but it is this same encounter that is thematically central to the *Celestina*.

is the lovers and the woof, the rogues and prostitutes who further their love, who plot against it, who envy it, who fear its consequences, and who in general cross it in many different ways and directions. The comparison with the weaving of a piece of cloth must be insisted upon. It helps to free us from dramatic modes of imagination, modes fully as misleading as those pertinent to the novel. To read the *Celestina* as it should be read, one must be prepared for its generic peculiarity. The acts are not really acts (in Act XI nothing "happens" whereas in Act XII everything does). The climax is not really a climax (Rojas made no mistake in inserting into the first sixteen-act version five new acts separating love from death). And the motives are not really motives (although we are shown the psychological preparation for certain deeds at length and with great subtlety, Rojas is not concerned with setting up a coherent structure of cause and effect). Each state of consciousness interests him for its own sake. For example, the servants' inner humiliation and shamed realization of their own cowardice during Act XII help explain their unexpected and apparently uncharacteristic murder of Celestina. But Rojas is far more interested in witnessing the growth of these sentiments and listening to their expression than he is in setting them forth as motives for the homicide. In the same way he doesn't worry about explaining why marriage is out of the question for his lovers. He feels no need to fabricate a Montague-and-Capulet situation with the result that he has puzzled almost twenty generations of readers, trained motive-hunters all.

Let us sum up the generic strangeness of the *Celestina* in this way. Made exclusively of dialogue, it cannot present a narrative world, that fully textured and contoured reproduction of life which we expect of the novel. But at the same time it is undramatic. The drama necessarily imposes a geometry of motive, plot, and climax upon the process of living. Rojas is not interested in such geometry; he prefers to trace the vine-like twistings and growth of each consciousness through its multiple spoken encounters with others. Each life is a temporal path of words heard ironically until it is emptied out into space, silenced in death. And if Calisto and Melibea believe for a moment that erotic companionship has provided a culmination for their existences, they are quickly undeceived by the fatal misstep on the ladder. Even Melibea's suicide, so oratorically justified and prepared, is an empty gesture, a fatal posturing more than a catastrophe. These two may want to be Tristram and Iseult just as Don Quixote wants to be Amadis of Gaul, but the draining of myth from their universe has left them stranded. That is why their rhetoric sounds at times exaggerated and artificial.

This unique attention paid to conscious life following its own course through ramps of space and avenues of time may help explain an apparent weakness of the *Celestina:* the failure to endow its lives with sympathy—that is, the work does not elicit pity for the characters nor full recognition of them as fellow human beings. Rojas' ironic objectivity is so merciless, his malice so unhindered, and his skill so uncanny that we come to know his characters (as we know most of our colleagues) too well to care for them. As we listen, we understand them ever more deeply; we become ever more fascinated with their misguided prudence and their heedlessness of real danger. But they never touch us as human beings who suffer. Their weaknesses are ours, but, in spite of all their preoccupation with love and hate, they are neither lovable nor detestable. They would be out of place in tragedy yet they are not comic types. Why do they fail in this way? Because they are only lives, not persons. Bonds of sympathy between man and man depend ultimately on what we *are*. And the *Celestina*'s inhabitants *are* nothing; they merely exist. They are independent, psychically intricate, pulsating lives, but they are not men and women. They are not in the sense that Don Quixote, or Achilles, Macbeth, or even Huck Finn are men, men who for good or ill, in one way or another, with doubt or confidence, pull themselves erect from out of the time of their lives and say, "I am."

There is one exception, and it is great enough to lift the *Celestina* above the ranks of the world's near-masterpieces—that is to say, works of intense poetic cohesion and striking originality of theme (for example, *Tamburlaine, Fiammetta,* the *Satyricon*) which have nonetheless lost contact with succeeding generations. Celestina herself is the exception, and, at the human center of the literary world in which she lives, she, unaided by her fellow citizens, triumphs over history. Celestina begins as a type, the go-between, and when Pármeno describes her for the first time, he sets movement, sheer "going," at the foundation of her life:

> If she walks through a crowd of a hundred women and one of them calls her "Old Whore," all unembarrassed she'll turn her head and answer with a cheerful look. Everyone knows her at receptions, parties, weddings, guild meetings, funerals, and everywhere people get together. Why, if she happens by a pack of dogs, they'll bark the same thing at her.

We too are permitted to witness her movement. Through the eyes of the other characters we see her skirts fly, or at other times, her bent-over figure trudging along as she calculates her next move. And they not only see her; they frequently interpret for us the sentimental significance of her changes of pace: triumphant jubilation, hesitancy in the face of danger, or physical caution as she maneuvers her aged body among the stones and pitfalls of the mediaeval pavement. As we follow her along, however, we quickly realize she is more than a go-between, a mere carrier of disruptive messages. She also serves, wheedles, suggests, influences, and, ultimately, directs all the lives around her. Her movement has a human force which distinguishes her from all the others. Except for her own murder, everything that happens in the *Celestina* is instigated by her. She is the dictator of nature's avid republic, the puppet mistress not only of her clients but of all the lives that impinge upon her vital horizon. It does not matter that she is corrupt and corrupting, infinitely calculating, or cold to everything except the physical stimulations of alcohol, danger, and sex. It doesn't matter that she is old, scarred, corporeally grotesque, scuttling like a spider around her broken-down old house, taking inventory of her batwings, cosmetics, and gallows-teeth. It doesn't matter that socially she is the core of the city's infection. What ultimately comes to matter is her courage, her mental fierceness (in Stendhalian coexistence with her talent for cold logic), her belief in herself and her way of life—a vital confidence which all the others in their momentary desires and anxieties never begin to approach.

Let us listen to Celestina herself expressing her basic stamina, her vocational density of being, in one of her last speeches: She has just been threatened by Sempronio with exposure to public shame:

> Who do you think I am, Sempronio? [she asks sarcastically] When did you save me from whoredom? Hold your tongue; don't shame my gray hair. I'm an old woman such as God made me and not the worst of the lot. I live by my profession as untarnished as any other professional. I don't seek out clients. They send for me at home, or they come to my house and ask my help. Whether my life be good or bad, God alone stands as witness to my heart. And don't try to bully me in your anger! Justice is equal for everyone, and all can appeal to it. Although I'm a woman, they'll listen to me just as much as they will to you, all sleek and combed. Leave me alone in my house to my own fortune.

Much earlier she had talked about "maintaining her honor," just as if she were a knight. And in her marvelous soliloquy of doubt and decision in Act IV, she made up her mind to brave entrance into Melibea's house by asking herself the same proverbial question Cortés was to use when he persuaded his men to follow him on the fearful march inland: "Where shall the ox go if he leaves the plow?" All this is, of course, ironical on Rojas' part. With supreme cynicism he imputes to a sink of human degradation the centrally admired trait of the Spanish world (the one trait shared by the Cid and Don Quixote): integral maintenance of the self in the face of all adverse circumstances. Yet this very imputation, this granting of a firm core of being to Celestina's life, awakens in the reader a special feeling—a kind of intense human involvement—for her. At the lowest level this amounts to appalled admiration as we watch her at her infernal work. But beyond that, and in spite of whatever moral principles the reader may adhere to, there is set into operation that basic sympathy lacking for the other characters.

As we have seen, Rojas was a master artisan of life, both a discoverer and a conqueror of the inner world where life becomes aware of itself. But life in words, as in flesh, is tricky stuff; it doesn't hold still and it is hard to rule. In the case of Celestina he made a life that got away from him, that set up its own being—for all of us to come to, as she herself might have said. Thus it was that before many editions had been printed, the *Tragicomedia of Calisto and Melibea* came to be called simply the *Celestina.* Celestina was the center of its human appeal and of its human repugnance, so much the center that, aside from affirmation or negation, she took over the literary world in which she lived. Like Don Quixote or Lazarillo of Tormes, or Don Juan Tenorio, Celestina stepped out beyond her author's intentions and began to live an authentic and ever-renewed life in the imagination of century after century of readers. Through this heroic antiheroine, they (we in our turn) have not only relived viciousness and sheer degradation but have done so as a human experience. In this, I think, lies the superiority of Celestina over the great villains, the Iagos and Agrippinas, of world literature. It is in this unique, incredible, seemingly impossible coexistence not of human beings but of full humanity with evil, that the final importance of the *Celestina* is to be found.

What Was Modernism?

HARRY LEVIN

A NEW APARTMENT BUILDING in New York City, according to a recent announcement, has been named The Picasso. Though I have not had the pleasure of seeing it, I would suggest that it ought to be hailed as a landmark, indicating that we Americans have smoothly rounded some sort of cultural corner. Heretofore it has been more customary to christen our apartments after the landed estates or the rural counties of England, as if by verbal association to compensate for the rootless transience of metropolitan living. A few years ago the name of Picasso, as household god, would have conjured up notions of a jerrybuilt structure and a Bohemian ambience. Prospective tenants, in their perennial quest for comfort and security, would have been put off by a vision of collapsible stairways, rooms without floors, trapezoidal kitchenettes, or neighbors with double faces and blue-green complexions. But in the meanwhile the signature has brought untold wealth and unquestioned prestige to its signer, and now it becomes a warrant of domestic respectability. If this is not an arrival, no painter can ever be said to have arrived. But where? At the latest and strangest phase of a restless career, where previous arrivals have always been points of departure.

We must admit that our eponymous hero has met with more appropriate recognitions, notably the retrospective gathering of Picasso's works, exhibited in several cities on the occasion of his seventy-fifth birthday. That was indeed a retrospect: not only of the productivity wherewith a single man could fill a museum, but of the versatility that enabled him to master such varied styles and numerous media. To follow his progression from room to room and period to period—from drawing and painting to sculpture and ceramics, or from Romanticism and Impressionism to Cubism and Primitivism—was to recapitulate the history of art. Above the labels of the catalogue loomed the dynamic personality of the artist, not merely a school in himself but a whole succession of schools, seeking to outrival his own work at every subsequent stage as well as the work of so many earlier artists. If there was any text he was born to illustrate, it was Ovid's *Metamorphoses.* The conceiving eye that could turn a broken mechanical toy into a monstrous ape or a sacrificial goat, the shaping hand that could transform a terra-cotta pitcher into an archaic goddess of love, such are the faculties that Marcel Proust must have had in mind when he described the impact of great painters as "*une métamorphose des choses.*" Emerson, a favorite writer of Proust's, had described the poetic process as "a metamorphosis of things."

Pablo Picasso, who will be eighty next year, is unique in his field, but not in his artistic eminence. In the sister art of music, we think at once of the protean achievement of Igor Stravinsky, his junior by one year. There, with due allowance for technical differences, we seem to note a similar tendency, which some bewildered cataloguers might have labelled Ultraism. This is the will to change, in other words that metamorphic impetus, that systematic deformation, that reshaping spirit which must continually transpose its material and outdistance itself in a dazzling sequence of newer and newest manners. Picasso was asked by a conventional person who admired his classical illustrations, "Since you can draw so beautifully, why do you spend your time making those queer things?" He answered succinctly, "That's why." He might have countered with another question: why retrace familiar lines? Similarly Stravinsky might have replied, to hearers aware that his departures were firmly grounded upon past mastery of his craft: why go on repeating the recognized chords? There are other possible modalities, though they may sound discordant the first time you hear them. The original composer is he who must try them, in the interests of further discovery.

Since more and more combinations have been tried, more and more possibilities have been exhausted, and the problems of experimentation have become harder and harder. The public, of course, is shocked; it prefers the accustomed harmonies to the neoteric experiments, and it finds cubist projections unrecognizable. However, the development of the arts is registered through a series of shocks to the public—which, after all, in buying cars or clothes, accepts the principle of planned obsolescence. At its own pace, it too is animated by "the need for a constant refreshment," as has been pointed out by James Johnson Sweeney, who as Director of the Guggenheim Museum has done so much to supply that need. The shift of taste fits in with a dialectical pattern of revolution and alternating reaction, as the breaking of outmoded images gives way to the making of fresh ones. Hence the successful iconoclast frequently ends as an image-maker. Witness T. S. Eliot, whose career has been a literary parallel to Stravinsky's or Picasso's. Since his conversion to the Anglican Church and his naturalization as a British subject, we have come to view him as a living embodiment of tradition. Yet he emerged as an experimentalist, whose problematic endeavors startled and puzzled his early readers.

This realignment corresponds with the usual transition from the *enfant terrible*, who is naturally radical, to the elder statesman, who is normally conservative. But it does not explain why such grand old men as Bernard Shaw and André Gide, several years after their respective deaths, still seem so alive and so much younger than their survivors. It does not account for the patricidal attacks, launched against Modernism in general and Mr. Eliot in particular, by angry middle-aged men such as Karl Shapiro, whose rallying cry is *In Defence of Ignorance*. It throws no light on the charlatanical fame that has accrued to Picasso's younger compatriot, Salvador Dalí, for turning back his limp and dripping watches. Yet one of the spokesmen for a resurgent conservatism, Peter Viereck, throws out a meaningful hint, when he speaks of "the revolt against revolt." And the Institute of Modern Art at Boston has officially marked the mid-century transition by changing its name to the Institute of Contemporary Art. Now, we are all contemporaries; about that we have no option, so long as we stay alive. But we may choose whether or not we wish to be modern, and the present drift seems to be toward the negative choice and away from the hazards of controversial involvement.

"An intellectual deliverance is the peculiar demand of those ages which are called modern." So Matthew Arnold had declared in his inaugural lecture "On the Modern Element in Literature." But though that lecture was delivered at Oxford in 1857—the year that inaugurated French modernism by dragging both *Madame Bovary* and *Les Fleurs du Mal* through the lawcourts—it was not much more than another of Arnold's pleas for classicism. By recourse to his criteria, which were those of high civilization, Sophocles and Lucretius could be ranked among the moderns. It remained for the late Edwin Muir to work out the implications of this relativistic conception, applying it also to the Renaissance and to such nineteenth-century prophets as Nietzsche. Muir's sharply pointed paragraphs in *The New Age*, collected under a pseudonym as *We Moderns* in 1918, were republished in the United States two years later with a polemical introduction by H. L. Mencken. Modernity, they argued, does not necessarily mean the very latest thing; rather it is a program of cultural emancipation, "a principle of life itself" which can only be maintained by "constantly struggling." The struggle of the moment was against such reactionaries as Chesterton and such derivatives as Galsworthy. The long-range conflict would meet those forces which, recognizing the challenge of modernism, damn it as heresy in every sphere.

Today we live in what has been categorized—by whom but Arnold Toynbee?—as the Post-Modern Period. Looking back toward the Moderns, we may feel as Dryden did when he looked back from the Restoration to the Elizabethans, contrasting earlier strength with later refinement. "Theirs was the giant race before the Flood. . . . The Second Temple was not like the First." But, we may console ourselves by reflecting, there are times of change and times that seek stability; a time for exploring and innovating may well lead into a time for assimilating and consolidating. We may well count ourselves fortunate in that we can so effortlessly enjoy those gains secured by the pangs of our forerunners. Lacking the courage of their convictions, much in our arts and letters simply exploits and diffuses, on a large scale and at a popular level, the results of their experimentalism. F. Scott Fitzgerald, because he managed to catch some of the glamor that finally caught him, has himself been sentimentalized as a hero of biography, fiction, and drama. Compare his own reckless hero of the Twenties, the great and flamboyant Gatsby, with a typical protagonist of the Fifties—the decent, judicious, respectable Arthur Winner in James Gould Cozzens' *By Love Possessed*—and you can measure how far we have advanced into the middle age of the Twentieth Century.

Compare a militant novel of the Thirties—let us say John Steinbeck's *Grapes of Wrath*—with a penitent novel of the Forties, Lionel Trilling's *Middle of the Journey*, and you can locate the turn that came *nel mezzo del cammin*. World War II was the Flood; but the Temple had been crumbling and the giant race disappearing through what W. H. Auden, retrospectively and rather too severely, called "a low dishonest decade." Some of the talents were prematurely sacrificed: Guillaume Apollinaire,

García Lorca. Others survived without honor in their own countries, as Ezra Pound and Boris Pasternak did for such different reasons. Many of their amiable juniors were led astray by those "enemies of promise" which Cyril Connolly demurred at but did little to resist. The query "Who killed Dylan Thomas?" has prompted some maudlin accusations. The poignant fact about James Agee's writing, much of it published posthumously, is his uneasiness about not living up to his genuine promise. The gifted J. D. Salinger, who writes so movingly of adolescent confusions, has yet to free himself from them. Our colleges are full of writers in residence, who offer courses in "creative" writing, and publish embittered novels whose principal source of interest is the noncoincidental resemblance between their colleagues and their characters.

Though our Miltons may not be glorious, they are both vocal and pampered. Poetry has become a caucus-race, where there are prizes for all the participants and where there are virtually no spectators. The little magazines that "died to make verse free," as people used to say, have been resurrected on the campuses, where they specialize in the stricter Provençal forms. Joyce's books, which were burned and censored during his lifetime, have become a happy hunting ground for doctoral candidates; while his dishevelled disciple, Samuel Beckett, is the subject of an article in a current issue of *PMLA*. One of my intermittent nightmares is based on two tons of Thomas Wolfe's manuscripts now reposing in a vault of the Houghton Library, and the thought that future scholars will gain reputations by putting back what the editors cut out. It is significant that Lawrence Durrell's tetralogy, one of the very few ambitious novels to appear in Britain latterly, takes place in the self-consciously decadent city of Alexandria. "Art," as Thomas Mann announced and illustrated in *Doktor Faustus*, "is becoming criticism." In the same vein John Crowe Ransom, who turned from poet to critic some thirty years ago, lately announced that literature has been moving from an age of creation into an age of criticism.

Mr. Ransom, interviewed on his retirement from his influential chair as teacher and editor at Kenyon College, stressed the happier aspects of the prevailing situation: the necessity for thoughtful rereading, the opportunities for self-cultivation and renewed understanding of the existent classics. An instance might be the revival of Henry James, far more dominant now than he ever was in his day. These are valid and absorbing pursuits, and I am too ingrained an academic myself to deplore the amenities of the Academy. Then too, it must be conceded, there are positive advantages to living in an epoch which technology has enriched with esthetic appliances, so that our acquaintance with music and with the fine arts is vastly augmented by long-playing records and photographic reproductions. But this is reproduction, not production; we are mainly consumers rather than producers of art. We are readers of reprints and connoisseurs of High Fidelity, even as we are gourmets by virtue of the expense account and the credit card. For our wide diffusion of culture is geared to the standardizations of our economy, and is peculiarly susceptible to inflationary trends. The independence of our practitioners, when they are not domesticated by institutions of learning, is compromised more insidiously by the circumstances that make art a business.

The prosperous and the established, *The Just and the Unjust,* find their mirror in the novels of Mr. Cozzens, as opposed to that concern for the underprivileged which novelists used to profess. Genius, more understanding than misunderstood, rises to worldly success in the shrewd fiction of C. P. Snow, where science and scholarships provide the means for "the new men" to enter "the corridors of power." From England we hear of young men who are angry, presumably at the various conformities which they sum up in their conception of an Establishment. It is not quite so clear what is beating our so-called "beat generation"; they seem to be rebels without a cause, born too late in a world too old. Jack Kerouac, in *On the Road,* has produced a document which fills some of us with the wistful feeling that experience must somehow have passed us by. Yet his friends, for all their violent whims, do not seem to be having nearly so good a time as Hemingway's playboys in *The Sun Also Rises.* The school associated with San Francisco, for whatever a personal impression may or may not be worth, looks very much like Greenwich Village transported across the continent long after its heyday. It exemplifies the cultural lag rather than the advance-guard.

As it happens, I have been somewhat associated with the publishing firm known as New Directions, which was founded in the late Nineteen-Thirties by my college friend, James Laughlin. In spite of its vanguard title, it has been primarily engaged in fighting a rear-guard action. The leading innovators on its list have been Ezra Pound and William Carlos Williams, both of whom are advanced septuagenarians nowadays. The other day I noticed a reference to the annual miscellany, *New Directions,* which was characterized as "the accepted place for off-beat publication." Here is an interesting contradiction in terms, which reveals a deeper contradiction in our standards. Whether it expresses the nonconformist's yearning for conformity or the conformist's urge toward nonconformity, it gives with one hand what it takes away with the other. It weighs the notion of acceptance against the compound, "off-beat," which is so characteristic an expression of the mid-century. The noun "beat" accords with the terminology of jazz; as an ungrammatical participle, the same word carries certain sado-masochistic overtones, e.g. "beat-up." Rounded off by a Slavic suffix, which may be either affectionate or contemptuous, and which must have been reinforced by the Sputnik, it has become an epithet for the fashion of being flagrantly unfashionable, "beatnik."

However, its underlying connotation seems to derive from the cop who is off his beat, the man in uniform who has gone off duty and strayed into unfamiliar territory. Thus it subserves the ambivalent curiosity of the denizens of a well-grooved society about whatever may lie beyond its beaten paths. It represents an ineffectual effort to vary the cliché, and probably owes its currency to those whose own beat is Madison Avenue. A cognate phrase, "off-Broadway," is more concrete in specifying the relationship between that main thoroughfare, the precinct of uniformity, and its bypaths, where novelty may perchance be encountered. Legitimate drama, all but superseded on Broadway by musical comedy, has had to improvise its theaters in devious lofts and makeshift basements. Shaw's *Pygmalion,* in its Broadwayized version of Covent Garden, *My Fair Lady,* is the soaring index of this trend. Like those bland composites to which Hollywood reduces imported ideas, it is an entrepreneurial accomplishment, another by-product of the middleman's pragmatic philosophy as stated by Pope:

> Be not the first by whom the new are tried,
> Nor yet the last to lay the old aside.

That sentiment is reversed paradoxically when an advertisement for *Esquire,* the haberdashery magazine, salutes its *clientèle* as "the aware moderns who are the first to embrace a new idea and speed it upon its way to becoming the popular fashion." Well, we Post-Moderns like to eat our cake and keep it, to take a chance on a sure thing. We tipsters want to call the long shot while hogging the inside track, to take credit for originality without risking unpopularity. Hence we congratulate ourselves upon our broadmindedness because *Lady Chatterley's Lover* is now a best-seller after thirty years of suppression.

Thirty years constitute nature's round number for the span from infancy through maturity, and consequently a kind of basic rhythm for reckoning the progresses and regressions of mankind. Thirty years is just about the age-difference between a playboy and an academician: consider the case history of Jean Cocteau. What is generally regarded as the Irish Renascence began in 1892 with Yeats's *Countess Cathleen* and terminated in 1922 with Joyce's *Ulysses.* Broader movements, succeeding one another, are comparable in their periodicity. Thus, if we start with Wordsworth's manifesto of 1800, we observe that the continental triumph of Romanticism dates from 1830. Shortly before the end of another cycle, this gives way to the countertendencies toward Positivism, Realism, and Naturalism; whereas, when we move from the Sixties to the Nineties, the latest watchwords are Symbolism, Estheticism, and Decadence. It will be seen that a revolutionary generation tends to be succeeded by a reactionary one; to put it less politically and more psychologically, there seems to be a cyclic oscillation between tough and tender minds. That would help to explain the phenomenon of the hard-boiled Nineteen-Twenties, recoiling as it were from the softness of the *fin du siècle.* It might also set the acknowledged weaknesses of the Fifties into clarifying perspective.

But nostalgia for the vigorous youth of our century is a weakness in which we need not indulge ourselves; nor would it serve any purpose to draw invidious comparisons between our immediate contemporaries and our elders. The average life is privileged to span two generations, and we live at least in the afterglow of the Moderns. Insofar as they were ahead of their time, we can even claim to be nearer to them. Furthermore, each generation has three decades, in which either to gather momentum after a wavering start, or else to subside from a powerful beginning. Accordingly, the manic Twenties declined into the depressive Thirties, which yielded in turn to the war-interrupted Forties. If the countermovement of the Fifties seems to have begun unpromisingly, we may take comfort in expecting the Sixties to proceed on a rising plane, looking toward the next watershed in the Nineteen-Eighties. There George Orwell's object-lesson gives us pause, and we shift with relief to a backward glance and a less complex set of variables. We can examine the material factors, chart the framing conditions, and project the hypothetical curves of artistic activity. Yet we have no means of predicting how the human sensibilities, in their most individualized manifestations, will respond.

The best we can do is recognize when those responses have occurred with a special resonance. But that point cannot be established by generalizations; let me particularize instead, with a handful of titles and names and dates. Among the latter, 1922 stands out as the year of Proust's death, of the publication of his central volume, *Sodome et Gomorrhe,* and the first appearance of his work in England. English letters had likewise to absorb the twofold shock of *Ulysses* and *The Waste Land.* And if this was not enough for the reviewers, D. H. Lawrence offered them *Aaron's Rod,* Virginia Woolf *Jacob's Room,* and Katherine Mansfield *The Garden Party.* Readers of poetry faced not merely the Georgian anthology but Hardy's *Late Lyrics and Earlier,* Yeats's *Later Poems,* and Housman's *Last Poems*—it sounded rather autumnal, but the harvest grew with reaping. Lytton Strachey's *Books and Characters* was more narrowly *de l'époque,* while Max Beerbohm's *Rossetti and his Circle* was an antiquarian curio. Among the highlights of the season in France were *Charmes,* Valéry's collection of verse, and the first installment of Martin du Gard's *Les Thibault.* Germany saw Bertolt Brecht's first play, *Baal,* and *Die Sonette an Orpheus* by Rainer Maria Rilke. Americans were reading Sinclair Lewis' *Babbitt* and being scandalized by Eugene O'Neill's *Anna Christie.*

Though I have been highly selective, the list is sufficient to justify an *annus mirabilis*—or would be, if there were not others comparably brilliant. Let us therefore sample another year, jumping arbitrarily to 1924, when Franz Kafka died, scarcely known, since his novels would only be published during the next three years. The greatest event for the critics was Thomas Mann's masterwork, *Der Zauberberg.* The noisiest, perhaps, was the Surrealist Manifesto, which proved to be something of an anticlimax; but Valéry counterbalanced it with his first collection of critical prose, *Variété;* while Gide braved scandal by signing *Corydon.* America witnessed Sherwood Anderson's autobiography, *A Story-Teller's Story,* Marianne Moore's salient volume of poetic *Observations,* and William Faulkner's first book, also in verse, *The Marble Faun.* In Britain, George Moore waxed more reminiscent than ever with *Conversations in Ebury Street;* T. E.

Hulme's posthumous *Speculations* were to have continuing influence on criticism and poetry; each of the three Sitwells contributed to the ebullition by bringing out a book; and Bernard Shaw was inspired to touch his heights by the theme of *Saint Joan*. E. M. Forster's *Passage to India* may have been an omen as well as a milestone; for it was his most important novel to date, and it is the last that Mr. Forster has given us.

Everyone can multiply for himself these modern instances; while students of Russian or Spanish literature can point to additional flowerings which were either transplanted or nipped in the bud. Futurism, as Joyce foresaw, had no future; Marinetti fell in line behind Mussolini; and Hitler was to proscribe Modernism as degenerate art or *Kulturbolschewismus*. We hardly need to underline the pressures or constraints that limited the epoch so poignantly, *entre deux guerres*, to Mr. Forster's "long week-end," 1918–1939. Nor could we blame the generation confronted with the task of continuing to write, if they found it hard to forgive such knowledge. Yet at this distance we can perceive, with increasing clarity, that the modernistic movement comprises one of the most remarkable constellations of genius in the history of the West. And while some of its lights are still among us, before they have all been extinguished, we should ask ourselves why they have burned with such pyrotechnic distinction. What, if anything, have such figures in common, each of them vowed to idiosyncracy, practising a divergent medium, formed in a disparate background? Above all, the elementary circumstance that they happen to be coeval, more or less; that they are all, or would have been, in their eighth decade today. But what, if we are not to beg the question, was the *Zeitgeist* they shared? What was there in the air they breathed that differed from the intellectual climate of their successors or predecessors?

All of them grew up in the late Nineteenth Century and matured in the early Twentieth, reaching their prime in the period between the wars. The Nineteenth was not so well organized as the Eighteenth, nor so deeply speculative as the Seventeenth, nor so richly magniloquent as the Renaissance. But, as the apogee of middle-class liberalism, it permitted a maximum of leeway for the emergence of individuality; it educated individuals thoroughly; it collected art and fostered science; it cultivated human relationships; it developed temperament and talent. Into its world the Modernists were born, and yet they were not quite shaped by it. To it they often hark back, with that acute sensibility which they have reserved for their own impressions of adolescence. Had they been born any earlier, they might have felt—with Henry Adams—that they had missed a still earlier boat. Had they been Mid-Victorians, they might have poured their creative energies into causes that they now could take for granted. If they had reached maturity in the Nineties, their views would have inevitably been colored by the outlook of the Decadents. But they took the *fin du siècle* in youthful stride; for them, it was not so much the end of one century as it was the beginning of another.

One of the determining characteristics of modern man, which influences the role he plays and relates him to pre-existing phenomena, is the awareness of chronology. We who are children of the Twentieth Century never experienced the excitement of welcoming it. Our casual habit of predating centuries makes us insensitive to the West's first realization that its second millennium was now in sight. The bliss that Wordsworth inhaled at the dawning of the French Revolution had been a disillusioning adumbration. "Years of the modern! years of the unperform'd!" Such had been Whitman's prologue to a performance which he anticipated all the more keenly because, as he chanted, "No one knows what will happen next." At all events, things would be happening; and those whose existence falls within the limits of a single century may well envy those who cross temporal boundaries and have a chance to inscribe their names on history's blank pages. How terribly much it must have meant to James Joyce, as an eighteen-year-old university student, to have set his ambitions down on paper and dated them "1900!" Here was the brave new world that had been heralded by his mentor Ibsen, by Nietzsche whose death came that very year, by Tolstoy and those other Proto-Moderns who had been breaking the images that had stood in its way.

One of the assumptions about World War I was that it had settled history. Its sequel was to teach T. S. Eliot that "History is now and England." But the interval thought of itself in the present tense, separating modernity from history. The past was over; the present was happily more comfortable—though unhappily less colorful, as Miniver Cheevy and other time-snobs lamented. Ernest Hemingway's first book of stories was aptly entitled *In Our Time,* and its grasp of immediacy was heightened by its reminiscences of battle. His intensive concentration on the instant, which imparts a film-like quality to his fiction, is pinpointed in "The Snows of Kilimanjaro," when a polyglot series of synonyms runs through the mind of a dying writer: "Now, *ahora, maintenant, heute. . . .*" Whatever the language, the meaning is imminence; and that "nowness" is a precondition of the search for newness, for what Whitman had termed "the unperform'd." To perform the unperformed! *La nouvelle revue française!* "The Great English Vortex!" The sense of novelty, of potentialities being opened up, does not seem any less eager because it is juxtaposed to the inherited sense of the past and the pleasures of retrospection. Everyman, in his more thoughtful moods, is conscious of his overwhelming patrimony as heir of all the ages; and his relation to them takes the guise of an endless stroll among the masterpieces of their invisible museum.

Time was of the essence, not only for the metaphysician Bergson, but for the innumerable poets, novelists, painters, and scientists who worked in the dimension he formulated. Vainly did Wyndham Lewis assail the time-consciousness of his contemporaries. As the Gracehoper retorted to the Ondt, in Joyce's fable, "Why can't you beat time?" The lifework of Proust was precisely such an attempt, the attempt of an aging dilettante to make up for lost time by recapturing the past, repudiating its ephemeral concerns and crystallizing its highest moments through an appeal to the timelessness of art. Yeats pursued the same objective symbolically, when he pictured himself abandoning the earthbound sphere of nature and setting sail for the timeless art-city, Byzantium. His poet, Michael Robartes, had desired to remember forgotten beauty. The feeling of belatedness has the habitual effect of stimulating the act of memory, along with the stylistic consequence of sounding echoes, evoking reverberations, and playing with *pastiche*. When Pound advised disciples to "make it new," he was repeating a maxim as old as Confucius, and was well aware of the irony; for his studies in the Renaissance had won him insights into the processes of cultural renewal, and shown him how renovation could be innovation.

What I have ventured to call the metamorphic impetus seems to have resulted from this paradoxical state of feeling belated and up-to-date simultaneously, and of working experimental transformations into traditional continuities. But there are other preconditions of Modernism, geographical as well as historical. Joyce and Picasso, Eliot and Stravinsky have another trait in common—alas, too common among the uncommon artists of our time. How few of them have lived out their careers in the lands of their origin! To be sure, migration is a civilizing force, and sojourn abroad has been a classic step in the artistic *curriculum vitae*. Unfortunately we have had to learn, through dint of wars, revolutions, and political persecutions, the distinction between expatriation and exile. The hyphenated German-Jewish Czech, Kafka, though he did not live to share it, clairvoyantly sketched the plight of the Displaced Person. Mann, who was destined to become a Transatlantic nomad, had situated his magic mountain in neutral Switzerland. There, in the International Sanitorium Berghof, his Teutonic hero undergoes successive exposure to a Swiss physician, an Italian poet, a Polish priest, a Dutch businessman, and a Russian mistress. Then, having gained an education while regaining his health, he is lost in combat with the Allies.

The catchphrase employed by continental architects, "The International Style," might be very appropriately extended to other works of the Twenties. Many of them were composed in Paris, the capital of between-the-wars cosmopolitanism. "The School of Paris"—a topographical designation for unacademic painting—was presided over by our expatriate Spaniard, Picasso, who now has his monument in New York. Paris was the inevitable headquarters for those Russian dancers, designers, and choreographers who staged Stravinsky's ballets. It was where a famous generation of Americans got temporarily lost, under the Sybilline tutelage of Gertrude Stein. Meanwhile, in an apartment near the Etoile, the self-exiled Irishman Joyce was carefully elaborating the most minute and comprehensive account that any city has ever received from literature—his account of his native Dublin. *Ulysses* is of its time, in endeavoring to arrest the eighteen hours of time it exhaustively chronicles. Nineteenth-century novelists, especially Balzac, had set forth the complexities of the metropolis, but through a sequence of loosely connected novels where more or less conventional narrative was filled in with sharply detailed observation. Joyce's unexampled contribution was a gigantic yet rigorously experimental design, which controlled the accumulating details as they fell into place.

It is the metamorphic impetus that provides this controlling device: the transmutation of Dublin citizens into mythical archetypes out of the *Odyssey*. In the novel, as Naturalism had left it, the environment came dangerously close to swamping the personages. That was not the fault of the Naturalists, but of the situations with which they dealt. The dehumanization of art, if I may build upon a useful phrase from Ortega y Gasset, mirrors the dehumanization of life. Joyce, by resorting to metamorphosis and even to mock-apotheosis, was trying to rehumanize his characters; and he succeeded in giving them contour, if not stature. Journalistic novelists like John Dos Passos and Jean-Paul Sartre, seeking a panoramic or kaleidoscopic approach to the urban scene, have imitated Joyce's structural methods. But the problem, to which the French *Unanimistes* and the German proponents of the *Gesamtkunstwerk* have also addressed themselves, goes beyond—

or else within—the matter of structure. If the object is unity, that must bear an organic connection to the multiplicity; its collective pattern must be revealed and confirmed through individual lives; its outward view of social interaction must be combined with an inner focus on psychological motivation.

Hence the old-fashioned type of rounded fictional character, standing between the narrator and the reader, seems to dissolve in the stream of consciousness, which directly and transparently conveys a flow of impression and sensation from the external world. Though the novelist need not utilize the internal monologue, increasingly he approximates to the voice and the viewpoint of his protagonist. The very completeness of the ensuing intimacy forces him to fall back upon the raw materials of his own autobiography, refining them into self-portraiture of the artist. The intensity of Proust's introspection pushed him to the point where he disclosed an abyss between the *moi* and everything else. Gide, by writing his novel about a novelist writing a novel, *Les Faux-monnayeurs,* including his novelist's journal, and then publishing the journal he kept while writing that novel, *Le Journal des Faux-monnayeurs,* demonstrated that first-person narrative may become a double mirror reflecting infinity. Fiction was spurred to such feats of self-consciousness by the revelations of psychoanalysis: the Freudian probing for unconscious motives, the Jungian search for universal patterns. It may be an exaggeration to argue that human nature changed in 1910, but Virginia Woolf was bold enough to do so, though probably unaware that the International Psychoanalytical Association had been founded in that year.

That argument was a measured overstatement, put forward in defending the new Georgian novelists against such Edwardians as Arnold Bennett. Mrs. Woolf knew that it would have just about as much validity as the assertion that sunsets have changed since Monet and the Impressionists undertook to paint them. It was true, in the sense that characterization had changed, that people too were being visualized through the eyes of other people, and that another metamorphosis was thereby being effected. The author of *Orlando* understood that permutations so subtle and subjective might have a circumscribing effect on the novel. Most flexible of genres, it readily focuses either upon the recesses of the self or the expanses of society; and the Twenties took it to both extremes, sometimes at once, with their mental analyses and their monumental constructs. Here is where Ultraism may have attained its *ne plus ultra.* Joyce himself could go no farther than *Finnegans Wake;* few others could get that far; and later novelists have understandably made no attempt to press beyond *Ulysses.* This has stirred some critics to announce that the novel is an obsolete or dying form. One cannot deny that it seems to be regressing toward the plane of documentary realism, where at best it may be indistinguishable from reportage or good journalism.

But fiction is doomed to failure in its competition with fact. What it possesses that non-fiction lacks is fantasy—that is to say, the projective power of the imagination, which confers value and significance on the stuff of our everyday apprehension by rearranging and transmuting it. Thus the apparent sordidness and purposelessness of our day with Leopold Bloom in Dublin are transmuted into a symbolic reënactment of Homer's epic. Some of those cross-references seem far-fetched, and others grimly ironic; yet, as a whole, they interpret for us data which would otherwise be meaningless. Joyce's use of myth makes the past a key to the present. More than that, wrote T. S. Eliot in his review of *Ulysses,* "It has the importance of a scientific discovery." Future writers would take advantage of it, as he predicted; and even then he had just finished his *Waste Land,* which abounded in flashbacks and parallels. In that least heroic and most fragmentary of epics, he exorcized the blight of contemporaneous London by tracing through it the outline of a quest for the Holy Grail. A timeless ritual, a timely critique, I. A. Richards commented that it completed the severance between poetry and belief. But, in the long run, it proved to be a station on Mr. Eliot's pilgrimage toward faith.

It is not surprising that Modernism, the product of cities, should be so impelled to recreate the image of cities. One of the greatest Modernists, in this respect, is Charlie Chaplin, who has so brilliantly rendered the metropolis in all its frustrations and incongruities. For T. S. Eliot, London is "unreal"; but its apparition is that of Vienna, Athens, Jerusalem, or Alexandria; and his elegiac vision becomes prophetic when he imagines "falling towers." The prophecy was apocalyptically fulfilled by the bombings of the next war, which Mr. Eliot— combining his own observation as air-raid warden with a reminiscence from Dante's *Inferno*—has powerfully invoked in the last of his *Four Quartets.* That he should proceed by musical analogy, finding his inspiration in the austere but imposing string quartets of the later Beethoven, is still another trait of his generation. Poets' poets and novelists' novelists, painters' painters and musicians' musicians, they were profoundly versed in their own particular crafts, and so whole-heartedly devoted to craftsmanship that they attempted to transfer it from one art to another. Writers borrowed thematic techniques from Wagner, who himself had aimed at a synesthesia, to be induced by music in conjunction with other arts. Poetry encompassed painting and music, when Wallace Stevens presented—after Picasso—his *Man with a Blue Guitar.*

The thought that a man of letters should consider himself a practitioner of the fine arts, or that he should be designated professionally as an artist, is a legacy from Flaubert's generation which is not likely to outlast Joyce's by long. The cult of intransigent artistry, which both men practised as devoutly as if it were their religious vocation, is embodied in and elucidated by the latter's *Portrait of the Artist as a Young Man,* where the archetypal figure is Daedalus, the fabulous Greek artificer, and the epigraph is a line about him from Ovid's *Metamorphoses:* "*Et ignotas animum dimittit in artes.*" Joyce was clearly inviting the application to himself: "And so he turned his mind to unknown arts." Paul Valéry discerned a historical prototype in the artist-engineer of the Italian Renaissance, and paid his homage in two essays upon the method of Leonardo da Vinci. He made his own apologia through the personage of M. Teste (M. Tête, Mr. Head), whose cerebral soliloquies begin with the unabashed admission: "*La bêtise n'est pas mon fort.*" Stupidity has decidedly not been the forte of the Modernists; they have left that virtue to their Post-Modern attackers, who can now write in defence of ignorance. If M. Teste seems arrogant, let them make the most of that last infirmity. He was just as firm, in refusing to suffer fools, as they are weak in appealing to philistines.

Though recent literature prides itself upon its outspokenness, there remains one organ of the body which it is almost taboo to mention, and that is the brain. What may seem a sin, on the part of the Moderns, is that they were preoccupied with the minds of their characters, and—what is worse—that they make serious demands upon the minds of their readers. This cannot be lightly forgiven by an era whose culture-heroes are persistently mindless—whether they be the good-hearted goons of John Steinbeck, the epicene slobs of Tennessee Williams, or the analphabetic gladiators of the later Hemingway. But popularity was excluded, by definition, from the aims of the writers I have been discussing; their names did not figure upon the best-seller lists of their day; many others did, which are now forgotten. The aura of obscurity or unintelligibility which may still occasionally tinge these intellectuals, in some degree, emanates from their refusal to advertise themselves or to talk down to their audience in the hope of enlarging it. That, for them, would indeed have been a treason of the clerks. Their ultimate quality, which pervades their work to the very marrow, is its uncompromising intellectuality. Like the intelligentsia of old Russia or the class of Mandarins in China, they looked upon letters as a way of life.

But this may have presupposed, along with their own dedication, other conditions which may no longer be possible. The extraordinary spread of higher learning has lowered it, and introduced a large amount of dilution. The highbrows and the low-brows have intermarried, and their children are—exactly what Virginia Woolf dreaded most—all middlebrows. Instead of a tension between the uncomprehending majority and the saving remnant—or, if you will, between sensible citizens and long-haired coteries—there has been a *détente,* a relaxation, and a collaboration for mutual profit between the formerly intractable artist and the no longer hostile bourgeoisie. Out of it there seems to be emerging a middlebrow synthesis, the moderated expression of our mid-century. But that is a subject notoriously better appreciated by professors of sociology and experts on mass communication than it is by old-fashioned scholars or modernist critics. Nor do I wish to imply that all of our talents, responding to technological pressure and economic attraction, have become mere purveyors of entertainment. On the contrary, many of them profess an engagement of the sincerest kind to the responsibilities of common welfare. The Modernists did not have to make such commitments, because they were not threatened by such urgencies. Hence they could strive for artistic perfection in single-minded detachment.

Alfred North Whitehead was strongly convinced that the early Twentieth Century was one of the greatest epochs in the march of intellect. Though he was thinking basically of mathematics and physics, he held a lively belief in the interplay between the sciences and the humanities. He concurred with the opinion that Wordsworth, writing from the opposite vantage-point, had expressed in the opening year of the Nineteenth Century:

> If the labours of Men of science should ever create any material revolution, direct or indirect, in our condition, and in the impressions which we habitually receive, the Poet will sleep then no more than at present; he will be ready to follow the steps of the Man of science, not only in those general indirect effects, but he will be at his side, carrying sensation into the midst of the objects of the science itself.

Certainly such a material revolution has taken place; the arts have struggled to adapt themselves to it; and we gain a fuller comprehension of the modern artist, if we envision him—in Wordsworth's terms—at the side of the scientist. The partnership, however uneasy, has intensified his curiosity and sharpened his preoccupation with his own technique. He has been encouraged to experiment, not by blindly accepting hypotheses as Zola did in his *roman expérimental,* but rather as Valéry did in transferring to poetry the lessons he had learned from geometry, or in taking for his motto *"ars non stagnat."* Successful experiment involves trial and error and incidental waste, as scientists know. This is a necessary function performed, upon the fringes of the arts, by that continued ferment of willed eccentricity whose products we can usually dismiss. But "the two cultures," as Sir Charles Snow has lately reminded us, are still too far apart. What should draw them together, more than anything else, is the shared recognition that conjointly they cover an area which man has set aside for the free play of painstaking intelligence.

Science no longer underprops our world view with rationalistic or positivistic reassurances. It has undergone a modernist phase of its own, and seen its solid premises subverted by such concepts as relativity and indeterminacy. Where, then, can we turn for illumination? Can we come to no more helpful conclusion than the message that E. M. Forster discerned in the Marabar Caves of India? "Everything exists; nothing has value." Critics of the Moderns have accused them of being deficient in a sense of values, of believing in nothing beyond that negativistic credo. However, to reread Eliot's "Fire Sermon," or Kafka's "Parable of the Law," or Mann's farewell to his soldier-hero, or Proust's commemoration of a great writer's death, or Joyce's hallucinating encounter between a sonless father and a fatherless son, is to feel the glow of ethical insight. A younger and more plain-spoken writer whom we have lost much too soon, Albert Camus, received the Nobel Prize three years ago for having "illuminated the problems of the human conscience in our time."

That citation recalls the warning of an earlier French moralist, Rabelais, at the very dawn of modernity, that "*science sans conscience*" would bring ruin to the soul. Joyce's young artist, Stephen Dedalus, pledged himself to create the "uncreated conscience" of his people. Has it not been the endeavor of his generation to have created a conscience for a scientific age?

Spring, 1960.

Madame Bovary

HENRI PEYRE

IT MAY BE that more powerful, more disturbing, more profoundly psychological novels than *Madame Bovary* exist in French literature. *La Chartreuse de Parme* and *A la Recherche du Temps Perdu* have more poetry; Balzac's and Zola's best works have more imaginative strangeness. There is a spiritual dimension in Rousseau's Julie, even in Mauriac's Thérèse, which modern readers may miss in Flaubert's adulteress. But no other French novel has produced such an impact and none perhaps stands out as such a milestone in the development of art. Before *Madame Bovary*, great novels had been composed, by Defoe, Fielding, Jane Austen, Abbé Prévost, Laclos, Gogol, and, of course, by Stendhal and Balzac. But the art of fiction conquered its true letters of nobility with Flaubert. With him it became established on a par with tragedy, epic, or lyric poetry.

Madame Bovary [1] has been called the one "perfect" novel in

[1] In writing this essay I have made liberal use of passages included in my introduction to the 1950 Modern Library edition of *Madame Bovary*, no longer in print.

existence. It has no grave flaws. It is harmoniously structured. It maintains a certain aloofness from life and yet it is impeccably true to life. It unfolds with ominous inevitability. Every one of its sentences is calculated and polished as no fictional prose has ever been. The result corresponds, almost to a fault, to what its author had intended. With this book, the novel, for the first time perhaps since *Don Quixote,* over which Flaubert had long pondered, produced a classic. "The work is a classic," pronounced Henry James, "because the thing such as it is, is ideally done and because it shows that in such doing eternal beauty may dwell."

The book is as timely today as it was in 1857. It will long continue to be read by the practitioners of the art of fiction, by many women who fondly identify themselves with the heroine, by boys and girls in schools and colleges to whom the novel is a revelation of life and art. It affords, moreover, a moral lesson of the most exalted order, neither obtrusive nor childish. It has received the consecration of being adapted, with dubious success, to the stage and to the screen. Social scientists currently refer to it as to a storehouse of accurate observation on provincial France; some even hail it as a portrayal of the typical French married woman, although many French husbands would disagree. Few things are more difficult than to create a literary type who goes on living with a life of its own and whom we recognize daily around us: as Molière had created Tartuffe and the would-be gentleman and Harpagon, Flaubert has given existence to Emma Bovary, to Monsieur Homais, even to kindly and pathetic Charles, "the eternal husband." A philosophical system called "Bovarysm" has even been evolved, by Jules de Gaultier, out of the character in whom Flaubert first diagnosed the evils brought about by romantic self-deception.

With the critics and connoisseurs, Flaubert's reputation has stood the test of time with remarkable endurance. He has lately been attacked in his own country by Proust, who charged him with being too unimaginative a stylist, by Malraux (in the preface to *Le Temps du Mépris*), who blamed him for his refusal of "commitment" and for dipping all his characters in the mud, instead of ennobling his heroes through virile fraternity. Valéry made fun of that ascetic Saint Anthony of literature, who disbelieved in everything but the polishing of cadences and accurate documenting for his imaginative creations. Sartre derided even more bitterly the devotee of art for art's sake who aimed at hypothetical posterity, and branded him as responsible for the Commune! A woman critic, Mme Claude-Edmonde Magny, railed at the incompetence of Flaubert, a confirmed bachelor, in rendering the intimate scenes in which Emma stripped herself in the fashion of a century ago: "She undressed brutally, tearing off the thin lace of her corset, which whistled around her hips like a gliding adder."

But the trend of critical opinion in France is already reversing itself and, after the great vogue of Dostoevski in the nineteen twenties, of Balzac in the nineteen forties, the young are again being attracted to Flaubert. Stendhal, as a person, with his shyness, his ironic independence of spirit, the naturalness of his tone, speaks to many of us more intimately. Proust was more daring and a far surer artist. But the majority of students of *Madame Bovary* continue to praise an author who unflinchingly faced all the problems of the art of fiction and solved them with admirable integrity. Joyce and Kafka owed much to him, indeed stemmed from him. The critic and novelist Allen Tate, writing in *The Sewanee Review* in 1944, could assert that "Flaubert created modern fiction." The novelist and memorialist Osbert Sitwell confessed in 1938, in a book entitled *Trio,* apropos of Dickens and Hardy, that "never, perhaps, can we hope to bring forth a novelist of such imaginative perfection, so polished, and at the same time so full of fire, as Flaubert." He chided Hardy for seemingly not realizing that he was living in a post-Flaubertian era, that is, after "Flaubert had altered the whole speed and machinery of the novel, altered it for ever." Ernest Hemingway could salute Flaubert's bust, as he walked in the Luxembourg Gardens, as "one that we believe in, whom we loved unstintingly." On April 12,

1957, the anonymous reviewer of the *Times Literary Supplement* saluted the author of *Madame Bovary* a century after the appearance of that novel as "the greatest virtuoso who ever practised prose fiction. . . . The creator of the modern novel, the source of nearly every important advance made since the middle of the last century."

Gustave Flaubert was one of the many French writers who came from Normandy—from Malherbe and Corneille to Maupassant and Gide, they have been many. He was born at Rouen on December 12, 1821. He was not, however, as has often been asserted, a true son of the sturdy Vikings who, ten centuries earlier, had invaded the west coast of France. Flaubert's own father had come from Champagne and adopted Normandy as his home. The novelist grew up among the farmers and townsmen of provincial France. Like Balzac before him, like Mauriac in the century that followed, he was to discover in provincial life a much richer domain for a novelist's observation than in a large metropolis. *Madame Bovary* bears the subtitle: "Provincial Manners." For, in a small town, one lives in a glass house. Everyone spies upon everyone else, kindly or maliciously. Many barriers prevent the easy gratification of one's desires or vices. Restraints and prohibitions thus exacerbate passions, direct mental life inwards, and drive rebellious souls to frustration and tragedy. "The provincial woman," wrote Balzac in a fragment on *La Femme de Province,* "has but two ways of being; either she resigns or she revolts. . . . The provincial woman has a heart and uses it very little or very badly, which is worse."

The majority of French writers and artists since the Revolution have been sons of the middle class rising in revolt against the bourgeoisie and sketching scathing caricatures of the very class which had nurtured them and bought (or refused to buy) their books. Flaubert was no exception. His family was well to do, and he is one of the few novelists who never had to overproduce, never were tempted by money or journalism. In his own father, young Gustave probably observed many of the features of the bourgeois: solid moral and professional virtues, respectability, a sense of traditions, fear of innovations, a positive turn of mind, and little emotion in the presence of beauty. It was his own blood that the novelist unflinchingly ridiculed. Indeed, and if it be true that we secretly hate ourselves most heartily, it was himself that Flaubert felt lurking behind Madame Bovary, the dreamy Salammbo, St. Anthony, even behind the pitiful puppets of Bouvard and Pécuchet avid for Faustian knowledge. He never recoiled before analyzing his own weaknesses.

Like Proust, Flaubert was the son of a doctor. His father was the chief surgeon of the Hôtel-Dieu, the Rouen hospital, and was succeeded by one of his two sons, Achille. As a boy, living in a picturesque apartment in the courtyard of the hospital, Gustave used to climb over a wall and look at the corpses in the dissection room. It is possible that the paternal profession developed in the son an early habit of self-analysis and some premature sadness. Flaubert's most famous novels are analytical and in some respects scientific in their apparent objectivity. Sainte-Beuve, the most influential though seldom the most perspicacious critic of the time, concludes his article on *Madame Bovary* in 1857 with the famous titles: "A son and a brother of distinguished surgeons, Flaubert holds his pen as others do a scalpel. Anatomists and physiologists, everywhere do I find you!"

Young Flaubert probably owed even more to his generation. He came into the world approximately at the same time as Leconte de Lisle, Baudelaire, Renan, the elder Goncourt, and, in the arts, as Chassériau, Courbet, Méryon, Gounod, César Franck. The men of that age group felt overwhelmed by the greatness and fecundity of the Romantic generation which had preceded them by some twenty years. Their own vitality was unequal to that of earlier giants like Balzac, Hugo, Michelet, Berlioz, and Delacroix. Yet, as their inheritors, they found themselves filled with the same dissatisfaction with the real world, the same nostalgic yearning for exotic climates and earlier ages, and the same exacerbation of sensibilities—an exacerbation which they were prone to cultivate rather than assuage. In fact, while the Romantics had plunged into the world without in order to change it, Flaubert, Baudelaire, and their contemporaries were more inclined to delve into the world within. They observed society, man and themselves more closely. They became intoxicated with books —like Emma Bovary. They studiously fed their despair, which set them above the common man and the bourgeois.

Flaubert's youth was steeped in melancholy, through no exterior cause, and his fiction was to be obstinately pessimistic—as was, at around the same time, that of Hawthorne and Melville, and of Turgenev, and a little later, of Zola and Hardy. Such stress laid on the darker side of life is often a mark of strength in young men and an assertion on their part that, much being wrong with the world, their coming into life was not altogether useless. It also accompanies the ebullience of adolescents and the mysterious spiritual changes parallel with their physical growth. Literature, discovered at a receptive age and contrasting with prosaic life in provincial schools, was a very important influence on Flaubert and his young friends. They reveled in Chateaubriand, Hugo, Byron. Flaubert soon added Goethe, Shakespeare, Rabelais, Cervantes, and the classics of antiquity to his favorite group of great writers, whom he contrasted with modern decadence. Suicide haunted him and his school friends, and they thought of madness as a relief for their overheated brains. When he hit upon Balzac's *Louis Lambert,* Flaubert was profoundly impressed and thought he recognized the life of one of his friends, whose too fervid cerebral life had collapsed into insanity. The madness of Tasso, of Hamlet, of Lear was then a favorite theme with writers and painters; when Flaubert first read *King Lear,* he felt like grinding Corneille and Racine with a pestle and painting with the powdered residue the walls of latrines. The expression of his literary enthusiasms was often colorful.

Three events marked Flaubert's life before he came into his

own as a writer. The first, when he was fourteen and a half years old, in August 1836, was the apparition of a woman who said a few words to him on the beach at Trouville. She was a young mother, living with a vulgar and shady business man. Young romantic Gustave thought he fell in love with her, dreamed of her for years, hardly ever saw her again, but considered the platonic and adolescent affair as the great love of his life. Then, in January 1844, he was struck with a nervous crisis which has (mistakenly, it is probable) been called epilepsy. It was the first of a series of violent and recurrent nervous fits which filled Flaubert with apprehension and drove him to lead a hermit's life, dreaming his impossible dreams, chiseling his style in the seclusion of Le Croisset, near Rouen. Flaubert was also lastingly impressed by a long trip which he took to the Near East in 1849–51. He visited not only Egypt, Syria, and Palestine but also Greece and Turkey. Antiquity always held a fascination for him. He always regretted not having lived in ages when, as he imagined, men were more virile, pagan society less addicted to hypocrisy and anguish than ours, and ugliness and stupidity less prevalent.

Flaubert began by writing several semi-biographical works, which he wisely refrained from rushing into print. He distrusted his own hyper-romantic lyricism. He finally decided to curb his youthful intemperance and to submit himself to the prosaic delineation of contemporary life. For five years he labored over the subject of *Madame Bovary*. He confided his harrowing scruples as a craftsman and proclaimed his lofty artistic ideals to Louise Colet, who was his mistress for several years and, as he called her, his "Muse." At last the novel appeared, first serially and with a few cuts imposed by timid editors in the *Revue de Paris* late in 1856, then in book form in 1857. The author won instant fame, but he was sued for immorality. The Second Empire was an era of stuffy, Pharisaic prudery; to his vehement indignation, Flaubert, the son of a respectable Rouen surgeon, was charged with having driven realism to licentious excesses and with having thrown before the public "a heap of manure." He was acquitted, vindicated at the trial, and the artistic and moral integrity of the volume was publicly recognized.

After 1857 Flaubert's outward life was uneventful. He lived for his work and, without ever falling prey to the temptation of overproduction to which writers not infrequently succumb once success has crowned their efforts, continued to perfect his novels with the utmost care. In *Salammbô* (1862), he returned to his romantic and archaeological vision of antiquity; in *L'Education Sentimentale* (1869)—a work which in the minds of many vies with *Madame Bovary* as his masterpiece and into which Flaubert poured even more of himself—he painted a vivid picture of the young men of his generation. Next, he attempted a philosophical and historical resurrection of the early Christian era in *La Tentation de Saint-Antoine* (1874), wrote his celebrated *Trois Contes,* and left a satiric epic, *Bouvard et Pécuchet,* uncompleted when he died in 1880. His voluminous *Correspondance* is the most revealing and the richest of all the letters left by the novelists of France; it is a treasure house of reflections on art and beauty, often couched in the raciest of styles and expressed with a spontaneous verve which contrasts with the labored style of his novels.

A strong tendency toward more pronounced realism in French fiction had been evident for some years before the publication of *Madame Bovary.* The advent of democracy and the industrial revolution had, since the early years of the century, enlarged the reading public; that public now voiced its need for a literature depicting the actual conditions of daily life and unheroic heroes and heroines with whom it could sympathize. Then the painter Courbet and a minor novelist, Champfleury, had waved the banner of Realism and advocated brutality in rendering life as it is, crude and vulgar, even dull and monotonous. The underlying philosophy of the age inclined to determinism and positivism: man was a mere product of forces and of circumstances; science claimed to disregard everything supernatural and mysterious, and to be content with analysis and mastery of the palpable and the measurable in the universe.

The "realistic" label was at once affixed to Flaubert's novel. It depicted the average life in a French province with minute attention and details; it excluded lyrical flights and moral reactions on the part of the author; it eschewed the conventional artificiality of a happy ending and, generally speaking, the wooliness and pathos prevalent in Romanticism. Yet Flaubert was to protest indignantly against the term "Realism," to him a "disgusting insult." "I execrate what is commonly termed 'realism,'" he wrote. Repeatedly he vented his anger against his prosaic subject and his ridiculous and pathetic provincial characters.

It is true that he had borrowed extensively from reality and modeled much of his plot upon it. Homais, Bournisien, and Léon had actually existed. Charles Bovary had been Flaubert's schoolmate, a country doctor whose wife was the daughter of a well-to-do farmer. She was fond of novels, indulged in luxury, took a lover, and committed suicide in 1848. Delamare was her real name. In addition, Flaubert lent to his heroine some of the features of Louise Colet, and even more of the wife of one of his friends, the sculptor Pradier, who then enjoyed great fame. Louise Pradier had also lived a disorderly life of debts and sordid love affairs.

But he transposed and transformed all that he had closely observed in real life. Reality was but his starting point; he aimed at truth, that is, at some generality, and he deserves to be called not a realistic but a classical writer. "What mechanics lurk in naturalness, and how many wiles [ruses] are needed in order to reach truth," he exclaimed in 1853 to Louise Colet. To a gentleman from the Ardennes who had questioned him about the models for his book, he replied on June 4, 1857: "I had no model posing for me. Madame Bovary is a purely fictitious character. . . . If I had followed reality, my portraits would be less true to life, because I should then have had individuals in view, while in fact I was trying to reproduce general types." Flaubert was never interested in photographic imitations of life. No genuine artist can be, for photography does not look at things; it passively registers them. But the artist, in looking at them, eliminates, selects, distorts, transforms into consciousness and thought. Flaubert's truth is not abstract and depersonalized, as truth in literature was apt to be before the moderns asserted their need for colorful reality. It is local and particular at the start, but far reaching and universal after it has been exalted to the plane which is that of literature worthy of the name: life, not copied, but selected and intensified.

Flaubert also differed from the realists in that he refused to cut off a slice of life arbitrarily and offer it as a novel. To him, a novel was a work of art, the primary condition for which was structure, "that architectural conception of work," as Walter Pater later defined it, "which foresees the end in the beginning and never loses sight of it, and in every part is conscious of the rest, till the last sentence does but, with undiminished vigor, unfold and justify the first." Such a description might have been inspired by *Madame Bovary*. It is a superbly constructed novel. If anything, it is too tightly built, for it almost excludes the sense of mystery, the sudden eruption of life through the framework of the work of art, which ought to be the attribute of very great books. Flaubert never loses control of his plot; he never quite allows his characters to carry him where he had not planned to take them.

The first scene affords a foretaste of the whole novel. Charles is already the placid and baffled victim of the pranks of other schoolboys, as he will die a helpless victim—"It is the fault of fatality!" is the pathetic phrase with which he leaves this world. His schoolboy's cap, somewhat heavily described by Flaubert, has several tiers, as later does the house from which Emma and Rodolphe will watch the "Comices agricoles." It symbolizes the circles of stupidity which emanate from poor Charles and those which spread from the provincial city. In his admirable analysis of *The Craft of Fiction*, Percy Lubbock demonstrates the supreme skill of the novelist whose subject was Emma, not Charles Bovary, but who chose to describe first the environment and the husband who will make her what she will become. The prelude and the epilogue, the prospect and the final retrospect, are calculated to have exactly the same length. Charles's career slowly unfolds. He marries first, at his mother's bidding, a dry-hearted widow older than himself. He is starved of sentiment, ready to fall in love when his wife dies. Already we realize that his mother and his first wife have stultified him and that, with all his good will, he will remain clumsy and stupid. Emma will exercize no influence over him.

The scene is now laid for the appearance of the heroine. Flaubert avoided the highly dramatic scenes dear to some novelists and the flashbacks that would interrupt the slow grinding of the characters by life. He bent his effort to secure the collaboration of time and the lapse of time becomes a powerful factor in the life of bored Emma and in her ultimate downfall. The slow-witted doctor visited the farm where Emma's father was laid up. His horse shied away as he arrived, as in a premonition of the perils to come. Pale, frail Emma attracted him. Marriage, even without love, provided her with an escape. The date was 1838 (Emma's death will occur in 1846). The celebrated Norman wedding was described by Flaubert in the manner of Breughel, or of Rabelais, whom he always admired, though with more tense, satirical mockery. The couple lived at Tostes; but disillusionment was soon to dispel the very few illusions that Emma might have harbored.

The elegant ball at the castle set her dreaming of what might have been and filled her with disgust at Charles's clumsiness. Her mad waltz turned her head. She treasured the cigar case found by Charles on the road as they were gloomily returning from the feast. Her nerves on edge, resentful of her life's dreary emptiness, Emma threw her nuptial bouquet into the fire. She lost her fanciful greyhound as they moved away from Tostes, a forewarning of her forthcoming caprices and of her own aimlessness. The plaster statue of the priest which she had kept in her garden collapsed and broke: her own piety was likewise brittle. Nothing is whispered about her sex life and its probable disappointments.

Flaubert was not prudish; he merely was discreet and set things in their right place. Emma's disappointment and her cravings were not sexual but sentimental.

Emma and Charles moved to the larger town of Yonville. But the same provincial dullness prevailed there. The night of arrival at the inn is masterfully described by the novelist, as in an old English print or in a Flemish picture, but with glimpses of insight into the reaction of the dismayed Emma. There were the apothecary and his family, and his pompous platitudes and well-meaning helpfulness; the tax-collector Binet; Léon, prone to dreaming of other horizons and of sentimental expansiveness; the stagecoach driver. These people of good will and of limited imagination will henceforth encircle her as in a prison. Emma's last avenues of escape are soon to be closed. Her only child is a daughter and she takes only slight interest in her; maternity fails to bring fulfillment to her. Her husband is a clumsy lover, an exasperatingly dull companion: he does not share her interest in books, her feeling for nature, her aspirations to a fuller life. Out of ambition, she urges him to undertake an operation upon the club-footed stableman: it ends in abject humiliation for the would-be surgeon. The net is woven even more closely around captive Emma. She had a few remnants of religion from her convent education; but her visit to the priest, on a mellow spring day when she feels nostalgically drawn to her girlish dreams of pious purity, ends in one more disappointment. The abbé Bournisien is as "borné," as limited and callous as other men around her. Rodolphe alone, with his seductive manners, his condescension toward all the boorish people around him and her, attracts her and all the dreams started by the cheap romantic literature that she had absorbed are crystallized around him.

Flaubert labored hard over the scene of the agricultural fair. "Bouilhet [Flaubert's friend and literary mentor] insists it will be the finest scene in the book," he reported to Louise Colet. The stress is not on Emma's own thoughts: she tries to banish any which might enter her mind and to forget and deceive herself.

We are not shown the scene through her lenses; we watch it as a dramatic episode, with the Councillor's speech on progress and the humble devotion of farmers. Again, there are several superposed tiers: Emma and the ironical Rodolphe, who feels her weakening; the officials blessing the crowd with their eloquence; the plebeian mass of peasants and animals down below, and the humble, bewildered woman who, having served for fifty years or more in the same farm, finally receives a reward. With all the novelist's objectivity, with his sedulous avoidance of facile contrasts, the old peasant woman's dignity serves as a foil to Emma's growing irresponsibility. There is comedy in the "Comices agricoles," but comedy of a wry and sardonic sort, as in the rest of the novel. As he disposed the varied scenes of his book into an elaborate whole, Flaubert repeatedly commented on the difficulty of catching the "comic spirit" dear to Meredith. He could not match Cervantes' masterpiece which he admired so highly; his own characters were too prosaic. "The prodigious thing about *Don Quixote*," he wrote, "is the absence of art and that perpetual fusion of illusions and reality which makes it such a comical and such a poetical book."

Rodolphe became Emma's lover, after a ride in the meadows and the woods. She felt confident that they would elope together, to the land of the sun and of art, Italy. Rodolphe encouraged her illusions and, frightened perhaps by the fierce determination and the male ambition which Baudelaire detected in Emma, "that bizarre androgyne," he took to flight and left her desperate. Charles nursed her, soothed her nervousness; he may have half understood her trouble, but he preferred silence or willful ignorance of the obvious. He was aware of his own clumsiness with words and in matters of feeling. He himself offered her the opportunities to go to Rouen and to meet other temptations. Her own indifference to her husband was turning into something physical —she was actually repelled by the sight of his stodgy fingers, by his vulgar manners and the heaviness of his conversation. Even weak, effeminate Léon, now working in an office in Rouen, appeared like a romantic diversion to Emma, and she threw herself into a second adulterous affair after a chance meeting with him at the theatre. The scene of their assignation, the Rouen cathedral, is a masterpiece of progressive revelation of two characters and in the subtle use of symbolic details. Emma arrived with a letter which she intended to deliver to Léon, recoiling before the decisive step and voicing her fear of the tragedy which, she was dimly aware, would come from another adulterous liaison. Then she and Léon observed every detail of the cathedral with the beadle, the Lady Chapel, the statue of Diane de Poitiers (one of the great "amoureuses" of the past whose ranks Emma had with elation hoped to join when she first had a lover), the representation of the Damned in Hell. She felt her resolution inwardly weakening and was anxious to gain time. At last they left the church and took the famous ride in the coach which revolted the conventional or the hypocritical moral denunciators of the novel when it first appeared. Through the window of the carriage, she threw to the winds the little bits of her torn letter.

Emma came to scorn her second lover, whom she intimidated and lorded over. "He was *her* mistress," Flaubert remarked, without indulging in psychological remarks upon the feminine submissiveness of Léon or on the virility of Emma. Baudelaire was less discreet in his 1857 essay that analyzes her imagination, her sudden power in making a decision and acting upon it, her generous and "masculine" way of giving herself: "Madame Bovary, through all that is most energetic and most ambitious in her, and also all that is most dreamy, has remained a man." But when she needed Léon most, to the point of urging him to steal in order to pay her debts, he failed her. She had turned into a frightening fury. Everyone else failed her. The money lender, Monsieur Lheureux, evinced not a sign of pity. The notary, Monsieur Guillaumin, would have provided the money, but only if she yielded to his desire. She walked out of his office, indignant, quivering with rage. Rodolphe, too, recoiled from her requests in fear and in avarice. Death loomed as the only recourse and the inevitable retribution. She swallowed the poison. In a ludicrous and gruesome fight, the free thinker Homais and the priest argued above her dying gasps. The raucous voice of the blind man outside sang as she passed away. Yet with faultless skill, Flaubert knew that the story was not to end, conventionally, with Emma's death. The point of view, in the Jamesian sense of the craft of fiction, had been alternately Emma's or Flaubert's himself. But how did Charles, with all his half-voluntary blindness, see his wife and judge her? "Weren't you happy? . . . I did all I could," were among his last words to dying Emma. Later he discovered letters which revealed to the full her adultery. He sequestered himself in despondency, enjoying the bitter voluptuousness of his grief, paid off the debts, and, when he chanced to meet Rodolphe, whispered, "I don't blame you now," adding "the only fine sentence he ever coined," says Flaubert cruelly: the famous "It is the fault of fatality!" Monsieur Homais, meanwhile, prospered and received the Cross of the Legion of Honor.

Alfred de Vigny, in his *Journal d'un Poète* (which Flaubert could not have read), reported the story of the dying Cervantes who was asked whom he had intended to portray in *Don Quixote:* "Myself," he answered. Flaubert's oft-quoted statement echoed it: "Madame Bovary, c'est moi." The advocate of impersonality in art had identified himself with his creation. The solitary hermit of letters had become each of his characters in turn, the fatuous and pitiable loving woman, the romantic devotee of literary illusions, the humiliated husband, the scorned bourgeois, the free thinker Homais. For Flaubert, as for Balzac, who described that same intoxication with escape from oneself in *Facino Cane,* writing was a way of multiplying his own personality. In a letter to Louise Colet on December 23, 1853, he had confided:

> It is a delightful thing to write, no longer to remain oneself, but to wander around in the whole creation of which one speaks. Today for example, man and woman all together, lover and mistress at onc and the same time, I took a ride on horseback in a forest in an

> autumn afternoon under yellow leaves, and I was the horses, the leaves, the wind, the words which were exchanged and the red sun which half closed their eyelids drowned in love.

Flaubert's method is varied and always held in check by a lucid workman whose every effect was deliberate. It is alternately "scenic" and "panoramic," to use the characterization of Percy Lubbock. Flaubert describes the scenery as the characters might have seen it and as he himself thought it was. He relates the past of his creatures insofar as it is relevant, supplements the dialogue and the narrative with his own analysis of the heroes' unexpressed thoughts. At times he talks with the voice and the style of Emma or of Charles or of Homais; at other moments, he is the omniscient novelist analyzing his creations. Now he stresses the incidents of the tale as they may have unfolded, for example in the agricultural fair, now the impression received from such incidents by the leading characters, as for instance at the ball given at the castle. Thus we know Emma from the inside and we sympathize with her; at the same time, we judge her and foresee the doom that lies in store for her. The author's tone verges on satire, as in *Don Quixote,* but it also half conceals pity. The reader must, like the novelist, remain at some aesthetic distance from Emma, or else he would identify himself with her aspirations and with her idealism. He must also be made aware of the falseness in her feelings, of the silliness of some of her reveries. Flaubert's implicit blame is psychological, not moral. As the book draws to its close and the dice are irretrievably loaded against poor Emma, the tone becomes more serene and tragic. The novel has become the full inheritor of the French classical tragedy.

Next to structure and its rendering of the Norman atmosphere, in which Flaubert excelled, the characterization of *Madame Bovary* has merited the highest praise. Even the minor characters are unforgettable. Rodolphe is no conventional seducer: he is inwardly empty, calculating, and selfish, but he fascinates Emma for a while, until she finds him out. He is not Emma's conventional antithesis; he is like a masculine Emma or, as an American scholar, Lawrence E. Harvey, contended, "a liberated Emma who has achieved the sort of success she yearns for and fails to find." Léon, too, is no mere adjunct to Emma's virile personality. He is sensitive, effeminate, cowardly, like most men who place security and professional comfort before love, like all the men whom unfortunate Emma approaches; actually he is very much like her own husband, and he enjoys the superiority over him of being superficially fond of literature and music. The country doctor's wife has hardly been lucky with the men whose understanding she desperately craved and sought. None of them is a criminal; yet each of them is an egotist who will accept a woman's love as long as it brings a little pleasure and prestige, but who will recoil as soon as it may involve sacrifices on his part or become too impassioned, and thus a hindrance. Madame Bovary towers over them, but she lacks the audacity to be a truly dominating fury, a criminal Lady Macbeth. Flaubert was living in an age of common men, or so he thought; and he eschewed heroes whom Shakespeare or Racine would have portrayed.

Homais is a creation worthy of Molière. Flaubert hated the complacent silliness of the bourgeois, discoursing in ready-made pomposities but inwardly empty. Yet he refrained from turning Homais into a mere caricature. He endowed the apothecary with many modest virtues. He made him diligent, kindly to others, tenderhearted in his crude way, eager to learn; like the would-be gentleman Monsieur Jourdain, Homais believes in education and in giving his children wider opportunities than his own humble parents had enjoyed. He fights a war against the village priest, who is almost too thick-skinned and devoid of spirituality to appear convincing. Homais, along with Monsieur Lheureux, emerges from the story as the real victor. Like Chekhov's characters from the lower classes who buy and exploit the cherry orchard after the romantic owners had to forsake it, the two men win in the end and, as did the bourgeoisie under Louis-Philippe, they will construct a new order out of the ruins of the old.

Charles, too, is a trifle overstressed and occasionally fails to win our total "suspension of disbelief." He is incorrigible in his stupidity and blindness, clumsy at games and dancing, and desperately trite in conversation, but kindly and devoted, if incurably awkward, where his wife is concerned. Yet he is not merely comical, like Molière's cuckolds. He is rather pathetic. The distinctive feature of his personality is an utter want of personality. His mere presence exasperates his wife. She soon discerns in him a triple lack: of intelligence, of imagination, of will power. Men refuse to recognize themselves in such a hopelessly mediocre being; yet it is hinted that many women have been attracted to the novel because they recognized their husbands in the village doctor.

Emma herself is probably as well-rounded a woman's portrait as we possess in literature. Flaubert drew her with great delicacy as well as with force. He made her an individualized person, whose character is explained by many a local circumstance, and yet also a general type, as broadly true as any woman in Balzac or Tolstoy. Well could he write, while he was slowly sketching her features, on August 14, 1853: "My poor Madame Bovary suffers and cries at the same time in twenty villages."

She has been judged in conflicting ways. We are less impressed today by her wrong-doings than by the ineluctable series of events which sealed her lamentable fate. She is a peasant girl with some callousness of feeling, and her maternal passion is never very powerful. She has little religious conviction and not overmuch sense of duty; yet there is no deep corruption in her. She has developed a taste for reading, like Stendhal's Julien Sorel or Hardy's Jude the Obscure, and lives in a world of escape. She cannot endure either boredom or the discrepancy between her dreams and reality. At bottom, she is not very intelligent and her will is not firm. She revolts against the trivialities of her married life, insists upon living her dreams, and she falls a victim to her own imprudence and to the selfishness of others. She is cruelly made to atone for her sins. Flaubert symbolized in her the malady of the modern soul: Bovarysm. As Jules de Gaultier defines the term, an excessive development of our sensibility has made us too prone to suffering; we fret at our inability to satisfy our sensual or sentimental needs; our imagination, sharpened by self-analysis, and by the reading of much romantic literature, anticipates and colors reality, and reality then proves disappointing to us. Emma, journeying to Rouen to meet her lover, constantly promised herself a deep felicity in his arms, "then she confessed to herself that she felt nothing extraordinary." Instead of accepting others and ourselves as they and we are, we are the playthings of relentless self-deception, and sincerely insincere. Reality wreaks its revenge.

The innermost conviction of Flaubert and of several of his contemporaries—such as Gautier, the Parnassian poets, and the champions of "art for art's sake"—was that the world is wrong; it has little significance and no justification, except in its beauty. Flaubert's religion was the cult of art and style. Man himself can redeem his littleness only by perceiving and creating beauty. He repeatedly described himself as an ascetic or as a mystic—a mystic without a God, who found his Absolute in art. The art-for-art's-sake doctrine that he professed asserted the total independence of art from politics and from all contemporary agitation, from religion, from ethics. Art should be self-contained and self-supporting, "like a star," said Flaubert. It should never be didactic. It should borrow nothing from what is transitory: political quarrels, social problems, economic values, moral ideals dependent upon a certain society and its implicit creed. The artist is a saint who curbs his own passions and prejudices: he must not reveal himself in his work and must aim at truth alone, which will outlive us "when old age shall this generation waste." He depicts life as it appears to him, but extracts the permanent from ephemeral contingency and the universal from shifting particularity.

Such an emphasis on beauty may not be altogether salutary for a novelist. Virginia Woolf, who should have known, declared that "a profound poetic sense is a dangerous gift for the novelist."

Flaubert was endowed with that dangerous gift, and thereby ran the risk of banishing life from his tales. Yet he realized that beauty ought not to exclude the animated truth of everyday life. "One must," he confessed at the end of his *Notes de Voyage* on Carthage, "through the beautiful and in spite of it, fashion something true and alive."

Flaubert believed in style and, as his disciple, Maupassant, specified, "in one manner, and one only, an absolute one, of expressing an object in all its color and all its intensity." Few of us today commune in such a religion of style and while the structure of *Madame Bovary* wins universal praise, its style meets with many a bitter criticism. The purists have detected a large number of provincialisms and even of errors in the volume: foreign readers are broader minded and those minor lapses, which in his day might well have kept Flaubert from entering the French Academy, do not irk us. The vocabulary is concrete and precise, but not particularly evocative. Balzac's is much richer and Proust's more sensitive and varied. Syntax was Flaubert's chief concern. He hunted down the relative pronouns "qui" and "que" mercilessly, as ponderous and ambiguous. Like many Latins, Flaubert was by nature prone to an oratorical style, with sonorous cadences and a multiplicity of interrogations. "How on earth had she proceeded, she who was so intelligent, to make that mistake once again?" wonders Emma. Or, at the beginning of the novel, "How is it that Charles returned to the farm, since M. Rouault was now cured?" Those rhetorical questions fitted in especially well with Flaubert's characteristic devices: the use of the imperfect and of indirect discourse.

The imperfect tense was for him the best means of suggesting the static and the monotonous, the unbearable duration of the hours that bored Emma and that weighed heavily upon the dull little towns where she, her husband, and their friends had to draw out their eventless lives. Indirect discourse enabled the novelist to render the corrosive, insidious reflections which entered the minds of those of his characters who revolted at their unbearable ennui. The notions or the visions flitting through them were thus expressed, not in direct speech and dialogue, which would reveal them too blatantly to others, but in indirect discourse in the imperfect tense. "That husband of hers knew nothing, wished nothing. He believed her to be happy, and she would resent that well-seated quietude." Or, in the characteristic passage of Part I, chapter IX, that Erich Auerbach analyzed in his *Mimesis:*

> It was above all at meal times that she could no longer endure it, . . . The whole bitterness of existence seemed to her to be served on her plate and, as the boiled beef steamed, there rose from the depths of her soul other exhalations of sickening insipidity. Charles was slow at eating; she would nibble a few hazel nuts, or else, leaning on her elbow, she would amuse herself, with the point of her knife, at drawing lines on the oilcloth.

The grinding boredom of Emma, her impatience with Charles, soon to develop into exasperation, and the banal vulgarity of her life are here presented through her mind. Flaubert expresses what his heroine inwardly felt but could not herself put into such words.

Flaubert labored most assiduously over comparisons and over the rhythm of his sentences. In a famous indictment of Flaubert's style, Proust found fault with the banality of his metaphors and of his laborious comparisons. It must be confessed that these epic comparisons, reminiscent of Chateaubriand, often fall flat and seldom conjure up a vivid vision. They usually draw a parallel between a feeling and an exterior object: "She would stop, paler and trembling more than the poplar leaves which swung above her head." "The memory of Rodolphe remained deep in her, more solemn and motionless than a king's mummy in a subterranean passage." The Rouen Cathedral is compared to a gigantic boudoir; the carriage in which Emma and Léon ride after leaving the cathedral is "more sealed than a tomb and tossed about like a ship." There is something strained and awkward in these comparisons. Perhaps Flaubert labored too long over them. Stendhal and Balzac, who wrote faster, wrote also with greater naturalness.

As to the cadences of his sentences, they too smack of artificiality. Flaubert's mother would upbraid him angrily: "Your mania for sentences dried up your heart." He would repeat them for hours, balance them skillfully, want them to be musical but without the effeminate softness of much poetic prose: his is often the triadic rhythm into which French prose readily falls. A sentence is made up of three segments, the longest being any of the three, the shortest sometimes the first and often the last, thus closing the rhythmical sentence with a knell of finality. A division into four segments would tend to become too obviously symmetrical. Very short sentences, such as Voltaire, Mérimée, and Hemingway cherished, can, in the long run, produce an impression of disconnectedness and fail to convey the effects of slow corrosion of the characters by time at which Flaubert aimed. But some monotony ensues in *Madame Bovary.* Paradoxically, the style, on which Flaubert spent such painstaking labor, appears to our contemporary eyes as perhaps the least admirable part of his art.

Yet, when all is said, Flaubert retains the rare merit of allowing no dross in his metal. He never used three words where one could suffice. He never resorted to padding or superfluous rhetoric; his sentences never lapse into jargon, obscurity, pathos; they are robust and muscular, "male" as he desired them to be. Flaubert's art is doubtless a trifle too self-conscious and over-calculated, but such restraint was needed in 1850–60 to establish fiction as an autonomous art form. John Galsworthy, in his *Castles in Spain and other Scripts,* remarked that the English novel, fine and rich as it can be, "has, from *Clarissa Harlowe* to *Ulysses,* been inclined to self-indulgence; it often goes to bed drunk." Flaubert's certainly does not. His lesson is one of restraint, finish, and artistic integrity.

Dostoevsky in *Crime and Punishment*

PHILIP RAHV

> *When thought is closed in caves*
> *Then love shall show its roots in deepest hell.*
> —WILLIAM BLAKE

IS THIS THE TYPE of narrative nowadays called a psycho-thriller? Yes, in a sense it is, being above all, in its author's own words, the psychological account of a crime. The crime is murder. But in itself this is in no way exceptional, for the very same crime occurs in nearly all of Dostoevsky's novels. Proust once suggested grouping them together under a single comprehensive title: The Story of a Crime.

Where this novel differs, however, from the works following it is in the totality of its concentration on that obsessive theme. Virtually everything in the story turns on Raskolnikov's murder of the old pawnbroker and her sister Lizaveta, and it is this concentration which makes the novel so fine an example of artistic economy and structural cohesion. Free of distractions of theme and idea, and with no confusing excess or over-ingenuity in the manipulation of the plot, such as vitiates the design of *A Raw Youth* and reduces the impact of *The Idiot, Crime and Punishment* is the one novel of Dostoevsky's in which his powerful appeal to our intellectual interests is most directly and naturally linked to the action.

The superiority of this work in point of structure has been repeatedly remarked upon, but what has not been sufficiently noted is its extraordinary narrative pace. Consider the movement of Part I, for instance. In this comparatively short section (coming to 84 pages in Constance Garnett's translation), we get to know the protagonist fairly well, to know the conditions of crushing poverty and isolation under which he lives and the complex origins of his "loathsome scheme"; we see him going through a rehearsal-visit to the victim's flat; we listen to Marmeladov's sermon in the pothouse, to the recital of his domestic woes, including the circumstances that forced his daughter Sonia to become a prostitute; we witness the drunken old man's homecoming and the hysterical violence with which he is received by his wife; then we read with Raskolnikov the long letter from his mother, learning a good deal about his family situation; we dream with him the frightful dream, looking at once to the past and to the future, of the beating to death of the little mare; finally, after several more scenes of the strictest dramatic relevance, we are brought to a close-up of the double murder, probably the most astonishing description of its kind in fiction, and watch the murderer returning to his lodgings where, after putting back the axe under the porter's bench, he climbs the stairs to sink on his bed in blank forgetfulness.

Thus in this first section of seven chapters a huge quantity of experience is qualitatively organized, with the requisite information concerning the hero's background driven into place through a consummate use of the novelistic device of foreshortening, and with the swift narrative tempo serving precisely as the prime means of controlling and rendering credible the wild queerness of what has been recounted. For this wild queerness cannot be made to yield to explanation or extrinsic analysis. To gain our consent—to enlist, that is, our poetic faith—the author must either dramatize or perish, and for full success he must proceed with the dramatic representation at a pace producing an effect of virtual instantaneousness. To have secured this effect is a triumph of Dostoevsky's creative method—a triumph because the instantaneous is a quality of Being rather than of mind and not open to question. As the vain efforts of so many philosophers have demonstrated, Being is irreducible to the categories of explanation or interpretation.

The artistic economy, force and tempo of Part I is sustained throughout the novel. (The epilogue, in which hope and belief play havoc with the imaginative logic of the work, is something else again.) There is no wasted detail in it, none that can be shown to be functionally inoperative in advancing the action and our insight into its human agents. And it is important to observe that the attaining of this fullness and intensity of representation is conditional upon Dostoevsky's capacity to subdue the time element of the story to his creative purpose. Readers not deliberately attentive to the time-lapse of the action are surprised to learn that its entire span is only two weeks and that of Part I only three days. Actually, there is no real lapse of time in the story because we are virtually unaware of it apart from the tension of the rendered experience. Instead of time lapsing there is the concrete flow of duration contracting and expanding with the rhythm of the dramatic movement.

Least of all is it a chronological frame that time provides in this novel. As the Russian critic K. Mochulsky has so aptly remarked, its time is purely psychological, a function of human consciousness, in other words the very incarnation of Bergson's *durée réele*.[1] And it is only in Bergsonian terms that one can do it justice. Truly, Dostoevsky succeeds here in converting time into a kind of progress of Raskolnikov's mental state, which is not

[1] K. Mochulsky, *Dostoevskii: zizn i tvorchestvo* (Paris, 1947), p. 243 ff.

actually a state but a process of incessant change eating into the future and expanding with the duration it accumulates, like a snowball growing larger as it rolls upon itself, to use Bergson's original image.

This effect is partly accomplished by the exclusion from Raskolnikov's consciousness of everything not directly pertaining to his immediate situation. From beginning to end he is in a state of crisis from which there is no diversion or escape either in memory or fantasy. The import of what he thinks, feels, and remembers is strictly functional to the present. Thus he thinks of his mother, who is involved in the action, with distinct alternations of feelings, while his dead father hardly exists for him. He belongs to the past, and so far as Raskolnikov is concerned the past is empty of affect. The one time he evokes his father's figure is in the anguished dream of the beating to death of the little mare, and his appearance in that dream is singularly passive, manifestly carrying with it no charge of emotion. This dream, enacting a tragic catharsis, is introduced with calculated ambiguity. Is the dreamer actually remembering an episode of his childhood or is he imagining the memory? In any case, though the dream is of the past its meaning is all in the present. The pitiful little mare, whipped across the eyes and butchered by Mikolka and a crowd of rowdy peasants, stands for all such victims of life's insensate cruelty, in particular such victims as Sonia and Lizaveta whose appeal to Raskolnikov is that of "poor gentle things . . . whose eyes are soft and gentle." Also, the mare stands above all for Raskolnikov himself, and in embracing her bleeding head in a frenzy of compassion it is himself he is embracing, bewailing, consoling. He is present in the dream not only as the little boy witnessing an act of intolerable brutality but as at once its perpetrator and victim too. The dream's imagery is entirely prospective in that it points ahead, anticipating the murder Raskolnikov is plotting even while exposing it as an act of self-murder. Its latent thought-content is a warning that in killing the pawnbroker he would be killing himself too, and it is indeed in this light that he understands his deed afterwards when, in confessing to Sonia, he cries out: "Did I murder the old woman? I murdered myself, not her! I crushed myself once and for all, forever." The cathartic effect of the dream is such that upon awakening he recovers the sense of his human reality, feeling "as though an abscess that had been forming in his heart had suddenly broken . . . he was free from that spell, that sorcery, that obsession." But the catharsis is momentary, and he no sooner hears that the pawnbroker will be alone in her flat the next evening than he is again gripped by his obsession.

Another instance of the functional character of Raskolnikov's memory is the way he recalls the invalid girl to whom he had once been engaged. "I really don't know," he says, "what drew me to her then . . . she was always ill. If she had been lame or hunchback, I believe I would have liked her even better." This is a meaningful admission, and it is curious that the numerous commentators on the novel should have unanimously ignored it. It is as if they all wanted to spare Sonia. For what prompts this memory if not his involvement with Sonia, who is in her own way ill too? In the eyes of the world and likewise of Raskolnikov in some of his moods she is a morally deformed creature, an outcast, and "a religious maniac" to boot. Physically too, the description of the invalid girl has much in common with that of Sonia.

Yet, for all his living in the present, Raskolnikov wills and acts with his whole past back of him; and it is for a very good reason that we are not permitted to gain a privileged understanding of his past in the sense of entering a series of his mental states anterior to the action. By denying us such intimacy the author effectively prevents us from rationalizing the mystery of the crime and its motive—the mystery which is never really solved but toward the solution of which everything in the novel converges. Now the study of Dostoevsky's manuscripts has shown that he was himself disturbed no end by the indefiniteness and uncertainty of Raskolnikov's motive, and he wrote a note reminding himself that he must once and for all clear up the uncertainty and isolate the "real" motive in order "to destroy," as he put it, "the indefiniteness and explain the murder this way or that way" (*tak ili etak*). Fortunately he was able to forget this injunction as the novel progressed. For his basic idea of his hero's motivation is such as to identify it with the totality of his consciousness, and to have changed that conception to a more conventional one would have led to the withering of that fine insight; and what that insight comes to, in the last analysis, is that human consciousness is inexhaustible and incalculable. It cannot be condensed into something so limited and specific as a motive. The consciousness is ever obliging in generating a sufficiency of reasons, but it is necessary to distinguish between reasons and motives. Not that motives have no existence; they exist, to be sure, but only on the empirical plane, materializing in the actual practice of living, primarily in the commitment of action. Existentially speaking, the acting man can be efficient and self-assured only insofar as his consciousness is non-reflective. Raskolnikov, however, is above all a man of reflection, and his crime is frequently described in the book as a "theoretical" one, "theoretical" not only in the sense of its being inspired by a theory but also in the sense that theory, that is to say abstraction, is of its very essence: no wonder he carries out the murder in the manner of a sleep-walker or of a man falling down a precipice. The textual evidence shows that what his crime mainly lacks is empirical content, and that is what some critics had in mind, I think, in defining it as a pure experiment in self-cognition. Thus it can be said of this murderer that he produces a corpse but no real motive. His consciousness, time and again recoiling upon itself in a sickening manner, consumes motives as fast as it produces them.

Crime and Punishment may be characterized as a psycho-thriller with prodigious complications. It is misleading, however, to speak of it as a detective story, as is so often done. It is nothing of the sort, since from the outset we know not only the murderer's identity but are also made to enter into some of his innermost secrets. True, the story is almost entirely given over to detection

—not of the criminal, though, but of his motive. Inevitably it turns out that there is not one but a whole cluster of motives, a veritable *embarras de richesses,* and if the criminal himself is in his own fashion constrained to take part in the work of detection it is because he is soon lost in the maze of his own motivation. Never quite certain as to what it was exactly that induced him to commit murder, he must continually spy on himself in a desperate effort to penetrate his own psychology and attain the self-knowledge he needs if he is to assume responsibility for his absurd and hideous act. And this idea of him as the criminal in search of his own motive is precisely what is so new and original in the figure of Raskolnikov.

His knowing and not knowing is in a sense the worst of his ordeal. He is aware of several motives that keep eluding him as his thought shifts among them, and there are times when they all seem equally unreal to him. To sustain himself in the terrible isolation of his guilt he must be in complete possession of a single incontrovertible motive representing his deepest self, his own rock-bottom truth. But he no sooner lays hold of this truth than he catches himself in a state of mind that belies it, as, for example, in the scene when right after burying the loot—a purse and some trinkets of jewelry—he suddenly stops in the street to confound himself with a simple and terrifying question:

> If it had all really been done deliberately and not idiotically, if I really had a certain and definite object, how is it that I did not even glance into the purse and didn't know what I had there. Then why have I undergone these agonies and have deliberately undertaken this base, dirty and degrading business?

This is but one of several passages in which the abstraction, so to speak, of the crime, its lack of empirical substance, is brought home to us. There is an intrinsic incongruity between this criminal and his crime which is exhibited by the author with masterful indirection, and nowhere to better effect than when Raskolnikov makes his confession to Sonia. In the course of it, though straining as hard as he can to discover and at long last seize the motive that impelled him, he still cannot stop wavering and giving various and contradictory explanations of his act. He begins by stating that he murdered "for plunder," but when Sonia cries: "You were hungry! It was to help your mother? Yes?" he at once retracts that explanation, muttering: "No, Sonia, no . . . . I was not so hungry . . . . I certainly did want to help my mother, but that's not the real thing either . . . ." A little later he adds that if he had simply killed the old pawnbroker because of hunger he would be *happy* now, exclaiming that he really wanted to become a Napoleon and that is why he killed her. Yet still later we hear him say that the argument from Napoleon is "all nonsense" as he reverts to the explanation from poverty and simple need. Soon enough, however, he strikes again the Napoleonic note, accounting for the murder now as a matter of wanting to have the daring: "I only wanted to have the daring . . . that was the whole cause of it"; he claims that he killed "not to gain wealth and power" but for himself alone so as to find out quickly whether "he was a louse like everybody else or a man," whether he was a "trembling creature" or one who has "the right" to step over barriers. Still another cause, more immediately psychological in bearing, is introduced when he speaks of his airless cupboard of a room, that room where he turned sulky and sat "like a spider," where he would not work but simply lay for hours thinking. It is chiefly this perpetual thinking, this desperate resort to sheer reflection, which is the source of the mystifications that torment him. Though it is his consciousness which did him in, it is to his empirical self that he absurdly looks for the justification it cannot supply; so that in the end, for all the keenness with which he explicates his act to Sonia, we are still left with a crime of indeterminate origin and meaning.

The indeterminacy is the point. Dostoevsky is the first novelist to have fully accepted and dramatized the principle of uncertainty or indeterminacy in the presentation of character. In terms of novelistic technique this principle manifests itself as a kind of hyperbolic suspense—suspense no longer generated merely by the traditional means and devices of fiction, though these are skilfully brought into play, but as it were by the very structure of human reality. To take this hyperbolic suspense as a literary invention pure and simple is to fail in comprehending it; it originates rather in Dostoevsky's acute awareness (self-awareness at bottom) of the problematical nature of the modern personality and of its tortuous efforts to stem the disintegration threatening it. Thus Raskolnikov, like Stavrogin and other protagonists of Dostoevsky's, is represented throughout under the aspect of modernity (the examining magistrate Porfiry Petrovitch sees him very specifically as "a modern case") understood as spiritual and mental self-division and self-contradiction. It is in this light that the search for the true cause of the crime becomes ultimately intelligible, the search that gives the novel at once its form and meaning, taking us where no psycho-thriller before or after *Crime and Punishment* has ever taken us, into a realm where only the sharpest psychological perception will see us through and into another realm still where our response to ideas is impetuously solicited: ideas bearing on crime and its relation to psychic illness on the one hand and to power and genius on the other; ideas about two kinds of human beings, ordinary and extraordinary, with the former serving as mere material for the latter who arrogate to themselves the right "to overstep the line" and remove moral obstacles at will; ideas concerning the supernal value of suffering and the promise of deliverance in Christ.

The principal characters (Raskolnikov, Svidrigailov, and others) are the carriers of these ideas, and if we are not to sever the unity of thought and action, theory and practice, prevailing in the Dostoevskyean world, it is necessary to take their ideas for what they are, without reducing them, with the purely psychological critics, to a species of "interesting" rationalizations, or, with the formalistic critics, to mere "fictive matter" drawn fortuitously from the intellectual sphere. That we must first of all regard the ideas as dramatic motivation goes without saying; but that should not deter us from also accepting them as given on the level of thought. "I killed not an old woman but a principle," declares Raskolnikov. What is that principle and why does he want to kill it? The answer to such questions has been much simplified or, worse, still, credulously taken for granted.

From the Christian standpoint Raskolnikov is easily enough perceived to be a kind of Lazarus whom Sonia strives to raise from the dead. Yet if he comes forth from the tomb it is only after experiencing the ecstasy and terror of having touched for one moment the secret springs of freedom and power. "What, then, is to be done?" asks Sonia. This is indeed the fateful question which reverberates throughout the whole of Russian literature and to which all the leaders of Russian thought, from Chaadayev to Lenin, sought to provide an answer. Raskolnikov, too, accepts the challenge. "Break what must be broken," he replies, "once and for all, and take the suffering on oneself. . . . Freedom and power! Over all trembling creation and all the antheap! . . . That is the goal, remember that!" No wonder that though apparently renouncing that goal in yielding to Sonia's entreaties that he save himself through penance and submission, he nevertheless remains essentially unrepentant to the end. At the very least it can be said that he remains so deeply divided in his mind as to give himself up more because of confusion and despair than because of any real change of heart. About his regeneration we are told only in the epilogue, when at long last the pale sickly faces of the murderer and the saintly prostitute become "bright with the dawn of a new future." But this happy Siberian aftermath is the beginning of something altogether new and different. As the author observes in the last paragraph of the text, it "might be the subject of a new story but our present story is ended." [2]

[2] It might indeed have been the subject of a new story. However, Dostoevsky, as a number of critics have noted, appears to have been incapable of carrying out his declared intention to depict the renewal of life on Christian foundations. On this score the late Leo Shestov made one of the most sardonic notations: "*Crime and Punishment* ends with the promise to picture the Christian rebirth of the hero.

We, as critical readers, cannot overmuch concern ourselves with such intimations of ultimate reconcilement and salvation. Our proper concern is with the present story, with the story as written.

Dostoevsky wrote the first of his four great novels in monthly installments for the *Russky Vestnik,* where it ran serially between January and December, 1866. He was following his usual course of producing a long work under the immediate pressure of editors and printers. In this instance, however, he appears to have encountered very few difficulties in meeting the magazine's schedule. And the ease with which he accomplished the actual composition may have been partly due at least to the fact that the narrative mode he had adopted after considerable experimenting and much vacillation, the mode, that is, of telling the story from the standpoint of the "omniscient author," justified itself in practice, allowing him to make the most of his material without strain or hindrance.

The strain had indeed told on him in the late months of 1865,

---

His words sound as if he were binding himself with a sacred vow. And, in point of fact, as a professed teacher of humanity, was not Dostoevsky in duty bound to let us in on the secret of the new reality and fresh possibilities that opened up to Raskolnikov? Yet our preceptor never managed to fulfill that sacred vow. The same promise is encountered again in his foreword to *The Brothers Karamazov,* where we are told that in order to portray his real hero, Alyosha, he would need to write still another volume, as if the existing book with its thousand pages lacked sufficient space to accommodate the 'new life.' In the three novels he produced after *Crime and Punishment* there is no mention of the sacred vow. Prince Myshkin cannot be taken into account here. If he is the one representing the 'renewal' awaiting mankind . . . then there is no point whatever in looking toward the future. . . . No, compared to Dostoevsky's other heroes Prince Myshkin is a misfit. This novelist understood only restless, fractious, struggling people whose search is never ended. No sooner did he undertake to show us a man who has found himself and achieved tranquillity than he fell into fatal banalities. One thinks, for instance, of the elder Zosima's dreams of 'the coming wonderful union of men.' What is this 'wonderful union' if not another of those idyllic pictures of the future which even the socialists—so maliciously ridiculed in his cellar by the narrator of *Notes from Underground*—have by now learned to do without?" *Dostoevskii i Nitsshe: filosofiya tragedii* (St. Petersburg, 1903).

when while living in Wiesbaden he had written an incomplete draft of the novel in the form both of a diary and of a murderer's confession. Those versions turned out to be so unsatisfactory, chiefly because of the cramping effects of the method of narration in the first person, that he was forced to scrap them. The economy of interest he had been trying to enforce by means of that method proved to be too much of a good thing, and he now took exactly the opposite tack, expanding the interest where formerly he had compressed it. Into the new expansive scheme he introduced the figures of Svidrigailov and Porfiry Petrovitch, who have nothing in common besides the fact that both represent possible attitudes toward Raskolnikov, viewpoints or perspectives enabling us to see at once more clearly and more variously the significance of his case. Dostoevsky also introduced into his revised scheme the basic elements of a tale, entitled *The Drunkards,* which he had just sketched out in outline and in which he was proposing to enter into "all the ramifications" of the then rather topical subject of alcoholism rampant among the city poor, with the emphasis falling on "the picture of a family and the bringing up of children under such circumstances." It is in this somewhat fortuitous manner, or so it would seem on the face of it, that the Marmeladov sequence, so reminiscent of the author's earlier vein in its pathos of indigence and harrowing exposition of the Petersburg misery, as the Russians are wont to call it, came to be included in the account of Raskolnikov's crime.

But the fortuitousness is more apparent than real. There is an inner logic, both of content and structure, in his combination of subject matter from which the novel gains enormously—and this can be said even while conceding that the rather stagey woes of the Marmeladovs are inducive of some moments of weariness. A somewhat Dickensian family with deviations toward Russian intensity, they are of course the very embodiment of the Petersburg misery. But Raskolnikov is also a child of that misery, patently belonging to the world of the insulted and injured, though in him the humility and submissiveness of that world's human mixture are turned inside out. He is the first of its inhabitants to attempt its redemption by making a bid, in however futile and hideous a fashion, for freedom and power.

Intrinsically his figure is a composite of the typical protagonists of Dostoevsky's earlier and later fiction. Morbidly estranged as he is from life and ceaselessly brooding in his cupboard of a room, he at once brings to mind certain traits of the underground man as well as of the daydreaming recluse portrayed in such stories of the 1840's as "The Landlady" and "White Nights"—the recluse who, suffering from nearly pathological depression and nameless guilt-feelings, keeps to himself and lives a life of wishful fantasy. At the same time Raskolnikov represents a startling departure from the recluse type in that, having overcome the latter's masochistic need for self-abasement, his aggression is no longer turned inward but outward. He is quite as much a fantast as the daydreaming recluse, but his fantasy has left behind it all *Schwärmerei* and noble aspiration *à la* Schiller: it has taken on the color of blood. A complete egoist on one side of his nature at least and a surprisingly candid one at that, he is filled with the wrath of outraged pride and a furious impatience to break out from his trapped existence even at the risk of self-destruction. Moreover, to see him from this angle of vision, as the Dostoevskyean hero in process of evolution, is to note another new element in him, namely, that he is an intellectual *pur sang*, recklessly yielding himself to the passion of thought and caught at last in the toils of an idea, mastered by it to the point of monomania. Thus the novel of which he is the protagonist has a double aspect. In virtue of its carryover of the theme of the Petersburg misery it brings to a close the series of so-called social narratives which, from *Poor Folk* to *The Insulted and Injured,* is dominated by a consistent motif that has been aptly defined as that of "the impotent protest of powerless people." In its second aspect, however, the novel throws off the limitations of the earlier theme, attaining the higher goals of its author's greater or ultimate period.

Raskolnikov's involvement with the Marmeladov clan enabled Dostoevsky to solve what must have been his main compositional problem: How to portray with entire cogency a hero who is a solitary and monomaniac acting throughout in a mood of "morbid irritability" verging on madness without succumbing to him, that is to say, without letting him take the lead to the degree of making the world over in his image? This is but another way of formulating one of the principal difficulties which forced Dostoevsky to abandon the first versions of the book. For to have permitted Raskolnikov, as first-person narrator, to absorb the story unto himself would surely have resulted in its impoverishment, producing an impression of life closing in, a claustrophobic effect diminishing the hero's stature in our eyes and turning him into an altogether special case.[3] And this is where the Marmeladovs come in exactly, that for all the grimness of their situation and its grotesque features they still somehow exist within the bounds of the normal, whereas Raskolnikov is decidedly outside it; hence their presence adds considerably to the story's quota of circumstantial realism, helping to overcome the hazard implicit in Raskolnikov's malaise. For we must keep in mind that his story, which on one side is an account of a crime open to explanation on the seemingly objective grounds of material need and a sinister "nihilistic" theory, is converted on the subjective side into an analysis of an extreme pathological condition or soul-sickness, if you will.

The episodes dealing with Svidrigailov, the would-be seducer of Raskolnikov's sister Dounia, have an engrossing interest of their own, but they also serve the same functional purpose of reducing the protagonist's remoteness from the common human measure. In order to heighten the dramatic tension and explore to

[3] The special or clinical case is precisely what no master of the narrative medium will let himself in for. Dostoevsky did let himself in for it once, in the early nouvelle, *The Double,* which, for all its startling effects, cannot be rated otherwise than as a failure. He never repeated that youthful error. In lesser talents, however, this error becomes habitual, for in coping with the extremes of morbidity or irrationality they are frequently lured into betraying the shared sense of human reality.

the end the complex meanings of Raskolnikov's plight, it was positively necessary to involve him in intimate human associations, notwithstanding the feeling of absolute aloneness, or "agonizing, everlasting solitude," into which he is plunged by his murderous act. It is a feeling brought on by the guilt he refuses to acknowledge and strains every nerve to repress; and what better way was there of dramatizing the struggle within him between guilt and scornful pride than by showing him entering almost in spite of himself into relations with people who for reasons both good and bad are intent on penetrating his isolation? Sonia, his "chosen bride" and Christian mentor, is of course the chief agent of this turn of the plot, but so in his own paradoxical fashion is Svidrigailov. The latter, however, is so fascinating a character in his own right, exercising an appeal nearly matching that of the hero, that at times he threatens to run away with the story; certainly the scene of his suicide and of the dream-haunted night that precedes it are perfectly realized incidents and among the marvels of the book. It must have called for the nicest management on the author's part to hold him to his subordinate position. But that was only part of the task Dostoevsky set himself in undertaking to unify the three thematic elements at his disposal: the major theme of Raskolnikov's crime and its consequences and the strongly contrasted minor themes of the lowly and good Marmeladovs on the one hand and of the wealthy immoralist Svidrigailov on the other. And it is the achieved integration with its fine contrapuntal effects which makes for verisimilitude of a higher order, for novelistic truth and density, and for structural cohesion.

But though the Svidrigailov sequence is successfully integrated into the main action, there is no denying that he is invested with an originality and expressive power that invite comment. It will not do to see him, in the fashion of most critics of Dostoevsky, as being merely Raskolnikov's double, representing the pole of self-will in his character. The formal abstractness of this traditional approach to Svidrigailov cannot do him justice; and so far as the element of self-will is concerned, Raskolnikov, like all "the children of darkness" in Dostoevsky, has more than enough of it in himself and is in no need of Svidrigailov's services. No, the latter has an independent existence in the novel though his position in it is structurally subordinate; his function is not simply that of ministering to its hero. There is no innate relationship between the two, no affinity of the mystical order such as is posited in so many Dostoevsky studies. Actually Svidrigailov enters the novel by way of the external plot or intrigue (his pursuit of Dounia), yet once he is in it he provides the story not only with an additional perspective on Raskolnikov but also with the psychosexual vitality which it otherwise lacks, for both Raskolnikov and Sonia are singularly sexless. Svidrigailov exemplifies a distinct character-type in Dostoevsky, the type of the nihilist in the realm of sensuality. He is a more elaborate and refined version of the rather coarse-grained libertine Valkovsky in *The Insulted and Injured* and he anticipates the figures of Stavrogin and the elder Karamazov in the later novels (like Stavrogin he is guilty of outraging a little girl). In this character-type, sensuality becomes a flight from the vertiginous consciousness of freedom and from a kind of ennui which has gone beyond the psychological and has acquired a metaphysical status. Thus Svidrigailov believes in ghosts who "are as it were shreds and fragments of other worlds" and who appear only to people whose psyche is prepared to receive them. He rejects all dogma, including that of the atheists, as he is given to relativizing all possible ideas, whether of belief or unbelief. Whereas Raskolnikov does not believe in a future life, Svidrigailov speculates that perhaps the future life does exist but that there are only "spiders there or something of that sort."

> We always imagine eternity as something beyond our conception, something vast, vast! But why must it be vast? Instead of all that, what if it is one little room, like a bathhouse in the country, black and grimy and spiders in every corner, and that's all eternity is?

As for vice, he chides Raskolnikov for his moral prejudices, contending that in sexual vice

> there is at least something permanent, founded indeed upon nature and not dependent on fantasy, something present in the blood like an ever-burning ember, forever setting one on fire and maybe not to be quickly extinguished even with years. You agree that it's an occupation of a sort.

Admitting that it is a disease, like everything that exceeds moderation, he defends his indulgence in it by claiming that to give it up would mean that he would be forced to shoot himself. Clearly, his métier is not the simple-minded villainy of melodrama but a species of objective cruelty (as in his doing away with his wife and driving his footman to suicide), which is in a sense a form of meditation upon life beyond good and evil translated into practice. Therefore he is at the same time capable of acts of sympathy and kindness, as when he helps the Marmeladov orphans and lets Dounia go after cornering her. Good and evil are never ends to him but simply the available, even if sometimes redundant, means of convincing himself that it is possible to continue living. Hence the actions he performs strike one as transpiring somewhere outside himself, for they are at bottom experiments conducted by a self which is itself an experimental projection.

It has been observed often enough that every literary artist genuinely an innovator creates his own audience. This is certainly true of Dostoevsky, in whose sphere we have now learned to move without undue strain but who shocked his contemporaries by his open and bold reliance on melodrama and by the seeming fantasticality of his characters. The Russian reader had learned by that time to identify the unhurried, equable, lifelike realism of writers like Turgenev, Goncharov and Tolstoy with the higher norms of the novel; and what those writers scrupulously avoided above all was the sensational and excessive. Dostoevsky was hard put to it to persuade the reader that he too, despite his startling deviations from the newly-established norms, was a realist. Hence while writing *Crime and Punishment* he fretted over the thought that his story would gain no credence from the public; and since he had long been trying to defend himself against the charge of insufficient regard for the real, he was pleased to note, shortly after the appearance of the first installment of the novel, that a crime curiously similar to the one he was describing had been committed by a Moscow student and reported in the newspapers. He at once seized upon this item as confirming his own "special view" of the relation between art and actuality.

> What the majority call fantastic and exceptional, [he wrote to the critic Strakhov] sometimes signifies to me the very essence of reality . . . . In every issue of the newspapers you come upon accounts of the most real facts and amazing coincidences. For our writers, who are unconcerned with them, they are fantastic. But being facts they are reality none the less.

But this appeal to actual life—formless, disorderly and inconsequent life with its "most real facts and amazing coincidences"—is unworthy of the genius of Dostoevsky. In spite of his opposition to such radical-minded simplifiers of the relation of art and life as Chernishevsky, Dobroliubov and Pisarev, critics exceedingly influential in their time, he was himself far from immune to the idea then prevailing in his intellectual milieu that the work of art was useless and perhaps even immoral in its inutility unless directly validated by life or "reality," understood in the simplest empirical sense of these terms. Dostoevsky was after all a Russian writer of his generation, a generation ideologically inspired to exalt life over art and seeking to justify the latter by citing the gifts of illumination and hopes of betterment it ostensibly brings to life. Where Dostoevsky twisted that common assumption to suit his creative practice was by claiming to discern the essence of reality not in its typical everyday manifestations but in the exceptional and fantastic. He was unable to go beyond that formula toward the assertion of a symbolic rather than literal correspondence between life and the fictive worlds of his own devising. Hence the speciousness of his argument from life in his literary apologetics, as in his pointing to life's "amazing coincidences" in the letter to Strakhov quoted above. The fact is that no coincidence copied from life can make in the least plausible the kind of coincidences, even the minor ones, you find in *Crime and Punishment,* such as the prosperous and respectable bourgeois Luzhin turning up in the same slum-lodging with the starving Marmeladov family or Svidrigailov, a rich man, finding no better place to stay in Petersburg than in the very same house where Sonia lives, a house in which his flat adjoins the room where she practices her trade and conducts those incredible conversations with Raskolnikov upon which he eavesdrops with the greatest relish. It is plain that Svidrigailov is situated where he is in order to make it possible for him to learn Raskolnikov's secret at the same time as he confides it to Sonia; an important turn of the plot depends on it. This is a calculated coincidence different in kind from those, however improbable, that life offers. It belongs to the stock-in-trade of melodrama, and Dostoevsky learned the use of it in his assiduous reading of Hoffmann, Dickens, Balzac, Sue, and a host of lesser authors of crime-thrillers and adventure stories.

It is in literature rather than in unprocessed life that you find some of the sources of this novel, including its major plot-element of a murder committed by someone who stands in no personal relation to the victim. Also, the Napoleon motif, on which so many changes are rung by Dostoevsky, is clearly transposed by him to a Petersburg setting from mid-nineteenth-century French fiction, Balzac and Stendhal in particular, both of whom glorified Napoleon (the former covertly and the latter overtly) and justified their ambitious plebeian heroes by appealing to his illustrious example. Thus Raskolnikov may be seen as a Russian version of

Julien Sorel and Eugène de Rastignac—the young man on the make who comes to the capital from the provinces intent on a career and a conquest. It is especially Balzac's *Le Père Goriot* that suggests an influence in the design of Raskolnikov's story. In his essay on Dostoevsky [4] Georg Lukacs mentions the anecdote of the Chinese Mandarin in Balzac's novel as containing the hint that the Russian writer might have developed. The relevant passage is worth citing in full. It occurs in a dialogue between Rastignac and his friend the medical student Bianchon:

> "What makes you look so serious?" asked the medical student taking his arm [Rastignac's] to walk up and down in front of the palace with him.
>
> "I am bothered by troublesome thoughts."
>
> "Of what kind are they? You know that thoughts can be cured."
>
> "How?"
>
> "By yielding to them."
>
> "You are laughing at me, without knowing what I mean. Have you read Rousseau?"
>
> "Do you remember the place where he asks the reader what he would do, if he could become rich by killing an old mandarin in China, by the sole act of his will, without stirring from Paris?"
>
> "Yes."
>
> "Well?"
>
> "Pooh! I have already come to my thirty-third mandarin."
>
> "Don't joke. Come, suppose you knew it were possible, and that a nod from you would do it, should you consent?"
>
> "Is he a very old mandarin? But young or old, sick or well, my goodness—the deuce. No, I shouldn't."

And Bianchon concludes his argument in favor of sparing the Chinese by warning Rastignac against a rash solution of the problem posed at "the entrance of life," against the attempt to cut that Gordian knot with his sword. "If you mean to act thus," he says, "you must be an Alexander or else you will be sent to the

[4] *Der russische Realismus in der Weltliteratur* (Berlin, 1949), p. 178.

gallows." Unlike Rastignac, however, Dostoevsky's hero confides in no one and sets out to cut the Gordian knot without in the least resembling an Alexander or a Napoleon, though hoping that his crime might possibly prove him to belong to their superior breed.

It seems to me, too, that Dostoevsky drew on *Le Père Goriot* for far more than the germinal anecdote of the Chinese Mandarin. Svidrigailov's posture *vis-à-vis* Raskolnikov is in certain respects strongly reminiscent of Vautrin's relation to Rastignac in Balzac's novel. We know that Svidrigailov is missing from the early drafts of *Crime and Punishment*, and it is not improbable that when it came to composing the final version Dostoevsky decided to introduce a character playing Vautrin to his own Rastignac. Consider that both Vautrin and Svidrigailov are older men who assume the role of mentors in the ways of the world, that both have insinuating manners and appear cheerful and obliging when it suits them, that both are sexual deviants (the Frenchman is a homosexual and the Russian has very special tastes in underage girls), and that both are predatory types who make no secret of their immorality. Moreover, some of the ideas that Vautrin communicates to Rastignac turn up in Raskolnikov's thought virtually without modification, as if he had absorbed the lesson addressed to his French prototype. Vautrin declares, for instance, that there are but two courses open to a man, blind obedience or open revolt, and that he can make his way in the world either

> by the splendor of genius or the adroitness of corruption. He must burst like a cannon-ball into the ranks of his fellow-men, or he must move among them like the pestilence. Honesty is of no use. Men yield to the power of genius; they hate and calumniate it . . . but they yield to it if it persists, and kneel to it when they find that they cannot suppress it.

There is a remarkable parallel between this formulation and Raskolnikov's view, passionately expounded to Sonia, that

> whoever is strong in mind and spirit will have power over men. Anyone who is greatly daring is right in their eyes. . . . I divined that power is only vouchsafed to the man who dares to stoop and pick it up. There is only one thing, one thing needful: one has only to dare.

Clearly, Vautrin's genius who bursts like a cannon-ball among his fellow-men bears an uncommon resemblance to Raskolnikov's criminal of genius who dares assert the right inherent in his superiority and whose criminality is soon forgiven or forgotten as he becomes a lawgiver and leader among men. However, in constructing Raskolnikov's theory of the relation between power and genius, Dostoevsky borrowed from more than one source; Balzac is but one of them.

It is possible to speak if not of a school then surely of a Petersburgian genre in Russian literature, of which Dostoevsky is in fact the leading practitioner. Pushkin's "The Bronze Horseman" is doubtless the outstanding poem of that genre, as Gogol's "The Overcoat" is the outstanding story and *Crime and Punishment* the outstanding novel. One must be aware of its author's profound response to Petersburg and of the masterly way in which he appropriated it to imaginative purposes in order to perceive that as the scene of Raskolnikov's crime the city is one of the essential constituents of the story, more foreground than background, a unique urban setting charged with multiple meanings, of which one of the more urgent emerges from Dostoevsky's preoccupation with the Petersburg misery and his depiction of it in a manner demonstrating his solidarity with its victims. As a novelist of the modern metropolis he was of course in the line of Balzac and Dickens, by whom he was greatly influenced, though there is a marked difference in his representation of the city and theirs. Balzac's Paris, as Arnold Hauser has remarked, is still a romantic wilderness, "a theatrical setting painted in chiaroscuro contrasts, a fairyland in which dazzling riches and picturesque poverty live side by side,"[5] whereas Dostoevsky describes the metropolis in somber colors, taking us into its reeking taverns and coffin-like rooms, bringing to the fore its petty-bourgeois and proletarian types, its small shopkeepers and clerks, students, prostitutes, beggars, and derelicts. True as this is, there is also something else in Dostoevsky's vision of Petersburg, a sense not so much of romance as of poetic strangeness, a poetic emotion attached to objects in themselves desolate, a kind of exaltation in the very lostness, loneliness, and drabness which the big city imposes on its inhabitants, as is so poignantly brought out in the scene when in an evening hour Raskolnikov stops on a street corner to listen to a sentimental song ground out on a barrel-organ and sung by a girl in a cracked and coarsened voice.

> "Do you like street music?" said Raskolnikov, addressing a middle-aged man standing idly by him. The man looked at him, startled and wondering.
>
> "I love to hear singing to a street organ," said Raskolnikov, and his manner seemed strangely out of keeping with the subject. "I like it on cold, dark, damp evenings—they must be damp—when all the passers-by have pale green, sickly faces, or better still when the wet snow is falling straight down, where there's no wind—you know what I mean? and the street lamps shine through it. . . ."
>
> "I don't know. . . . Excuse me. . . ." muttered the stranger, frightened by the question and Raskolnikov's strange manner. . . .

Catching Raskolnikov talking to himself on the street, Svidrigailov says to him: "This is a town of crazy people. . . . There are few places where there are so many gloomy, queer influences on the soul of man as in Petersburg." There is indeed something peculiarly Petersburgian about Raskolnikov, and not merely in the sense that he belongs to its "proletariat of undergraduates." The crime he commits—in the idea of it, namely, which is so strange an amalgam of the abstract and artificial with the sheerly fantastic—corresponds intrinsically to the character of this city,

[5] *The Social History of Art,* (New York, 1952), II, 854.

frequently described in exactly such terms.[6] It is in the heat and stench of its slums, as he wanders endlessly through the streets, that Raskolnikov spawns his idea, which he himself likens to "a spell, a sorcery, an obsession." And afterwards, having carried his idea to its terrible conclusion, though not at all in the bravura manner of a Napoleon but rather like a man deprived of reason and will power by mental illness, on the very next day he resumes his wanderings about the city in a state more often than not bordering on delirium.

St. Petersburg was far more the capital of the Russian empire than of the Russian land. It was erected on the Finnish marshland with cruel haste and at the cost of many lives by the edict of Peter the Great, who undertook, with the savage rationality typical of belated and alien converts to progress, to transform his backward domain all at once into an efficient state militarized along modern lines. The self-will and precipitate style of this operation brought into being a city without roots in the past or in

[6] The ambiguity of Petersburg in its odd blending of the real and the unreal is what Dostoevsky tried mainly to capture. In *A Raw Youth* there is an especially suggestive passage in which young Arkady speaks of a Petersburg morning as being at the same time infinitely prosaic and infinitely fantastic.—"On such a wild Petersburg morning, foul, damp and foggy, the wild dream of some Hermann out of Pushkin's 'Queen of Spades' (a colossal figure, an extraordinary and regular Petersburg type . . . the type of the Petersburg period) might, I believe, strike one as a piece of solid reality. A hundred times over, in such a fog, I have been haunted by a strange and persistent fancy: 'What if this fog should part and float away? Would not all this rotten and slimy town go with it, rise up with the fog, and vanish like smoke, and the old Finnish marsh be left as before and in the midst of it, perhaps, to complete the picture, a bronze horseman on a panting, overdriven steed?' "

The bronze horseman is Falconet's statue of Peter the Great, but implicitly the reference is of course to Pushkin's famous poem of that title. Hermann is the protagonist of Pushkin's story "The Queen of Spades," in whom some scholars have discerned an early model of Raskolnikov. For, like Dostoevsky's hero, Hermann is under the spell of Napoleon and he too, daring all on one throw, kills an old woman in an attempt to wrest from her the secret that will make his fortune. What the two characters share, basically, is the Petersburgian power-urge combined with the peculiar Petersburgian dreaminess.

the vast rural hinterland, the center of alienation and of everything novel and foreign violating the national traditions and the patriarchal mode of life. It was in Petersburg that in a fashion peculiar to it the imperial bureaucracy exerted itself to westernize the country from above while the turbulent and seditious "proletariat of undergraduates," impelled by other motives and a nobler vision, strove to effect the same end from below. Thus the material brutality of the caste pressing down upon society from the top met its counterpart in the tragic spiritual brutality of the dissident intelligentsia forcing the issue lower down.

No wonder the Slavophils hated Petersburg. Khomaikov, a leading ideologue of their faction, spoke of it as a city of dead beauty, where "all is stone, not only the houses but the trees and inhabitants as well." The Marquis de Custine, visiting the capital in 1839, could not believe that it would endure. "I have seen no place that is more penetrated with the instability of human beings," he wrote. Penetrated with the instability of human beings—a marvelously apt phrase which we can apply to the Dostoevskyean world as a whole with but a slight shift of context. You will find this singular instability in Raskolnikov, to be sure, but you will also find in him more than a trace of that savage rationality characterizing the champions of the Petersburg period in Russian history and subsequently the revolutionary elite. He emerges from that "literate world of reckless youth," as Bakunin called it, in which the latter professed to see the hope of the revolution, and he is the epitome of those traits of which Alexander Herzen gave an account of incomparable precision in his *Memoirs.*

> We are greatly given [he noted] to theoretical pedantry and argumentativeness. This German propensity is in us associated with a special national element—which we might call the Araktcheyev [7] element—a ruthlessness, a passionate rigidity, and an eagerness to

[7] Alexis Araktcheyev (1769–1834), a high official and trusted adviser of Alexander I in the closing years of his reign, put into effect such inordinately cruel administrative practices as to give rise to the dread term *Araktcheyevchina.*

> dispatch their victims. To satisfy his grenadier ideal, Araktcheyev flogged living peasants to death; we flog to death ideas, arts, humanity, past leaders, anything you like. In dauntless array we advance step by step to the limit and overshoot it, never sinning against logic but only against *truth;* unaware, we go on further and further, forgetting that real sense and real understanding of life are shown precisely in stepping short before the extreme. . . .

In truth Raskolnikov is one of those young men whose coming was foreshadowed with fear by Joseph de Maistre, the author of *Soirées de St. Pétersbourg,* when he observed, in discussing the peasant uprisings of the eighteenth century, headed by such leaders as Emelian Pugachev, an obscure and illiterate Cossack, that if another such revolt ever took place in Russia it would be headed by a Pugachev "armed with a university degree." But the hour of the university Pugachevs had not quite struck when Raskolnikov set out entirely on his own, cut off from any social effort or collective historical action, to remove "certain obstacles." Proclaiming the necessity of breaking once and for all what must be broken, in other words, of killing not simply an old woman but the principle of authority bolstered by the moral law, he yet proceeds to commit not an act of political terror but another crime altogether that inevitably stamps him as no more than a common criminal, a criminal from egoism. He is a dissenter and rebel (*raskol,* the word from which his name derives, means schism or dissent), in essence the type of revolutionary terrorist of that period, whose act of terror is somehow displaced into a private object. The terrorist is a political criminal, and if he is to be vindicated at all it is by an appeal to historical necessity; no such appeal is open to Raskolnikov.

Of course he has at his disposal a theory justifying his crime, and I have already indicated one source of it in Balzac. Another and more important source, to my mind, is Hegel's concept of the historic hero (the agent of the World-Spirit) and his victims. The enormous influence of the Hegelian philosophy in Russia during the late 1830's and the 1840's is well known; the period of this influence coincides with Dostoevsky's youth and it would have been impossible for him to escape it. But that he was in fact concerned with it is shown, moreover, by his letter (of February 22, 1854) from Siberia to his brother Mikhail asking that he send him, among other books, Hegel's *Philosophy of History*.[8] It is strange that this source, far from esoteric, should have been overlooked. I imagine that scholars and critics have been so carried away by the apparent analogy between Raskolnikov (in his theory of himself, that is) and Nietzsche's Superman as to have missed a more substantial likeness, though one which is more in the nature of a caricature than an exact replica. It is only in the vulgarized popular version of the Superman that Raskolnikov's theory reminds us of him; so far as Nietzsche's actual idea of the Superman goes, as a product of a mutation of the human species, there is no resemblance. It is in Hegel rather that we discover a direct and obvious source of Raskolnikov's notion of inferior and superior men, the superior ones having the right to commit breaches of morality while their inferiors are obliged to mind their business, which is to stay put in the common rut. Now what Dostoevsky has done in devising Raskolnikov's justification is to convert into a theory of human nature what is in Hegel not a psychological theory at all but a theory of men as subjects and objects of history. Hegel's world-historical individual—such as Alexander or Caesar or Napoleon, the very names invoked by Dostoevsky's protagonist—performs the grandiose tasks set for him by the *Weltgeist* irrespective of moral considerations; he can do no other, for, as Hegel puts it, "the history of the world moves on a higher level than that of morality." These heroes may "treat other great and even sacred interests inconsiderately—a conduct which subjects them to moral reprehension. But so mighty a figure may trample down many an innocent flower, crush to

[8] "Send me the Koran, and Kant's *Critique of Pure Reason,* and if you have the chance of sending me anything not officially, then be sure to send Hegel, particularly Hegel's *Philosophy of History.* Upon that depends my whole future."

pieces many things in its path." Thus as the subject of history he rides roughshod over its mere objects or victims. Dostoevsky gives us a parody-version of Hegel's theory of two types of men by abstracting it from its historical logic. This enables him to entangle Raskolnikov in what is in truth a comedy of mistaken identity: an obvious victim of the historical process—a small man in search of personal security and happiness—laughably taking himself for its hero. In this sense he is no better than a clown, and he does indeed laugh at himself from time to time.

> One sudden idea made him laugh. Napoleon, the pyramids, Waterloo, and a wretched skinny old woman, a pawnbroker with a red trunk under her bed. . . . It's too inartistic. A Napoleon creep under the old woman's bed! Ugh, how loathsome!

However, though Raskolnikov refuses the historical action of the political rebel, and, instead of throwing a bomb at a general or even the Czar himself, he crushes the skull of an old woman with an axe, there is still something in his deed, for all its weird abjectness and ugliness, which in some sense comes through to us as a protest against the Petersburg misery and the ethics justifying it. One cannot but agree with Alberto Moravia's statement in his essay "The Marx-Dostoevsky Duel" that though "Raskolnikov had not read Marx and regards himself as a superman beyond good and evil, he was already, in embryo, a people's commissar." [9] Moravia is one of the very few Western commentators on the novel who has not overlooked its aborted political meaning, which emerges again and again, as when Raskolnikov dissociates himself from his friend Razumihin's abuse of the socialists. He understands very well that rebellion can take another form, the collective form advocated by the socialists. After all, what the socialists want, he remarks to himself, is the happiness of all. As it happens, however, he is not the one "to put his little brick into the happiness of all," for what he wants is to live prop-

[9] Alberto Moravia, in *Encounter,* November 1956.

erly here and now. Into his manuscript Dostoevsky inserted the following passage (later deleted) into a speech of Raskolnikov's: "What care I what will come to pass in the future. Is it possible to live at present? I cannot pass by with indifference all these horrors, this suffering and misery. I want power." Power for what purpose? Presumably to do good, to alleviate the suffering and misery. He is in a state of fatal self-contradiction, however, in that he attempts to further a common end of an altruistic character with egoistical and purely private means. In order to test his strength he needs more than anything else the support of a social faith. This is plainly seen by the examining magistrate, Porfiry Petrovitch, who is the one figure in the story who can be said manifestly to speak for the author, and it is he who says to Raskolnikov:

> You made up a theory and then were ashamed that it broke down and turned out to be not at all original! It turned out something base, that's true, but you are not hopelessly base! . . . How do I regard you? I regard you as one of those men who would stand and smile at their torturer while he cuts their entrails out, if only they have found faith or God.

It is significant that the phrase is "faith *or* God," not faith *in* God, as if to say that there are other faiths besides the traditional one.

That Raskolnikov stands in an inauthentic relation to his crime is thus confirmed by the author's spokesman in the novel. The crime does not truly belong to him, and that is the reason he affects us as being almost ludicrously inadequate to his deed, as when he faints in the police station the day right after the murder, even though there is as yet no suspicion attached to him, and calls attention to himself in other ways too. In spite of all his protestations to the contrary, he is prostrate with guilt and the yearning for punishment. It is not that he lacks the strength to kill and bear the responsibility for it to the end, but that he killed for himself alone, deranged by unconscious urges and over-conscious theories, rather than for the common cause to which his "nihilistic" generation was dedicated; and that is also the secret of Sonia's hold on him. There is no social substance in his anarchic individualism, as there is none in Sonia's idea of Christian salvation.

Sonia, "the eternal victim so long as the world lasts," is a small thin girl of eighteen, every feature of whose face reflects "a sort of insatiable compassion." Raskolnikov turns to her in his need because, as he tells her: "We are both accursed, so let us go together." She is the very embodiment of meekness and humility (far more so than Myshkin or Alyosha), and only Dostoevsky, with his uncanny powers of representation, could have brought her to life without blundering into mawkish sentimentality. But though he so brilliantly persuades us of her reality as a novelistic creation, this in itself in no sense constitutes a "proof" of her idea of Christian salvation. She proves quite as much the Nietzschean negation of it. It appears to me that it is precisely in his characterization of Sonia, rather than of Raskolnikov, that Dostoevsky's insight coincides with that of Nietzsche; the fact that the Russian arrives at that insight by way of assent, and the German by way of dissent, is scarcely to the point here. Thus Nietzsche speaks in his *Antichrist* of "that queer and sick world into which the Gospels introduce us—as in a Russian novel, a world into which the scum of society, nervous disorders, and 'childlike' idiocy seem to be having a rendezvous." Sonia is truly an inhabitant of that world, and she has the stirring charm of the mixture it exhibits—"a mixture of the sublime, the sickly and the childlike." Nowhere in literature do we find so striking a confirmation of Nietzsche's idea of the evangelical type as in the figure of Sonia. What is that type? It is one in whom "the incapacity for resistance becomes morality," who experiences "any resistance, even any compulsion to resist, as unendurable *displeasure* . . . and finds blessedness (pleasure) only in no longer offering any resistance to anybody, neither to evil nor to him who is evil—love as the only, as the *last* possible way of life." Significantly, Sonia's faith is not one that has been attained through struggle.

When Raskolnikov challenges her faith, she answers with simple pathos: "What should I be without God?" This is the kind of faith which, as Nietzsche said, "has been there from the beginning; it is as it were an infantilism that has receded into the spiritual."[10] Plainly, Sonia's faith is of a sort that offers no solution to Raskolnikov, whose spiritual existence is incommensurable with hers. No wonder that the epilogue to the novel, in which he finally seems to be preparing himself to accept her outlook, has struck many readers as implausible and out of key with the work as a whole.

A few weeks after Dostoevsky's death in January 1881 a terrorist of the People's Will party by the name of Andrey Zhelyabov took part in the successful attempt on the life of Alexander II. He was caught and brought to trial, and this is what he had to say to the court:

> I was baptized in the Orthodox Church but I reject Christianity, although I acknowledge the essential teaching of Jesus Christ. This essential teaching occupied an honored place among my moral incentives. I believe in the truth and righteousness of that teaching and I solemnly declare that faith without works is dead and that every true Christian ought to fight for the truth and for the rights of the oppressed and the weak, and even, if need be, to suffer for them. Such is my creed.

Evidently the blood he shed did not weigh on Zhelyabov's conscience, for he went to his death on the gallows calm and impenitent. Raskolnikov, cheated of Zhelyabov's fate, goes to a Siberian prison in the same state of perplexity and outrage with which he undertook to carry out his "loathsome scheme." But, then, it was a hideous old harpy he killed, not the Czar of all the Russias.

Whatever the manifest theme of the novel, its latent theme is not that of crime as such or the criminal's innate need of pun-

[10] *The Portable Nietzsche*, edited by Walter Kaufmann (New York, 1954), p. 602 ff.

ishment but the right to violent rebellion. It was the violence that Dostoevsky condemned, even as he was secretly drawn to it, fearing that if let loose it would tear down the authority both of heaven and earth, and Raskolnikov goes down to defeat to prove his creator right.

In its aspect as a polemic against the radical generation of the 1860's—whose obscurantist rationalism and notion of enlightened self-interest as the motive-force of human conduct Dostoevsky began satirizing in *Notes from Underground*—the novel depends on the sleight-of-hand of substituting a meaningless crime for a meaningful one. But if that were all, *Crime and Punishment* would not be the masterpiece it undoubtedly is. The very substitution of one type of crime for another set problems for Dostoevsky which he solved brilliantly by plunging his hero into a condition of pathology which ostensibly has nothing to do with the "heroic" theory by means of which he justifies himself. In his article "On Crime" Raskolnikov wrote that the perpetration of a crime is always accompanied by illness, and that is an exact description of his own case, though he believes himself to be another kind of criminal altogether, one acting from rational calculation and in the interests of a higher idea; the irony of his self-deception is among the finest effects of the book. And it is astonishing how well Dostoevsky was able to preserve the unity of his protagonist's character, to present him as all of a piece in spite of the fact that we are dealing not with one but with several Raskolnikovs. There is Raskolnikov the altruist and there is Raskolnikov the egoist, "a despot by nature"; there is the crypto-revolutionary Raskolnikov and there is the self-styled genius who demands power as his right and as the guaranty of his freedom; then of course there is the neurotic who acts out his illness through a murder intellectually rationalized but inexplicable except in terms of an unconscious drive. After all, he conceives an "insurmountable repulsion" to Alyona Ivanonva, the old moneylender, weeks before he elaborates his murderous plan. Dostoevsky confronted the hazard of these contradictions with unequalled mastery. His capacity to combine them creatively in a single brain and a single psyche, while staving off the danger of incoherence at one end and of specious reconciliation at the other, is the measure of the victory scored in this novel by the imaginative artist in him over the ruthless polemicist.

The Posthumous History of the Enlightenment

GREGOR SEBBA

NOWHERE DID the Enlightenment run its course more consistently than in France, and nowhere was its influence upon literature more profound. In France, the emancipation of Reason became the dominant theme in the evolution of literature and society as well as of thought, from seventeenth-century rationalism to the brief, climactic epiphany of Universal Reason. This is the evolution we wish to trace in its broadest lines, for the sake of the curious transformation it effected upon French literature, and for its relevance today.

I

There is an ancient statue of a seated woman in St. Peter's Church at Louvain, the old Catholic university town. In the severity of its line, bearing, and expression, in the stark simplicity of its symbolism, it reflects the attitude of the Early Middle Ages. *Sapientia* (Wisdom) sits erect, head raised, eyes straight forward; on her arm she holds the infant Jesus. On her lap lies an open book, and the finger of her right hand points at it with a commanding gesture.

This is all, for there are no unknown realms of knowledge to conquer: everything that man can know, everything he needs to know for his own good, is already known—is "in the book." All he has to do is read it. The book contains the knowledge of the world which he can find by the light of his reason, knowledge which the ancients have already found. But since this knowledge is not enough for his salvation, God in His mercy revealed to him that portion which he cannot find by the power of reason. *Sapientia* is therefore both human and divine. She is teacher, mistress, Mother of God, mother of the God who, in becoming man, had to become a child—and a child must learn.

In the Enlightenment, the symbolization of knowledge becomes tumultuous and chaotic. Gone is the strength and discipline, the clarity and nobility of *Sapientia*. The frontispiece to a then popular Dutch work on the natural sciences [1] is a typical example. It is a picture of struggle. Light bursts through black, billowing clouds that all but cover the sky. Light streams from the lovely, shining, naked figure of a woman in the sky: Truth, holding up a radiating crystal. There is another light in the sky, a small disk labelled ΘΕΟΣ (God), from which a feeble beam falls on the superhuman figure below that dominates the picture, a majestic woman, standing on a pedestal, labelled *Magistra rerum*. She is Nature, the teacher of all things; she has just taken the blindfold from the eyes of the philosopher kneeling at her feet, and for the first time he beholds the world as it is. No wonder his face expresses awe—and perplexity. For this world is brimming over with things, each one as important as the next, all of them calling for attention at once: sun, moon, stars, comets, rainbow, lightning, volcanoes, ocean and earth teeming with life, botanical and zoological specimens, fossils, minerals; and strewn

[1] In the seventh edition (Amsterdam, 1759) of Bernard Nieuwentydt's *Het regt gebruik der wereld beschouwingen*, first published in 1714.

about the messy scene, the tools and products of scientific observation: telescope and microscope, magic lantern, astrolabe, barometer, compass, mathematical tables. . . . The philosopher pays no attention to them as yet. He gazes at Truth high in the sky, her radiant light eclipsing the small, pale, ineffective disk in the center, which needs the inscription ΘΕΟΣ to avoid being mistaken for a natural phenomenon. Soon the philosopher's sole guide and teacher will be Nature. She alone has her feet on the ground; her hand points to all the things he is to investigate.

To attain knowledge is to learn to read the book of Nature. The Book of the Middle Ages is gone; or rather, it has been transformed; what once was Wisdom has become the blindfold now removed from the thinker's eyes.

The seventeenth century in France had found the symbol for the break-through of Reason: Light dispersing Night. In this classical age, there was but one great sun breaking through, the sun of Reason or Truth, for the two were at one. The new light shone on a curiously vacant, curiously geometrical scene.

II

Renaissance and Reformation had broken the medieval mold. They had destroyed the universality of the Church and opened the globe to European exploration and dominance; they had laid the philosophical and scientific foundations for the great break-through. Now, in the age of the Baroque, Reason emerges as the supreme arbiter. It proceeds to design the world in its own image, and the design is Cartesian. Reason is not only the ultimate judge of all truth man can attain by his own effort; it is also the fountainhead of all knowledge of the world. In his *Principles of Philosophy,* Descartes paints a vast picture of Nature. Do you want to know what keeps the stars moving on their tracks? What makes the magnet attract iron? What goes on in the body of a man suddenly gripped by anger? Reason will tell you. All you have to do is draw inevitable conclusions from one irrefutable premise.

At Versailles, Le Nôtre designs nature. Out of the historical and cultural landscape he carves the miracle of geometrical space that is Versailles. A main axis runs straight ahead, as far as the eye can see. From focal points, avenues radiate like spokes of a wheel. The trees that line them are molded into solid, unbroken green walls with plane surfaces. The park is laid out *more geometrico:* squares, hexagons, circles. Trees and shrubs are shaped into Euclidian solids: globes, cones, prisms. Too bad the trunks cannot be transformed too. Versailles is a system. The system is all-comprehensive, nothing is left out. In this Garden of Reason, everything is a work of art and all arts are one. Between the foliage walls, Molière performs the comedy he wrote for the occasion, to music contributed by Lully. Afterwards, the royal party will float down the Grand Canal on barges, towards a fairy palace front erected for the pleasure of one night, outlined with countless lights. As the music from the barges approaches, the statues that stand on the cornices and parapets come to life and dance a ballet. Fountains rise and play; night becomes day as five thousand rockets simultaneously rise into the sky to form, for one glorious moment, a gigantic dome which bursts into a shower of stars slowly descending to earth. In these great Fêtes de Versailles the permanent and the fleeting are fused into one; all arts contribute to the supreme event, the creation of a sensuous universe for one night, a superb symbol for the first age of Reason, the age of Order, of System. Reason does not search for order, it constructs it. What it needs for the work, it finds within itself.

III

As the century nears its end, the climate changes. The great systems do not look so attractive any more. Worse still, the taste for systematization, is on the wane. Stubborn fact undermines it. To cope with fact, reason turns to a more potent source of knowledge: observation. In doing so, it becomes anti-Cartesian; it turns from construction to analysis.

The beautiful geometrical world becomes cluttered up with objects and tools; everything wants to be in the picture. More important, Reason, in becoming analytical, becomes destructive. Tired of building, it begins to tear apart, then to tear down. It attacks any and every belief that hampers free investigation; it turns upon the social and political system, it corrodes faith. Assuredly, this is also a time of construction, of laying lasting foundations. But most of the constructive work is done outside France. Newton and Locke open Voltaire's eyes, and both these men are English. There is not one philosopher, not one scientist, in France to rank with the giants across the Channel; instead, there is a host of *philosophes,* men of the world, of literature, of thought, able, inquisitive, enormously versatile. They push out from the bridgehead secured in the seventeenth century, when science won its claim to autonomy. The great enemy, theology, had concluded a truce which left the battlefield in the hands of the scientist. Now the *philosophes* prepare the second break-through; they carry the battle into the field of social and political institutions, into the fields of education and of religion itself. During the first half of the eighteenth century, a destructive critical attack on human institutions is pressed forward; the criticism flows from an odd assembly of first principles which as yet go unchallenged because they are so reasonable and so good. For this is still an age of faith, an age of confidence, of optimism. Man is good, Reason is powerful, Light conquers Night. Before long, the idea of Progress will rise in time to dominate the next century. Meanwhile, Reason inexorably moves on to the third stage.

Having riddled and hollowed out the edifice of institutions and beliefs, Reason must take the next step, and again it is in France that this step is taken. Reason will once more proceed to create a world in its own image, this time in the realm not of thought or of art but of action. The French Revolution is the climax of the Enlightenment.

IV

What enables Reason to proceed from thought to action is, paradoxically, the strength it receives from a revolt against rationalism. In the field of literature, the revolt is pressed in the name of sentiment. While this current gradually builds up, the mood of thought also changes. By the middle of the century, the *philosophe* is no longer the hopeful optimist he was, even though his belief in the supreme *value* of simple goodness, tolerance, and justice is unshaken. It is the facts that disturb him. Is man really the rational being who will resolutely do the right thing, once the blindfold has been taken from his eyes? "Like Montesquieu and Vauvenargues somewhat earlier, neither Voltaire nor Diderot, Helvétius nor Holbach, could believe in the integral goodness of man." [2] An undercurrent of pessimism runs beneath the surface of confidence in the liberating power of reason, and the undercurrent is strong. But help comes from an unexpected quarter: out of that simmering, growing revolt that looks to feeling for the certainty that neither reason nor observation can give. From the ranks of the *philosophes* a solitary figure detaches itself and establishes a position of enormous strength: Jean-Jacques Rousseau.

This is the Rousseau as the Enlightenment knew him, not the Jean-Jacques *we* know. In the *Nouvelle Héloise,* in *Emile,* in the *Discourses* and the *Contrat Social,* the heart revolts against the brain. Not reasoning but sentiment, feeling, leads man to the truth. To the *philosophe,* this is treason. But the prophet of sentiment, of the heart, of feeling, does not destroy the reign of reason. He gives it the one thing it still lacks: the fire of passionate commitment. Just when the activist Voltaire is driven towards pessimism and resignation, when his first principles begin to sound hollow in his own ears, Rousseau gives eighteenth-century rationalism the implacable, intolerant belief in absolutes that are not

[2] Henry Vyverberg, *Historical Pessimism in the French Enlightenment* (Harvard University Press, 1958), p. 84.

imposed upon man from outside or from above but enshrined in his own heart. And so the men of the French Revolution were right after all when they canonized both of them, Voltaire and Rousseau, the arch-enemies, as fathers of the Revolution, and when they laid them to final rest in the same Pantheon and placed their busts side by side in every municipal office. They had a right to *their* Rousseau. The other Rousseau, the Jean-Jacques of the last autobiographical writings, plunging down to the very depths of the soul to find out what man is in all his nakedness, this Rousseau had to wait almost a century and a half to find understanding.

V

The Enlightenment was not kind to poetic genius. Not the eighteenth but the sixteenth and seventeenth centuries were the golden age, in France as well as in England, Holland, and Spain. No figure of the Enlightenment in these countries compares with Rabelais, Montaigne, Racine, Molière, with Milton and Shakespeare, with Cervantes and Calderòn. The French Enlightenment produces no great lyric poetry, no great epic, no great drama. As to comedy, Marivaux is the rightful heir of the great age before him; he is to Molière as the Rococo is to the Baroque. What kills poetry is the habit of precision, exactness, pedantry, generality, idealization. Diderot has to counsel writers to give their heroes a wart or some other slight blemish to rescue them from being vacuous clichés. The French language, foaming and swirling in Rabelais, had become staid and deep in Montaigne; then, under the influence of Malherbes and Vaugelas, its poetic vocabulary shrinks, its grammar hardens: Racine will say all he wants to say in a mere two thousand vocables; but how plastic, how supple, how real in its classical simplicity is this language of his! Now, in the Enlightenment, desiccation sets in. Poetic language becomes thin, character degenerates to type, abstraction replaces full-blooded conceptualization.

But there is another side to the picture. Poetry is dead but prose flourishes. From all sides, new words pour into the language of the educated: from daily life, from the arts and crafts, from science and philosophy. Voltaire creates a brilliant style that intoxicates the brain, even if it leaves the heart cold; he moves the reader by persuasion, not by empathy. But the heart too, that delicate heart of the age of Reason, receives its due: the literature of sentiment develops a style and language of its own that delights and transports the reader. Then as the century passes the half-way mark, areas open up of which the golden age was innocent, areas of darkness into which the rays of liberating Reason do not penetrate. There is a cold fascination with evil in the *Liaisons dangereuses* of Laclos; the Marquis de Sade creates the anti-world to enlightened Reason; Diderot the writer probes a universe which is as equivocal, as dubious, as that of Thomas Mann; Jean-Jacques, in his last solitude, passes from what others call reality into the true world of the dream. These descents into the darkness of the self are a revolt against the very notion of Enlightenment.

The revolt, however, remains hidden. The stuff is there, but it does not enter the fabric of the age. This is as it ought to be, as it almost always is. Just as next year's buds are already formed under today's foliage, so the literature of tomorrow is already there in the bud when the literature of today is in full bloom. The Enlightenment knew the Diderot of the *Encyclopédie,* the friend of d'Alembert, the *philosophe;* the manuscript of his *Neveu de Rameau* remained lost until Goethe discovered, translated, and published it. The Enlightenment knew the Rousseau of the great writings of his middle life, of the bare ten or twelve years "when he wrote books," as he said of himself; the profound autobiographical work of his last twenty years remained unpublished until after his death. However, it was the literature flowering openly in the age of Enlightenment that bore fruit in the French Revolution; for if the age was unkind to poetry, it was a great age for literature as a social force.

VI

In his brilliant book on the philosophy of the Enlightenment, Ernst Cassirer finds its decisive and lasting contribution to consist, not in any original or novel doctrines, but in the peculiar *form* of philosophizing it developed. The problems and concepts of the past are no longer treated as finished products: they become forces of action. Mere results are now turned into imperatives. The same, *mutatis mutandis,* is true of the literature of the French Enlightenment, and with even greater force. Literature becomes the universal medium, the universal frame of discourse, and the discourse is a revolutionary one, however elegant or tame it may sound. This universe is coextensive with the world of men capable of action, whatever their social position: the readers of today will be the actors of tomorrow. Compared with our own world in which everybody can read, it is narrow; compared to the world of the ancient régime, it is all-comprehensive. It reaches from the King of Prussia, the King of Poland, to the juvenile delinquent of Geneva, from the court to the café, from the mathematician to the pretty girl with those big, blue eyes and a convent education. And literature is more than belles-lettres. The *philosophe* will write anything, from stale drama and dull verse to the flaming encyclopedia article and the exhilarating treatise on the nature of God or the cause of the tides. In his hands, the language becomes an educated, universal tool in which any and every problem can be discussed without the use of the jargon of the specialists. The very eclipse of pure poetry makes it possible for the literati to be encyclopedic and to fuse thought, sentiment, and elegance into a style characteristic of the age. For the first time, writing becomes a profession; but the new class of professional writers is not yet isolated; imperceptibly it shades off into the wider circle of amateur writers and, beyond them, into the general educated public. More important, the writer (professional or amateur) presents everybody's ideas in everybody's language.

No college course is needed to understand Voltaire, the *Contrat Social* is as easy to grasp as *Das Kapital* is difficult, and even philosophy makes delectable reading. Literature thus becomes a potential vehicle of action. What makes it an actual revolutionary force is not the ideas it expresses, but its *style*.

The writer of the Enlightenment is no Hamlet. Though a thinker, he is not one sicklied o'er with the pale cast of thought. His thought is as close to action as an untriggered bomb. It is at the limit, at times beyond the limit, of pure thought.

It is a commonplace to say that ideas in themselves are not socially effective, that if they are not to remain on paper they must become *somebody's* ideas, and must be acted upon. The question is, *why* are some ideas acted upon and others not? To say that the idea must be disseminated and that the circumstances must be right is not saying much. Ideas are constantly disseminated, the air is full of them; and circumstances are always right for *some* idea. It might be more helpful to recognize that an idea, to become effective, must become both more and less than a pure idea. So long as an idea remains in the realm of thought, it remains a disembodied spirit. This spirit can be a mighty one, capable of moving other ideas; it may carry conviction, but conviction is not unassailable. In the realm of the mind, argument is king—subject to revision. To become socially effective, the idea must harden into a social fact. It must become embodied in an image, a slogan, a program, a style; it must become palpable, tangible, emotive. In brief, it must be incarnated. The incarnated idea ceases to be a matter of argument, criticism, discussion, analysis, or persuasion. It becomes a matter of life and death. What French literature did for the ideas of the Enlightenment (which were old ideas) was precisely this: it brought them down from the empyrean of thought onto the field of action. It hardened them; it converted arguments of thought into causes of events. And the transformation was achieved by style.

VII

Let us consider the problem of "the miracle." In the old order of ideas, the miracle held a strategic place. An all-powerful God must be able to upset the normal course of events; the miracle proves that power. But such power is incompatible with autonomous natural order. If the miracle has natural causes, it is no miracle; if it *is* a miracle, then the natural order of cause and effect is valid only until further notice from Above. The idea of natural order did not call for the rejection of the idea of a Supreme Being, but it did require keeping that Supreme Being out of the machinery of nature. Hence the attack upon the miracle, an attack which was subversive in the seventeenth and became destructive in the eighteenth century. What made the second attack destructive was that it passed beyond the stage of argumentation. An examination of two texts dealing with the same theme will show how.

Saul has lost his asses; God directs him to Samuel, and he becomes king. This is how Spinoza, in the seventeenth century, handles the subject:

> In the first book of Samuel, ix.15, 16, it is related that God revealed to Samuel that he would send Saul to him; yet God did not send Saul to Samuel as people usually send one man to another. His "sending" was merely the ordinary course of nature. Saul was looking for the asses he had lost, and was thinking of going home without them, when at the suggestion of his servant he went to the prophet Samuel, to learn from him where he might find them. From no part of the narrative does it appear that Saul had any command from God to visit Samuel, beyond this natural motive.[3]

Everything has natural causes that fully explain it. The biblical story, closely examined, does not contradict this. No divine inter-

[3] Spinoza, "A Theologico-Political Treatise (1670)," ch. 6. in *The Chief Works of Benedict de Spinoza* (Dover, 1951), I, 89. (R. H. M. Elwes' translation, slightly modified.)

vention is needed to explain why Saul went to Samuel, no mandate of God *praeter hunc Naturae ordinem,* "beyond this order of Nature."[4] The style of Spinoza's examination is the style of argument. The effectiveness of argument depends entirely upon its soundness in fact, premises, and logic. Hence the argument is open to criticism and counter-argument, and Spinoza makes no attempt to lift it out of this realm. On the contrary, he invites discussion, confident that the argument will stand up. Even if shaken, it will leave behind the seeds of reasonable doubt. The entirely logical operation remains in the realm of thought, and thus outside the realm of action.

One century later, Voltaire goes into the same case, and immediately pushes beyond it:

> If a young peasant, looking for his asses, finds a kingdom, this does not happen every day; if another peasant [David] cures his king of an attack of madness by playing the harp, this is an even rarer case; but that this little harp player should become king because he somewhere happened to run into a village priest who pours a bottle of olive oil over his head, this is more miraculous still.[5]

For Voltaire, the case is open and shut. His style is the style of the *fait accompli.* It puts any potential opponent into the position of a fool who wants to argue about what is beyond argument. Spinoza was still respectful. He carefully lifted the veil from the idol, carefully examined what was underneath, and invited his readers to see for themselves. Voltaire jauntily walks through the church, his hat on his head, hands in his pockets; in passing, he kicks the idol, to enjoy the hollow sound. His style is close to the style of action; but while it creates contempt for the idol, it is not destructive. Contempt is still an attitude, destruction is action.

[4] Elwes mistranslates: "beyond this natural motive," a typically nineteenth-century misunderstanding.

[5] Voltaire, "David" (first paragraph), *Dictionnaire philosophique,* London, 1767.

With Rousseau, however, the literary style of the Enlightenment becomes a style of action.

Rousseau, to be sure, has at least three different styles, only one of which concerns us here. There is the narrative style ("I was born at Geneva in 1712, the son of Isaac Rousseau, a citizen of that town, and Suzanne Bernard, his wife. My father's inheritance, being a fifteenth part of only a very small property which had been divided among as many children" *etc.*); there is the elegiac dream style of *Rousseau Juge de Jean-Jacques* and of the *Rêveries;* and there is what we shall call the *manifesto style:*

<table>
<tr><td>Man is born free,</td><td>and everywhere he is in chains.</td></tr>
<tr><td>I may not be better,</td><td>but at least I am different.</td></tr>
<tr><td>The infant is bound up
in swaddling clothes,</td><td>the corpse is nailed down
in his coffin.</td></tr>
<tr><td>I have resolved on an enterprise
which has no precedent,</td><td>and which, once it is completed,
will have no imitator.</td></tr>
</table>

This is the style of action. It does not argue, neither does it ridicule. It makes manifest, and what it manifests are the two parts of one fact, split apart, with an ominous pause between them. In that pause lies the conclusion, unstated. The two parts are like electrical poles, with a gap between them. The current cannot flow. But a spark will leap from pole to pole, if the tension is high enough. This leap is a shock—and it is action. The mind is forced to *act.* The two parts of the fact are passively received, but the unstated conclusion engages the will as well as the mind. It forces the mind into union with the will, which is the condition of revolutionary action. The first and third examples mobilize the will to freedom against constraint. The second and the fourth mobilize the individual's will to be unique, regardless of morals, custom, or tradition.

At its height, the manifesto style goes to extremes in keeping argument out of fact:

> L'homme est né libre, *et* partout il est dans les fers.
> Man is born free, *and* everywhere he is in chains.

One would expect "but," not "and," and this is what Rousseau originally wrote: "et *cependant*. . . ." However, "but" is a reasoning word. It spells out the contrast between the two statements linked in the sentence, and invites us to think about the nature of the connection. This is why it had to go, making room for the revolutionary "AND": Man is born free, *and* everywhere he is in chains. Now the cold, brutal fact stands free from the entanglements of thought; now it is a body blow, a shock. In the style of this one sentence, the revolutionary character of French eighteenth-century literature reveals itself.

Hypertension distinguishes the manifesto style from the outwardly similar style of playful argumentative antithesis. We find it before as well as after Rousseau. The first sentence is ascribed to Luther, called before the Reichstag (Diet) of Worms, 1521: the second opens the *Communist Manifesto* by Marx and Engels, 1848:

> Hier stehe ich, ich kann nicht anders.
> Here I stand, I cannot do otherwise.

> Ein Gespenst geht um in Europa, das Gespenst des Kommunismus.[6]
> A specter is haunting Europe, the specter of Communism.

And again, in that echo of the French Revolution—the last sentences of the *Communist Manifesto,* in the English translation authorized by Engels himself:

> Die Proletarier haben nichts zu verlieren als ihre Ketten.
> Sie haben eine Welt zu gewinnen.
> Proletarier aller Länder, vereinigt euch!

[6] Note the disquieting drum rhythm of the German phrase:
— — ⊥ — ⊥ — — ⊥ —, — — ⊥ — — — ⊥ —.

The proletarians have nothing to lose but their chains.
They have a world to win.
Working men of all countries, unite!

As democracy, once a revolutionary force, becomes a possession to be defended, the tocsin call of the *Contrat Social* yields to a discursive style which wraps masses of qualifications around every sharp point to make it feel comfortable. Remote echoes of the democratic manifesto style still appear in Woodrow Wilson's wartime speeches and addresses:

The day has come to *conquer* or to *submit*.
If the forces of autocracy can
divide us, they will *overcome* us.

But the style is already weak, overgrown with professorial and rhetorical academese from which it frees itself only at the climax, as in this passage:

[WEAK MANIFESTO STYLE:]

These are American principles,
American policies. We could stand for no other.

[ACADEMESE:]

And yet they are the principles and policies of forward-looking men and women everywhere, of every nation, of every enlightened community.

[TRUE MANIFESTO STYLE:]

They are the principles of mankind, and must prevail.

The hypertension that leads to the flash of the Revolution will not subside. A hitherto unknown energy drives civilized man forward. The idea of Progress, rising to dominance toward the end of the Enlightenment, reflects this drive. But, by a curious misunderstanding, the dynamics of the situation are seen from the viewpoint of goals, as an unending journey towards an ever better, ever more reasonable life, towards ever greater mastery of the world. But while it is easy to see the difference between Light and Darkness, Error and Truth, Superstition and Enlightenment, it is hard to scc any essential difference between those goals that stretch into the future as far as the eye can see.

In the last resort, the idea of Progress turns out to be another eschatology, except that the *eschaton* is already here in principle and in essence. How could this aspect of gradual progression from goal to similar goal, this notion of an ever-better carrot dangling forever just beyond reach, satisfy the restless nineteenth century? It could do so because emphasis imperceptibly shifted from the goal to the effort, from the gains to the energy driving towards them. Again, literature was to provide the perfect formula for this shift. Faust, the Faust of Goethe's *Part One*, symbolizes striving *per se*, striving so eternal, so unstillable, so elemental, that the question: "What is he striving for?" never arises. It is true that *der faustische Mensch*, Faust-like Man, has a superhuman job before him, carrying the new order into the four corners of the earth, wiping out hunger, pain, and cruelty. But after this has been achieved, happiness will reign unbroken; only its hues will change from age to age. No wonder eternal striving becomes an end in itself, and an insurance against boredom.

Faust is a symbol of the restless progress of contemporary science. Unchallenged, scientific man goes on from triumph to triumph, insatiable, ever striving, transforming nature and the human world. His operations are the same under capitalism and under communism. Scientific management is at home in the churches as well as in business and industry. Long before the advent of the electronic computer, human computors and calculators had come to invade, pervade, and master every field of activity but one: man's self-representation in literature, art, and creative thought. And oddly enough, the image in which the man of Reason recognizes himself is the image of the dark, bottomless pit. The hidden buds of the literature of the Enlightenment have opened; the leaves are dark, the blossoms phosphorescent, and the fruit is bitter. Our hearts no longer leap up at the drum beats of the *Contrat Social;* our heads do not swim at Voltaire's elegant maliciousness which sends the heavy idols of the past swirling as if they were made of papier-mâché. Diderot's *Encyclopédie* and Bayle's *Dictionnaire* have become library ornaments; what we now read is *Candide, Le Neveu de Rameau, Jacques le fataliste.* It takes a peculiar taste to be still entranced by the *Nouvelle Héloïse,* but in the hell of *Rousseau Juge de Jean-Jacques* and the heartbreaking solitude of the *Rêveries,* we find ourselves at home. We discover the labyrinth of the Second Part of *Faust,* we who prefer Beethoven's late quartets to the *Eroica.*

VIII

This divorce between art and literature, on one hand, science and daily life, on the other, is frightening. Like Faust we know that two souls live in our breast. Unlike Faust, we find these two souls living together in peaceful coexistence. Our literature, unlike that of the eighteenth century, does not aim at making the world a better, more reasonable place. It does not have to persuade us any more that the world is not so good as it might be, that it can be improved, and that the only one who can improve it is man himself. Literature need no longer strengthen our belief in the powers of "science," the term taken as denoting any and every application of rational, methodical analysis. What Descartes had boldly held out, in 1637, to a doubtful age, has become a commonplace: that reason, rightly used, shall reveal the web of causes and effects,—"and thus make us masters and possessors, as it were, of nature." It is hard to understand, now that it has come to pass, how foreign and utopian this sentence sounded more than three hundred years ago; but we might remember the eighteenth-century image of the philosopher down again on his knees at Nature's feet, enraptured by Truth in the sky—three generations after Descartes had envisioned him proudly standing alone, his foot planted on the prostrate body of Nature. Today we neither kneel nor stand, we move about in a familiar world whose frontiers are incessantly pushed outward. We no longer capitalize the word Nature; indeed, we no longer use it to denote the universe. We no longer speak of the "mastery and possession" of nature. Our term is "control," and this term marks the distance between the awe and tension of those pioneering days and cool, businesslike contemporary rationalism.

But the Enlightenment has left us with two legacies, not one: rationalism and the search for the self. In 1776, Jean-Jacques, knowing that his time is almost up, prepares his final account. For twenty years a question has been gnawing him, driving him out of human companionship into solitude; for his spectacular ten years as a *philosophe* were but a ghastly, fatal mistake for which, he says, he has been paying ever since. Now he is ready to ask that question: "But I, divorced from my contemporaries and from all, *what am I?* This is what I still have to find out." The bluster of the opening page of the *Confessions* ("If I am not better, at least I am different") was but a blind. Now the question is out. And what does Jean-Jacques—what does contemporary man—find when he goes inward? He finds, not the master and possessor of nature, but nature's strangest child; not an ascertainable order, but a marvelous labyrinth: questions without answer, problems without solution, impasses.

What divides Western man from the men behind the Iron Curtain is precisely this: that we have accepted both legacies of the past, while they accept but one, the scientific, rationalistic legacy. In their world the optimism of the early eighteenth century still prevails; men still believe that they are fighting the battle of Light against Darkness; control is extended not only over nature but over man, subjecting his society, art, thought, the individual himself, to the plan. But if the intellectual climate is rationalistic, materialistic, activist, anti-religious, literature still proves recalcitrant. Their writers cry out, and the stifled cry comes *de profundis,* out of that darkness we know so well. Rationalism, scientism, is putting man into space, but literature shows him still caught in the labyrinth of soul and world.

It is one of the little ironies of history that the first man to go into the space to be tamed had the untamed name Gagarin, meaning Wild Duck. This particular wild duck had all the astro- or cosmonautic virtues, particularly prompt response to orders, self-control, hard will, and hard optimism. These are not virtues that thrive in the labyrinth. The man in the labyrinth wonders what it is all about; he worries about who and what he is. His descents into the abysses of the soul, assuming he is neither schizophrenic nor insensitive, will dampen his zest for the wild black yonder, his eagerness to plant his foot and his flag on unconquered moons and stars, and his determination to liberate, here on earth, all the non-liberated from their oppressors and from themselves.

Literature in quest of the self can become revolutionary at any time, teaching us to walk past the new idols and kick them to hear the hollow sound. The question is whether the effect would be revolutionary or counter-revolutionary, and the answer depends on the premises. Those willing to draw the final consequences from the victory of Reason must proceed to control man as the last step in the mastery and possession of nature. They must reconstruct man. They must take out of him those anxieties and despairs, those doubts, this longing to plunge into the abysses of the self. If literature blocks this reconstruction, the new Enlighteners must treat it as counter-revolutionary. Others see in that very literature of the labyrinth proof of the inevitable revolt of man against the attempt to un-man him. Still others see nothing; they are organization men during office hours, and wild ducks in their spare time. And this is where we stand now, struggling with what the era of Enlightenment has left us.

On the Modern Element in Modern Literature

LIONEL TRILLING

THE TITLE I HAVE GIVEN to this essay makes reference to a lecture which Matthew Arnold delivered a little over a century ago. I cannot expect a quick and general recognition of the allusion, for this particular one of Arnold's lectures is not widely known. "On the Modern Element in Literature" has a signal importance in its author's career—it was Arnold's first lecture as Professor of Poetry at Oxford, and it inaugurated not only his professorship but his career in criticism. The lecture as it was delivered in 1857 was a great success, but Arnold was not pleased with it; he never wanted it to be part of the canon of his work, he never put it into any of the volumes of critical essays he brought out in his lifetime.[1] Yet he did not entirely disown it; after the passage of a decade he published it in *Macmillan's Magazine*, explaining that

[1] The lecture, although republished from time to time, was for many years difficult to come by, but in 1961 it was made accessible in *Essays, Letters, and Reviews by Matthew Arnold*, edited by Fraser Neiman (Harvard University Press) and in *On the Classical Tradition*, edited by R. H. Super, the first volume of the projected *Complete Prose Works of Matthew Arnold* (The University of Michigan Press).

he did so because it made a certain point about the nature of Hellenism which at that time needed to be made. He apologized for the inadequacy of the piece in a prefatory note, speaking of its deficiencies in content, but more emphatically of its wrongness of tone. He said that it was composed in a style which he had since learned to dislike, what he called the style of the "doctor" rather than in the style which he called that of the "explorer." In describing the rejected style as that of the doctor, Arnold very likely had in mind the Scriptural injunction which he liked to quote, "Be ye not called Rabbi," that is to say, Be ye not called doctor—be ye not one who claims to have the doctrine.

At this distance of time from him, we incline to think of Arnold as the doctor *par excellence,* as the man above all others writing in English who fixed the critical doctrine and handed it down. But he thought of himself in quite the opposite way, as a spirit *ondoyant et divers,* flexible and various, as a mind peculiarly individual and personal, asking the question which, as he said, Goethe had taught modern Europe to ask: "But is it true? Is it true for *me*?" In his own sense of himself as a critic, he was the explorer, with all that the word may suggest of freedom, curiosity, risk.

I shall presently recur to Arnold's lecture in a substantive way, but I refer now to Arnold's remarks about its style in order to find sanction for the mode in which I shall deal with my subject. I have the intention of talking about a certain theme which appears frequently in modern literature—so frequently, indeed, and in so striking a manner, that it may be said to constitute one of the shaping and controlling ideas of our epoch. I can identify it by calling it the disenchantment of our culture with culture itself—it seems to me that the characteristic element of modern literature, or at least of the most highly developed modern literature, is the bitter line of hostility to civilization which runs through it. It happens that my present awareness of this theme is involved in a personal experience, and I am impelled to speak of the theme not abstractly but as it actually exists for me, with the husks of my experience clinging untidily to it. If Arnold is right, if the critic should be the explorer rather than the doctor, then the avowedly personal mode cannot be wholly unbecoming to him, it is not inappropriate to the critic's function to talk about his personal experience of an idea. And I shall go so far in doing this as to describe the actual circumstances in which the experience took place. These circumstances are pedagogic—they consist of some problems in teaching modern literature to undergraduates and my attempt to solve these problems. And perhaps I ought to admit at once that, as much as about modern literature itself, I am talking about the teaching of modern literature. I know that pedagogy is a depressing subject to all persons of sensibility, and yet I shall not apologize for speaking about it because the teaching of literature and especially modern literature constitutes one of the most salient and significant characteristics of the culture of our time. Indeed, if we are on the hunt for *the* modern element of modern literature, we might want to find it in the susceptibility of modern literature to being made into an academic subject.

Here, then, is my experience.

For some years I have taught the course in modern literature in Columbia College. I did not undertake the course without misgiving and I have never taught it with an undivided mind. My doubts do not refer to the value of the literature itself, only to the educational propriety of its being studied in college. These doubts persist in the face of my entire awareness that the relation of our collegiate education to modernity is no longer an open question. The unargued assumption of most curriculums is that the real subject of all study is the modern world; that the justification of all study is its immediate and presumably practical relevance to modernity; that the true purpose of all study is to lead the young person to be at home in, and in control of, the modern world. There is really no way of quarreling with this belief, nor with what follows upon it, the framing of curriculums of which the substance is chiefly contemporary or at least makes ultimate reference to what is contemporary.

It might be asked why anyone should *want* to quarrel with this assumption. To that question I can only return a defensive, eccentric, self-depreciatory answer. It is this: that to some of us, as we go on teaching, if we insist on thinking of our students as the creators of the intellectual life of the future, there comes a kind of despair. It does not come because our students fail to respond to ideas, rather because they respond to ideas with a happy vagueness, a delighted glibness, a joyous sense of power in the use of received or receivable generalizations, a grateful wonder at how easy it is to formulate and judge, at how little resistance language offers to their intentions. When that despair strikes us, we are tempted to give up the usual and accredited ways of evaluating education, and instead of prizing responsiveness and aptitude, we set store by some sign of personal character in our students, some token of individual will. We think of this as taking the form of resistance and imperviousness, of personal density or gravity, of some power of supposing that ideas are real, a power which will lead a young man to say, "But is this really true—is it true for me?" And to say this not in the modern way, not following the progressive educational prescription to "think for yourself," which means to think in the progressive pieties rather than in the conservative pieties (if any of the latter do still exist), but to say it from his sense of himself as a person rather than as a bundle of attitudes and responses which are all alert to please the teacher and the progressive community.

We can't do anything about the quality of personal being of our students, but we are led to think about the cultural analogue of a personal character that is grave, dense, and resistant—we are led to think about the past. Perhaps the protagonist of Thomas Mann's story, "Disorder and Early Sorrow" comes to mind, that sad Professor Cornelius with his intense and ambivalent sense of history. For Professor Cornelius, who is a historian, the past is dead, is death iself, but for that very reason it is the source of order, value, piety, and even love. If we think about education in the dark light of the despair I have described, we wonder if perhaps there is not to be found in the past that quiet place at which a young man might stand for a few years, at least a little beyond the competing attitudes and generalizations of the present, at least a little beyond the contemporary problems which he is told he can master only by means of attitudes and generalizations, that quiet place in which he can be silent, in which he can *know* something—in what year the Parthenon was begun, the order of battle at Trafalgar, how Linear B was deciphered: almost anything at all that has nothing to do with the talkative and attitudinizing present, anything at all rather than variations of the accepted formulations about *anxiety,* and *urban society,* and *alienation,* and *Gemeinschaft* and *Gesellschaft,* all the matter of the academic disciplines which are founded upon the modern self-consciousness and the modern self-pity. The modern self-pity is certainly not without its justification; but, if the grounds for our self-pity are ever to be overcome, we must sometimes wonder whether that task is likely to be accomplished by minds which are taught in youth to accept these sad conditions of ours as ineluctable, and as the only right objects of contemplation. And quite apart from any practical consequences, there is the simple aesthetic personal pleasure of having to do with young minds, and maturing minds, which are free of cant, which are, to quote an old poet, "fierce, moody, patient, venturous, modest, shy."

This line of argument I have called eccentric and maybe it ought to be called obscurantist and reactionary. Whatever it is called, it is not likely to impress a Committee on the Curriculum. It was, I think, more or less the line of argument of my department in Columbia College, when, up to a few years ago, it decided, whenever the question came up, not to carry its courses beyond the late nineteenth century. But our rationale could not stand against the representations which a group of students made to our dean and which he communicated to us. The students wanted a course in modern literature—very likely, in the way of students, they said that it was a scandal that no such course was being offered in the College. There was no argument that could stand against this expressed desire: we could only capitulate, and then, with pretty good grace, muster the arguments that justified our doing so. Was not the twentieth century more than half over? Was it not nearly fifty years since Eliot wrote "Portrait of a Lady"? George Meredith had not died until 1909, and even the oldest among us had read one of his novels in a college course—many American universities had been quick to bring into their purview the literature of the later nineteenth century, and even the early twentieth century; there was a strong supporting tradition for us. Had not Yeats been Matthew Arnold's contemporary for twenty-three years?

Our resistance to the idea of the course had never been based on an adverse judgment of the literature itself. We are a department not only of English but of comparative literature, and if the whole of modern literature is surveyed, it could be said—and we were willing to say it—that no literature of the past matched the literature of our time in power and magnificence. Then too, it is a difficult literature, and it is difficult not merely as defenders of modern poetry say that all literature is difficult. We nowadays believe that Keats is a very difficult poet, but his earlier readers did not. We now see the depths and subtleties of Dickens, but his contemporary readers found him as simply available as a plate of oysters on the half shell. Modern literature, however, shows its difficulties at first blush; they are literal as well as doctrinal difficulties, and they are to be dealt with by young men brought up with a lax secondary education and an abstract and generalized college education—if our students are to know their modern literary heritage, surely they need all the help that a teacher can give?

These made cogent reasons for our decision to establish, at long last, the course in modern literature. They also made a ground for our display of a certain mean-spirited, last-ditch vindictiveness. I recall that we said something like, "Very well, if they want the modern, let them have it—let them have it, as Henry James says, full in the face. We shall give the course, but we shall give it on the highest level, and if they think, as students do, that the modern is the facile, the easily comprehended, let them have their gay and easy time with Yeats and Eliot, with Joyce and Proust and Kafka, with Lawrence, Mann, and Gide."

Eventually the course fell to me to give. I approached it with an uneasiness which has not diminished with the passage of time —it has, I think, even increased. It arises, this uneasiness, from my personal relation with the works that form the substance of the course. Almost all of them have been involved with me for a long time—I invert the natural order not out of lack of modesty but taking the cue of W. H. Auden's remark that a real book reads us. I have been read by Eliot's poems and by *Ulysses* and by *Remembrance of Things Past* and by *The Castle* for a good many years now, since early youth. Some of these books at first rejected me; I bored them. But as I grew older and they knew me better, they came to have more sympathy with me and to understand my hidden meanings. Their nature is such that our relationship has been very intimate. No literature has ever been so shockingly personal as ours—it asks every question that is forbidden in polite society. It asks us if we are content with our marriages, with our family lives, with our professional lives, with our friends. It is all very well for me to describe my course in the college catalogue as "paying particular attention to the role of the writer as a critic of his culture"—this is sheer evasion: the questions asked by our literature are not about our culture but ourselves. It asks us if we are content with ourselves, if we are saved or damned—more than with anything else, our literature is concerned with salvation. No literature has even been so intensely spiritual as ours. I do not venture to call it religious, but certainly it has the special intensity of concern with the spiritual life which Hegel noted when he spoke of the great modern phenomenon of the secularization of spirituality.

I do not know how other teachers deal with this extravagant personal force of modern literature, but for me it makes difficulty. Nowadays the teaching of literature inclines to a considerable technicality, but when the teacher has said all that can be said about formal matters, about verse-patterns, metrics, prose conventions, irony, tension, etc., he must confront the necessity of bearing personal testimony. He must use whatever authority he may possess to say whether or not a work is true; and if not, why not; and if so, why so. He can do this only at considerable cost to his privacy. How does one say that Lawrence is right in his great rage against the modern emotions, against the modern sense of life and ways of being, unless one speaks from the intimacies of one's own feelings, and one's own sense of life, and one's own wished-for way of being? How, except with the implication of personal judgment, does one say to students that Gide is perfectly accurate in his representation of the awful boredom and slow corruption of respectable life? Then probably one rushes in to say that this doesn't of itself justify homosexuality and the desertion of one's dying wife, certainly not. But then again, having paid one's *devoirs* to morality, how does one rescue from morality Gide's essential point about the supreme rights of the individual person, and without making it merely historical and totally academic?

My first response to the necessity of dealing with matters of this kind was resentment of the personal discomfort it caused me. These are subjects we usually deal with either quite unconsciously or in the privacy of our own conscious minds, and if we now and then disclose our thoughts about them, it is to friends of equal age and especial closeness. Or if we touch upon them publicly, we do so in the relative abstractness and anonymity of print. To stand up in one's own person and to speak of them in one's own voice to an audience which each year grows younger as one grows older—that is not easy, and probably it is not decent.

And then, leaving aside the personal considerations, or taking them merely as an indication of something wrong with the situation, can we not say that, when modern literature is brought into the classroom, the subject being taught is betrayed by the pedagogy of the subject? We have to ask ourselves whether in our day too much does not come within the purview of the academy. More and more, as the universities liberalize themselves, and turn their beneficent imperialistic gaze upon what is called Life Itself, the feeling grows among our educated classes that little can be experienced unless it is validated by some established intellectual discipline, with the result that experience loses much of its personal immediacy for us and becomes part of an accredited societal activity. This is not entirely true and I don't want to play the boring academic game of pretending that it *is* entirely true, that the university mind wilts and withers whatever it touches. I must believe, and I do believe, that the university study of art is capable of confronting the power of a work of art fully and courageously. I even believe that it can discover and disclose power where it has not been felt before. But the university study of art achieves this end chiefly with works of art of an older period. Time has the effect of seeming to quiet the work of art, domesticating it and making it into a classic, which is often another way of saying that it is an object of merely habitual regard. University study of the right sort can reverse this process and restore to the old work its freshness and force—can, indeed, disclose unguessed-at power. But with the works of art of our own present age, university study tends to accelerate the process by which the radical and subversive work becomes the classic work, and university study does this in the degree that it is vivacious and responsive and what is called non-academic. In one of his poems Yeats mocks the literary scholars, "the bald heads forgetful of their sins," "the old, learned, respectable bald heads," who edit the poems of the fierce and passionate young men.

> Lord, what would they say
> Did their Catullus walk this way?

Yeats, of course, is thinking of his own future fate, and no doubt there is all the radical and comical discrepancy that he sees between the poet's passions and the scholars' close-eyed concentration on the text. Yet for my part, when I think of Catullus, I am moved to praise the tact of all those old heads, from Heinsius and Bentley to Munro and Postgate, who worked on Codex G and Codex O and drew conclusions from them about the lost Codex V—for doing only this and for not trying to realize and demonstrate the true intensity and the true quality and the true cultural meaning of Catullus's passion and managing to bring it somehow into eventual accord with their respectability and baldness. Nowadays we who deal with books in universities live in fear that the World—which we imagine to be a vital, palpitating, passionate, reality-loving World—will think of us as old, respectable, and bald, and we see to it that in our dealings with Yeats—to take him as the example—his wild cry of rage and sexuality is heard by our students and quite thoroughly understood by them as—what is it that we eventually call it?—a significant expression of our culture. The exasperation of Lawrence and the subversiveness of Gide, by the time we have dealt with them boldly and straightforwardly, are notable instances of the *alienation of modern man as exemplified by the artist*. "Compare Yeats, Gide, Lawrence, and Eliot in the use which they make of the theme of sexuality to criticize the deficiencies of modern culture. Support your statement by specific references to the work of each author." Time: one hour. And the distressing thing about our examination questions is that they are not ridiculous, they make perfectly good sense—such good sense that the young person who answers them can never again know the force, the terror, of what has been communicated to him by the works he is being examined on.

Very likely it was with the thought of saving myself from the necessity of speaking personally and my students from the betrayal of the full harsh meaning of a great literature that I first taught my course in as *literary* a way as possible. A couple of decades ago the discovery was made that a literary work is a structure of words: this doesn't seem a surprising thing to have learned except in its polemical tendency, which is to urge us to minimize the amount of attention we give to the poet's social and personal will, to what he wants to happen outside the poem as a result of the poem; it urges us to fix our minds on what is going on inside the poem. For me this polemical tendency has been of the greatest usefulness, for it has corrected my inclination to pay attention chiefly to what the poet *wants.* For two or three years I directed my efforts toward dealing with the matter of the course chiefly as structures of words, in a formal way with due attention paid to the literal difficulty which marked so many of the works. But it went against the grain. It went against my personal grain. It went against the grain of the classroom situation, for formal analysis is best carried on by question-and-answer, which needs small groups, and the registration for the course in modern literature in any college is sure to be large. And it went against the grain of the authors themselves—structures of words they may indeed have created, but these structures were not pyramids or triumphal arches, they were manifestly contrived not to be static and commemorative but mobile and aggressive, and one does not describe a quinquireme or a howitzer or a tank without estimating how much *damage* it can do.

Eventually I had to decide that there was only one way to give the course, which was to give it without strategies and without conscious caution. It was not honorable, neither to the students nor to the authors, to conceal or disguise my relation to the literature, my commitment to it, my fear of it, my ambivalence toward it. The literature had to be dealt with in the terms it announced for itself. As for the students, I have never given assent to the modern saw about "teaching students, not subjects"—I have always thought it right to teach subjects, believing that if one gives his first loyalty to the subject, the student is best instructed. So I resolved to give the course with no considerations in mind except my own interests. And since my own interests lead me to see literary situations as cultural situations, and cultural situations as great elaborate fights about moral issues, and moral issues as having something to do with gratuitously chosen images of personal being, and images of personal being as having something to do with literary style, I felt free to begin with what for me was a first concern, the animus of the author, the objects of his will, the things he wants or wants to have happen.

I went so far in my cultural and non-literary method as to decide that I would begin the course with a statement of certain themes or issues that might especially engage our attention. I even went so far in non-literariness as to think that my purposes would best be served if I could contrive a "background" for the works we would read—I wanted to propose a history for the themes or issues that I hoped to discover. I did not intend that this history should be either very extensive or very precise. I wanted merely a *sense* of a history, some general intuition of a past. And because there is as yet no adequate general work of history of the culture of the last two hundred years, I asked myself what books of the age just preceeding ours had most influenced our literature, or, since I was far less concerned with showing influence than with discerning a tendency, what older books might seem to fall into a line the direction of which pointed to our own literature and thus might serve as a prolegomenon to the course.

It was virtually inevitable that the first work that should have sprung to mind was Sir James Frazer's *The Golden Bough,* not, of course, the whole of it, but certain chapters, those that deal with Osiris, Attis, and Adonis. Anyone who thinks about modern literature in a systematic way takes for granted the great part played in it by myth, and especially by those examples of myth which tell about gods dying and being reborn—the imagination of death and rebirth, reiterated in the ancient world in innumerable variations that are yet always the same, captivated the literary mind at the very moment when, as all accounts of the modern age agree, the most massive and compelling of all the stories of resurrection had lost much of its hold upon the world.

Perhaps no book has had so decisive an effect upon modern literature as Frazer's. It was beautifully to my purpose that it had first been published ten years before the twentieth century began. Yet forty-three years later, in 1933, Frazer delivered a lecture, very eloquent, in which he bade the world be of good hope in the face of the threat to the human mind that was being offered by the Nazi power. He was still alive in 1941. Yet he had been born in 1854, three years before Matthew Arnold gave the lecture "On the Modern Element in Literature." Here, surely, was history, here was the past I wanted, beautifully connected with our present. Frazer was wholly a man of the nineteenth century, and the more so because the eighteenth century was so congenial to him —the lecture of 1933 in which he predicted the Nazi defeat had as its subject Condorcet's *Progress of the Human Mind;* when he took time from his anthropological studies to deal with literature, he prepared editions of Addison's essays and Cowper's letters. He had the old lost belief in the virtue and power of rationality. He loved and counted on order, decorum, and good sense. This great historian of the primitive imagination was in the dominant intellectual tradition of the West that, since the days of the pre-Socratics, has condemned the ways of thought that we call primitive.

In short, Frazer—at least in his first or conscious intention—was a perfect representative of what Matthew Arnold meant by a modern age. And perhaps nothing could make clearer how the conditions of life and literature have changed in a hundred years than to note the difference between the way in which Arnold defines the modern element in literature and the way in which we must define it.

If we speak of modernity, we should have it in mind that the terms of the endowment of the Poetry Chair at Oxford required that the Professor lecture on the ancient literatures and that he speak in Latin. This will suggest that Arnold's making the idea of modernity the subject of his inaugural was not without its subversiveness. Arnold met the requirement of dealing with the classic writers—his lecture is about the modern element in the ancient literatures. But he asked for permission to lecture in English, not because he was unable to speak in Latin but because he wished to be understood by more than scholars. Permission was granted by the University, with what reluctance I do not know, or with what sad sense that another bastion of the past had fallen, and in an English which was perhaps doctoral but certainly lucid, Arnold undertook to decline what he called the modern element.

Arnold used the word modern in a wholly honorific sense. So much so, indeed, that he seems to dismiss all temporal idea from the word and makes it signify certain timeless intellectual and civil virtues. A society, he said, is a modern society when it maintains a condition of repose, confidence, free activity of the mind, and the tolerance of divergent views. A society is modern when it affords sufficient material well-being for the conveniences of life and the development of taste. And, finally, a society is modern when its members are intellectually mature, by which Arnold means that they are willing to judge by reason, to observe facts in a critical spirit, and to search for the law of things. By this definition Periclean Athens is for Arnold a modern age, Elizabethan England is not; Thucydides is a modern historian, Sir Walter Raleigh is not.

I shall not go into further details of Arnold's definition or description of the modern.[2] I have said enough, I think, to suggest what Arnold was up to, what he wanted to see realized as the desideratum of his own society, what ideal he wanted the works of intellect and imagination of his own time to advance. And at what a distance his ideal of the modern puts him from our

[2] I leave out of my summary account the two supreme virtues that Arnold ascribes to the most successful examples of a "modern" literature. One is the power of effecting an "intellectual deliverance," by which Arnold means leading men to comprehend the "vast multitude of facts" which make up "a copious and complex present, and behind it a copious and complex past." The other is "adequacy," the ability to represent the complex high human development of a modern age "in its completest and most harmonious" aspect, doing so with "the charm of that noble serenity which always accompanies true insight."

present sense of modernity, from our modern literature! To anyone conditioned by our modern literature Arnold's ideal of order, convenience, decorum, and rationality might well seem to reduce itself to the small advantages and excessive limitations of the middle-class life of a few prosperous nations of the nineteenth century. Arnold's historic sense presented to his mind the long, bitter, bloody past of Europe, and he seized passionately upon the hope of true civilization at last achieved. But the historic sense of our literature has in mind a long excess of civilization to which it ascribes the bitterness and blood both of the past and of the present and of which it conceives the peaceful aspects to be mainly contemptible—its order achieved at the cost of extravagant personal repression, either that of coercion or that of acquiescence; its repose otiose; its tolerance either flaccid or capricious; its material comfort corrupt and corrupting; its taste a manifestation either of timidity or of pride; its rationality attained only at the price of energy and passion.

For the understanding of this radical change of opinion nothing is more illuminating than to be aware of the doubleness of mind of the author of *The Golden Bough.* I have said that Frazer in his conscious mind and in his first intention exemplifies all that Arnold means by the modern. He often speaks quite harshly of the irrationality and the orgiastic excesses of the primitive religions he describes, and even Christianity comes under his criticism both because it stands in the way of rational thought and because it can draw men away from intelligent participation in the life of society. But Frazer had more than one intention, and he had an unconscious as well as a conscious mind. If he deplores the primitive imagination, he does not fail to show it as also wonderful and beautiful. It is the rare reader of *The Golden Bough* who finds the ancient beliefs and rituals wholly alien to him. It is to be expected that Frazer's adduction of the many pagan analogues to the Christian mythos will be thought by Christian readers to have an adverse effect on faith, it was undoubtedly Frazer's purpose that it should, yet many readers will feel that Frazer makes all faith and ritual indigenous to humanity, virtually biological; they feel, as DeQuincey put it, that not to be at least a *little* superstitious is to lack generosity of mind. Scientific though his purpose was, Frazer had the effect of validating and even of seeming to propose to modern times those old modes of experiencing the world which, beginning with the Romanticists, modern men have sought to revive in order to escape from positivism and common sense.

The direction of the imagination upon great and mysterious objects of worship is not the only means men use to liberate themselves from the bondage of quotidian fact, and although Frazer can scarcely be held accountable for the ever-growing modern attraction to the extreme mental states, to rapture, ecstasy, and transcendance, which are achieved by drugs, trance, music and dance, orgy, and derangement of personality, yet he did provide a bridge to the understanding and acceptance of these states, he proposed to us the idea that the desire for them and the use of them for heuristic purposes is a common and acceptable manifestation of human nature.

This one element of Frazer's masterpiece could scarcely fail to suggest the next of my prolegomenal works. It is worth remarking that its author is in his own way as great a classical scholar as Frazer himself—Nietzsche was the Professor of Classical Philology at the University of Basel when, at the age of 27, he published his essay, *The Birth of Tragedy*. After the appearance of this stunningly brilliant account of Greek civilization, of which Socrates is not the hero but the villain, what can possibly be left to us of that rational and ordered Greece, that modern, that eighteenth-century, Athens that Arnold so entirely relied on as the standard for judging all civilizations? Professor Kaufmann is right when he warns us against supposing that Nietzsche exalts Dionysus over Apollo and tells us that Nietzsche "emphasizes the Dionysiac only because he feels that the Apollonian genius of the Greeks cannot be fully understood apart from it." But no one reading Nietzsche's essay for the first time is likely to heed this warning. What will reach him before due caution intervenes, before he becomes aware of the portentous dialectic between Dionysus and Apollo, is the excitement of his sudden liberation from Aristotle, the joy that he takes in his willingness to believe the author's statement that, "art rather than ethics constitutes the essential metaphysical activity of man," that tragedy has its source in the Dionysiac rapture, "whose closest analogy is furnished by physical intoxication," and that this rapture, in which "the individual forgets himself completely," was in itself no metaphysical state but an orgiastic display of lust and cruelty, "of sexual promiscuity overriding every form of tribal law." This sadic and masochistic frenzy, Nietzsche is at pains to insist, needs the taming hand of Apollo before it can become tragedy, but it is the primal stuff of the great art, and to the modern experience of tragedy this explanation of it seems far more pertinent than Aristotle's, with its eagerness to forget its origin in its achievement of a noble *apatheia.*

Of supreme importance in itself, Nietzsche's essay had for me the added pedagogic advantage of allowing me to establish an historical line back to William Blake. Nothing is more characteristic of modern literature than its discovery and canonization of the primal, non-ethical energies, and the historical point could be made the better by remarking the correspondence of thought of two men of different nations and separated from each other by a good many decades, for Nietzsche's Dionysus and Blake's Hell are much the same thing.

Whether or not Joseph Conrad read either Blake or Nietzsche I do not know, but his *Heart of Darkness* follows in their line. This very great work has never lacked for the admiration it deserves, and it has been given a kind of canonical place in the legend of modern literature by Eliot's having it so clearly in mind when he wrote *The Waste Land* and his having taken from it the epigraph to "The Hollow Men." But no one, to my knowledge, has ever confronted in an explicit way its strange and terrible message of ambivalence toward the life of civilization. Consider that its protagonist Kurtz is a progressive and a liberal and that he is the highly respected representative of a society which undertakes to represent itself as benign, although in fact it is vicious. Consider too that he is a practitioner of several arts, a painter, a writer, a musician, and into the bargain a political orator. He is at once the most idealistic and the most practically successful of all the agents of the Belgian exploitation of the Congo. Everybody knows what truth about him Marlow discovers—that Kurtz's success is the result of a terrible ascendancy he has gained over the natives of his distant station, an ascendancy which is derived from his presumed magical or divine powers, that he has exercised his rule with the extreme of cruelty, that he has given himself to unnamable acts of lust. This is the world of the darker pages of *The Golden Bough.* It is one of the great points of Conrad's story that Marlow speaks of the primitive life of the jungle not as being noble or charming or even free but as being base and sordid—and for *that* reason compelling: he himself feels quite overtly its dreadful attraction. It is to this devilish baseness that Kurtz has yielded himself, and yet Marlow, although he does indeed treat him with hostile irony, does not find it possible to suppose that Kurtz is anything but a hero of the spirit. For me it is still ambiguous whether Kurtz's famous deathbed cry, "The horror! The horror!" refers to the approach of death or to his experience of savage life. Whichever it is, to Marlow the fact that Kurtz could utter this cry at the point of death, while Marlow himself, when death threatens him, can know it only as a weary greyness, marks the difference between the ordinary man and a hero of the spirit. Is this not the essence of the modern belief about the nature of the artist, the man who goes down into that hell which is the historical beginning of the human soul, a beginning not outgrown but established in humanity as we know it now, preferring the reality of this hell to the bland lies of the civilization that has overlaid it?

This idea is proposed again in the somewhat less powerful but still very moving work with which I followed *Heart of Darkness,*

Thomas Mann's *Death in Venice*. I wanted this story not so much for its account of an extravagantly Apollonian personality surrendering to forces that, in his Apollonian character, he thought shameful—although this was certainly to my purpose—but rather for Aschenbach's fevered dreams of the erotic past, and in particular that dream of the goat-orgy which Mann, being the kind of writer he is, having the kind of relation to Nietzsche he had, might well have written to serve as an illustration of what *The Birth of Tragedy* means by religious frenzy, the more so, of course, because Mann chooses that particular orgiastic ritual, the killing and eating of the goat, from which tragedy is traditionally said to have been derived. A notable element of this story in which the birth of tragedy plays an important part is that the degradation and downfall of the protagonist is not represented as tragic in the usual sense of the word—that is, it is not represented as a great deplorable event. It is a commonplace of modern literary thought that the tragic mode is not available even to the gravest and noblest of our writers. I am not sure that this is the deprivation that some people think it to be and a mark of our spiritual inferiority. But if we ask why it has come about, one reason may be that we have learned to think our way back through tragedy to the primal stuff out of which tragedy arose. If we consider the primitive forbidden ways of conduct which traditionally in tragedy lead to punishment by death, we think of them as being the path to reality and truth, to an ultimate self-realization. We have always wondered if tragedy itself may not have been saying just this in a deeply hidden way, drawing us to think of the hero's sin and death as somehow conferring justification, even salvation of a sort—no doubt this is what Nietzsche had in mind when he said that "tragedy denies ethics." What tragedy once seemed to hint, our literature now is willing to say quite explicitly. If Mann's Aschenbach dies at the height of his intellectual and artistic powers, at the behest of a passion that his ethical reason condemns, we do not take this to be a defeat, rather a kind of terrible rebirth: at his latter end the artist knows a reality that he had until now refused to admit to consciousness.

This being so, how fortunate that the Anchor edition of *The Birth of Tragedy* should include Nietzsche's *The Genealogy of Morals*. For here, among many other ideas most pertinent to the *mystique* of modern literature, was the view of society which is consonant with the belief that art and not ethics constitutes the essential metaphysical activity of man and with the validation and ratification of the primitive energies. Nietzsche's theory of the social order dismisses all ethical impulse from its origins—the basis of society is to be found in the rationalization of cruelty: as simple as that. Nietzsche has no ultimate Utopian intention in saying this, no hope of revising the essence of the social order, although he does believe that its pain can be mitigated. He represents cruelty as a social necessity, for only by its exercise could men ever have been induced to develop a continuity of will: nothing else than cruelty could have created in mankind that memory of intention which makes society possible. The method of cynicism which Nietzsche pursued—let us be clear that it is a method and not an attitude—goes so far as to describe punishment in terms of the pleasure derived from the exercise of cruelty: "Compensation," he says, "consists in a legal warrant entitling one man to exercise his cruelty on another." There follows that most remarkable passage in which Nietzsche describes the process whereby the individual turns the cruelty of punishment against himself and creates the bad conscience and the consciousness of guilt which manifests itself as a pervasive anxiety. Nietzsche's complexity of mind is beyond all comparison, for in this book which is dedicated to the liberation of the conscience, Nietzsche makes his defense of the bad conscience as a decisive force in the interests of culture. It is much the same line of argument that he takes when, having attacked the Jewish morality and the priestly existence in the name of the health of the spirit, he reminds us that only by his sickness does man become interesting.

From *The Genealogy of Morals* to Freud's *Civilization and Its Discontents* is but a step, and some might think that, for pedagogic purposes, the step is so small as to make the second book supererogatory. But although Freud's view of society and culture has indeed a very close affinity to Nietzsche's, Freud does add certain considerations which are essential to our sense of the modern disposition.

For one thing, he puts to us the question of whether or not we want to *accept* civilization. It is not the first time that the paradox of civilization has been present to the mind of civilized people, the sense that civilization makes men behave worse and suffer more than does some less developed state of human existence. But hitherto all such ideas were formulated in a moralizing way—civilization was represented as being "corrupt," a divagation from a state of innocence. Freud had no illusions about a primitive innocence, he conceived no practicable alternative to civilization. In consequence there was a unique force to the question he asked: whether we wished to accept civilization, with all its contradictions, with all its pains—pains, for "discontents" does not accurately describe what Freud has in mind. He had his own answer to the question—his tragic, or stoic, sense of life dictated it: we do well to accept it, although we also do well to cast a cold eye on the fate that makes it our better part to accept it. Like Nietzsche, Freud thought that life was justified by our heroic response to its challenge.

But the question Freud posed has not been set aside or closed up by the answer that he himself gave to it. His answer, like Nietzsche's, is essentially in the line of traditional humanism—we can see this in the sternness with which he charges women not to interfere with men in the discharge of their cultural duty, not to claim men for love and the family to the detriment of their free activity in the world. But just here lies the matter of Freud's question that the world more and more believes Freud himself did not answer. The pain that civilization inflicts is that of the instinctual renunciation that civilization demands, and it would seem that fewer and fewer people wish to say with Freud that the loss of instinctual gratification, emotional freedom, or love, are compensated for either by the security of civilized life or the stern pleasures of the moral masculine character. The possibility of options different from the one that Freud made is proposed theoretically by two recent books, Herbert Marcuse's *Eros and Civilization* and Norman O. Brown's *Life Against Death.*

With Freud's essay I brought to a close my list of prolegomenal books for the first term of the course. I shall not do much more than mention the books with which I introduced the second term, but I should like to do at least that. I began with *Rameau's Nephew,* thinking that the peculiar moral authority which Diderot assigns to the envious, untalented unregenerate protagonist was peculiarly relevant to the line taken by the ethical explorations of modern literature. Nothing is more characteristic of the literature of our time than the replacement of the hero by what has come to be called the anti-hero, in whose indifference to or hatred of ethical nobility there is presumed to lie a special authenticity. Diderot is quite overt about this—he himself in his public character is the deuteroganist, the "honest consciousness," as Hegel calls him, and he takes delight in the discomfiture of the decent, dull person he is by the Nephew's nihilistic mind.

It seemed to me too that there was particular usefulness in the circumstance that this anti-hero should avow so openly his *envy,* which Tocqueville has called the ruling emotion of democracy, and that, although he envied anyone at all who had access to the creature-comforts and the social status which he lacked, what chiefly animated him was envy of men of genius. Ours is the first cultural epoch in which many men aspire to high achievement in the arts and, in their frustration, form a dispossessed class which cuts across the conventional class lines, making a proletariat of the spirit.

Although *Rameau's Nephew* was not published until fairly late in the century, it was known in manuscript by Goethe and Hegel; it suited the temper and won the admiration of Marx and Freud for reasons that are obvious. And there is ground for supposing that it was known to Dostoevsky, whose *Notes from Un-*

derground is a restatement of the essential idea of Diderot's dialogue in terms both more extreme and less genial. The Nephew is still on the defensive—he is naughtily telling secrets about the nature of man and society. But Dostoevsky's underground man shouts aloud his envy and hatred and carries the ark of his self-hatred and alienation into a remorseless battle with what he calls "the good and the beautiful," mounting an attack upon every belief not merely of bourgeois society but of the whole humanist tradition. The inclusion of *Notes from Underground* among my prolegomenal books constituted something of a pedagogic risk, for if I wished to emphasize the subversive tendency of modern literature, here was a work which made all subsequent subversion seem like affirmation, so radical and so brilliant was its negation of our pieties and assumptions.

I hesitated in compunction before following *Notes from Underground* with Tolstoy's *Death of Ivan Ilytch,* which so ruthlessly and with such dreadful force destroys the citadel of the commonplace life in which we all believe we can take refuge from ourselves and our fate. But I did assign it and then two of Pirandello's plays which, in the atmosphere of the sordidness of the commonplace life, undermine all the certitudes of the commonplace, common-sense mind.

From time to time I have raised with myself the question of whether my choice of these prolegomenal works was not extravagant, quite excessively tendentious. I have never been able to believe that it is. And if these works do indeed serve to indicate in an accurate way the nature of modern literature, a teacher might find it worth asking how his students respond to the strong dose.

One response I have already described—the readiness of the students to engage in the process that we might call the socialization of the anti-social, or the acculturation of the anti-cultural, or the legitimization of the subversive. When the term-essays come in, it is plain to me that almost none of the students have been taken aback by what they have read: they have wholly contained the attack. The chief exceptions are the few who simply do not comprehend, although they may be awed by, the categories of our discourse. In their papers, like poor hunted creatures in a Kafka story, they take refuge first in misunderstood large phrases, then in bad grammar, then in general incoherence. After my pedagogical exasperation has run its course, I find that I am sometimes moved to give them a queer respect, as if they had stood up and said what in fact they don't have the wit to stand up and say: "Why do you harry us? Leave us alone. We are not Modern Man. We are the Old People. Ours is the Old Faith. We serve the little Old Gods, the gods of the copybook maxims, the small, dark, somewhat powerful deities of lawyers, doctors, engineers, accountants. With them is neither sensibility nor *angst.* With them is no disgust—it is they, indeed, who make ready the way for 'the good and the beautiful' about which low-minded doubts have been raised in this course, that 'good and beautiful' which we do not possess and don't want to possess but which we know justifies our lives. Leave us alone and let us worship our gods in the way they approve, in peace and unawareness." Crass, but—to use that interesting modern word which we have learned from the curators of museums—authentic. The rest, the minds that give me the A papers and the B papers and even the C+ papers, move through the terrors and mysteries of modern literature like so many Parsifals, asking no questions at the behest of wonder and fear. Or like so many seminarists who have been systematically instructed in the constitution of Hell and the ways to damnation. Or like so many *readers,* entertained by moral horror stories. I asked them to look into the Abyss, and, both dutifully and gladly, they have looked into the Abyss, and the Abyss has greeted them with the grave courtesy of all objects of serious study, saying: "Interesting, am I not? And *exciting,* if you consider how deep I am and what dread beasts lie at my bottom. Have it well in mind that a knowledge of me contributes materially to your being whole, or well-rounded, men."

In my distress over the outrage I have conspired to perpetrate upon a great literature, I wonder if perhaps I have not been reading these papers too literally. After all, a term-essay is not a diary of the soul, it is not an occasion for telling the truth. What my students might reveal of their true feelings to a younger teacher they will not reveal to me; they will give me what they conceive to be the proper response to the official version of terror I have given them. I bring to mind their faces, which are not necessarily the faces of the authors of these unperturbed papers, nor are they, not yet, the faces of fathers of families, or of theater-goers, or of buyers of Modern Paintings: not yet. I must think it possible that in ways and to a degree which they keep secret they have responded directly and personally to what they have read.

And if they have? And if they have, am I the more content?

What form would I want their response to take? It is a teacher's question that I am asking, not a critic's. We have decided in recent years to think of the critic and the teacher of literature as one and the same, and no doubt it is both possible and useful to do so. But there are some points at which the functions of the two do not coincide, or can be made to coincide only with great difficulty. Of criticism we have been told, by Arnold, that "it must be apt to study and praise elements that for fulness of spiritual perfection are wanted, even though they belong to a power which in the practical sphere may be maleficent." But teaching, or at least undergraduate teaching, is not given the same licensed mandate—cannot be given it because the teacher's audience, which stands before his very eyes, as the critic's audience does not, asks questions about "the practical sphere," as the critic's audience does not. For instance, on the very day that I write this, when I had said to my class all I could think of to say about *The Magic Mountain* and invited questions and comments, one student asked, "How would you generalize the idea of the educative value of illness, so that it would be applicable not only to a particular individual, Hans Castorp, but to young people at large?" It makes us smile, but it was asked in all seriousness, and it is serious in its substance, and it had to be answered seriously, in part by the reflection that this idea, like so many ideas encountered in the books of the course had to be thought of as having reference only to the private life; that it touched the public life only in some indirect or tangential way; that it really ought to be encountered in solitude, even in secrecy, since to talk about it in public and in our academic setting was to seem to propose for it a public practicality and thus to distort its meaning. To this another student replied; he said that, despite the public ritual of the classroom, each student inevitably experienced the books in privacy and found their meaning in reference to his own life. True enough, but the teacher sees the several privacies coming together to make a group, and they propose—no doubt the more because they come together every Monday, Wednesday, and Friday at a particular hour—the idea of a community, that is to say, "the practical sphere."

This being so, the teacher cannot escape the awareness of certain circumstances which the critic, who writes for an ideal, uncircumstanced reader, has no need to take into account. The teacher considers, for example, the social situation of his students —they are not of patrician origin, they do not come from homes in which stubbornness, pride, and conscious habit prevail, nor are they born into a culture marked by these traits, a culture in which other interesting and valuable things compete with and resist ideas; they come, mostly, from "good homes" in which authority and valuation are weak or at least not very salient and bold, so that ideas have for them, at their present stage of development, a peculiar power and preciousness. And in this connection the teacher will have in mind the peculiar prestige that our culture, in its upper reaches, gives to art, and to the ideas that art proposes—the agreement, ever growing in assertiveness, that art yields more truth than any other intellectual activity. In this culture what a shock it is to encounter Santayana's acerb skepticism about art, or Keats's remark, which the critics and scholars never take notice of, presumably because they suppose it to be an aberration, "This is the very thing in which consists poetry; and if so it is not so fine a thing as philosophy—For the same reason that an eagle is not so fine a thing as a truth." For many students no ideas that they will encounter in any college discipline will equal in force and sanction the ideas conveyed to them by modern literature.

The author of *The Magic Mountain* once said that all his work could be understood as an effort to free himself from the middle class, and this, of course, will serve to describe the chief intention of all modern literature. And the means of freedom which Mann prescribes (the characteristic irony notwithstanding) is the means of freedom which in effect all of modern literature prescribes. It is, in the words of Clavdia Chauchat, "*se perdre et même . . . se laisser dépérir,*" and thus to name the means is to make plain that the end is not merely freedom from the middle class but freedom from society itself. I venture to say that the idea of losing oneself up to the point of self-destruction, of surrendering oneself to experience without regard to self-interest or conventional morality, of escaping wholly from the societal bonds, is an "element" somewhere in the mind of every modern person who dares to think of what Arnold in his unaffected Victorian way called "the fulness of spiritual perfection." But the teacher who undertakes to present modern literature to his students may not allow that idea to remain in the *somewhere* of his mind; he must take it from the place where it exists habitual and unrealized and put it in the conscious forefront of his thought. And if he is committed to an admiration of modern literature, he must also be committed to this chief idea of modern literature. I press the logic of the situation not in order to question the legitimacy of the commitment, or even the propriety of expressing the commitment in the college classroom (although it does seem odd!) but to confront those of us who do teach modern literature with the striking actuality of our enterprise.

The Contributors

M. H. ABRAMS—Frederic J. Whiton Professor of English, Cornell University. Author: *The Mirror and the Lamp: Romantic Theory and the Critical Tradition; The Milk of Paradise; A Glossary of Literary Terms.* Editor: *The Poetry of Pope; Literature and Belief; English Romantic Poets;* etc.

JACQUES BARZUN—Seth Low Professor of History, Dean of Faculties and Provost, Columbia University. Author: *Darwin, Marx, Wagner; The Energies of Art; Classic, Romantic, and Modern;* etc. Translator: Diderot's *Rameau's Nephew;* Flaubert's *Dictionary of Accepted Ideas;* etc.

ERIC BENTLEY—Brander Matthews Professor of Dramatic Literature, Columbia University. Author: *What Is Theatre?;* etc. Translator: Brecht's *Mother Courage;* etc. Editor: *Seven Plays by Bertolt Brecht; The Classic Theatre; The Modern Theatre;* etc.

GERMAINE BRÉE—Professor of French Literature, Institute for Research in the Humanities, University of Wisconsin. Author:

Marcel Proust and Deliverance from Time; Camus; etc. Coauthor (with Margaret Guiton): *An Age of Fiction.* Editor: *Great French Short Stories;* etc.

CLEANTH BROOKS—Gray Professor of Rhetoric, Yale University. Author: *The Well-Wrought Urn; Modern Poetry and the Tradition.* Coauthor (with William K. Wimsatt, Jr.): *Literary Criticism: a Short History;* (with Robert Penn Warren) *Understanding Poetry; Understanding Fiction.*

CALVIN S. BROWN—Alumni Foundation Distinguished Professor of English, University of Georgia. Author: *Music and Literature: A Comparison of the Arts; Tones into Words: Musical Compositions as Subjects of Poetry;* etc. Editor: *The Reader's Companion to World Literature;* etc.

STANLEY BURNSHAW—Lecturer in Literature, New York University. Author: *Early and Late Testament; The Sunless Sea; The Bridge;* etc. Translator: *André Spire and His Poetry.* Editor: *The Poem Itself.*

JOHN CIARDI—Poetry Editor, *Saturday Review.* Author: *As If; I Marry You; In the Stoneworks; How Does a Poem Mean;* etc. Translator: Dante's *Inferno, Purgatorio.* Editor: *Mid-Century American Poets.*

EDWARD DAHLBERG—Author: *Bottom Dogs; Can These Bones Live; The Flea of Sodom; The Sorrows of Priapus;* etc. Coauthor (with Herbert Read): *Truth Is More Sacred.*

ÁNGEL DEL RÍO—Late Professor of Spanish and Director of the Hispanic Institute in the United States, Columbia University. Author: *Historia de la literatura española; Federico García Lorca: Vida y obra; Estudios galdosianos;* etc. Coeditor (with Amelia del Río): *Antología general de la literatura española.* Editor, *Revista Hispánica Moderna.*

LEON EDEL—Professor of English, New York University. Author: *Henry James: The Untried Years; James Joyce: The Last Journey; Literary Biography; The Modern Psychological Novel.*

JOHN GASSNER—Sterling Professor of Playwriting and Dramatic Literature, Yale University. Author: *Form and Idea in Modern Theatre; Masters of the Drama; Theatre at the Crossroads;* etc. Editor: *A Treasury of the Theatre; Producing the Play;* etc.

STEPHEN GILMAN—Professor of Romance Languages, Harvard University. Author: *Cervantes y Avellaneda; The Art of "La Celestina"; Tiempo y formas temporales en el "Poema del Cid."*

HARRY LEVIN—Irving Babbitt Professor of Comparative Literature, Harvard University. Author: *James Joyce: A Critical Introduction; The Power of Blackness: Hawthorne, Poe, Melville; The Overreacher: A Study of Christopher Marlowe; The Question of Hamlet; Contexts of Criticism;* etc.

HENRI PEYRE—Chairman of the Department of Romance Languages and Sterling Professor of French, Yale University. Author: *Writers and Their Critics; Shelley et la France; L'Influence des littératures antiques sur la littérature française moderne;* etc.

PHILIP RAHV—Professor of English, Brandeis University, and co-editor (with William Phillips): the *Partisan Review*. Author: *Image and Idea; Discovery of Europe.* Editor: *Great Short Novels of Henry James; Great Russian Short Novels; Literature in America: A Critical Anthology;* etc.

GREGOR SEBBA—Professor of the Liberal Arts, Graduate Institute of the Liberal Arts, Emory University. Author: *Bibliographia Cartesiana, 1800–1960.* Editor: *Georgia Studies.* Contributor: *Goethe on Human Creativity; The Poem Itself; Truth and Symbol.*

LIONEL TRILLING—Professor of English, Columbia University. Author: *The Liberal Imagination; The Opposing Self; Matthew Arnold; The Middle of the Journey; Freud and the Crisis of Our Culture; A Gathering of Fugitives; E. M. Forster.*

Index